Infectious Disease

Contributors

John N. Goldman, MD, Book Editor[1]
Professor Emeritus
Pennsylvania State University College of Medicine
Hershey, Pennsylvania

Thomas Fekete, MD, FACP, Associate Editor[1]
Professor of Medicine
Associate Professor of Microbiology
Temple University Medical School
Philadelphia, Pennsylvania

Emily J. Erbelding, MD, MPH[2]
Associate Professor of Medicine
Division of Infectious Diseases
Johns Hopkins Bayview Medical Center
Baltimore, Maryland

Stephen Gluckman, MD, FACP[1]
Professor of Medicine
University of Pennsylvania School of Medicine
Chief Infectious Disease Clinical Services
Hospital of the University of Pennsylvania
Philadelphia, Pennsylvania
Visiting Professor of Infectious Diseases
University of Botswana

Joseph A. Hassey, MD[1]
Clinical Assistant Professor of Medicine
Drexel University College of Medicine
Department of Medicine
Division of Infectious Diseases
Abington Memorial Hospital
Abington, Pennsylvania

Fred A. Lopez, MD, FACP[2]
Richard Vial Professor of Medicine
Professor and Vice Chair
Louisiana State University Department of Medicine
Assistant Dean
Louisiana State University School of Medicine
New Orleans, Louisiana

Carlene A. Muto, MD, MS[1]
Medical Director of Infection Control and Hospital
   Epidemiology

University of Pittsburgh Medical Center (UPMC)
Presbyterian Center for Quality Improvement and
   Innovation, UPMC Health System
Associate Professor of Medicine and Epidemiology
Division of Infectious Diseases
University of Pittsburgh School of Medicine
Pittsburgh, Pennsylvania

Judith A. O'Donnell, MD[2]
Associate Professor of Clinical Medicine
Division of Infectious Diseases
University of Pennsylvania School of Medicine
Hospital Epidemiologist and Director
Department of Infection Prevention and Control
Penn Presbyterian Medical Center
Philadelphia, Pennsylvania

William R. Short, MD, MPH[2]
Assistant Professor of Medicine
Division of Infectious Diseases
Jefferson Medical College of Thomas Jefferson University
Philadelphia, Pennsylvania

Allan R. Tunkel, MD, PhD, MACP[1]
Professor of Medicine
Drexel University College of Medicine
Chair, Department of Medicine
Monmouth Medical Center
Long Branch, New Jersey

Editor-in-Chief

Patrick C. Alguire, MD, FACP[1]
Director, Education and Career Development
American College of Physicians
Philadelphia, Pennsylvania

Infectious Disease Reviewers

Robert D. Arbeit, MD, FACP[2]
Rabeh Elzuway, MD[1]
Thomas E. Finucane, MD, FACP[1]
John D. Goldman, MD, FACP[1]
Duane R. Hospenthal, MD, PhD, FACP[2]
Leigh K. Hunter, MD, FACP[2]
Jeffrey L. Jackson, MD, FACP[1]
Richard H. Moseley, MD, FACP[1]

Michael W. Peterson, MD, FACP[1]
Peter H. Wiernik, MD, FACP[2]
John Zurlo, MD[2]

Infectious Disease ACP Editorial Staff

Margaret Wells, Managing Editor
Sean McKinney, Director, Self-Assessment Programs
Charles Rossi, Senior Associate of Clinical Content Development
John Murray, Editorial Coordinator

ACP Principal Staff

Steven E. Weinberger, MD, FACP[2]
Deputy Executive Vice President
Senior Vice President, Medical Education and Publishing

D. Theresa Kanya, MBA[1]
Vice President, Medical Education and Publishing

Sean McKinney[1]
Director, Self-Assessment Programs

Margaret Wells[1]
Managing Editor

Charles Rossi[1]
Senior Associate of Clinical Content Development

Becky Krumm[1]
Senior Staff Editor

Ellen McDonald, PhD[1]
Senior Staff Editor

Amanda Neiley[1]
Staff Editor

Katie Idell[1]
Production Administrator/Editor

Valerie Dangovetsky[1]
Program Administrator

John Murray[1]
Editorial Coordinator

Shannon O'Sullivan[1]
Editorial Coordinator

Developed by the American College of Physicians

---

1. Has no relationships with any entity producing, marketing, re-selling, or distributing health care goods or services consumed by, or used on, patients.

2. Has disclosed relationships with entities producing, marketing, re-selling, or distributing health care goods or services consumed by, or used on, patients. See below.

Conflicts of Interest

The following contributors and ACP staff members have disclosed relationships with commercial companies:

Robert D. Arbeit, MD, FACP
Employment
Paratek Pharmaceuticals
Stock Options/Holdings
Paratek Pharmaceuticals

Emily J. Erbelding, MD, MPH
Employment
Johns Hopkins University
Research Grants/Contracts
Health Services Resource Administration, King Pharmaceuticals
Consultantship
Accordia Global Health Foundation (formerly known as the Academic Alliance for Care and Prevention of AIDS in Africa)

Duane R. Hospenthal, MD, PhD, FACP
Speakers Bureau
Merck, Pfizer

Leigh K. Hunter, MD, FACP
Employment
Methodist Health Systems
Speakers Bureau
Cubist

Fred A. Lopez, MD, FACP
Royalties
UpToDate

Judith A. O'Donnell, MD
Employment
Spouse works for Viropharma

William R. Short, MD, MPH
Consultantship
Abbott, Tibotec, Gilead
Speakers Bureau
Tibotec, Gilead, Merck

Steven E. Weinberger, MD, FACP
Stock Options/Holdings
Abbott, GlaxoSmithKline

Peter H. Wiernik, MD, FACP
Research Grants/Contracts
Favrille, Celgene
Honoraria
Celgene

John Zurlo, MD
Research Grants/Contracts
Tibotec, Gilead

American College of Physicians

MKSAP® 15

Medical Knowledge Self-Assessment Program®

Infectious Disease

Acknowledgments

The American College of Physicians (ACP) gratefully acknowledges the special contributions to the development and production of the 15th edition of the Medical Knowledge Self-Assessment Program® (MKSAP 15) of Scott Thomas Hurd (Senior Systems Analyst/Developer), Ricki Jo Kauffman (Manager, Systems Development), Michael Ripca (Technical Administrator/Graphics Designer), and Lisa Torrieri (Graphic Designer). The Digital version (CD-ROM and Online components) was developed within the ACP's Interactive Product Development Department by Steven Spadt (Director), Christopher Forrest (Senior Software Developer), Ryan Hinkel (Senior Software Developer), John McKnight (Software Developer), Sean O'Donnell (Senior Software Developer), and Brian Sweigard (Senior Software Developer). Computer scoring and reporting are being performed by ACT, Inc., Iowa City, Iowa. The College also wishes to acknowledge that many other persons, too numerous to mention, have contributed to the production of this program. Without their dedicated efforts, this program would not have been possible.

Continuing Medical Education

The American College of Physicians is accredited by the Accreditation Council for Continuing Medical Education (ACCME) to provide continuing medical education for physicians.

The American College of Physicians designates this educational activity for a maximum of 166 *AMA PRA Category 1 Credits*™. Physicians should only claim credit commensurate with the extent of their participation in the activity.

AMA PRA Category 1 Credit™ is available from July 31, 2009, to July 31, 2012.

Learning Objectives

The learning objectives of MKSAP 15 are to:
- Close gaps between actual care in your practice and preferred standards of care, based on best evidence
- Diagnose disease states that are less common and sometimes overlooked and confusing
- Improve management of comorbidities that can complicate patient care
- Determine when to refer patients for surgery or care by subspecialists
- Pass the ABIM certification examination
- Pass the ABIM maintenance of certification examination

Target Audience

- General internists and primary care physicians
- Subspecialists who need to remain up-to-date in internal medicine
- Residents preparing for the certifying examination in internal medicine
- Physicians preparing for maintenance of certification in internal medicine (recertification)

How to Submit for CME Credits

To earn CME credits, complete a MKSAP 15 answer sheet. Use the enclosed, self-addressed envelope to mail your completed answer sheet(s) to the MKSAP Processing Center for scoring. Remember to provide your MKSAP 15 order and ACP ID numbers in the appropriate spaces on the answer sheet. The order and ACP ID numbers are printed on your mailing label. If you have not received these numbers with your MKSAP 15 purchase, you will need to acquire them to earn CME credits. E-mail ACP's customer service center at custserv@acponline.org. In the subject line, write "MKSAP 15 order/ACP ID numbers." In the body of the e-mail, make sure you include your e-mail address as well as your full name, address, city, state, ZIP code, country, and telephone number. Also identify where you have made your MKSAP 15 purchase. You will receive your MKSAP 15 order and ACP ID numbers by e-mail within 72 business hours.

Disclosure Policy

It is the policy of the American College of Physicians (ACP) to ensure balance, independence, objectivity, and scientific rigor in all its educational activities. To this end, and consistent with the policies of the ACP and the Accreditation Council for Continuing Medical Education (ACCME), contributors to all ACP continuing medical education activities are required to disclose all relevant financial relationships with any entity producing, marketing, re-selling, or distributing health care goods or services consumed by, or used on, patients. Contributors are required to use generic names in the discussion of therapeutic options and are required to identify any unapproved, off-label, or investigative use of commercial products or devices. Where a trade name is used, all available trade names for the same product type are also included. If trade-name products manufactured by companies with whom contributors have relationships are discussed, contributors are asked to provide evidence-based citations in support of the discussion. The information is reviewed by the committee responsible for producing this text. If necessary, adjustments to topics or contributors' roles in content development are made to balance the discussion. Further, all readers of this text are asked to evaluate the content for evidence of commercial bias so that future decisions about content and contributors can be made in light of this information.

Resolution of Conflicts

To resolve all conflicts of interest and influences of vested interests, the ACP precluded members of the content-creation committee from deciding on any content issues that involved generic or trade-name products associated with proprietary entities with which these committee members had relationships. In addition, content was based on best evidence and updated clinical care guidelines, when such evidence and guidelines were available. Contributors' disclosure information can be found with the list of contributors' names and those of ACP principal staff listed in the beginning of this book.

Educational Disclaimer

The editors and publisher of MKSAP 15 recognize that the development of new material offers many opportunities for error. Despite our best efforts, some errors may persist in print. Drug dosage schedules are, we believe, accurate and in accordance with current standards. Readers are advised, however, to ensure that the recommended dosages in MKSAP 15 concur with the information provided in the product information material. This is especially important in cases of new, infrequently used, or highly toxic drugs. Application of the information in MKSAP 15 remains the professional responsibility of the practitioner.

The primary purpose of MKSAP 15 is educational. Information presented, as well as publications, technologies, products, and/or services discussed, is intended to inform subscribers about the knowledge, techniques, and experiences of the contributors. A diversity of professional opinion exists, and the views of the contributors are their own and not those of the ACP. Inclusion of any material in the program does not constitute endorsement or recommendation by the ACP. The ACP does not warrant the safety, reliability, accuracy, completeness, or usefulness of and disclaims any and all liability for damages and claims that may result from the use of information, publications, technologies, products, and/or services discussed in this program.

Publisher's Information

Unauthorized Use of This Book Is Against the Law

MKSAP 15 ISBN: 978-1-934465-25-7
Infectious Disease ISBN: 978-1-934465-34-9

Printed in the United States of America.

For order information in the U.S. or Canada call 800-523-1546, extension 2600. All other countries call 215-351-2600. Fax inquiries to 215-351-2799 or e-mail to custserv@acponline.org.

Errata and Norm Tables

Errata for MKSAP 15 will be posted at http://mksap.acponline.org/errata as new information becomes known to the editors.

MKSAP 15 Performance Interpretation Guidelines with Norm Tables, available December 31, 2010, will reflect the knowledge of physicians who have completed the self-assessment tests before the program was published. These physicians took the tests without being able to refer to the syllabus, answers, and critiques. For your convenience, the tables are available in a printable PDF file at http://mksap.acponline.org/normtables.

Table of Contents

Viral Infections

New Principles in Antibiotics

Infectious Disease

Infections of the Central Nervous System

Bacterial Central Nervous System Infections

Meningitis

Major changes in the epidemiology of bacterial meningitis have occurred in the United States, primarily owing to the availability of conjugate vaccines that confer protection against the common meningeal pathogens. In the latest surveillance data released by the Centers for Disease Control and Prevention (CDC), *Streptococcus pneumoniae* was the most common etiologic agent of bacterial meningitis (61%), followed by *Neisseria meningitidis* (16%), group B streptococcus (14%), *Haemophilus influenzae* (7%), and *Listeria monocytogenes* (2%).

Meningitis caused by *S. pneumoniae* may occur in conjunction with other suppurative foci of infection (for example, pneumonia, otitis media, mastoiditis, sinusitis, endocarditis, or in the setting of head trauma with cerebrospinal fluid [CSF] leak). Initial studies of a heptavalent conjugate pneumococcal vaccine demonstrated an efficacy of 97.4% in preventing invasive pneumococcal disease in fully vaccinated children, leading the American Academy of Pediatrics Committee on Infectious Diseases to recommend vaccination for all infants younger than aged 2 years. Since licensure of this vaccine in 2000, invasive pneumococcal disease incidence among the target population of children younger than 5 years has decreased. The use of the vaccine has also reduced invasive pneumococcal disease incidence among unvaccinated populations including adults, indicating herd immunity in those who did not receive vaccination. The overall rate of pneumococcal meningitis caused by serotypes in the 7-valent conjugate pneumococcal vaccine has declined, but disease caused by serotypes 19A, 22F, and 35B, which are not contained in the vaccine, has increased. A 13-valent conjugate pneumococcal vaccine containing additional serotypes was being studied at the time of publication.

N. meningitidis meningitis usually occurs in children and young adults. Patients with deficiencies in certain complement components (see Repeated Infections) are predisposed to infection with neisserial species, including *N. meningitidis*. In 2005, the U.S. Food and Drug Administration approved licensure of a meningococcal conjugate vaccine against serogroups A, C, Y, and W135 (Menactra®) (MCV-4) for protection against *N. meningitidis*–induced disease in persons aged 11 to 55 years. The CDC's Advisory Committee on Immunization Practices recommended routine immunization with MCV-4 for pre-adolescent children aged 11 or 12 years and "catch-up" vaccination for previously unvaccinated teens entering high school and for college freshmen. Other recommended groups are microbiologists with frequent exposure to *N. meningitidis*, travelers to hyperendemic areas of the world, and patients with a history of splenectomy or functional asplenia. This vaccine may also provide herd immunity by decreasing nasopharyngeal colonization. MCV-4 does not provide protection against serogroup B meningococcus, which may be responsible for up to 30% of all cases of invasive meningococcal disease in the United States.

Group B streptococcal meningitis is an important cause of meningitis in neonates. Disease in adults has been associated with underlying conditions or settings, including diabetes mellitus, cardiac disease, malignancy, collagen vascular disorders, alcoholism, liver and kidney disease, corticosteroid use, and HIV infection.

Meningitis caused by *L. monocytogenes* occurs rarely in the United States, although it represents approximately 20% of cases in the neonatal population. Outbreaks have been associated with consumption of contaminated cole slaw, raw vegetables, milk, cheese, and processed meats, implicating the gastrointestinal tract as the usual portal of entry. Disease is associated with extremes of age (neonates and persons >50 years), alcoholism, malignancy, immune suppression, diabetes mellitus, liver and kidney disease, iron overload, collagen vascular disorders, pregnancy, HIV infection, and use of antitumor necrosis factor-α agents such as infliximab and etanercept.

H. influenzae type b is now a rare cause of bacterial meningitis in the United States since the licensure and routine use of *H. influenzae* type b conjugate vaccines. Gram-negative bacilli (*Klebsiella* species, *Escherichia coli*, *Serratia marcescens*, and *Pseudomonas aeruginosa*) may cause meningitis in patients following neurosurgical procedures or head trauma, or in association with disseminated strongyloidiasis in the hyperinfection syndrome. *Staphylococcus aureus* meningitis usually occurs in the postneurosurgical period or after head trauma, but it may also develop in patients with diabetes mellitus, alcoholism, chronic kidney disease requiring hemodialysis, injection drug use, endocarditis, and malignancy. Coagulase-negative staphylococci are the most common cause of meningitis in patients with CSF shunts.

Adult patients with bacterial meningitis classically present with fever, headache, nuchal rigidity, and signs of cerebral dysfunction, although insidious onset with lethargy or obtundation and variable signs of meningeal irritation may be present in elderly patients, especially in the setting of diabetes mellitus or cardiopulmonary disease. The diagnosis of acute bacterial meningitis is established by CSF analysis (**Table 1**). The initial management approach to the patient with acute meningitis is shown in **Figure 1**. Once there is suspicion of acute bacterial meningitis, blood cultures must be obtained and a lumbar puncture immediately performed to determine whether the CSF findings are consistent with the clinical diagnosis. In some patients, the clinician may not emergently perform the lumbar puncture (that is, secondary to the inability to obtain CSF or the concern that the clinical presentation is caused by a central nervous system [CNS] mass lesion, in which case a CT scan of the head will be performed before lumbar puncture). CT scan before lumbar puncture should be performed in patients who are immunocompromised, have a history of CNS disease, present with new-onset seizures, or have an abnormal level of consciousness, focal neurologic deficit, or papilledema. It has also recently been suggested that lumbar puncture should be delayed in patients with clinical signs of impending brain herniation because of the risk for precipitating brain herniation, even in those with a normal CT. These clinical signs include a deteriorating level of consciousness (particularly a Glasgow Coma Scale score of <11), brain stem signs (including pupillary changes, posturing, or irregular respirations), and a very recent seizure. In those patients in whom the lumbar puncture is delayed, blood cultures must be obtained and appropriate adjunctive and antimicrobial therapy (**Table 2**) given before lumbar puncture. Once CSF analysis is performed, targeted antimicrobial therapy (**Table 3**) can be initiated in patients with a positive Gram stain result.

Once an etiologic agent is identified and antimicrobial susceptibility has been performed, specific antimicrobial therapy should be started (**Table 4**).

Administration of adjunctive dexamethasone should be strongly considered in patients with acute bacterial meningitis, because clinical trials have established the benefit of adjunctive dexamethasone on adverse outcomes and death in adults with suspected or proven pneumococcal meningitis. In patients with pneumococcal meningitis caused by strains that are highly resistant to penicillin or cephalosporins, careful follow-up for possible dexamethasone-associated adverse clinical outcomes is critical because there are insufficient outcome data on patients treated with adjunctive dexamethasone who are subsequently found to have meningitis caused by these resistant bacteria. In this circumstance, repeat CSF analysis should be performed in any patient who has not responded clinically after 48 hours of appropriate antimicrobial therapy.

Appropriate timing of dexamethasone administration in patients with suspected or proven bacterial meningitis is crucial. Dexamethasone (0.15 mg/kg every 6 hours for 2 to 4 days) should be administered with or just before the first dose of antimicrobial therapy for maximal benefit. There are insufficient data in adults with pneumococcal meningitis to know whether dexamethasone administration after antimicrobial therapy offers any outcome benefit.

KEY POINTS

- The meningococcal conjugate vaccine against serogroups A, C, Y, and W135 (MCV-4) is recommended for pre-adolescent children aged 11 or 12 years; unvaccinated teens entering high school and college freshmen requiring "catch-up vaccination"; microbiologists with frequent exposure to *Neisseria meningitidis;* travelers to hyperendemic areas of the world; and patients with a history of splenectomy or functional asplenia.

- The meningococcal conjugate vaccine against serogroups A, C, Y, and W135 (MCV-4) does not provide protection against serogroup B meningococcus, which may be responsible for up to 30% of all cases of invasive meningococcal disease in the United States.

- Fever, headache, nuchal rigidity, and signs of cerebral dysfunction are the classic symptoms of bacterial meningitis, although insidious onset with lethargy or obtundation and variable signs of meningeal irritation may be present in elderly patients.

- The diagnosis of acute bacterial meningitis is established by cerebrospinal fluid analysis.

- In patients with bacterial meningitis in whom Gram stain results are negative or lumbar puncture is delayed, empiric antimicrobial therapy should be initiated based on patient age and the underlying condition.

- Patients with bacterial meningitis who received adjunctive dexamethasone experienced fewer unfavorable outcomes or death.

Brain Abscess

Before the advent of HIV infection, about 1500 to 2500 patients received treatment for brain abscesses in the United States annually. Mortality rates now range from 0 to 24%, compared with previous rates of 30% to 60%. This decrease can be attributed to the availability of more effective antimicrobial regimens, new surgical techniques, and the availability of CT scanning, which allows early diagnosis and monitoring of patients with brain abscesses.

The most common mechanism of brain abscess formation is spread from a contiguous focus of infection, most often originating in the middle ear, mastoid cells, or paranasal sinuses. A second mechanism of brain abscess formation is hematogenous spread from a distant focus of infection. These abscesses are usually multiple and multiloculated and confer a higher mortality rate than those arising from contiguous foci of infection. The most common source of initial infection in adults with brain abscesses is chronic pyogenic lung disease, but hematogenous spread to the brain may also result from wound and skin infections, osteomyelitis, pelvic infection,

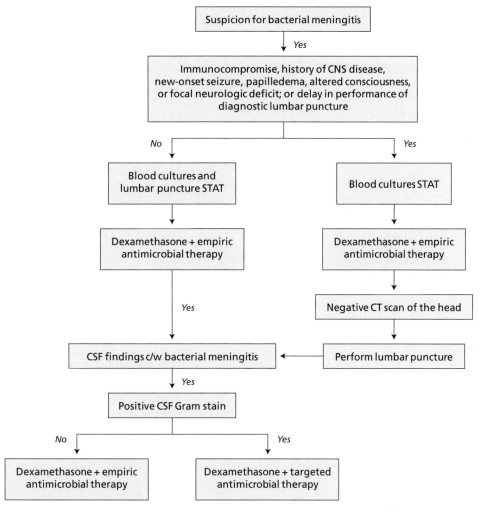

FIGURE 1.
Management algorithm for adults with suspected bacterial meningitis.

CNS = central nervous system; c/w = consistent with; CSF = cerebrospinal fluid.

Reprinted with permission from Tunkel AR, Hartman BJ, Kaplan SL, Kaufman BA, Roos KL, Scheld WM, et al. Practice guidelines for the management of bacterial meningitis. Clin Inf Dis. 2004; 39:1267–84. Copyright 2004 Infectious Diseases Society of America.

TABLE 1 Typical Cerebrospinal Fluid Findings in Patients with Acute Meningitis		
CSF Parameter	**Bacterial**	**Viral**[a]
Opening pressure (mm H_2O)	200-500[b]	≤250
Leukocyte count (µL)	1000-5000 (1000-5000 × 10^6/L)[c]	50-1000 (50-1000 × 10^6/L)
Leukocyte differential	Neutrophils	Lymphocytes[d]
Glucose	<40 mg/dL (2.2 mmol/L)[e]	>45 mg/dL (2.5 mmol/L)
Protein	100-500 mg/dL (1000-5000 mg/L)	<200 mg/dL (2000 mg/L)
Gram stain	Positive in 60-90%[f]	Negative
Culture	Positive in 70-85%	Negative

CSF = cerebrospinal fluid.

[a]Primarily nonpolio enteroviruses (echoviruses and coxsackieviruses).

[b]Values exceeding 600 mm H_2O suggest the presence of cerebral edema, intracranial suppurative foci, or communicating hydrocephalus.

[c]Range may be <100 to >10,000 cells/µL (100-10,000 × 10^6/L).

[d]May have a neutrophil predominance early in infection, but gives way to lymphocyte predominance over the first 6-48 hours.

[e]The CSF:serum glucose ratio is ≤0.40 in most patients.

[f]Likelihood of a positive Gram stain correlates with number of bacteria in CSF.

TABLE 2 Empiric Antimicrobial Therapy for Purulent Meningitis Based on Patient Age and Underlying Condition

Predisposing Factor	Common Bacterial Pathogens	Antimicrobial Therapy
Age 0-4 weeks	*Streptococcus agalactiae, Escherichia coli, Listeria monocytogenes, Klebsiella* species	Ampicillin + cefotaxime; or ampicillin + an aminoglycoside
Age 1-23 months	*Streptococcus pneumoniae, Haemophilus influenzae, S. agalactiae, Neisseria meningitidis, E. coli*	Vancomycin + a third-generation cephalosporin[a,b,c]
Age 2-50 years	*S. pneumoniae, N. meningitidis*	Vancomycin + a third- generation cephalosporin[a,b,c]
Age >50 years	*S. pneumoniae, N. meningitidis, L. monocytogenes,* gram-negative bacilli	Vancomycin + ampicillin + a third-generation cephalosporin[a,b]
Basilar skull fracture	*S. pneumoniae, H. influenzae,* group A β-hemolytic streptococci	Vancomycin + a third-generation cephalosporin[a]
Postneurosurgery or head trauma	*Staphylococcus aureus,* coagulase-negative staphylococci (especially *Staphylococcus epidermidis*), gram-negative bacilli (including *Pseudomonas aeruginosa*)	Vancomycin + either ceftazidime or cefepime or meropenem
Cerebrospinal fluid shunt	*S. aureus,* coagulase-negative staphylococci (especially *S. epidermidis*), gram-negative bacilli (including *P. aeruginosa*), diphtheroids (including *Propionibacterium acnes*)	Vancomycin + either ceftazidime or cefepime or meropenem

[a]Cefotaxime or ceftriaxone.

[b]Some experts would add rifampin if dexamethasone is given.

[c]Add ampicillin if the patient has risk factors for *Listeria monocytogenes* or infection with this organism is suspected.

TABLE 3 Targeted Antimicrobial Therapy Recommendations for Bacterial Meningitis[a]

Microorganism	Antimicrobial Therapy
Streptococcus pneumoniae[b]	Vancomycin + a third-generation cephalosporin[c,d]
Neisseria meningitidis	A third-generation cephalosporin[c]
Listeria monocytogenes	Ampicillin or penicillin G[e]
Streptococcus agalactiae	Ampicillin or penicillin G[e]
Haemophilus influenzae type b[f]	A third-generation cephalosporin[c]

[a]Based on presumptive pathogen identification by cerebrospinal fluid Gram stain.

[b]Pending in vitro susceptibility testing, assume that the pneumococcal isolate is highly resistant to penicillin and use combination therapy.

[c]Cefotaxime or ceftriaxone.

[d]Addition of rifampin may be considered.

[e]Addition of an aminoglycoside may be considered.

[f]Pending in vitro susceptibility testing, assume that the microorganism produces β-lactamase.

cholecystitis, endocarditis, and other intraabdominal infections. Trauma is the third pathogenic mechanism of brain abscess formation, secondary to an open cranial fracture with dural breach or to neurosurgery or foreign-body injury. Brain abscess is cryptogenic in about 20% of patients.

Patients with brain abscesses commonly have headache, with severe pain usually located on the same side of the head as the abscess that is gradual or acute in onset and that may not be relieved by aspirin or other over-the-counter medications. Neck stiffness, changes in mental status, and vomiting may also occur.

Physical examination findings may include fever (45% to 50%), neurologic deficits (about 50%), and seizure (about 25%), with tonic-clonic seizures a very common occurrence in patients with frontal abscesses.

MRI is more sensitive than CT in the diagnostic evaluation of brain abscess and offers significant advantages in the early detection of cerebritis and satellite lesions and identification of spread of inflammation into the ventricles and subarachnoid space. On T1-weighted nonenhanced images, the capsule of the abscess reveals a thin-walled ring that is isointense to slightly hyperintense relative to the brain, and hypointense on T2-weighted images; after gadolinium administration, the abscess shows a ring or, less commonly, multiloculated enhancement.

The use of CT scanning in patients with suspected brain abscess has allowed stereotactic CT-guided aspiration to facilitate microbiologic diagnosis and guide antimicrobial therapy. During aspiration, specimens should be obtained for Gram stain and for cultures to identify aerobic and anaerobic organisms and mycobacteria and fungi. Other special stains, such as the acid-fast stain for mycobacteria, the modified acid-fast stain for *Nocardia* species, and special stains for fungi (for example, mucicarmine and methenamine silver) should be performed to aid in the diagnosis.

After appropriate neuroimaging is performed, emergent surgery is required in patients with brain abscess, with excision or stereotactic aspiration of all lesions greater than 2.5 cm in diameter. When all abscesses are 2.5 cm in diameter or less, the largest lesion should be aspirated to facilitate diagnosis

TABLE 4 Recommendations for Specific Antimicrobial Therapy for Bacterial Meningitis Based on Pathogen and In Vitro Susceptibility Testing

Microorganism	Standard Therapy	Alternative Therapies
Streptococcus pneumoniae		
Penicillin MIC <0.1 µg/mL	Penicillin G or ampicillin	Third-generation cephalosporin[a]; chloramphenicol
Penicillin MIC 0.1-1.0 µg/mL	Third-generation cephalosporin[a]	Meropenem; cefepime
Penicillin MIC ≥2.0 µg/mL; or cefotaxime or ceftriaxone MIC ≥1.0 µg/mL	Vancomycin + a third-generation cephalosporin[a,b]	A fluoroquinolone[c]
Neisseria meningitidis		
Penicillin MIC <0.1 µg/mL	Penicillin G or ampicillin	Third-generation cephalosporin[a]; chloramphenicol
Penicillin MIC 0.1-1.0 µg/mL	A third-generation cephalosporin[a]	Chloramphenicol; a fluoroquinolone; meropenem
Listeria monocytogenes	Ampicillin or penicillin G[d]	Trimethoprim-sulfamethoxazole
Streptococcus agalactiae	Ampicillin or penicillin G[d]	Third-generation cephalosporin[a]; vancomycin
Haemophilus influenzae		
β-Lactamase-negative	Ampicillin	Third-generation cephalosporin[a]; cefepime; chloramphenicol; a fluoroquinolone; aztreonam
β-Lactamase-positive	Third-generation cephalosporin[a]	Chloramphenicol; cefepime; a fluoroquinolone; aztreonam
Escherichia coli and other Enterobacteriaceae[e]	Third-generation cephalosporin[a]	Aztreonam; meropenem; a fluoroquinolone; trimethoprim-sulfamethoxazole
Pseudomonas aeruginosa	Ceftazidime[d] or cefepime[d]	Aztreonam[d]; meropenem[d]; a fluoroquinolone[d]
Staphylococcus aureus		
Methicillin-sensitive	Nafcillin or oxacillin	Vancomycin; meropenem
Methicillin-resistant	Vancomycin[f]	Trimethoprim-sulfamethoxazole; linezolid; daptomycin
Staphylococcus epidermidis	Vancomycin[f]	Linezolid

MIC = minimal inhibitory concentration.

[a]Cefotaxime or ceftriaxone.

[b]Addition of rifampin should be considered if the organism is sensitive and if the ceftriaxone MIC is >2 µg/mL.

[c]No clinical data available; would use newer fluoroquinolones with in vitro activity against *S. pneumoniae* (e.g., moxifloxacin). Many experts would not use a fluoroquinolone as single-agent therapy but would combine with vancomycin or a third-generation cephalosporin such as cefotaxime or ceftriaxone.

[d]Addition of an aminoglycoside should be considered.

[e]Choice of specific antimicrobial therapy should be guided by in vitro susceptibility test results.

[f]Consider addition of rifampin.

and identification of microorganisms. Once abscess material is aspirated for use in microbiologic and histologic studies, empiric antimicrobial therapy consisting of abscess cavity–penetrating agents should be initiated based on the likely pathogenesis of infection (**Table 5**). After the infecting pathogen(s) have been isolated, antimicrobial therapy can be modified for optimal treatment. However, even when only a single pathogen is isolated, pathogenesis of spread to the CNS should be considered in the selection of antimicrobial agents because certain bacteria such as anaerobes may not be identified by routine culture techniques. Six to 8 weeks of antimicrobial therapy is generally recommended in patients with adequate surgical drainage, with regular follow-up neuroimaging studies for 3 months to evaluate the therapeutic response.

KEY POINTS

- The most common mechanisms of brain abscess formation are from a contiguous focus of infection, hematogenous spread from a distant focus of infection, or trauma.

- MRI is more sensitive than CT in the diagnostic evaluation of brain abscess and offers early detection of cerebritis and satellite lesions and identification of spread of inflammation into the ventricles and subarachnoid space.

- After appropriate neuroimaging is performed, emergent surgery is required in patients with brain abscess, with excision or stereotactic aspiration of all lesions greater than 2.5 cm in diameter.

TABLE 5 Recommendations for Empiric Antimicrobial Therapy in Patients with Bacterial Brain Abscess Based on Predisposing Condition

Predisposing Condition	Usual Bacterial Isolates	Antimicrobial Regimen
Otitis media or mastoiditis	Streptococci (aerobic or anaerobic); *Bacteroides* species; *Prevotella* species; Enterobacteriaceae	Metronidazole + a third-generation cephalosporin[a]
Sinusitis	Streptococci, *Bacteroides* species; Enterobacteriaceae; *Staphylococcus aureus*; *Haemophilus* species	Vancomycin + metronidazole + a third-generation cephalosporin[a]
Dental sepsis	Mixed *Fusobacterium*, *Prevotella*, and *Bacteroides* species; streptococci	Penicillin + metronidazole
Penetrating trauma or after neurosurgery	*S. aureus*, streptococci; Enterobacteriaceae; *Clostridium* species	Vancomycin + a third-generation cephalosporin[a]
Lung abscess, empyema, bronchiectasis	*Fusobacterium*, *Actinomyces*, *Bacteroides*, and *Prevotella* species; streptococci; *Nocardia* species	Penicillin + metronidazole + a sulfonamide[b]
Endocarditis	*S. aureus*, streptococci	Vancomycin + gentamicin

[a]Cefotaxime or ceftriaxone; use cefepime if *Pseudomonas aeruginosa* is suspected.

[b]Trimethoprim-sulfamethoxazole; include if *Nocardia* species are suspected.

Subdural Empyema

Subdural empyema (an infectious process occupying the space between the dura mater and arachnoid membrane surrounding the brain) accounts for 15% to 20% of all localized intracranial infections, with mortality rates of approximately 10% to 20%. The most common conditions predisposing to cranial subdural empyema are otorhinologic infections, especially of the paranasal sinuses, which are affected in 50% to 80% of patients, followed by the mastoid cells and the middle ear in 10% to 20%. Metastatic infection is present in only about 5% of patients.

Several bacterial species have been isolated in patients with cranial subdural empyema, including aerobic streptococci (25% to 45%), staphylococci (10% to 15%), aerobic gram-negative bacilli (3% to 10%), and anaerobic streptococci and other anaerobes (from 33% to as high as 100% in some series in which careful culturing was performed); polymicrobial infections are common. Surgical cultures do not yield growth in 7% to 53% of cases, presumably because of prior administration of antimicrobial therapy or failure to use proper techniques for anaerobic cultures.

The diagnosis of cranial subdural empyema should be considered in any patient presenting with meningeal signs and a focal neurologic deficit. MRI, which is the diagnostic imaging procedure of choice, provides better clarity of detail than CT in the diagnosis of cranial subdural empyema and is particularly helpful in detecting subdural empyemas located at the base of the brain, along the falx cerebri, or in the posterior fossa. MRI can also differentiate extra-axial empyemas from most sterile effusions and subdural hematomas. T1-weighted images show mass effect and hypointense areas of purulence, which are hyperintense on T2-weighted images.

Subdural empyema is a medical and surgical emergency. Surgery is needed because antimicrobial agents alone do not reliably sterilize the empyema. Cultures of purulent material can be used to guide antimicrobial therapy based on Gram stain results and predisposing factors for infection. Given the likelihood of polymicrobial infection from paranasal sinusitis, an empiric regimen of vancomycin, metronidazole, and an agent with broad in vitro activity against aerobic gram-negative bacilli such as cefepime, ceftazidime, or meropenem is reasonable, pending microorganism identification and in vitro susceptibility testing.

The goals of surgical therapy are to achieve adequate decompression of the brain and to evacuate the empyema completely. The optimal surgical approach (that is, drainage via burr holes or craniotomy) is controversial, although some studies have demonstrated a better outcome for patients who undergo craniotomy drainage versus burr-hole surgery.

KEY POINTS

- The most common conditions predisposing to cranial subdural empyema are otorhinologic infections, especially of the paranasal sinuses, followed by infection of the mastoid cells and the middle ear.
- Metastatic infection is present in only about 5% of patients with cranial subdural empyema.
- In the diagnosis of subdural empyema, MRI is preferred to CT.
- In patients with suspected subdural empyemas, MRI can differentiate extra-axial empyemas from most sterile effusions and subdural hematomas.
- Subdural empyema is a surgical emergency requiring adequate decompression of the brain and evacuation of the empyema.
- Empiric treatment of subdural empyema includes vancomycin, metronidazole and either cefepime, ceftazidime, or meropenem.

Epidural Abscess

Epidural abscess is a localized collection of pus between the dura mater and overlying skull or vertebral column. Spinal epidural abscess usually occurs secondary to hematogenous dissemination from foci elsewhere in the body to the epidural space (50% of patients) or by contiguous extension (30% of patients) from conditions such as vertebral osteomyelitis. Bacteremia may be an important predisposing factor to development of epidural abscess because the incidence of spinal epidural abscess is increased in patients who use injection drugs. Diabetes mellitus is also an important risk factor, present in up to 50% of patients. The infecting microorganism in most patients with spinal epidural abscess is *S. aureus* (50% to 90%), with more cases in recent years caused by methicillin-resistant *S. aureus* (MRSA). Gram-negative bacilli (especially *E. coli* and *P. aeruginosa*) are present in 12% to 17% of patients, and aerobic and anaerobic streptococci are isolated in 8% to 17%. A primary source of infection is not identified in 20% to 40% of patients with epidural abscess.

The triad of symptoms in patients with spinal epidural abscess consists of fever, spinal pain, and neurologic deficits, but all three symptoms are present in only a few patients on presentation. Early diagnosis and intervention are crucial because, left untreated, symptoms of epidural abscess progress sequentially from pain to potentially irreversible paralysis. Signs and symptoms of cranial epidural abscess are the result of infection and the slowly expanding intracranial mass. Diagnosis is often delayed because cranial epidural abscess is often a complication of another localized infection (sinusitis or mastoiditis) that dominates the clinical focus.

MRI is the diagnostic procedure of choice in patients with suspected spinal epidural abscess. MRI is recommended over CT because it can better facilitate visualization of the spinal cord and epidural space in both sagittal and transverse sections and can help to identify accompanying osteomyelitis, intramedullary spinal cord lesions, and diskitis.

Therapy for spinal epidural abscess consists of prompt surgical decompression, abscess drainage, and long-term antimicrobial therapy. Empiric antimicrobial therapy must include an antistaphylococcal agent (that is, vancomycin pending microorganism identification and in vitro susceptibility testing) plus coverage for aerobic gram-negative bacilli with an agent such as cefepime, ceftazidime, or meropenem, especially in patients with a history of spinal procedure or injection drug use.

Patients with spinal epidural abscess and neurologic dysfunction represent a surgical emergency and require laminectomy with decompression and drainage to minimize the likelihood of permanent neurologic sequelae. Antimicrobial therapy alone can be used in patients who have localized pain or radicular symptoms without long-tract findings, although these patients require frequent neurologic examinations and serial MRI studies to demonstrate resolution of the abscess; emergency surgical decompression should be performed in any patient with an increasing neurologic deficit, persistent severe pain, or increasing fever or persistent leukocytosis. Although emergent decompressive laminectomy is not indicated in patients with paralysis of more than 24 to 36 hours' duration, it may still be needed to treat the epidural infection

and control sepsis. In patients receiving antimicrobial therapy alone, identification of the causative pathogen may be attempted by CT-guided needle aspiration, which is important in guiding appropriate drug therapy.

KEY POINTS

- Spinal epidural abscess usually occurs secondary to hematogenous dissemination from foci elsewhere in the body to the epidural space, by contiguous extension, or may be associated with transient bacteremia.
- MRI is the diagnostic procedure of choice in patients with suspected spinal epidural abscess.
- Therapy for spinal epidural abscess consists of prompt surgical decompression, abscess drainage, and early empiric antimicrobial therapy.
- Although emergent decompressive laminectomy is not indicated in patients with epidural abscess and paralysis of more than 24 to 36 hours' duration, it may still be needed to treat the epidural infection and control sepsis.

Viral Central Nervous System Infections

Viral Encephalitis

Encephalitis is defined by the presence of an inflammatory process in the brain associated with clinical evidence of neurologic dysfunction. Various pathogens cause encephalitis, most of which are viruses. The most commonly identified viral causes of encephalitis in the United States are herpes simplex virus, West Nile virus, and the enteroviruses, followed by other herpesviruses such as varicella-zoster virus. However, the cause of encephalitis remains unknown in 32% to 75% of patients despite extensive testing. Furthermore, approximately 10% of patients initially thought to have an infectious cause for their encephalitis are ultimately found to have a noninfectious condition. All patients with suspected encephalitis should undergo neuroimaging (preferably MRI) and CSF analysis with appropriate serologic or nucleic acid amplification tests to identify the causative agent. Recommended studies, including additional tests on specimens outside the CNS, are guided by specific epidemiologic clues (see below). Although the cause of encephalitis remains unidentified in many cases, identifying the cause is important for facilitating prognosis, potential prophylaxis, patient and family counseling, and initiating public health interventions.

Epidemiologic clues helpful in identifying etiologic agents in patients with encephalitis include season of the year; geographic locale; prevalence of disease in the local community; patient immune status; and history of travel, recreation, occupation, insect contact, animal contact, and vaccination. Clinical presentation and certain physical examination findings, such as rash, pulmonary findings, and neurologic presentation, may also be informative. Although these clues may be suggestive of certain causes of encephalitis, the etiologic diagnosis is based on identifying microorganisms in specimens from outside or within the central nervous system (CNS). Specimens from outside the CNS include specific fluid cultures (blood, nasopharynx, sputum, and urine), direct fluorescent antibody testing (for example, of skin lesions), tissue biopsies with use of nucleic acid amplification tests such as polymerase chain reaction (PCR), and serologic testing. For serologic testing, measurement of acute and convalescent serum IgG titers is useful for the retrospective diagnosis of infection by a causative agent, although this testing is generally not useful in guiding specific therapy because a diagnosis may not be confirmed for several weeks following the acute illness.

MRI is the diagnostic neuroimaging procedure of choice in patients with suspected encephalitis, although it generally does not differentiate a specific cause of encephalitis from another. Results of electroencephalography are generally nonspecific but can identify nonconvulsive seizure activity in those who are confused, obtunded, or comatose. Unless contraindicated, CSF analysis is essential in patients with viral encephalitis and typically reveals a mononuclear pleocytosis and mild or moderately elevated protein concentration; however, a few patients (approximately 3% to 5%) with severe CNS viral infections, including herpes simplex encephalitis, can have completely normal CSF. The presence of virus-specific IgM in CSF usually indicates CNS disease, because IgM antibodies do not readily cross the blood-brain barrier. The development of nucleic acid amplification tests such as PCR has greatly increased the ability to establish a diagnosis of CNS infection, especially herpesvirus infection. CSF cultures are of limited value in isolating viral causes of encephalitis. Brain biopsy is used only rarely to identify the cause of encephalitis but should be considered in patients with encephalitis of unknown cause whose condition deteriorates neurologically despite acyclovir therapy.

Herpes Simplex Encephalitis

Herpes simplex virus is one of the most common causes of identified sporadic encephalitis worldwide, accounting for 5% to 10% of cases. Herpes simplex virus type 1 occurs more commonly in adults, and herpes simplex virus type 2 occurs more commonly in neonates.

Clinical features of herpes simplex encephalitis include fever, hemicranial headache, language and behavioral abnormalities, memory impairment, cranial nerve deficits, and seizures. On T1-weighted MRI, edema and hemorrhage in the temporal lobes and hypodense areas and nonhomogeneous contrast enhancement may be identified. Bilateral temporal lobe involvement is nearly always pathognomonic for herpes simplex encephalitis but is a late development. More than 90% of patients with herpes simplex encephalitis documented by CSF PCR have abnormalities on MRI of the brain. In more than 80% of patients with herpes simplex encephalitis, electroencephalography

demonstrates a temporal focus that typically occurs between days 2 and 14 of symptom onset.

The reported sensitivity and specificity of CSF PCR is greater than 96% to 98% and 95% to 99%, respectively. CSF PCR results are positive early in the disease course and remain positive during the first week of therapy; false-negative results are observed when hemoglobin or other inhibitors are present in the CSF. The presence of fewer than 10 leukocytes/µL (10×10^6/L) in the CSF has also been associated with a higher likelihood for a negative CSF PCR result. Initially negative CSF PCR results for herpes simplex virus may become positive on repeat testing 1 to 3 days after treatment initiation in patients with herpes simplex encephalitis. Therefore, in undiagnosed cases of encephalitis in which patients have clinical features suggestive of this disease or temporal lobe findings on neuroimaging, a repeat CSF PCR on a second CSF specimen should be considered 3 to 7 days into therapy.

Although various viruses may cause encephalitis, specific antiviral therapy is generally limited to disease caused by the herpesviruses, especially herpes simplex virus. Acyclovir, 10 mg/kg intravenously every 8 hours for 14 to 21 days in patients with normal renal function, is the treatment of choice. However, despite the availability of specific antiviral therapy, mortality is 28% 18 months after treatment. Predictors of adverse outcome include patient age older than 30 years, depressed level of consciousness with a Glasgow Coma Scale score of less than 6, and symptom duration before starting acyclovir of greater than 4 days. Initiation of therapy fewer than 4 days after symptom onset has reduced mortality to 8%. Negative CSF PCR results at the completion of therapy in patients with herpes simplex encephalitis are associated with a better outcome, suggesting that a CSF PCR assay should be repeated at completion of therapy in patients who have not responded fully to treatment. Positive CSF PCR test results indicate the need for continuation of antiviral therapy.

Arboviral Encephalitis

Arboviruses are viral agents with avian or small mammalian reservoirs transmitted by mosquito or other arthropod vector, and they can lead to development of encephalitis. In the United States, the most important agents are the La Crosse virus, St. Louis encephalitis virus, Eastern equine encephalitis virus, and West Nile virus. Most people infected with arboviruses are presumed to have subclinical infection, although they may develop neuroinvasive disease.

In recent years, the West Nile virus has been identified as an important cause of encephalitis in the United States and has now been identified in almost all parts of the United States. Birds are the main reservoir of this virus in nature. Several species of mosquitoes can acquire the virus after biting a bird with high-level viremia. Besides mosquito-vector transmission, West Nile virus transmission may also occur through transfusion, transplantation, and breastfeeding. In patients with West Nile virus infection, an increased incidence of encephalitis exists in those older than 50 years (1 in 150 develop neuroinvasive disease) and who are immunocompromised.

Clinical features of neurologic infection with West Nile virus include tremors, myoclonus, parkinsonism, and poliomyelitis-like flaccid paralysis that may be irreversible. In recent years, IgM- and IgG-capture enzyme-linked immunosorbent assays have become the most useful and widely used tests for diagnosing arboviral encephalitis. However, cross-reactivity of serologic assays may occur, particularly among the flaviviruses such as Japanese encephalitis virus, St. Louis encephalitis virus, and West Nile virus. In areas in which multiple flaviviruses may cocirculate or in patients who have previously received vaccination against a related flavivirus such as Japanese encephalitis virus or yellow-fever virus, plaque-reduction neutralization testing is recommended.

In patients with encephalitis caused by flaviviruses and Eastern equine encephalitis virus, MRI may display a characteristic pattern of mixed-intensity or hypodense lesions on T1-weighted images in the thalamus, basal ganglia, and midbrain, which are hyperintense on T2-weighted and fluid-attenuated inversion recovery (FLAIR) imaging. These neuroimaging findings occur in about 30% of patients with West Nile virus encephalitis.

The detection of CSF IgM antibodies by enzyme-linked immunosorbent assay in patients with presumed flavivirus encephalitis is considered diagnostic of neuroinvasive disease. Approximately 90% of patients with neuroinvasive disease caused by West Nile virus will have detectable CSF IgM antibody titers 8 to 10 days after symptom onset, and these titers are still detectable more than 500 days after presentation; therefore, the presence of CSF IgM antibodies in patients with West Nile virus–associated neuroinvasive disease is suggestive of acute infection only in the setting of a compatible clinical syndrome. CSF PCR results are positive for West Nile virus in less than 60% of serologically confirmed cases.

Effective therapy is not available for arbovirus-induced encephalitis. Studies on the benefits of therapy with interferon alfa and interferon alfa-2b have been inconclusive or limited. A prospective, randomized trial is needed to support this approach.

One study of patients with West Nile virus encephalitis in Israel found no significant benefit in patients who took oral ribavirin, and treatment was possibly detrimental. However, multivariate analysis suggests that the use of ribavirin may have been a surrogate marker for use in sicker patients. Interferon alfa was used in a nonrandomized, nonblinded assessment of patients with West Nile virus encephalitis, but the results were inconclusive.

KEY POINTS

- Unless contraindicated, cerebrospinal fluid analysis is essential in patients with viral encephalitis and typically reveals a mononuclear pleocytosis and mild or moderately elevated protein concentration.

- The cerebrospinal fluid may be completely normal in about 3% to 5% of patients with viral encephalitis.

- Clinical features of herpes simplex encephalitis include fever, hemicranial headache, language and behavioral abnormalities, memory impairment, cranial nerve deficits, and seizures.

- Acyclovir is the treatment of choice in patients with herpes simplex encephalitis.

- Clinical features of West Nile virus encephalitis include tremors, myoclonus, parkinsonism, and poliomyelitis-like flaccid paralysis that may be irreversible.

- The detection of cerebrospinal fluid IgM antibodies by enzyme-linked immunosorbent assay in patients with presumed flavivirus encephalitis is considered diagnostic of neuroinvasive disease.

- Effective therapy is not currently available for arbovirus-induced encephalitis.

Bibliography

Bloch KC, Glaser C. Diagnostic approaches for patients with suspected encephalitis. Curr Infect Dis Rep. 2007;9(4):315-322. [PMID: 17618552]

Bode AV, Sejvar JJ, Pape WJ, Campbell GL, Marfin AA. West Nile virus disease: a descriptive study of 228 patients hospitalized in a 4-county region of Colorado in 2003. Clin Infect Dis. 2006;42(9):1234-1240. [PMID: 16586381]

Carpenter J, Stapleton S, Holliman R. Retrospective analysis of 49 cases of brain abscess and review of the literature. Eur J Clin Microbiol Infect Dis. 2007;26(1):1-11. [PMID: 17180609]

Darouiche RO. Spinal epidural abscess. N Engl J Med. 2006;355(19):2012-2020. [PMID: 17093252]

Dery MA, Hasbun R. Changing epidemiology of bacterial meningitis. Curr Infect Dis Rep. 2007;9(4):301-307. [PMID: 17618550]

Hsu HE, Shutt KA, Moore MR, et al. Effect of pneumococcal conjugate vaccine on pneumococcal meningitis. N Engl J Med. 2009;360(3):244-256. [PMID: 19144940]

Lu CH, Chang EN, Lui CC. Strategies for the management of bacterial brain abscess. J Clin Neurosci. 2006;13(10):979-985. [PMID: 17056261]

Osborn MK, Steinberg JP. Subdural empyema and other suppurative complications of paranasal sinusitis. Lancet Infect Dis. 2007;7(1):62-67. [PMID: 17182345]

Tunkel AR, Glaser CA, Bloch KC, et al. The management of encephalitis: clinical practice guidelines by the Infectious Diseases Society of America. Clin Infect Dis. 2008;47(3):303-327. [PMID: 18582201]

Tunkel AR, Hartman BJ, Kaplan SL, et al. Practice guidelines for the management of bacterial meningitis. Clin Infect Dis. 2004;39(9):1267-1284. [PMID: 15494903]

Prion Diseases

Introduction

Prions are pathogenic particles that produce disease when a conformational change develops in a normally occurring host protein, PrPC. This change is associated with the accumulation of prion protein, PrPSc, in neural tissues. All human prion diseases share several features, including a long incubation period, spongiform brain pathology without inflammation, normal cerebrospinal fluid, relentless symptomatic progression, and no specific treatment.

There are five human prion diseases, of which Creutzfeldt-Jakob disease (CJD) and variant Creutzfeldt-Jakob disease (vCJD) are the most common (**Table 6**).

KEY POINT

- All human prion diseases have a long incubation period, spongiform brain pathology without inflammation, normal cerebrospinal fluid, relentless symptomatic progression, and no specific treatment.

Creutzfeldt-Jakob Disease

CJD is the most common of the human prion diseases, with an annual incidence of less than 1 in 1,000,000 persons. Sporadic, familial, and iatrogenic forms occur with a relative frequency of 85%, 15%, and less than 1%, respectively. Mutations in a gene located on the short arm of chromosome 20 that encode for PrPC are highly associated with the development of familial CJD. Iatrogenic CJD has been transmitted by dural grafts, corneal transplants, contaminated neurosurgical instruments, and cadaveric pituitary hormones. CJD typically occurs between the ages of 50 and 70 years.

The main clinical features of CJD are dementia that progresses over months and startle myoclonus, although the latter may not be present early in the illness (**Table 7**). Many other neurologic abnormalities may occur; however, sensory and cranial nerve abnormalities are distinctly unusual in CJD.

The diagnosis of CJD can be established only by brain biopsy; however, when performed in the correct clinical setting, other less-invasive tests strongly support the diagnosis. CT is helpful only in excluding other diagnoses. Increased signal intensity in the putamen and head of the caudate on MRI of the brain suggests CJD. An abnormal cerebrospinal fluid protein 14-3-3 may have some utility in the diagnosis of CJD. It is neither sensitive nor specific enough to be diagnostic but might be helpful in evaluating a patient with suggestive symptoms and compatible MRI findings. CJD has no established treatment and is unvaryingly fatal.

KEY POINTS

- Dementia progressing over months, cerebellar and spinocerebellar findings, and startle myoclonus possibly developing later in the illness are characteristic of Creutzfeldt-Jakob disease.

- Sensory and cranial nerve abnormalities are distinctly unusual in Creutzfeldt-Jakob disease.

- Creutzfeldt-Jakob disease has no established treatment and is unvaryingly fatal.

Variant Creutzfeldt-Jakob Disease

vCJD was first described in the United Kingdom in 1995. vCJD is very likely caused by the transmission to humans of bovine spongiform encephalopathy ("mad cow" disease), a prion disease of cattle. vCJD differs in several ways from CJD. In particular, compared with CJD, vCJD has a much earlier age of onset and is typically characterized by psychiatric

TABLE 7 World Health Organization Diagnostic Criteria for Sporadic Creutzfeldt-Jakob Disease

Probable (all 4)

1. Progressive dementia

2. At least two of the following four clinical features: myoclonus; visual or cerebellar disturbance; pyramidal/extrapyramidal dysfunction; akinetic mutism

3. A typical electroencephalogram with the characteristic pattern of periodic sharp wave complexes, and/or a positive cerebrospinal fluid 14-3-3 assay with a clinical duration to death of less than 2 years

4. Routine investigations should not suggest an alternative diagnosis

Definite (the above clinical features plus at least one of the following)

1. Loss of neurons; gliosis; spongiform degeneration; or plaques positive for PrPSc on histopathology of brain tissue

2. Positive PrPSc staining following pretreatment of brain tissue with proteinase K to destroy PrPC reactivity

3. Positive histoblotting of brain tissue extracts for PrPSc after treatment with proteinase K to destroy PrPC reactivity

4. Transmission of characteristic neurodegenerative disease to experimental animals

5. Demonstration of *PRNP* gene mutations

TABLE 6 Prion Diseases[a]

Disease	Characteristic Features
Kuru	First prion disease described. Was endemic in Fore Indians of Papua New Guinea owing to ritual cannibalism. Characterized by tremors, ataxia, movement disorders, and progression to dementia and death within 2 years.
Gerstmann-Sträussler-Scheinker syndrome	Autosomal dominant. Described in more than 20 families. Characterized by progressive cerebellar degeneration, leading to dementia and death in 5 years.
Fatal familial insomnia	Characterized by progressive insomnia, confusion, hallucinations, autonomic dysfunction, endocrine abnormalities, and death within 1 year.

[a]Creutzfeldt-Jakob disease (CJD) and variant CJD, the two most common of the prion diseases, are described in the syllabus text.

symptoms. Unlike CJD, patients with vCJD have PrPSc in the lymph node and tonsillar tissue, which makes tonsillar biopsy a useful diagnostic test. Changes in the cattle industry have markedly decreased the incidence of this disease to fewer than five human cases per year worldwide.

> **KEY POINT**
>
> - Compared with Creutzfeldt-Jakob (CJD) disease, variant CJD has a much earlier age of onset and is characterized by a psychiatric presentation and the presence of PrPSc in lymph node and tonsillar tissue, making biopsy of the latter a useful diagnostic test.

Bibliography
Prusiner SB. Shattuck lecture—neurodegenerative diseases and prions. N Engl J Med. 2001;344(20):1516-1526. [PMID: 11357156]

Tschampa HJ, Kallenberg K, Urbach H, et al. MRI in the diagnosis of sporadic Creutzfeldt-Jakob disease: a study on inter-observer agreement. Brain. 2005;128(Pt 9):2026-2033. [PMID: 15958503]

Skin and Soft Tissue Infections

Introduction

Cellulitis is a bacterial skin infection involving the dermis and subcutaneous tissues. This infection is most frequently associated with dermatologic conditions involving breaks in the skin, such as eczema, tinea pedis, or chronic skin ulcers, and conditions leading to chronic lymphedema, such as mastectomy and lymph node dissections or saphenous vein grafts used in bypass surgery. See **Table 8** for cellulitis risk factors and associated etiologic pathogens.

The most common pathogens are *Staphylococcus aureus* and the β-hemolytic streptococci, especially group A β-hemolytic streptococci (GABHS). When infecting the skin and subcutaneous structures, *S. aureus* may also cause concomitant abscesses, furuncles, carbuncles and bullous impetigo. Erysipelas is a specific skin infection usually caused by GABHS that limits its involvement to the upper dermis and superficial lymphatics.

Cellulitis should be suspected in patients with the acute onset of spreading erythema, edema, pain or tenderness, and warmth. Fever, although common, is not uniformly present. Patients with severe disease may have associated systemic toxicity.

The diagnosis of erysipelas is based on classic physical examination findings, including well-demarcated, indurated borders; intense erythema; and significant edema. Erysipelas occurs most frequently in the extremities and, usually, at the site of preexisting chronic edema. Leukocytosis is often present, but this finding is nonspecific. Frequently, the diagnosis is based on clinical findings. A specific microbiologic

diagnosis is never established in most patients. Despite reports of pathogen identification in 5% to 35% of patients who undergo lesional aspiration and in 20% to 30% of patients who undergo punch biopsy, the lower figures are more consistent with clinical experience. Blood cultures are positive in only 5% of patients and appear to be most helpful when the infection is severe or involves immunocompromised hosts. Given their limited yield, needle aspiration, punch biopsy, and blood culture are not routinely recommended in mild disease. If there is concomitant abscess formation or an open wound with purulent material, culture is indicated.

An antimicrobial agent with activity against *S. aureus* and β-hemolytic streptococci should always be included in any regimen to treat a skin or soft tissue infection, and therapy can be narrowed if a causative organism is identified.

> **KEY POINTS**
>
> - The most common cellulitis pathogens are *Staphylococcus aureus* and the β-hemolytic streptococci, especially group A β-hemolytic streptococci.
> - Cellulitis should be suspected in patients with acute onset of spreading erythema, edema, pain or tenderness, warmth, and, occasionally, fever.

Community-acquired Methicillin-resistant *Staphylococcus aureus*

Novel community-acquired methicillin-resistant *S. aureus* (CA-MRSA) strains have emerged across the United States. These strains are distinct from hospital-acquired or health care–associated MRSA strains, have different virulence factors, and often have different antimicrobial susceptibility patterns. Most CA-MRSA isolates contain genes encoding the Panton-Valentine-Leukocidin (PVL) toxin, which is a cytotoxin that causes leukocyte and tissue destruction. CA-MRSA strains have a predilection for causing skin and soft tissue infection, in particular with abscess formation, and pneumonia. Initial cases of skin and soft tissue infections, including cellulitis with or without abscesses, occurred in children, student and professional athletes, prisoners, men who have sex with men, and American Indians. CA-MRSA strains continue to spread throughout the community and beyond these initially defined subpopulations, and many patients may not have identifiable risk factors.

Suspicion for CA-MRSA should be high in patients with purulent drainage or frank abscesses with associated cellulitis. Patients with mild cellulitis and no history of MRSA colonization or infection and no MRSA risk factors may be treated empirically with an oral antistaphylococcal penicillin agent such as dicloxacillin or an oral first-generation cephalosporin such as cephalexin. Broadened coverage for MRSA is appropriate when the local rate of MRSA isolation is relatively high.

TABLE 8 Cellulitis Pathogens Associated with Specific Behaviors/Risk Factors

Pathogen	Risk Factor	Comment
Streptococcus pneumoniae		Rarely seen. Can be a primary soft tissue infection or secondary cellulitis after bacteremia. Skin findings are similar to erysipelas.
Aeromonas hydrophila	Contact with, or participation in, recreational sports in freshwater lakes, streams, rivers (including brackish water); contact with leeches	Cellulitis nonspecific in clinical appearance; usually occurs after minor trauma to skin leads to inoculation of organism.
Vibrio vulnificus, other *Vibrio* species	Contact with salt water or brackish water; contact with drippings from raw seafood	May cause cellulitis through direct inoculation into skin or may be ingested, leading to bacteremia with secondary skin infection. Hallmark is hemorrhagic bullae in area of cellulitis lesion(s).
Erysipelothrix rhusiopathiae	Contact with salt water marine life (can also infect freshwater fish)	Cellulitis usually involves the hand or arm, and in those handling fish, shellfish, or, occasionally, poultry or meat contaminated with the bacterium. Causes erysipeloid disease.
Pasteurella multocida	Contact with cats	Cellulitis occurs as a result of cat scratch or bite.

Oral trimethoprim-sulfamethoxazole is usually recommended for empiric outpatient treatment of CA-MRSA. The tetracyclines doxycycline and minocycline may also be used as well as oral linezolid, which is expensive. Clindamycin is not recommended for empiric treatment of CA-MRSA infections owing to inducible resistance in these strains. However, clindamycin may be prescribed for patients in whom the isolate is sensitive and has tested negative for inducible resistance. In patients with moderate or severe cellulitis, hospitalization and intravenous antibiotics are indicated, and vancomycin should be considered, especially in the presence of known CA-MRSA risk factors or in a community where CA-MRSA strains occur commonly. In rare patients with vancomycin allergy and suspected or confirmed MRSA cellulitis, intravenous linezolid, daptomycin, or tigecycline may be prescribed.

Not all CA-MRSA soft tissue infections require antibiotic therapy. Focal skin infections such as follicular abscesses often can be treated successfully with incision and drainage if the lesion is less than 5 cm in diameter and is not associated with systemic symptoms. Patients with larger abscesses or systemic signs of infection should be managed with combination incision and drainage and appropriate antimicrobial therapy.

KEY POINTS

- Suspicion for community-acquired methicillin-resistant *Staphylococcus aureus* should be high in patients with purulent drainage or frank abscesses with associated cellulitis.
- Oral trimethoprim-sulfamethoxazole is recommended for empiric outpatient treatment of mild community-acquired methicillin-resistant *Staphylococcus aureus* soft tissue infection.

- In patients with moderate or severe cellulitis, hospitalization and intravenous antibiotics with agents such as vancomycin are appropriate.
- Focal skin infections, such as follicular abscesses, often can be treated successfully with incision and drainage if the lesion is less than 5 cm in diameter and is not associated with systemic symptoms.

Bite Wounds

Animal Bite Wounds

Recognizing the types of organisms that constitute the mouth flora of the biting animal and the skin flora of the patient is important in evaluating patients with bite wounds. *Capnocytophaga canimorsus,* a gram-negative rod, is the most commonly identified pathogen in the oral flora of dogs, but *Pasteurella multocida* may be present in 25% of dog bite-associated wounds. *C. canimorsus* can cause overwhelming sepsis in splenectomized patients or those with severe immunosuppression. *P. multocida* is a common microbe in the oral flora of cats and may be found not only in bite wounds but also in cat scratches. Anaerobes are commonly found in the mouths of cats and dogs. The oral flora of many reptiles, including snakes and turtles, contain various *Salmonella* species, and snakes can also harbor *Pseudomonas aeruginosa.*

Aspects of the history and physical examination in patients with animal bites are described in **Table 9**. Management of patients with animal bites includes adequate wound irrigation and debridement of devitalized tissue. Patients with deep bite wounds or fang-related injuries with puncture-like wounds should undergo radiographic evaluation for bone involvement. A rabies risk assessment should be performed, and in those for whom a credible risk exists, rabies immune globulin should be administered and a human diploid rabies vaccination series instituted. All cases of rabies

TABLE 9 Pertinent History and Physical Examination Points in the Evaluation of a Patient with a Bite Wound

Questions to Ask in the History

1. What type of animal was involved?

2. Where is the animal now?

3. Was the attack unprovoked, and what was the animal's behavior like prior to the injury?

4. When did the bite injury occur relative to time of presentation?

5. Does the patient have a history of splenectomy or a chronic illness that can lead to functional asplenia?

6. Does the patient take immunosuppressive drugs or have a chronic medical illness that causes immunosuppression?

7. Has the patient had a mastectomy/lymph node dissection?

8. When was the patient's last tetanus booster?

Important Physical Examination Findings

1. Location of bite

2. Depth of injury (puncture wound)

3. Range of motion and function of affected limb or adjacent joint

4. Presence or absence of tendon or joint involvement

5. Presence of nerve injury

6. Edema

7. Evidence of crush injury or devitalized tissue

8. Presence of findings consistent with infection, including cellulitis or purulent wound drainage

must be reported to the local health department, and, when possible, the biting animal should be captured and quarantined. Review of the patient's tetanus vaccination status is appropriate (see MKSAP 15 General Internal Medicine). Tetanus immune globulin and tetanus toxoid administration are indicated in patients who have not completed the vaccination series; tetanus toxoid is administered to those who have completed the series but in whom the last booster was more than 5 years ago.

In patients presenting immediately after injury, no definitive consensus exists on routine antimicrobial prophylaxis. Antibiotic prophylaxis is probably not necessary in patients presenting 24 hours or more after injury with no overt signs of infection. Prophylaxis should be considered for all patients with hand, face, and genital wounds; for injuries near joints; for those with significant crush injury; and for those with underlying immunosuppression. A 3- to 5-day course of amoxicillin/clavulanate is the first choice in therapy. Alternatives in patients with penicillin allergy include the combination of doxycycline or trimethoprim-sulfamethoxazole or a fluoroquinolone with an anaerobic agent such as clindamycin.

Patients with animal bites presenting with signs of infection and severe tendon, nerve, or crush injuries may

require hospitalization and intravenous antibiotic therapy. Intravenous antibiotic choices include ampicillin/sulbactam, other β-lactam/β-lactamase inhibitor combinations, cefoxitin, or ciprofloxacin plus clindamycin in patients with penicillin allergy. Patients who do not require hospitalization can be treated with the agents used in prophylaxis. Duration of treatment in patients with infected bite wounds is usually 7 to 14 days; longer courses are needed for patients with bone or joint involvement.

KEY POINTS

- Management of patients with animal bites includes adequate wound irrigation and debridement of devitalized tissue, radiographs for those with deep bite wounds or puncture-like wounds, and rabies and tetanus risk assessment.

- Prophylaxis with amoxicillin/clavulanate should be considered for all patients with hand, face, and genital bite wounds; for injuries near joints; for those with significant crush injury; and for those with underlying immunosuppression.

- Patients with animal bites presenting with signs of infection and severe tendon, nerve, or crush injuries may require hospitalization and intravenous ampicillin/sulbactam therapy.

Human Bite Wounds

Human bite wounds are associated with a much higher rate of infection than are animal bites and may be self-inflicted, such as paronychia or lip biting; occlusional injuries; or clenched-fist injuries from a punch to the face. The oral flora of humans include *Eikenella corrodens*, streptococci, staphylococci, *Haemophilus* species, and a multitude of anaerobes. Management of human bite wounds is similar to that of animal bites and includes irrigation, debridement, and radiographs, especially in patients with clenched-fist injuries. Antimicrobial prophylaxis consisting of a 3- to 5-day course of amoxicillin/clavulanate is appropriate in patients with human bite wounds without overt signs of infection. Patients with clenched-fist injuries have a high likelihood for tenosynovitis or infection in the deeper tissues of the hand and often require hospitalization. Consultation with a hand surgeon is appropriate in the management of patients with these injuries because surgical exploration and debridement are often required to control infection and maximize functional outcomes. Initial intravenous antibiotic therapy with ampicillin/sulbactam or a similar combination agent is an appropriate first-line regimen. Oral therapy can be substituted for intravenous therapy once infection stabilizes or improves. As for animal bite wounds, the patient's tetanus vaccination status should be reviewed (see MKSAP 15 General Internal Medicine).

- Human bite wounds are associated with a much higher rate of infection than are animal bite wounds.
- Management of human bite wounds includes irrigation, debridement, and radiographs, especially in patients with clenched-fist injuries.
- Antimicrobial prophylaxis consisting of a 3- to 5-day course of amoxicillin/clavulanate should be provided to patients who have sustained a human bite wound without overt signs of infection.

Diabetic Foot Infections

Diabetic foot infections usually begin after minor trauma in patients with diabetic peripheral neuropathy and arterial vascular disease and range in severity from mild, non–limb-threatening to limb- and life-threatening infections.

Non–limb-threatening infections are usually superficial. Affected patients do not have systemic signs of infection or toxicity and have minimal cellulitis surrounding an open wound or ulcer with no tissue ischemia. Staphylococci and streptococci are the most commonly associated pathogens.

Limb-threatening infections are characterized by extensive spreading cellulitis extending far beyond the wound or ulcer, with systemic illness and possible sepsis with ulcers deep into the subcutaneous tissue, and tissue ischemia. Limb-threatening infections are polymicrobial, and cultures in affected patients often grow multiple pathogens, including staphylococci, streptococci, enteric gram-negative rods, *P. aeruginosa*, and anaerobes.

Gram-negative rods and anaerobes are common pathogens in patients with moderate foot infections and those with repeated infections or chronic wounds. Superficial swabs of such wounds are not as helpful as deep tissue cultures obtained during surgical debridement. Patients with diabetic foot infections should be co-managed by vascular surgeons and wound management specialists. The possibility of osteomyelitis should be assessed in all patients with diabetic foot infections (see Osteomyelitis). Initial treatment for recurrent, moderate, and limb-threatening infections should be broad, including coverage for staphylococci (MRSA), streptococci, gram-negative rods such as *Pseudomonas* species, and anaerobes. Targeted antibiotic therapy should be based on culture results.

- Patients with non–limb-threatening diabetic foot infections due to staphylococci and streptococci do not have systemic signs of infection or toxicity and have minimal cellulitis surrounding an open wound or ulcer with no tissue ischemia.

- Limb-threatening diabetic foot infections are characterized by extensive spreading cellulitis extending far beyond the wound or ulcer, with systemic illness and possible sepsis with ulcers deep into the subcutaneous tissue, and tissue ischemia.
- Broad-spectrum antibiotics are the appropriate initial treatment for recurrent, moderate, and limb-threatening diabetic foot infections, including coverage for staphylococci, streptococci, gram-negative rods such as *Pseudomonas* species, and anaerobes.

Necrotizing Fasciitis

Necrotizing fasciitis is characterized by infection extending beyond the epidermis, dermis, and subcutaneous tissues to involve the fascia and, potentially, the underlying muscle. Infecting organisms elaborate toxins and produce enzymes that cause intense tissue inflammation, ischemia, and necrosis and, ultimately, overwhelming sepsis and death. Patients with suspected necrotizing fasciitis require immediate surgery.

Some cases are caused by GABHS, alone or with another pathogen such as *S. aureus*. Other cases are polymicrobial, with multiple pathogens, including *S. aureus*, streptococci, anaerobes, and gram-negative rods. Another well-described clinical entity is necrotizing fasciitis caused by *Vibrio vulnificus*, a gram-negative rod commonly found in the coastal waters of the Gulf of Mexico. Patients with *V. vulnificus*–associated necrotizing fasciitis often have underlying chronic liver disease or other immunocompromising conditions predisposing them to overwhelming infection.

Necrotizing fasciitis may occur as an extension of infection from a preexisting wound, including surgical wounds, chronic vascular or decubitus ulcers, or diabetic foot ulcers. Alternatively, this infection may develop without obvious skin or soft tissue injury, although bacterial entry may be facilitated by small breaks or minor microtrauma to the skin. Necrotizing fasciitis can involve any site, but most cases occur in the lower extremities. When this infection involves the male perineum, it is also known as *Fournier gangrene*.

Patients usually present acutely, with systemic illness characterized by fever, localizing symptoms, leukocytosis, and, possibly, sepsis or sepsis syndrome. The affected area is usually indurated (described as "woody"), erythematous, hot, edematous, and exquisitely painful, with pain disproportionate to the physical findings. Skin findings can progress rapidly over hours from initial erythema to a purplish, dusky, ischemic appearance, and, finally, to cyanosis and gangrene (**Figure 2**).

An MRI scan of the affected area may identify fascial-plane involvement in patients in whom the diagnosis is uncertain. Blood cultures should be obtained on admission. A Gram stain of expressed wound material may be helpful in identifying the presumptive etiologic organism; however, cultures of involved tissues should also be obtained during surgical debridement.

Timely surgical exploration to determine the extent of necrosis and debridement of all devitalized tissue are essential in patients with necrotizing fasciitis, and most patients require at least one second-look surgery.

Broad-spectrum antibiotics are appropriate initial empiric therapy for patients with suspected necrotizing fasciitis and should include coverage for *S. aureus*, including MRSA; streptococci, including GABHS; anaerobes; and gram-negative rods. Regimens consisting of vancomycin plus (1) piperacillin-tazobactam, (2) cefepime and metronidazole, or (3) meropenem are reasonable. Clindamycin should be part of the initial regimen when GABHS is suspected because a retrospective analysis showed greater efficacy for clindamycin compared with β-lactam antibiotics in patients with invasive infections. Clindamycin's greater efficacy in this setting may be related to its ability to suppress toxin production in these bacteria and remain active when bacteria are in a stationary growth phase. This consideration may be critical in necrotizing fasciitis in which large numbers of bacteria may be present at the site, have stopped reproducing, and are in stationary phase. Discontinuation of antimicrobials is appropriate once surgical debridement is not indicated and the patient has demonstrated clinical improvement, including the absence of fever for 2 to 3 days. Studies of the use of intravenous immune globulin in necrotizing fasciitis are conflicting, and, as of this writing, no recommendation on its use in streptococcal necrotizing fasciitis exists.

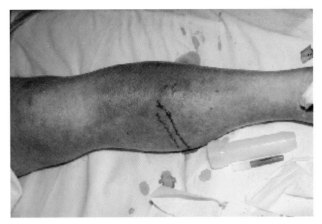

FIGURE 2.
Necrotizing fasciitis of the left calf of an elderly patient with peripheral arterial disease.

Reprinted with permission from Physicians' Information and Education Resource. http://pier.acponline.org/physicians/diseases/d197/FIGUREs/d197-FIGUREs.html. Accessed on July 14, 2009. Copyright 2009 American College of Physicians.

KEY POINTS

- Patients with necrotizing fasciitis usually present acutely, with systemic illness characterized by fever, localizing symptoms, leukocytosis, and, possibly, sepsis or sepsis syndrome.
- Timely surgical exploration to determine the extent of necrosis and debridement of all devitalized tissue are essential in patients with necrotizing fasciitis.
- Broad-spectrum antibiotics are appropriate initial empiric therapy for patients with suspected necrotizing fasciitis and should include coverage for *Staphylococcus aureus*, including methicillin-resistant *S. aureus*; streptococci, including group A β-hemolytic streptococci; anaerobes; and gram-negative rods.
- Clindamycin should be added to the regimen when infection with group A β-hemolytic streptococci is suspected in patients with necrotizing fasciitis.

Toxic Shock Syndrome

Toxic shock syndrome (TSS) is an infrequent, but life-threatening, infection in which bacterial toxins are produced and lead to septic shock. Specific toxin-producing strains of *S. aureus* cause TSS. Certain toxin-producing streptococci, in particular GABHS and groups B, C, F, and G β-hemolytic streptococci, can also cause TSS.

Staphylococcal TSS can occur when toxin-producing strains cause infection at any site in the body. Menstruation-associated TSS occurs in women who are using tampons, and nonmenstruation–associated TSS involves postpartum and surgical wounds, skin and soft tissue infections including abscesses, and nasal packings. Surgical wounds can become a portal of entry and are often colonized but not infected. Affected patients have no overt signs of wound infection when systemic toxicity develops. Staphylococcal TSS can occur in patients with *S. aureus* pneumonia, usually as a complication of influenza. Both methicillin-susceptible *S. aureus* and MRSA strains can produce toxic shock syndrome toxin-1 (TSST-1). The diagnostic criteria for staphylococcal TSS are outlined in **Table 10**.

Almost all cases of TSS are sporadic. However, cases of secondary transmission of GABHS-induced TSS to health care workers and close contacts have occurred. Contact isolation precautions should be initiated in patients with suspected invasive GABHS-induced disease, including TSS and necrotizing fasciitis, until completion of 24 hours of antibiotic therapy, as well as in those with draining wounds, until cessation of drainage or until there is minimal discharge containable by a dressing.

Streptococcal TSS can occur in the setting of any GABHS infection and has been reported as a complication of GABHS pharyngitis. Streptococci gain entry through the skin, vagina, or pharynx. Many surgical procedures, including hysterectomy, orthopedic procedures, and mammoplasty, have been associated with subsequent streptococcal TSS. Streptococcal skin and soft tissue infections may progress to necrotizing fasciitis and streptococcal TSS when the toxin-producing strains are the infecting organisms. Some patients

TABLE 10 Diagnostic Criteria for Staphylococcal Toxic Shock Syndrome

The presence of:

Fever >38.9 °C (102.0 °F)

Systolic blood pressure less than 90 mm Hg

Diffuse macular rash with subsequent desquamation, especially on palms and soles

Involvement of three of the following organ systems:

Gastrointestinal (nausea, vomiting, diarrhea)

Muscular (severe myalgia or fivefold or greater increase in serum creatine kinase level)

Mucous membrane (hyperemia of the vagina, conjunctivae, or pharynx)

Renal (blood urea nitrogen or serum creatinine level at least twice the upper limit of normal)

Liver (bilirubin, aspartate aminotransferase or alanine aminotransferase concentration twice the upper limit of normal)

Blood (platelet count <100,000/µL [100 × 10⁹/L])

Central nervous system (disorientation without focal neurologic signs)

Negative serologies for Rocky Mountain spotted fever, leptospirosis, and measles; negative cerebrospinal fluid cultures for organisms other than *Staphylococcus aureus*

Adapted with permission from Moreillon P, Aue Y-A, Glauser, MP. *Staphylococcus aureus.* In: Mandell GL, Dolin R, Bennett JE, eds. Principles and Practice of Infectious Disease. 6th ed. Philadelphia, PA: Churchill Livingstone; 2005:2331. Copyright 2004, Elsevier.

TABLE 11 Diagnostic Criteria for Streptococcal Toxic Shock Syndrome

Definite Case:

Isolation of GABHS from a sterile site

Probable Case:

Isolation of GABHS from a nonsterile site

Hypotension

The presence of two of the following findings:

Renal (acute renal insufficiency or failure)

Liver (elevated aminotransferase concentrations)

Skin (erythematous macular rash, soft tissue necrosis)

Blood (coagulopathy, including thrombocytopenia and disseminated intravascular coagulation)

Pulmonary (acute respiratory distress syndrome)

GABHS = group A β-hemolytic streptococci.

KEY POINTS

- Specific toxin-producing strains of *Staphylococcus aureus* and certain toxin-producing streptococci can cause toxic shock syndrome.

- Contact isolation precautions should be initiated in patients with suspected invasive group A β-hemolytic streptococci–induced disease, including toxic shock syndrome and necrotizing fasciitis, until completion of 24 hours of antibiotic therapy.

- Empiric broad-spectrum antibiotics, including clindamycin, are appropriate in any initial empiric regimen for possible toxic shock syndrome.

with streptococcal TSS may have only a history of nonpenetrating trauma, such as hematoma, bruising, and muscle strain. Streptococcal TSS may complicate varicella or influenza infections. The diagnostic criteria for streptococcal TSS are outlined in **Table 11**.

Patients with TSS are critically ill and require aggressive supportive measures. Initial examination of such patients should include inspection of the vaginal vault for identification and removal of retained foreign bodies and a careful skin examination for identification of any portal of entry and potential necrotizing fasciitis. Broad-spectrum antibiotics should be prescribed as they would in any patient with sepsis and can be narrowed once the culture results confirm the cause of the TSS. Some data suggest that the β-lactam antibiotics (penicillins, cephalosporins, and carbapenems) may actually increase TSST-1 production in *S. aureus*. Consequently, clindamycin is typically included in the initial empiric regimen for possible TSS, whether staphylococcal or streptococcal infection is suspected. In an observational study, patients with streptococcal TSS receiving intravenous immune globulin had a significantly better survival outcome compared with patients who did not receive intravenous immune globulin, and this agent can be considered as adjunctive treatment. The use of adjunctive intravenous immune globulin in staphylococcal TSS is even less well defined.

Bibliography

Anaya DA, Dellinger EP. Necrotizing soft tissue infection: diagnosis and management. Clin Infect Dis. 2007;44(5):705-710. [PMID: 17278065]

Darenberg J, Söderquist B, Normark BH, Norrby-Teglund A. Differences in potency of intravenous polyspecific immunoglobulin G against streptococcal and staphylococcal superantigens: implications for therapy of toxic shock syndrome. Clin Infect Dis. 2004;38(6): 836-842. [PMID: 14999628]

Fleisher GR. The management of bite wounds. New Engl J Med. 1999;340(2):138-140. [PMID: 9887167]

Fridkin SK, Hageman JC, Morrison M, et al; Active Bacterial Core Surveillance Program of the Emerging Infections Program Network. Methicillin-resistant Staphylococcus aureus in three communities [erratum in N Engl J Med. 2005;352(22):2362]. New Engl J Med. 2005;352(14):1436-1444. [PMID: 15814879]

Pallin DJ, Egan DJ, Pelletier AJ, Espinola JA, Hooper DC, Camargo CA Jr. Increased US emergency department visits for skin and soft tissue infections and changes in antibiotic choices, during the emergence of community-onset methicillin-resistant Staphylococcus aureus. Ann Emerg Med. 2008;51(3):291-298. [PMID: 18222564]

Prevention of Invasive Group A Streptococcal Infections Workshop Participants. Prevention of invasive group A streptococcal disease among household contacts of case patients and among postpartum and postsurgical patients: recommendations from the Centers for Disease Control and Prevention. Clin Infect Dis. 2002;35(8):950-959. [PMID: 12355382]

Ruhe JJ, Smith N, Bradsher RW, Menon A. Community onset methicillin-resistant Staphylococcus aureus skin and soft tissue infections: impact of antimicrobial therapy on outcome. Clin Infect Dis. 2007;44(6):777-784. [PMID: 17304447]

Stevens DL, Bisno AL, Chambers HF, et al: Infectious Diseases Society of America. Practice guidelines for the diagnosis and management of skin and soft tissue infections [erratum in Clin Infect Dis. 2006;42(8):1219]. Clin Infect Dis. 2005;41(10):1373-1406. [PMID: 16231249]

Stevens DL, Eron LL. Cellulitis and soft-tissue infections. Ann Intern Med. 2009;150(1):ITC11. [PMID: 19124814]

Swartz MN. Clinical practice. Cellulitis. N Engl J Med. 2004;350(9): 904-912. [PMID: 14985488]

Community-Acquired Pneumonia

Epidemiology and Cause

Community-acquired pneumonia (CAP) is defined as a case of infectious pneumonia in patients living independently in the community or in those hospitalized for less than 48 hours for other reasons because it is likely the inoculation occurred before admission. Five to 10 million cases of CAP occur annually in the United States, with almost 1 million in patients 65 years of age or older.

CAP has been classically differentiated clinically as typical or atypical. Typical CAP is defined as the rapid onset of high fever, productive cough, and pleuritic chest pain. The usual microorganisms include *Streptococcus pneumoniae*, *Haemophilus influenzae*, and *Moraxella catarrhalis*. Patients with atypical CAP may have low-grade fever, nonproductive cough, and no chest pain; *Mycoplasma pneumoniae*, *Chlamydophila* (formerly *Chlamydia*) *pneumoniae*, and *Legionella pneumophila* fall into this category. However, the initial symptoms and signs vary, and these presentations cannot be reliably used to establish a specific infectious cause. Potential infectious etiologies in patients with CAP, based on risk factors and underlying disorders, are shown in **Table 12**. See MKSAP 15 General Internal Medicine for discussion of preventive therapy for CAP.

KEY POINT

- Typical community-acquired pneumonia (CAP) is defined as the rapid onset of high fever, productive cough, and pleuritic chest pain, whereas atypical CAP may be characterized by low-grade fever, nonproductive cough, and no chest pain.

Diagnosis

Chest radiography is always indicated when CAP is suspected, although a radiographic image rarely identifies the causative agent. The presence of cavities with air-fluid levels suggests abscess formation (caused by staphylococci, anaerobes, or gram-negative bacilli), whereas the presence of cavities without air-fluid levels suggests tuberculosis or fungal infection.

If there is evidence of volume loss, bronchial obstruction must be excluded. Enlargement of mediastinal or hilar lymph nodes suggests fungal or mycobacterial infection. The presence of pleural fluid may indicate empyema possibly requiring thoracentesis.

Pathogen identification should be attempted before antimicrobial therapy is initiated, even though the overall low yield and infrequent positive impact on clinical care argue against specific diagnostic studies. Diagnostic testing is encouraged whenever the result is likely to change antimicrobial management; therapy may be broadened, narrowed, or completely changed, especially in patients in whom drug-resistant pathogens are isolated.

The most clear-cut indication for extensive diagnostic testing is in the critically ill patient with CAP. Pretreatment blood cultures and Gram stain and culture of an expectorated sputum sample (with fewer than 10 squamous cells and more than 25 leukocytes per low power field) should be performed in hospitalized patients with CAP. Although a well-performed Gram stain may reveal a single predominant microorganism, current data have not clearly correlated Gram stain findings with culture results of alveolar material. Patients with severe CAP should also undergo urine antigen tests for *L. pneumophila* and *S. pneumoniae*. However, the *Legionella* urine antigen test is positive only in cases caused by *L. pneumophila* serogroup I.

In intubated patients, an endotracheal aspirated specimen should be obtained. During the appropriate season and during epidemics of influenza, rapid antigen tests can be used to diagnose and distinguish between influenza A and B viruses. Serologic studies may be useful for epidemiologic purposes in the retrospective diagnosis of CAP. However, even with extensive laboratory testing, the specific microbiologic cause is established with certainty in only about 50% of patients.

KEY POINTS

- Chest radiography is always indicated when community-acquired pneumonia is suspected.

- On radiographic imaging, cavities with air-fluid levels in patients with severe community-acquired pneumonia suggest abscess formation, whereas cavities without air-fluid levels suggest tuberculosis or fungal infection.

- Enlargement of mediastinal or hilar lymph nodes suggests fungal or mycobacterial infection in patients with community-acquired pneumonia.

- Pathogen identification by diagnostic studies should be attempted before antimicrobial therapy is initiated in hospitalized patients with severe community-acquired pneumonia.

• Pretreatment blood cultures; Gram stain and culture of an expectorated sputum sample; endotracheal aspiration specimens in intubated patients; rapid antigen testing for influenza A and B virus, when appropriate; and urine antigen testing for *Legionella pneumophila* and *Streptococcus pneumoniae* should be performed in hospitalized patients with severe community-acquired pneumonia.

Initial Management

Assessing disease severity in patients with CAP helps to determine the initial site of care: outpatient, inpatient medical unit, or intensive care unit (ICU). Severity of illness scores such as the CURB-65 criteria (Confusion, Uremia, Respiratory rate, low Blood pressure, and age ≥65 years) may help predict a complicated course. Scoring 1 point for each positive criterion, patients with a score of 0 to 1 can be managed as outpatients, those with a score of 2 should be admitted to a hospital ward, and those with a score of 3 or higher often require ICU care. Another prognostic model is the Pneumonia Severity Index (PSI) from the Pneumonia Patient Outcomes Research Team. The PSI stratifies patients into five mortality risk classes: classes I and II encompass outpatients, class III encompasses patients requiring care in an observation unit or short-term hospitalization, and classes IV and V encompass inpatients (for more information, go to http://content.nejm.org/cgi/reprint/336/4/243.pdf). Although the use of objective admission criteria can decrease the number of hospitalized patients with CAP, subjective factors including a patient's ability to safely and reliably take oral medications and the availability of outpatient support resources should also be considered. Furthermore, in clinical practice, patients with low-risk PSI and CURB-65 scores may still be admitted to the ICU based on clinical judgment rather than objective scoring.

Direct admission to the ICU is required for patients with CAP who develop septic shock requiring vasopressors or who have acute respiratory failure requiring intubation and mechanical ventilation. Admission to an ICU or high-level monitoring unit is also recommended for patients with at least three of the following criteria: respiration rate greater than 30/min, arterial PO_2/FiO_2 ratio of 250 or less, multi-lobar infiltrates, confusion/disorientation, uremia (blood urea nitrogen ≥20 mg/dL [7.14 mmol/L]), leukopenia (leukocyte count <4000/μL [4 × 10^9/L]), thrombocytopenia (platelet count <100,000/μL [100 × 10^9/L]), hypothermia (core temperature <36.0 °C [96.8 °F]), and hypotension requiring aggressive fluid resuscitation.

KEY POINTS

• Patients with community-acquired pneumonia and a CURB-65 criteria (Confusion, Uremia, Respiratory rate, low Blood pressure, and age ≥65 years) score of 0 to 1 can be managed as outpatients, those with a score of 2 should be admitted to a hospital ward, and those with a score of 3 or higher often require admission to an intensive care unit.

• Direct admission to the intensive care unit is required for patients with community-acquired pneumonia who develop septic shock requiring vasopressors or have acute respiratory failure requiring intubation and mechanical ventilation.

Antimicrobial Therapy

S. pneumoniae is the most frequently isolated pathogen in patients with CAP, followed by nontypeable *H. influenzae* and *M. catarrhalis*. Various "atypical" organisms (for example, *M. pneumoniae*, *C. pneumoniae*, *Legionella* species, and various respiratory viruses) should also be considered. These organisms are rarely identified in clinical practice because, with the exception of some *Legionella* species and influenza viruses, rapid diagnostic tests are not available. Clinical features and risk factors for other potential microorganisms are shown in **Table 12**. Recommendations for empiric therapy are shown in **Table 13**. Once the microbial cause has been determined and in vitro susceptibility results are available, antimicrobial therapy should be modified for optimal treatment (**Table 14**).

Timing of First Antimicrobial Dose

The timing of the first dose of an antimicrobial agent in a patient with CAP is a core measure that has been targeted for reporting by hospitals in the United States to facilitate performance monitoring. Initial retrospective studies suggested a lower mortality rate among patients who received early antimicrobial therapy. In a review of the available data by the Infectious Diseases Society of America and the American Thoracic Society, a specific time frame for administration of the first dose of an antimicrobial agent was not recommended, although the authors believed that the first dose should be administered as soon as possible after a suspected diagnosis, preferably while the patient is still in the emergency department.

Antimicrobial Selection

Choice of empiric antimicrobial therapy in patients with CAP depends on resistance to commonly used antimicrobial agents and local susceptibility patterns. Although pneumococcal resistance to penicillin and cephalosporins has stabilized in recent years, pneumococcal resistance to macrolides continues to increase. The clinically relevant level of penicillin resistance in *S. pneumoniae* is a minimal inhibitory concentration

(MIC) of at least 4 µg/mL. Risk factors associated with β-lactam–resistant *S. pneumoniae* include age younger than 2 years or older than 65 years, β-lactam therapy within the preceding 3 months, alcoholism, medical comorbidities, immunosuppressive illness or immunosuppressive therapy, and exposure to a child in a day-care center. Recent treatment with antimicrobials such as the β-lactams, macrolides, or fluoroquinolones appears to be the most significant risk for β-lactam resistance. However, current resistance of pneumococci to β-lactam agents does not usually result in treatment failure in patients with pneumococcal pneumonia, even in the setting of bacteremia, as long as dosages of the antimicrobial agent are appropriate.

The number of pneumonia cases caused by community-acquired methicillin-resistant *Staphylococcus aureus* (CA-MRSA) has increased. Risk factors include end-stage renal disease, injection drug use, prior influenza, and prior antimicrobial therapy (especially with the fluoroquinolones). These strains more often contain a novel type IV SCC *mec* gene, and most contain a gene for Panton-Valentine leukocidin, a toxin associated with necrotizing pneumonia, shock, respiratory failure, and formation of abscesses and empyema. When CA-MRSA is the suspected cause of CAP, vancomycin or linezolid should be added to the treatment regimen.

Changing from Intravenous to Oral Therapy

Many antimicrobial agents have excellent oral bioavailability; therefore, in non-ICU patients who can eat and drink, it is possible to switch from intravenous to oral therapy. The change to oral therapy should be done by using the same agent or drug class as that being used intravenously in patients who are hemodynamically stable and improving clinically, able to ingest oral medications, and have a normally functioning gastrointestinal tract. As many as two thirds of all

TABLE 12 Possible Microbial Causes of Community-Acquired Pneumonia	
Clinical Presentation	**Commonly Encountered Pathogens**
Aspiration	Gram-negative enteric pathogens, oral anaerobes
Cough >2 weeks with whoop or posttussive vomiting	*Bordetella pertussis*
Lung cavity	Community-associated methicillin-resistant *Staphylococcus aureus*, oral anaerobes, endemic fungal pathogens, *Mycobacterium tuberculosis*, atypical mycobacteria
Epidemiology or Risk Factor	**Commonly Encountered Pathogens**
Alcoholism	*Streptococcus pneumoniae*, oral anaerobes, *Klebsiella pneumoniae, Acinetobacter* species, *M. tuberculosis*
Chronic obstructive pulmonary disease and/or smoking	*Haemophilus influenzae, Pseudomonas aeruginosa, Legionella* species, *S. pneumoniae, Moraxella catarrhalis, Chlamydophila pneumoniae*
Exposure to bat or bird droppings	*Histoplasma capsulatum*
Exposure to birds	*Chlamydophila psittaci*
Exposure to rabbits	*Francisella tularensis*
Exposure to farm animals or parturient cats	*Coxiella burnetii*
Exposure to rodent excreta	Hantavirus
HIV infection (early)	*S. pneumoniae, H. influenzae, M. tuberculosis*
HIV infection (late)	Those with early HIV infection plus *Pneumocystis jirovecii, Cryptococcus, Histoplasma, Aspergillus*, atypical mycobacteria (especially *Mycobacterium kansasii*), *P. aeruginosa*
Hotel or cruise ship stay in previous 2 weeks	*Legionella* species
Travel or residence in southwestern United States	*Coccidioides* species, hantavirus
Travel or residence in Southeast and East Asia	*Burkholderia pseudomallei*
Influenza activity in community	Influenza, *S. pneumoniae, Staphylococcus aureus, H. influenzae*
Injection drug use	*S. aureus*, anaerobes, *M. tuberculosis, S. pneumoniae*
Endobronchial obstruction	Anaerobes, *S. pneumoniae, H. influenzae, S. aureus*
Bronchiectasis or cystic fibrosis	*Burkholderia cepacia, P. aeruginosa, S. aureus*
Bioterrorism	*Bacillus anthracis, Yersinia pestis, Francisella tularensis*

Adapted with permission from Mandell LA, Wunderink RG, Anzueto A, et al. Infectious Diseases Society of America/American Thoracic Society consensus guidelines on the management of community-acquired pneumonia in adults. Clin Infect Dis. 2007;44(Suppl 2):S27-72. Copyright 2007, University of Chicago Press.

TABLE 13 Recommended Empiric Antimicrobial Therapy for CAP

Outpatient Treatment

Previously healthy and no use of antimicrobials within previous 3 months	Macrolide[a] or Doxycycline[b]
Presence of comorbid conditions (chronic heart, lung, liver or renal disease; diabetes mellitus; alcoholism; malignancies; asplenia; immunosuppressing conditions; or use of antimicrobials within the previous 3 months or risk of drug-resistant *Streptococcus pneumoniae*)	Respiratory fluoroquinolone[c] or β–lactam[d] plus a macrolide[a,e]

Inpatient Treatment

Non-ICU patient	Respiratory fluoroquinolone[c] or β–lactam[f] plus a macrolide[a,e]
ICU patient	β–lactam[g] plus either azithromycin or a respiratory fluoroquinolone[c] or if penicillin-allergic, a respiratory fluoroquinolone[c] and aztreonam

Special Concerns

Pseudomonas aeruginosa	An antipneumococcal, antipseudomonal β-lactam (piperacillin-tazobactam, cefepime, imipenem, or meropenem) plus either ciprofloxacin or levofloxacin or The above β–lactam plus an aminoglycoside and azithromycin or The above β–lactam plus an aminoglycoside and an antipneumococcal fluoroquinolone; if penicillin allergic, substitute aztreonam for the β-lactam
Community-associated methicillin-resistant *Staphylococcus aureus*	Add vancomycin or linezolid

CAP = community-acquired pneumonia; ICU = intensive care unit.

[a]Azithromycin, clarithromycin, or erythromycin.

[b]Weak recommendation.

[c]Levofloxacin, moxifloxacin, or gemifloxacin.

[d]Amoxicillin-clavulanate preferred; alternatives include ceftriaxone, cefpodoxime, and cefuroxime axetil.

[e]Doxycycline is an alternative to the macrolide.

[f]Cefotaxime, ceftriaxone, or ampicillin preferred; ertapenem for selected patients.

[g]Cefotaxime, ceftriaxone, or ampicillin-sulbactam.

patients have clinical improvement and meet criteria for a switch to oral therapy within the first 3 days. Hospital discharge should be considered for those who are candidates for oral therapy, for whom there is no need to treat any comorbidities, and for whom there is a safe home environment for continued care.

Duration of Antimicrobial Therapy

Most patients with CAP traditionally receive treatment for 7 to 10 days, although few studies have elucidated the optimal duration of antimicrobial therapy. Patients should receive treatment for a minimum of 5 days, be afebrile for 48 to 72 hours, and have no more than one associated CAP sign of clinical instability (pulse rate >100/min; respiration rate >24/min; systolic blood pressure <90 mm Hg; or arterial oxygen saturation <90% or arterial Po_2 <60 mm Hg on ambient air) before antibiotic therapy discontinuation. In a meta-analysis of 15 randomized, controlled trials, adults with mild to moderate CAP received safe and effective treatment with an antimicrobial treatment duration of 7 days or less. Reduction in patient exposure to antimicrobials may decrease drug resistance rates and cost and improve patient adherence and tolerability.

TABLE 14 Recommended Antimicrobial Therapy Based on Bacteria Identification in CAP

Bacterium	Preferred Therapies	Alternative Therapies
Streptococcus pneumoniae		
Penicillin MIC <2 µg/mL	Penicillin G, amoxicillin	Macrolide[a], oral cephalosporin[b], parenteral cephalosporin[c], clindamycin, doxycycline, respiratory fluoroquinolone[d]
Penicillin MIC ≥2 µg/mL	Agents chosen based on in vitro susceptibility, including cefotaxime, ceftriaxone, respiratory fluoroquinolone[d]	Vancomycin, linezolid, high-dose amoxicillin (3 g/d)
Haemophilus influenzae		
Non–β-lactamase producing	Amoxicillin	Fluoroquinolone[d,e], doxycycline, azithromycin, clarithromycin[f]
β-Lactamase producing	Second- or third-generation cephalosporin, amoxicillin-clavulanate	Fluoroquinolone[d,e], doxycycline, azithromycin, clarithromycin[f]
Mycoplasma pneumoniae or *Chlamydophila pneumoniae*	Macrolide[a], a tetracycline	Fluoroquinolone[d]
Legionella species	Fluoroquinolone[d,e], azithromycin	Doxycycline
Enterobacteriaceae	Third-generation cephalosporin, carbapenem[g,h]	β-Lactam/β-lactamase inhibitor combination[i]
Pseudomonas aeruginosa	Antipseudomonal β-lactam[j] plus ciprofloxacin or levofloxacin or an aminoglycoside	Aminoglycoside plus ciprofloxacin or levofloxacin
Acinetobacter species	Carbapenem[g]	Cephalosporin plus an aminoglycoside, ampicillin-sulbactam, colistin
Staphylococcus aureus		
Methicillin-susceptible	Antistaphylococcal penicillin[k]	Cefazolin, clindamycin
Methicillin-resistant	Vancomycin, linezolid	Trimethoprim-sulfamethoxazole
Anaerobes (aspiration)	β-Lactam/β-lactamase inhibitor[i], clindamycin	Carbapenem[g]
Chlamydophila psittaci	A tetracycline	Macrolide[a]
Coxiella burnetii	A tetracycline	Macrolide[a]
Bacillus anthracis	Ciprofloxacin, levofloxacin, doxycycline (usually with a second agent)	Other fluoroquinolone, β-lactam (if susceptible), rifampin, clindamycin, chloramphenicol
Yersinia pestis	Streptomycin, gentamicin	Doxycycline, fluoroquinolone
Francisella tularensis	Doxycycline	Gentamicin, streptomycin
Bordetella pertussis	Macrolide[a]	Trimethoprim-sulfamethoxazole

CAP = community-acquired pneumonia; MIC = minimal inhibitory concentration.

[a]Azithromycin, clarithromycin, or erythromycin.

[b]Cefpodoxime, cefprozil, cefuroxime axetil, cefdinir, cefditoren.

[c]Cefuroxime, ceftriaxone, cefotaxime.

[d]Levofloxacin, moxifloxacin, or gemifloxacin.

[e]Ciprofloxacin is appropriate for *Legionella* species and most gram-negative bacilli.

[f]Azithromycin is more active in vitro than clarithromycin against *Haemophilus influenzae*.

[g]Imipenem-cilastatin, meropenem, or ertapenem.

[h]Drug of choice if extended-spectrum β–lactamase producer.

[i]Piperacillin-tazobactam for gram-negative bacilli, ticarcillin-clavulanate, ampicillin-sulbactam, amoxicillin-clavulanate.

[j]Piperacillin, piperacillin-tazobactam, cefepime, ceftazidime, imipenem, meropenem.

[k]Nafcillin, oxacillin.

Adapted with permission from Mandell LA, Wunderink RG, Anzueto A, et al. Infectious Diseases Society of America/American Thoracic Society consensus guidelines on the management of community-acquired pneumonia in adults. Clin Infect Dis 2007;44(Suppl 2):S27-72. Copyright 2007, University of Chicago Press.

- *Streptococcus pneumoniae* is the most frequently isolated pathogen in community-acquired pneumonia, followed by nontypeable *Haemophilus influenzae* and *Moraxella catarrhalis*.

- Recommended empiric antibiotic treatment for previously healthy outpatients with community-acquired pneumonia and no history of antimicrobial use within the past 3 months includes a macrolide or doxycycline.

- Recommended empiric antibiotic treatment for outpatients with community-acquired pneumonia with comorbidities or hospitalized non–intensive care unit patients includes a respiratory fluoroquinolone or a β-lactam plus a macrolide.

- Recommended empiric antibiotic treatment for intensive care unit patients with community-acquired pneumonia includes a β-lactam plus either azithromycin or a respiratory fluoroquinolone.

- Risk factors associated with β-lactam–resistant *Streptococcus pneumoniae* include age younger than 2 years or older than 65 years, β-lactam therapy within the preceding 3 months, alcoholism, medical comorbidities, immunosuppressive illness or therapy, and exposure to a child in a day-care center.

- Risk factors for community-acquired methicillin-resistant *Staphylococcus aureus* include end-stage kidney disease, injection drug use, prior influenza, and prior antimicrobial therapy.

- When community-acquired methicillin-resistant *Staphylococcus aureus* is the suspected cause of community-acquired pneumonia, vancomycin or linezolid should be added to the treatment regimen.

- Patients with community-acquired pneumonia (CAP) should receive treatment for a minimum of 5 days, be afebrile for 48 to 72 hours, and have no more than one associated CAP sign of clinical instability (pulse rate >100/min; respiration rate >24/min; systolic blood pressure <90 mm Hg; or arterial oxygen saturation <90% or arterial PO_2 <60 mm Hg on ambient air) before antibiotic discontinuation.

Bibliography

Capelastegui A, España PP, Quintana JM, et al. Validation of a predictive rule for the management of community-acquired pneumonia. Eur Respir J. 2006;27(1):151-157. [PMID: 16387948]

Fee C, Weber EJ, Maak CA, Bacchetti P. Effect of emergency department crowding on time to antibiotics in patients admitted with community-acquired pneumonia. Ann Emerg Med. 2007;50(5):501-509. [PMID: 17913300]

Jackson ML, Neuzil KM, Thompson WW, et al. The burden of community-acquired pneumonia in seniors: results of a population-based study. Clin Infect Dis. 2004;39(11):1642-1650. [PMID: 15578365]

Jasti H, Mortensen EM, Obrosky DS, Kapoor WN, Fine MJ. Causes and risk factors for rehospitalization of patients hospitalized with community-acquired pneumonia. Clin Infect Dis. 2008;46(4):550-556. [PMID: 18194099]

Li JZ, Winston LG, Moore DH, Bent S. Efficacy of short-course antibiotic regimens for community-acquired pneumonia: a meta-analysis. Am J Med. 2007:120(9):783-790. [PMID: 17765048]

Mandell LA, Wunderink RG, Anzueto A, et al. Infectious Diseases Society of America/American Thoracic Society consensus guidelines on the management of community-acquired pneumonia in adults. Clin Infect Dis. 2007;44 Suppl 2:S27-S72. [PMID: 17278083]

Marrie TJ, Shariatzadeh MR. Community-acquired pneumonia requiring admission to an intensive care unit: a descriptive study. Medicine (Baltimore). 2007;86(2):103-111. [PMID: 17435590]

Rosón B, Fernández-Sabé N, Carratalà J, et al. Contribution of a urinary antigen assay (Binax NOW) to the early diagnosis of pneumococcal pneumonia. Clin Infect Dis. 2004;38(2):222-226. [PMID: 14699454]

Vanderkooi OG, Low DE, Green K, Powis JE, McGeer A; Toronto Invasive Bacterial Disease Network. Predicting antimicrobial resistance in invasive pneumococcal infections. Clin Infect Dis. 2005;40(9):1288-1297. [PMID: 15825031]

Yealy DM, Auble TE, Stone RA, et al. Effect of increasing the intensity of implementing pneumonia guidelines: a randomized, controlled trial. Ann Intern Med. 2005:143(12):881-894. [PMID: 16365469]

Tick-Borne Diseases

Lyme Disease

Several diseases have a human tick vector (**Table 15**). Lyme disease is caused by three closely related *Spirochete* species classified together as *Borrelia burgdorferi senso lato*. In the United States, most Lyme disease is caused by *B. burgdorferi senso stricto*, whereas in Europe and Asia, it is most often caused by *B. afzelii* and *B. garinii*. The vector for Lyme disease is the

TABLE 15 Tick-borne Diseases

Hard Ticks
  Rocky Mountain spotted fever
  Lyme disease
  Babesiosis
  Ehrlichiosis
  Anaplasmosis
  Tularemia
  Endemic typhus
  Southern tick-associated rash illness
  Powassan and other tick-borne encephalitides
  Tick typhus
    African tick typhus
    Mediterranean tick typhus
    Queensland tick typhus
  Colorado tick fever
Soft Ticks
  Relapsing fever

Ixodes scapularis tick (the deer tick); the reservoirs are small mammals such as deer and mice.

Lyme disease is characterized by three stages: early, disseminated, and late. Each stage is associated with different clinical presentations, which may overlap. Most early localized Lyme disease occurs in the summer and fall and is characterized by the erythema migrans (EM) rash, an expanding erythematous patch appearing 5 to 14 days after inoculation by an infected tick. Multiple EM lesions, reflecting spirochetemia, can occur. EM may be solid, show central clearing, manifest as target lesions, and, occasionally, vesiculate or develop a necrotic center (Figure 3).

The appearance of the EM rash should not be confused with the hypersensitivity reaction that occasionally results from the tick bite itself (**Table 16**). The differential diagnosis of EM is limited (**Table 17**). Patients with early Lyme disease may also have systemic symptoms including fever, myalgia, and arthralgia. In approximately 20% of patients, no EM rash is found and only systemic symptoms are present.

Early Lyme disease is usually diagnosed clinically because serologic test results are often negative at presentation and can become positive with clinical improvement. Early disseminated Lyme disease occurs weeks to months after a tick bite and may not be preceded by early-stage disease. Clinical manifestations are neurologic and cardiac. Neurologic syndromes include aseptic meningitis, cranial nerve palsies, and painful radiculopathies. Lyme carditis most often manifests as transient heart block, although severe myocarditis has been reported.

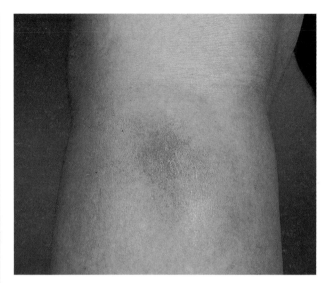

FIGURE 3.
Typical erythema migrans rash manifested as "target lesion" with central clearing.

Late Lyme disease occurs months to years after the initial inoculation, may occur without the evidence of early localized or early disseminated stages, and can have rheumatologic, neurologic, or cutaneous manifestations. Lyme arthritis is characterized by a mono- or oligoarthritis most commonly involving the knees. In affected patients, the synovial fluid is inflammatory, and positive synovial fluid polymerase chain

TABLE 16 Comparison of Erythema Migrans with Tick Bite Reaction		
Characteristics	**Erythema Migrans**	**Tick Bite**
Incubation period	5 to 14 days	Hours
Local symptoms	Rare	Pruritus
Size	>5 cm	<1 cm
Expands	Over days	Over hours
Resolves	Over weeks	Over days
Systemic symptoms	Common	Rare

TABLE 17 Differential Diagnosis of Erythema Migrans	
Differential Diagnosis	**Comments**
Streptococcal cellulitis	Streptococcal cellulitis progresses over hours rather than days and is very tender. Patients are often extremely ill.
Trauma such as burn	Patient should have suggestive history.
Fixed drug eruption	Patient should have suggestive history.
Dermatophyte infection	Has less erythema and evolves much more slowly than erythema migrans. Raised active border with central clearing.
Necrotic arachnidism	Should be considered as possible differential but only in endemic areas.

reaction test results for *B. burgdorferi* are diagnostic. Although arthralgia can occur in early Lyme disease, persistent diffuse arthralgia is not characteristic of late Lyme disease. Rarely, encephalitis characterized by subtle cognitive deficits may be noted. In Europe, the cutaneous disease acrodermatitis chronica atrophicans is an uncommon late manifestation.

In all patients with compatible symptoms and signs, serologic testing to confirm the diagnosis of Lyme disease is necessary except for those with typical EM.

A two-step approach should be used in the serologic diagnosis of Lyme disease. The initial serologic test is an enzyme-linked immunosorbent assay. Positive test results are confirmed with a Western blot analysis. Patients with non-specific symptoms, such as fatigue, myalgia, or arthralgia, should not be tested. In such patients with a low pretest probability for disease, a positive enzyme-linked immunosorbent assay is most likely a false-positive result. Repeat testing to determine whether antibody titers have declined after completion of antibiotic treatment is unnecessary because seroreactivity often persists for at least months after antibiotic treatment of early infection and for years after treatment of late infection. The diagnosis of neurologic involvement requires evidence of *B. burgdorferi* on cerebrospinal fluid polymerase chain reaction testing (insensitive) or intrathecal production of *B. Burgdorferi* antibodies.

There is considerable controversy concerning post–Lyme disease syndrome, also referred to as "chronic Lyme disease." However, despite the persistence of subjective symptoms after recommended treatment, no evidence of continued infection with *B. burgdorferi* exists, and treatment beyond that recommended is not beneficial and may be harmful. The notion that Lyme disease is difficult to treat has evolved because of overdiagnosis, not because patients do not respond to recommended treatment. For recommended treatment approaches, see **Table 18** and **Table 19**.

The primary prevention is avoidance and timely removal of ticks. Transmission of *B. Burgdorferi* does not occur until the tick has fed for at least 36 hours. Antimicrobial prophylaxis with a single dose of doxycycline, 200 mg, after a tick bite is not recommended in most circumstances but can be considered when all four of the following are present: (1) the attached tick is *Ixodes scapularis* and it has been attached for at least 36 hours as determined by the degree of engorgement or the time of likely exposure; (2) prophylaxis can be given within 72 hours of tick removal; (3) the local prevalence of infected ticks is greater than 20%; and (4) doxycycline is not contraindicated.

KEY POINTS

- Eighty percent of patients with Lyme disease develop erythema migrans, an erythematous patch occurring 5 to 14 days after inoculation; some have systemic symptoms only, some have both.
- Serologic testing is often negative in patients with early Lyme disease.
- Lyme carditis most often consists of transient heart block.
- Lyme arthritis typically presents as a mono- or oligoarthritis most commonly involving the knees.
- Seroreactivity often persists for at least months after antibiotic treatment of early infection and for years after treatment of late infection.

Babesiosis

Babesiosis is caused by *Babesia microti*, an intracellular protozoan parasite. Babesiosis is transmitted from rodents and cattle to humans by *Ixodes scapularis* ticks and occurs primarily in the northeastern United States with an epicenter in Cape Cod, Massachusetts, and the associated islands. Most infections are subclinical, but a nonspecific febrile illness can occur. Babesiosis should be considered in patients who have traveled to endemic areas and now have a nonfocal febrile illness with chills, sweats, myalgia, arthralgia, nausea, vomiting, or fatigue. On physical examination, fever, splenomegaly, hepatomegaly, and/or jaundice may be present.

Infection in patients with babesiosis and asplenia can cause a severe, life-threatening illness. Other risk factors for more severe disease include age older than 50 years and decreased cell-mediated immunity, underlying malignancy, and immunosuppressive therapy.

Diagnosis is established by identification of the organisms within erythrocytes on the peripheral blood smear. Antibody testing and polymerase chain reaction amplification of *Babesia* species DNA on blood specimens are also available in some areas.

Treatment is necessary for all symptomatic patients. The combination of quinine and clindamycin or atovaquone and azithromycin is effective. Because of its better side-effect profile, the latter combination is preferred, particularly for

---

TABLE 18 Treatment of Lyme Disease	
Preferred Oral Regimen	Dosage
Doxycycline	100 mg, twice daily
Amoxicillin	500 mg, three times daily
Cefuroxime axetil	500 mg, twice daily
Alternative Oral Regimen	
Azithromycin	500 mg, daily
Preferred Parenteral Regimen	
Ceftriaxone	2 g daily
Alternative Parenteral Regimen	
Cefotaxime	2 g every 8 hours
Penicillin G	3 to 4 million units every 4 hours

Data from Wormser GP, Dattwyler RJ, Shapiro ED, et al. (See reference list on p. 26).

TABLE 19 Indication, Route, and Duration of Therapy for Lyme Disease

Indication	Route	Duration (d) (range)
Erythema migrans	Oral	14 (14-21)
Cranial nerve palsy	Oral[a]	14 (14-21)
Meningitis	Parenteral	14 (10-28)
Cardiac	Oral or parenteral	14 (14-21)
Arthritis	Oral	28
Recurrent arthritis	Oral or parenteral	28
Antibiotic-refractory arthritis[b]	Symptomatic, no antibiotic	
Lyme-associated dementia	Parenteral	28

[a]90% of the time, oral treatment is successful. Parenteral treatment should be considered in patients with abnormal cerebrospinal fluid results if a lumbar puncture is performed (strong suspicion of central nervous system involvement due to prolonged headache and/or meningeal signs).

[b]Persistence of inflammatory arthritis for at least 2 months after completion of intravenous ceftriaxone or two courses of an oral regimen.

Data from Wormser GP, Dattwyler RJ, Shapiro ED, et al. (See reference list on p. 26).

non–life-threatening disease. Partial or complete erythrocyte exchange transfusions are indicated in patients with severe, complicated disease.

KEY POINTS

- Risk factors for severe illness in babesiosis are asplenia, age older than 50 years, cell-mediated immunity, underlying malignancy, and immunosuppressive therapy.

- Patients with suspected babesiosis should receive treatment with combinations of quinine and clindamycin or atovaquone and azithromycin.

Ehrlichiosis and Anaplasmosis

Ehrlichia chaffeensis and *Anaplasma phagocytophilum* are rickettsial-like organisms that infect leukocytes. *E. chaffeensis* causes human monocytic ehrlichiosis (HME) and *A. phagocytophilum* causes human granulocytic anaplasmosis (HGA). The reservoirs for HME are primarily deer, dogs, and goats, and the vector is the Lone Star tick. The reservoirs for HGA are deer and rodents, and the vector is the *Ixodes scapularis* tick.

The clinical syndromes of HME and HGA are very similar. After tick exposure and an incubation period of 5 to 10 days, the infection typically manifests with fever, headache, and myalgia. Although HGA and HME have been distinguished from Rocky Mountain spotted fever by the absence of a rash in the former, a nonspecific trunk rash can occur in up to 40% of patients with HME but is much less common in those with HGA. Severe disease can occur in HGA and HME, with multiorgan failure and a mortality rate of 3% in treated patients. In addition, HGA and HME should be considered among the differential diagnoses of patients with fever of unknown origin because symptoms can persist for several months in untreated patients.

Leukopenia and thrombocytopenia are characteristic. Diagnosis can be confirmed by demonstration of morulae (clumps of organisms in the cytoplasm of the appropriate leukocyte) on peripheral blood smear; however, this test is insensitive. Convalescent serologic testing is the most commonly used diagnostic test, and polymerase chain reaction testing is available in some areas.

Intravenous or oral doxycycline is the treatment of choice for HME and HGA. Empiric treatment is appropriate in patients with suspected disease to avoid the adverse outcomes associated with delayed treatment. Response to treatment can occur within 1 to 3 days, and treatment should be continued for several days after the patient has become afebrile. Treating pregnant women with doxycycline is not recommended but should be considered in women with life-threatening illness. Rifampin may be an alternative treatment option in pregnant women, although data were limited at the time of publication. Patients who do not respond to treatment may have coinfection with one of the other tick-associated illnesses. As with Lyme disease and babesiosis, active infection with HME and HGA does not cause a chronic fatiguing illness, and antimicrobial treatment for such patients is not indicated.

KEY POINTS

- In the proper clinical setting, fever, myalgia, arthralgia, leukopenia, and thrombocytopenia are suggestive of human monocytic ehrlichiosis and human granulocytic anaplasmosis.

- A nonspecific rash on the trunk can occur in up to 40% of patients with human monocytic ehrlichiosis; a rash is much less common in human granulocytic anaplasmosis.

- Convalescent serologic testing is the most commonly used diagnostic test in patients with human granulocytic anaplasmosis or human monocytic ehrlichiosis.

- Patients who do not respond to treatment for human granulocytic anaplasmosis or human monocytic ehrlichiosis may have coinfection with another tick-borne illness.

- Empiric treatment is appropriate in patients with suspected human granulocytic anaplasmosis or human monocytic ehrlichiosis to avoid the adverse outcomes associated with delayed treatment.

Rocky Mountain Spotted Fever

Rocky Mountain spotted fever is caused by *Rickettsia rickettsii*. The reservoir is humans, and the vectors are dog and wood ticks. The disease causes a febrile illness in the spring and summer throughout the Western hemisphere and is centered in the United States in the south central and southeast regions.

After a tick bite and an incubation period of 3 to 14 days, fever, headache, and myalgia develop. The characteristic rash begins as blanching erythematous macules around the wrists and ankles; lesions spread centripetally and become petechial. The rash is found in only 15% of patients on presentation but appears in most patients by day 4; however, the rash never develops in 10% of patients. The absence of the rash presents a diagnostic challenge because of the nonspecific nature of the presentation. Treatment must be initiated as soon as the infection is suspected, because the mortality rate increases from 6.5% to more than 20% when treatment is initiated more than 5 days after onset.

The standard diagnostic test is serologic testing using indirect fluorescent antibody or enzyme immunoassay, and it can take several weeks for positive seroconversion. The treatment of choice is doxycycline.

KEY POINTS

- The rash in Rocky Mountain spotted fever is characterized by blanching erythematous macules around the wrists and ankles; lesions spread centripetally and become petechial.

- Rash occurs in only 15% of patients with Rocky Mountain spotted fever on presentation, and it never occurs in 10%.

- Mortality increases from 6% to more than 20% when treatment is initiated more than 5 days after presentation in patients with Rocky Mountain spotted fever.

Bibliography

Chapman AS, Bakken JS, Folk SM, et al; Tickborne Rickettsial Diseases Working Group; Centers for Disease Control and Prevention. Diagnosis and management of tickborne rickettsial diseases: Rocky Mountain spotted fever, ehrlichioses, and anaplasmosis—United States: a practical guide for physicians and other health-care and public health professionals. MMWR Recomm Rep. 2006;55(RR-4):1-27. [PMID: 16572105]

Dhand A, Nadelman RB, Aguero-Rosenfeld M, Haddad FA, Stokes DP, Horowitz HW. Human granulocytic anaplasmosis during pregnancy: case series and literature review. Clin Infect Dis. 2007;45(5):589-593. [PMID: 17682993]

Swanson SJ, Neitzel D, Reed KD, Belongia EA. Coinfections acquired from ixodes ticks. Clin Microbiol Rev. 2006;19(4):708-727. [PMID: 17041141]

Wormser GP, Dattwyler RJ, Shapiro ED, et al. The clinical assessment, prevention, and treatment of Lyme disease, human granulocytic anaplasmosis, and babesiosis: clinical practice guidelines by the Infectious Diseases Society of America. Clin Infect Dis. 2006;43(9):1089-1134. [PMID: 17029130]

Urinary Tract Infections

Introduction

Urinary tract infections (UTIs) may involve only the lower urinary tract or the upper and lower urinary tract. A UTI in an individual with an indwelling urinary catheter, neurogenic bladder, stones, obstruction, immunosuppression, pregnancy, renal disease, or diabetes mellitus is defined as complicated and may predispose to treatment failure or require modified approaches to management owing to infection with antibiotic-resistant organisms. Women, particularly young, sexually active women, are at higher risk for UTIs than are men. Other UTI risk factors include diabetes, pregnancy, spermicide use (in women), urinary tract instrumentation, and neurogenic bladder–related voiding abnormalities.

Common symptoms and findings of UTIs include dysuria and urinary frequency and urgency, pyuria on urinalysis, and 10^5 or more colony-forming units (CFU)/mL of bacteria on quantitative urine culture. *Escherichia coli is* the isolated pathogen in more than 90% of patients with uncomplicated upper and lower UTIs.

KEY POINTS

- Risk factors for urinary tract infection include female sex (particularly in those sexually active), diabetes, pregnancy, spermicide use in women, urinary tract instrumentation, and neurogenic bladder–related voiding abnormalities.

- Symptoms and findings of urinary tract infection include dysuria and urinary frequency and urgency, pyuria, and 10^5 or more colony-forming units/mL of bacteria on urine culture.

Cystitis

Acute cystitis occurs most commonly among young, sexually active women, and may be self-limited and associated with few long-term consequences, but the symptoms may be distressing and disruptive. The constellation of new-onset urinary frequency, urgency, and dysuria, without an abnormal vaginal discharge, has a positive predictive value for acute cystitis of 90%. Presumptive therapy based on clinical symptoms in the setting of pyuria on urinalysis (without performing a urine culture) is an acceptable management strategy for acute, uncomplicated cystitis in young women. The urinalysis can be omitted in healthy women with acute cystitis if there are no complicating factors. When the diagnosis is not clear, the urine dipstick for leukocyte esterase and/or nitrite is an acceptable screening tool but may be less sensitive than microscopic urinalysis. A urine culture should be obtained for women with suspected cystitis if the diagnosis is not clear from the history and physical examination; if an unusual or antimicrobial-resistant organism is suspected; if the patient is pregnant; if therapeutic options are limited owing to medication intolerance; if the episode represents a suspected relapse or treatment failure after recent UTI treatment; and if any underlying complicating conditions are identified.

Commonly used antibiotics in nonpregnant women include trimethoprim, trimethoprim-sulfamethoxazole (TMP-SMX), nitrofurantoin, fluoroquinolones, and β-lactams. When possible, a 3-day regimen of TMP-SMX is recommended in patients with uncomplicated infection; short courses of fluoroquinolones have also proven successful, but the additional expense of these agents and resistance concerns with widespread use make them less preferred as initial therapy compared with TMP-SMX. In pregnant women with cystitis, a 3- to 7-day treatment regimen with an oral antimicrobial agent that is safe in pregnancy, such as amoxicillin or nitrofurantoin, is appropriate. Patients with complicated UTIs should be treated for 7 to 14 days with a fluoroquinolone.

Young men should receive short-course antibiotic regimens approved for women with cystitis. Diagnostic considerations in men with UTIs include urinary obstruction or other anatomic abnormalities.

KEY POINTS

- The constellation of new-onset urinary frequency and urgency and dysuria, without an abnormal vaginal discharge, has a positive predictive value for acute cystitis of 90%.
- Presumptive therapy based on clinical symptoms in the setting of pyuria on urinalysis (without performing a urine culture) with commonly used antibiotics such as trimethoprim-sulfamethoxazole is an acceptable management strategy for acute, uncomplicated cystitis in nonpregnant young women.
- Pregnant women with cystitis are treated for 3 to 7 days with amoxicillin or nitrofurantoin.
- Empiric treatment of complicated urinary tract infections includes 7 to 14 days with a fluoroquinolone.

Recurrent UTI

Up to 44% of young women treated effectively for acute cystitis experience a recurrent infection within the next year. Studies have shown women with a history of acute cystitis can recognize the symptoms of a recurrence and provide appropriate self-treatment. Other acceptable management approaches include phone triage and care by a medical provider. Self-treatment and phone triage allow for prompt access to antibiotics for symptomatic relief and result in greater convenience and health care savings compared with clinical evaluation. Preventive strategies for future recurrences include avoiding spermicides and prophylaxis with single-dose TMP-SMX, nitrofurantoin, or ciprofloxacin after sexual intercourse in women with two or more episodes of postcoital UTIs per year.

KEY POINTS

- Women with a history of acute cystitis can recognize the symptoms of urinary tract infection recurrence and provide appropriate self-treatment.
- Antibiotic prophylaxis with a single dose of an antibiotic after sexual intercourse can be considered in women with two or more episodes of postcoital urinary tract infections per year.

Pyelonephritis

Pyelonephritis typically occurs in the setting of ascending bacterial infection from the bladder. Diabetes and pregnancy are risk factors. Pyelonephritis, including abscess, can occur hematogenously in patients with staphylococcal bacteremia or endocarditis. Symptoms include those typical of cystitis as well as flank pain or abdominal pain and fever. Diagnosis is based on a characteristic clinical presentation, bacteriuria and pyuria on urinalysis, and urine culture demonstrating 10^4 or more CFU/mL of bacteria. Blood cultures are positive in 25% of patients.

Fluoroquinolones constitute first-line empiric oral therapy for patients with pyelonephritis who are clinically well enough for outpatient management. TMP-SMX, cephalosporins or other β-lactams, or aminoglycosides may also be appropriate depending on urine culture results and antimicrobial susceptibility testing. Parenteral therapy should be used initially in patients who are acutely ill, nauseated, or vomiting. The recommended duration of antibiotic therapy for uncomplicated pyelonephritis is at least 10 to 14 days. Imaging studies are indicated only in patients in whom an alternative diagnosis or a urologic complication is suspected. Ultrasonography of the kidneys and bladder is the appropriate initial imaging study. CT and MRI should be considered in patients with suggestive findings of an anatomic abnormality on ultrasound and in those with persistent or relapsing pyelonephritis despite a negative ultrasound.

KEY POINTS

- Oral fluoroquinolones constitute first-line empiric oral therapy for patients with pyelonephritis who are clinically well enough for outpatient management.
- Imaging studies in patients with possible pyelonephritis should be used only if an alternative diagnosis or a urologic complication is suspected.

Asymptomatic Bacteriuria

The prevalence of asymptomatic bacteriuria is higher among women than men and occurs more commonly in pregnancy, diabetic patients, and the elderly. Asymptomatic bacteriuria becomes more common among men at age 65 years or older. Treatment of asymptomatic bacteriuria in adult nonpregnant patients (including diabetic patients and the elderly) is generally not indicated but may be considered after recent indwelling urinary catheter removal, before an invasive urologic procedure, in neutropenic patients, or in patients with a urinary tract obstruction. Screening for and treatment of bacteriuria in pregnancy have been shown to be effective in preventing pyelonephritis.

KEY POINTS

- Treatment of asymptomatic bacteriuria in adult nonpregnant patients (including diabetic patients and the elderly) without urinary tract obstruction is not indicated.
- Screening for and treatment of asymptomatic bacteriuria in pregnant women are effective in preventing pyelonephritis.

Bibliography

Drekonja DM, Johnson JR. Urinary tract infections. Prim Care. 2008;35(2):345-367. [PMID: 18486719]

Lin K, Fajardo K; U.S. Preventive Services Task Force. Screening for asymptomatic bacteriuria in adults: evidence for the U.S. Preventive Services Task Force reaffirmation recommendation statement. Ann Intern Med. 2008;149(1):W20-W24. [PMID: 18591632]

Masson P, Matheson S, Webster AC, Craig JC. Meta-analyses in prevention and treatment of urinary tract infections. Infect Dis Clin North Am. 2009;23(2):355-385. [PMID: 19393914]

Smaill F, Vazquez JC. Antibiotics for asymptomatic bacteriuria in pregnancy. Cochrane Database Syst Rev. 2007;(2):CD000490. [PMID: 17443502]

Mycobacterium tuberculosis Infection

Introduction

Tuberculosis is second only to HIV infection in causing deaths from an infectious agent. Tuberculosis is more aggressive, contagious, and lethal in people with HIV-1–related immune dysfunction, and HIV-1 progresses more rapidly in people with active tuberculosis.

Epidemiology

In 2007, 13,293 tuberculosis cases were reported in the United States. Prevalence in foreign-born U.S. residents is 9.7 times higher than that in U.S.-born persons. Approximately 1% of U.S. cases are multidrug resistant (MDR), and of these, only two cases in 2007 and four in 2006 were extensively drug resistant (XDR).

KEY POINT

- Prevalence of tuberculosis in foreign-born U.S. residents is 9.7 times higher than that in U.S.-born persons.

Pathophysiology

Tuberculosis is caused by infection with *Mycobacterium tuberculosis*, an acid-fast–staining bacillus, which is inhaled into the respiratory system by airborne droplets. In the airways, alveolar macrophages ingest the bacteria but are unable to arrest multiplication of the organism, which ultimately destroys macrophages. Infected macrophages are also carried to lymph nodes, and in some patients, such as those with immunosuppression, they are carried to the bones, gastrointestinal tract, and other locations. These processes occur before immunity develops, heralded by reactivity to the tuberculin skin test (TST). Once immunity develops, a quiescent state usually occurs in which infection is recognized only by reactivity to tuberculin skin testing. In some patients, a pulmonary Ghon complex (localized parenchymal infection and lymph node involvement) may reach significant size and calcification status to be visible on radiographs. Malnutrition, immunosuppressed states, and stress are risk factors for primary progression or reactivation of quiescent tuberculosis.

KEY POINT

- Malnutrition, immunosuppressed states, and stress are risk factors for primary progression or reactivation of quiescent tuberculosis.

Clinical Manifestations

Patients with pulmonary tuberculosis are often asymptomatic. However, constitutional symptoms, including anorexia, fatigue, weight loss, chills, fever, night sweats, and local symptoms such as cough, may develop. Hemoptysis and chest pain from pleural involvement indicate advanced disease. The pulmonary examination is often minimally abnormal. HIV-infected or other immunocompromised patients often have no classic signs or symptoms of tuberculosis and have a greater likelihood of dissemination or extrapulmonary infection.

Diagnostic Testing

Tuberculin Skin Testing

The most common tuberculosis testing procedure is the TST. The procedure involves injecting purified protein derivative (PPD) intradermally and assessing the skin response to the antigen load. The induration—not the erythema—resulting within 48 to 72 hours is then measured. Various cutoff values are used, based on the patient's risk status, to increase the specificity of the test results (**Table 20**).

A booster effect whereby a negative TST result is followed by a positive reaction a few weeks later may occur and is caused by reactivation of immunity that may be remote. This phenomenon occurs more commonly in older patients with a remote history of latent tuberculosis, in those with nontuberculous mycobacterial infection, and in those who have received bacille Calmette-Guérin (BCG) vaccination; therefore, these populations are at lower risk for tuberculosis reactivation than persons with initially positive TST results, especially when the positive TST result represents a recent conversion. However, caution should be exercised when immunosuppressive therapy is planned. False-positive and false-negative TST results may occur, and approximately 20% of patients with active tuberculosis may not exhibit TST positivity. A history of BCG vaccination should not influence interpretation of the TST.

Interferon-γ Release Assays

The measurement of interferon-γ release by T lymphocytes specific for *M. tuberculosis* is a new test gaining popularity. Despite the Centers for Disease Control and Prevention's endorsing its use in all situations in which the TST is done, the test's lack of availability and requirement of testing the patient's blood within 12 hours of sample collection so that leukocytes are still viable have limited its use. Additionally, there are limited data on its use in children, persons recently exposed to tuberculosis, and immunocompromised hosts.

Culture and Other Diagnostic Methods

M. tuberculosis can be cultivated in the laboratory and identified on culture media. The long growth time of this organism decreases the effectiveness of this method in rapid treatment decisions, although more rapid culture tests that use polymerase chain reaction probes (median time to positivity, 10 days versus 28 days for conventional cultures) are more practical. Both methods involve viable organisms; therefore, drug susceptibility testing can be done.

Positive acid-fast stains of respiratory specimens are helpful in the diagnosis of tuberculosis infection but often are negative. In patients with suspected pleural tuberculosis, pleural biopsies should be considered because pleural fluid testing is associated with low sensitivity. Bronchoscopy may aid diagnosis in certain circumstances. Pathologic examination of specimens for granulomas, caseous necrosis, and bacilli is helpful but not pathognomonic for tuberculosis. Polymerase chain reaction–based assays are also increasingly being used, particularly in patients with suspected central nervous system infections, but are limited by their low sensitivity.

Radiographic Imaging

Chest radiographic abnormalities of reactivation tuberculosis classically include lesions in the apical-posterior segments of the upper lung and superior segments of the lower lobe. Cavitation may be present. Primary progressive tuberculosis may manifest as hilar lymphadenopathy or infiltrates in any

TABLE 20 Interpretation of Tuberculin Skin Test Results

Criteria for Tuberculin Positivity by Risk Group		
≥5 mm Induration	**≥10 mm Induration**	**≥15 mm Induration**
HIV-positive persons	Recent (<5 years) arrivals from high-prevalence countries	All others with no risk factors for TB
Recent contacts of active TB case	Injection drug users	
Persons with fibrotic changes on chest radiograph consistent with old TB	Residents or employees of high-risk congregate settings: prisons and jails, nursing homes and other long-term facilities for the elderly, hospitals and other health care facilities, residential facilities for patients with AIDS, homeless shelters	
Patients with organ transplants and other immunosuppressive conditions (receiving the equivalent of ≥15 mg/d of prednisone for >4 weeks)	Mycobacteriology lab personnel; persons with clinical conditions that put them at high risk for active disease; children age <4 years or exposed to adults in high-risk categories	

TB = tuberculosis infection.

part of the lung, similar to those found in bacterial pneumonia. Atypical or absent radiologic findings commonly occur in immunocompromised patients but may also occur in immunocompetent patients. Miliary tuberculosis may have the characteristic "millet seed" appearance. CT scans may identify abnormalities not yet visible on chest radiographs.

KEY POINTS

- In tuberculin skin testing, the induration—not the erythema—resulting within 48 to 72 hours is measured, with cutoff values determined according to risk factor status.

- A booster effect whereby a negative tuberculin skin test result is followed by a positive reaction a few weeks later may occur, most commonly in older patients with a remote history of latent tuberculosis, patients with nontuberculous mycobacterial infection, and those with bacille Calmette-Guérin vaccine history.

- The long growth time of *Mycobacterium tuberculosis* decreases the effectiveness of culture as a diagnostic method in rapid treatment decisions; however, cultures are essential for drug susceptibility testing.

- Chest radiographic abnormalities of reactivation tuberculosis classically include lesions in the apical-posterior segments of the upper lung and superior segments of the lower lobe.

Treatment

Because of increasing concerns of resistance, all patients with suspected/confirmed tuberculosis are treated with four-drug therapy with the first-line agents isoniazid, rifampin, pyrazinamide, and ethambutol for 2 months, followed by de-escalation of antimicrobial therapy once drug susceptibility of isoniazid and rifampin is established. These agents are then continued for 7 months, totaling a 9-month treatment course. Latent tuberculosis (positive TST result but no evidence of active disease) can be treated with a 9-month course of isoniazid. The toxicity profile of each drug must be addressed with patients before treatment is commenced (**Table 21**). In some instances, directly observed therapy may be warranted to increase drug adherence and prevent resistance.

Multidrug-Resistant and Extensively Drug-Resistant Tuberculosis

Multidrug-resistant (MDR) tuberculosis is defined as an isolate that exhibits decreased susceptibility to at least isoniazid and rifampin. Extensively drug-resistant (XDR) tuberculosis is a subtype of multidrug-resistant tuberculosis that is resistant to isoniazid and rifampin as well as any fluoroquinolone and at least one of three injectable second-line drugs.

Higher mortality is associated with these strains, especially XDR tuberculosis.

Vaccination

The bacille Calmette-Guérin vaccine is derived from an attenuated strain of *M. bovis* and is used worldwide except in the United States. The efficacy of this vaccine for preventing serious forms of tuberculosis (tuberculous meningitis and miliary tuberculosis) has been evaluated in recent meta-analyses and has been shown to be high in children (>80%). However, this protective effect for pulmonary tuberculosis in adults was not found.

KEY POINTS

- Because of increasing resistance concerns, all patients with suspected/confirmed tuberculosis are treated with four-drug therapy with isoniazid, rifampin, pyrazinamide, and ethambutol, followed by de-escalation of antimicrobial therapy once drug susceptibility is known.

- Higher mortality is associated with multidrug-resistant and extensively drug-resistant tuberculosis.

Bibliography

Centers for Disease Control and Prevention Web site. www.cdc.gov/tb. Updated June 1, 2009. Accessed July 17, 2009.

Escalante P. In the clinic. Tuberculosis. Ann Intern Med. 2009;150(11): ITC61-ITC614; quiz ITV616. [PMID: 19487708]

Gaba PD, Haley C, Griffin MR, et al. Increasing outpatient fluoroquinolone exposure before tuberculosis diagnosis and impact on culture-negative disease. Arch Intern Med. 2007;167(21):2317-2322. [PMID: 18039990]

Luetkemeyer AF, Charlebois ED, Flores LL, et al. Comparison of an interferon-gamma release assay with tuberculin skin testing in HIV-infected individuals. American Journal of Respiratory and Critical Care Medicine. 2007;175(7):737-742.

The role of BCG vaccine in the prevention and control of tuberculosis in the United States: a joint statement by ACET and the Advisory Committee on Immunization Practices. MMWR Recomm Rep. 1996;45(RR-4):1-18. [PMID: 8602127]

Nontuberculous Mycobacterial Infections

Introduction

Nontuberculous mycobacteria (NTM) are organisms ubiquitous in the environment. In humans, NTM isolates may or may not be pathogenic, whereas *Mycobacterium tuberculosis* isolates are always considered pathogenic. Determining whether NTM in a clinical specimen is a pathogen, environmental contaminant, or colonizer is the initial management step; only pathogenic infection requires treatment. Features suggestive of pathogenic infection include the species' likelihood for pathogenicity, the presence of many colonies on

TABLE 21 Antituberculosis Drugs

Agent	Side Effects	Notes
First-Line Medications		
Isoniazid	Rash; hepatic enzyme elevation; hepatitis; peripheral neuropathy; lupus-like syndrome	Hepatitis risk increases with age and alcohol consumption. Pyridoxine may prevent peripheral neuropathy. Adjust for renal failure.
Pyrazinamide	Hepatitis; rash; GI upset; hyperuricemia	May make glucose control more difficult in diabetic patients. Adjust for renal failure.
Rifampin	Hepatitis; rash; GI upset	Contraindicated or should be used with caution when administered with protease inhibitors and non-nucleoside reverse transcriptase inhibitors. Do not administer to patients also taking saquinavir/ritonavir. Colors body fluids orange.
Rifabutin	Rash; hepatitis; thrombocytopenia; severe arthralgia; uveitis; leukopenia	Dose adjustment required if taken with protease inhibitors or non-nucleoside reverse transcriptase inhibitors. Monitor for decreased antiretroviral activity and for rifabutin toxicity.
Rifapentine	Similar to rifampin	Contraindicated in HIV-positive patients (unacceptable rate of failure/relapse).
Ethambutol	Optic neuritis; rash	Baseline and periodic tests of visual acuity and color vision. Patients are advised to call immediately if any change in visual acuity or color vision. Adjust for renal failure.
Streptomycin	Auditory, vestibular, and renal toxicity	Avoid or reduce dose in adults >59 years. Monitor hearing and renal function tests. Adjust for renal failure.
Second-Line Medications[a]		
Cycloserine	Psychosis; convulsions; depression; headaches; rash; drug interactions	Pyridoxine may decrease CNS side effects. Measure drug serum levels.
Ethionamide	GI upset; hepatotoxicity; hypersensitivity	May cause hypothyroidism.
Kanamycin and amikacin	Auditory, vestibular, andrenal toxicity	Not approved by the FDA for TB treatment. Monitor vestibular, hearing, and renal function.
Ciprofloxacin, ofloxacin, levofloxacin, moxifloxacin, gatifloxacin	GI upset; dizziness; hypersensitivity; drug interactions	Not approved by the FDA for TB treatment. Should not be used in children.
Para-aminosalicyclic acid	GI upset; hypersensitivity; hepatotoxicity	May cause hypothyroidism, especially if used with ethionamide. Measure hepatic enzymes.

CNS = central nervous system; FDA = U.S. Food and Drug Administration; GI = gastrointestinal; TB = tuberculosis.

[a]Use these drugs in consultation with a clinician experienced in the management of drug-resistant TB.

Data from Centers for Disease Control and Prevention. Core curriculum on tuberculosis. www.cdc.gov/tb/webcourses/CoreCurr/index.htm. Published October, 2004. Accessed on July 23, 2009.

repeated culture, no other explanation for the symptoms, the nature of the clinical illness itself, and the presence of acid-fast bacilli in histologic specimens. NTM infections are noncontagious; persons infected with NTM do not require isolation.

NTM infections typically involve one of four syndromes: (1) slowly progressive pulmonary disease similar to *M. tuberculosis* infection and primarily caused by *M. kansasii* and *M. avium* complex (MAC) (also referred to as *M. avium-intracellulare*); (2) MAC- or *M. scrofulaceum*–related lymphadenitis; (3) disseminated disease in immunocompromised hosts caused by MAC or the rapidly growing mycobacteria (RGM) *M. abscessus*, *M. fortuitum*, and *M. chelonae*; and (4) cutaneous disease due to direct inoculation primarily with RGM, *M. marinum*, or *M. ulcerans*.

KEY POINT

- Determining whether nontuberculous mycobacteria isolated in a clinical specimen is a pathogen, environmental contaminant, or colonizer is the initial management step; only pathogenic infection requires treatment.

Mycobacterium avium complex

MAC infections are associated with several different clinical presentations. Elderly men with MAC infections typically have underlying pulmonary disease from cigarette smoking, with symptoms and radiographic findings similar to those found in *M. tuberculosis* infection (see *Mycobacterium tuberculosis* Infection). Elderly nonsmoking women more commonly have interstitial infiltrates involving the right middle lobe or the lingula characterized by chronic cough.

MAC-associated hypersensitivity pneumonitis occurs in immunocompetent patients and is related to hot tub exposure ("hot tub lung") (see MKSAP 15 Pulmonary and Critical Care Medicine). This condition responds to corticosteroids. MAC can also cause mycobacterial lymphadenitis and typically presents as disseminated disease in HIV-infected patients with very low CD4 cell counts.

MAC organisms are slow growing but grow well on standard mycobacterial media. Once colonies appear, they can be readily identified with nucleic acid probes. Pulmonary disease and lymphadenitis are diagnosed by sputum and fine-needle aspiration, respectively. Patients with disseminated disease often have positive blood cultures if specimens are obtained in isolator tubes.

Determining whether antimicrobial agents are warranted is the first step in MAC treatment. **Table 22** outlines guidelines for initiating treatment. The major drugs for treating MAC infections are clarithromycin or azithromycin plus ethambutol and rifampin or rifabutin. Streptomycin, amikacin, and fluoroquinolone antibiotics are second-line options. Treatment should continue for at least 1 year after the last positive culture is observed. Surgery can be useful if the disease is well localized. Disease is controlled with treatment in approximately 90% of patients.

KEY POINTS

- *Mycobacterium avium* complex–associated disease includes hypersensitivity pneumonitis ("hot tub lung"); tuberculosis-like infection in elderly smoking men; chronic right middle lobe/lingula infection and cough in nonsmoking elderly women; lymphadenitis; and disseminated disease in HIV-infected patients.

- The major drugs for treating *Mycobacterium avium* complex infections are clarithromycin or azithromycin plus ethambutol and rifampin or rifabutin.

Mycobacterium kansasii

M. kansasii infection almost always occurs in the lung and is clinically indistinguishable from *Mycobacterium tuberculosis* infection (see *Mycobacterium tuberculosis* Infection). Treatment consists of isoniazid, ethambutol, and rifampin. Although there is much less experience with the use of clarithromycin, this drug is active in vitro and appears to be clinically effective.

KEY POINT

- *Mycobacterium kansasii* infection almost always occurs in the lung, is clinically indistinguishable from *Mycobacterium tuberculosis* infection, and is treated with isoniazid, ethambutol, and rifampin.

TABLE 22 Guidelines for Initiating *Mycobacterium avium* Complex Treatment

Pulmonary Disease
1. Must have compatible illness and chest radiographic findings
2. Repeated isolation of the organism from respiratory specimens must be documented
3. Exclusion of other diagnostic explanations for the patient's findings must be established
Extrapulmonary Disease
1. Isolation of the organism from an ordinarily sterile site must be documented

Reprinted with permission from Griffith DE, Aksamit T, Brown-Elliott BA, et al; ATS Mycobacterial Diseases Subcommittee; American Thoracic Society; and Infectious Disease Society of America. An official ATS/IDSA statement: diagnosis, treatment, and prevention of nontuberculous mycobacterial diseases [erratum in Am J Respir Crit Care Med. 2007;175(7):744-745]. Am J Respir Crit Care Med. 2007;175(4):367-416. [PMID: 17277290] Copyright American Thoracic Society, 2007.

Rapidly Growing Mycobacteria

RGM (*M. abscessus, M. fortuitum,* and *M. chelonae*) are environmental organisms distinct from other mycobacteria by their rapid growth in culture. Cultures for RGM are generally positive within 1 week rather than the 2 to 6 weeks expected for other mycobacteria. They grow on routine culture media if kept for at least 1 week, in addition to media selective for mycobacteria.

RGM-associated pulmonary disease is typically chronic and most often caused by *M. abscessus*. Surgical RGM infections are associated with implantable prosthetic devices such as augmentation mammoplasty, prosthetic joints, or prosthetic heart valves. RGM should be considered in any purulent infection in which routine bacterial cultures are negative. Disseminated disease occurs rarely, developing only in patients with advanced stages of immunosuppression.

Drug susceptibility varies depending on RGM species. Most RGM are susceptible to clarithromycin and amikacin. Other potentially useful drugs include trimethoprim-sulfamethoxazole, the fluoroquinolones, the tetracyclines, imipenem, and cefoxitin. RGM are not susceptible to the standard antituberculosis drugs. Therapy should last a minimum of 4 months and possibly as long as several years in patients with severe infections.

KEY POINTS

- Rapidly growing mycobacteria are not susceptible to standard antituberculosis medications.

- Therapy for rapidly growing mycobacteria should last a minimum of 4 months and possibly as long as several years in patients with severe infections.

Bibliography

Griffith DE, Aksamit T, Brown-Elliott BA, et al; ATS Mycobacterial Diseases Subcommittee; American Thoracic Society; Infectious

Disease Society of America. An official ATS/IDSA statement: diagnosis, treatment, and prevention of nontuberculous mycobacterial diseases [erratum in Am J Respir Crit Care Med. 2007;175(7):744-755]. Am J Respir Crit Care Med. 2007;175(4):367-416. [PMID: 17277290]

Uslan DZ, Kowalski TJ, Wengenack NL, Virk A, Wilson JW. Skin and soft tissue infections due to rapidly growing mycobacteria: comparison of clinical features, treatment, and susceptibility. Arch Dermatol. 2006;142(10):1287-1292. [PMID: 17043183]

Vugia DJ, Jang Y, Zizek C, Ely J, Winthrop KL, Desmond E. Mycobacteria in nail salon whirlpool footbaths, California. Emerg Infect Dis. 2005;11(4):616-618. [PMID: 15829204]

Fungal Infections

Aspergillosis

Aspergillus is a ubiquitous mold found in soil and other moist environments throughout the world. Classically, the diseases caused by *Aspergillus* species are allergic bronchopulmonary aspergillosis, invasive aspergillosis, and aspergilloma (fungus ball).

Allergic bronchopulmonary aspergillosis is manifested by persistent severe asthma, expectoration of brown sputum that contains *Aspergillus* organisms, pulmonary infiltrates, and fibrosis. More recently, the designation of aspergilloma has been divided into chronic cavitary aspergillosis and single aspergilloma. Risk factors for invasive aspergillosis include prolonged and severe neutropenia, corticosteroid therapy, hematopoietic stem cell transplantation, solid organ transplantation, advanced AIDS, and chronic granulomatous disease. Mortality rates in patients with invasive aspergillosis are high, and aggressive treatment is always indicated.

Although the lung is the usual site of involvement in aspergillosis, other organs may occasionally be involved. The "halo sign" (nodules bordered by a ground-glass attenuation) on CT scan of the lung is the classic radiographic finding in pulmonary aspergillosis (**Figure 4**), but it is not specific because this finding is also associated with infections involving other filamentous fungi and some bacterial lung infections. *Aspergillus* usually can be recovered in culture from infected sites by bronchoalveolar lavage, transbronchial biopsy, needle aspiration, and video-assisted thoracoscopic biopsy. A definitive diagnosis requires histologic demonstration of the organisms in tissue. Often, it is not possible to obtain tissue for histologic examination in ill patients with a suspected diagnosis of invasive aspergillosis. Serologic tests used in the diagnosis of invasive disease include antigenic assays for detection of fungal components in blood, cerebrospinal fluid, and urine; galactomannan assays of blood or spinal fluid; and assays for (1-3)-β-D glucans. A polymerase chain reaction assay for detecting fungal DNA has been used experimentally and is associated with higher sensitivity and earlier results than culture for detection of *Aspergillus* species and zygomycetes in patients with histologically proven disease.

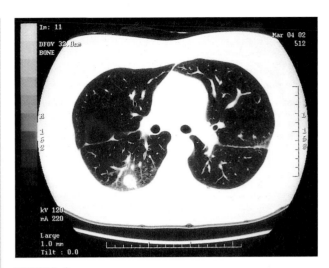

FIGURE 4.
CT scan of a patient with invasive pulmonary aspergillosis.
Note the nodule with a typical "halo sign" in the posterior right lung adjacent to the pleura.

Empiric therapy should be initiated in patients in whom aspergillosis is suspected. Voriconazole has emerged as the initial treatment of choice for invasive aspergillosis, whereas liposomal and lipid complex amphotericin B remain good alternatives for patients with voriconazole intolerance. The primary treatment for allergic bronchopulmonary aspergillosis is corticosteroids; the addition of itraconazole has been shown to have a corticosteroid-sparing effect. Voriconazole and posaconazole are alternatives to itraconazole.

KEY POINT

- Allergic bronchopulmonary aspergillosis is manifested by persistent severe asthma, expectoration of brown sputum that contains *Aspergillus* organisms, pulmonary infiltrates, and fibrosis.

Cryptococcosis

Cryptococcus has become a common opportunistic pathogen, associated mainly with HIV infection, and, less frequently, transplantation. The lungs are the presumed portal of entry, and pulmonary disease is one of the most common manifestations. Central nervous system (CNS) disease may also occur. Before the availability of amphotericin B, cryptococcal meningitis was uniformly fatal. Now, especially with the availability of the triazoles, most patients can be cured.

The diagnosis is established by growth of the organism in culture, demonstration of cryptococcal antigen in cerebrospinal fluid or blood, nucleic acid amplification techniques, or typical pathologic findings in tissues with special stains.

Mild pulmonary disease can be treated with fluconazole, itraconazole, or an amphotericin B lipid formulation. CNS disease is treated initially with a lipid formulation of amphotericin B for at least the first 2 weeks of therapy. Thereafter, the amphotericin B lipid formulation can be continued, or, more commonly, therapy can be switched to high-dose oral fluconazole for 6 to 10 weeks. Subsequently, maintenance therapy with a lower dose of fluconazole may be prescribed. Patients with late-stage HIV infection may require lifelong secondary prophylaxis with oral fluconazole.

> **KEY POINT**
> - Cryptococcal meningitis, a once uniformly fatal disease associated with HIV infection, and less frequently with transplantation, is now curable with the availability of amphotericin B and the triazoles.

Histoplasmosis

Histoplasma capsulatum is a dimorphic fungus that lives primarily in soil, often in association with bird or bat droppings, and is most commonly found in areas surrounding the great river valleys of the United States. Inhaled spores cause subclinical infection in most persons living in these areas. *H. capsulatum* may rarely be found in many other parts of the country, and it is also found in Central and South America and in parts of Europe. Point-source epidemics have been described in individuals who have been exposed to bird excrement, such as in chicken coops or wild bird nesting areas. Immunosuppressed patients and those with chronic pulmonary disease are most susceptible to developing clinical disease. In these populations, invasive and cavitary pulmonary disease; disseminated disease; or extrapulmonary localized disease in the adrenal glands, liver, pericardium, or CNS are common manifestations.

H. capsulatum urine antigen assays are sensitive and specific for detecting active disease, but confirmation requires recovery of organisms from infected foci, blood, or bone marrow, or detection in histopathologic specimens. Treatment should not be delayed until the diagnosis is confirmed.

Mild pulmonary disease in patients with *H. capsulatum* is most often self-limited and usually does not require treatment. Patients with moderate pulmonary disease with symptoms persisting for more than 4 weeks may be treated with itraconazole for 6 to 12 weeks. Patients with *H. capsulatum* with severe, acute, or chronic pulmonary disease require treatment with one of the amphotericin B lipid formulations for at least 2 weeks, followed by itraconazole for 12 weeks. Methylprednisolone may be added for patients with hypoxemia or evidence of bronchial obstruction for the first 1 to 2 weeks of therapy. Patients with disseminated disease require treatment with an amphotericin B lipid formulation for at least 1 to 2 weeks, followed by itraconazole for 12 months. Histoplasmosis-induced mediastinal fibrosis does not necessitate antifungal treatment unless there is evidence of active granulomatous disease, in which case itraconazole for 6 to 12

weeks is recommended. Treatment for *H. capsulatum* CNS infection consists of an amphotericin B lipid formulation for 4 to 6 weeks, followed by itraconazole for 12 months.

> **KEY POINT**
> - Mild forms of histoplasmosis may not require antifungal treatment, whereas more severe disease may be treated with amphotericin B or one of the newer triazoles.

Blastomycosis

Blastomyces dermatitidis is a dimorphic fungus found primarily in the southeastern United States; around the Great Lakes; in the states bordering on the Ohio, Missouri, and Mississippi rivers; and parts of New York. The portal of entry is usually the lungs, but direct inoculation through the skin also occurs (**Figure 5**).

Although the lungs are the most common site of infection, extrapulmonary disease is also common. The diagnosis is established by demonstration of typical findings on pathologic examination of tissue and demonstration of the organism in culture. Unlike histoplasmosis, most patients with blastomycosis require treatment. Patients with acute and severe disease require treatment with an amphotericin B lipid formulation, and those with mild or moderate disease require itraconazole therapy for at least 6 months or until all signs and symptoms of active disease have abated.

> **KEY POINT**
> - Patients with acute and severe blastomycosis require treatment with an amphotericin B lipid formulation, and those with mild or moderate disease require itraconazole therapy for at least 6 months or until all signs and symptoms of active disease have abated.

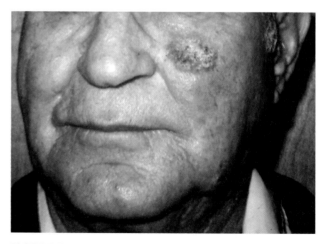

FIGURE 5.
Cutaneous blastomycosis on the left cheek of a patient with severe actinic skin changes.
This condition could have occurred secondary to direct inoculation into the skin or by hematogenous spread from a primary pulmonary focus.

Coccidioidomycosis

Coccidioides immitis is a dimorphic fungus that lives in soil in parts of Arizona, California, New Mexico, west Texas, and parts of northern Mexico (the Sonoran Desert). The disease is transmitted through inhalation of the arthroconidia, which are formed from the mycelia in soil. More than 50% of all infections are subclinical, but tens of thousands of clinical cases occur in endemic areas annually. The most common form of illness is acute or subacute pneumonia, with or without pleural effusions or empyema. As many as 10% of these acute or subacute infections lead to late sequelae consisting of pulmonary nodules or cavitary disease typified by cavities that are thin-walled and solitary or few in number. Less than 1% of the cases involve an extrapulmonary site such as the skin or the CNS. Most early infections resolve spontaneously, but patients with known infection require follow-up monitoring for several years to evaluate for a potential late recurrence. Persons of Filipino or African descent have an increased susceptibility to disseminated infection.

Diagnosis of coccidioidomycosis is based on clinical manifestations, classic radiographic findings, demonstration of the organism on culture or by special stains, histopathologic evaluation, and serologic demonstration of increased antibody titers. Clinical findings in acute disease may consist of brief, mild fever and malaise, progressing to flu-like symptoms, including fever, myalgia, and productive cough. Patients with more severe disease with empyema may have severe rigors, diaphoresis, high fever, pleuritic chest pain, dyspnea, cough, and headache. Chronic pulmonary disease may be present, with a productive cough and weight loss, with or without fever. Radiographic findings of acute disease may show small infiltrates; larger, more severe infiltrates; pleural effusions or empyema; and cavitary lesions. Radiographic findings in chronic coccidioidomycosis may show findings consistent with COPD, fibrosis, infiltrates and thin-walled cavities.

Drugs used to treat coccidioidomycosis include amphotericin B, ketoconazole, fluconazole, and itraconazole. Uncomplicated pulmonary infection in the immunocompetent host can be managed by periodic reevaluation. Immunosuppressed patients or those with disease progression require treatment with an amphotericin B lipid formulation or an azole for 3 to 6 months. Diffuse pneumonia in patients with coccidioidomycosis is usually treated initially with a 2- to 4-week course of an amphotericin B lipid formulation, followed by fluconazole or itraconazole for 1 year. Pulmonary cavitary disease may require surgical excision, and no antifungal treatment is required in patients in whom the lesion is removed entirely with no evidence of disease at the margins. Patients with severe immunodeficiency and coccidioidomycosis may require prolonged therapy with a triazole. CNS infection is generally treated with fluconazole, indefinitely.

Fusarium Infection

Although *Fusarium* species are often considered contaminants on culture, they may cause various infections, including localized cutaneous, nail, paranasal sinus, and ocular infection, as well as disseminated and invasive infection. Invasive infection usually develops only in immunocompromised patients. Cutaneous infection in immunocompromised patients may result from direct inoculation or hematogenous spread from another organ system. *Fusarium* skin infections occurring in immunosuppressed patients are almost always a cutaneous manifestation of a hematogenously disseminated fungal infection in patients with severe and prolonged neutropenia or severe lymphocyte dysfunction. Although amphotericin B, voriconazole, and posaconazole are active against *Fusarium* species, the prognosis of disseminated infections in these patients is poor because recovery usually depends on reestablishing adequate neutrophil counts.

The skin lesions of *Fusarium* infection cannot be differentiated from those associated with cutaneous infections caused by aspergillosis and the agents of mucormycosis or from many bacterial infections, such as *Pseudomonas* (**Figure 6**).

Biopsy should be done on cutaneous lesions for stain, culture, and histologic examination. Because the hyphae of *Fusarium* resemble those of *Aspergillus* in tissue samples, culture is the only way to confirm the diagnosis.

Pseudallescheria boydii and *Scedosporium apiospermum* Infections

Pseudallescheria boydii is the sexual state and *Scedosporium apiospermum* is the asexual state of a fungus that causes

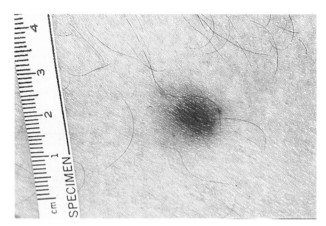

FIGURE 6.
Skin findings in a patient with *Fusarium* infection.

infection with increasing frequency in debilitated patients. This fungal pathogen is not found as often as is *Aspergillus*, although its clinical presentation and patient populations are similar to those of *Aspergillus*. *Pseudallescheria/Scedosporium* is indistinguishable from *Aspergillus* on histologic specimen sections in which it exhibits acute angle branching with slender mycelia. Clinically, *Pseudallescheria/Scedosporium* infections must be differentiated from *Aspergillus* infections, particularly because the former are uniformly resistant to the polyenes. These pathogens are reliably sensitive to voriconazole and posaconazole, which are the empiric therapies of choice in patients in whom these infections are suspected.

KEY POINT

- Voriconazole and posaconazole are the empiric therapies of choice in patients in whom *Pseudallescheria/Scedosporium* infections are suspected.

Antifungal Drug Resistance

Resistance to each of the main classes of antifungals is increasing. With the advent of standardized methods for testing fungal sensitivities, good information regarding susceptibility of specific fungi to multiple antifungal agents is becoming available. Fungal mechanisms of resistance appear remarkably similar to those of bacterial mechanisms of resistance (for example, efflux pumps, mutation of the target site, up-regulation of the target, and alternative pathway development). Currently, azole resistance appears to be more common than polyene and echinocandin resistance. Early studies suggest that in vitro resistance studies are good predictors of clinical effectiveness because cure is less often achieved when the fungus shows in vitro resistance to the antifungal in use.

Amphotericin B was formerly the mainstay of treatment for most serious deep fungal infections, but the introduction of more potent triazole antifungals and the use of the echinocandins have changed the prevention and management approach to these diseases. Although amphotericin B remains effective against most fungi, its side effect profile is often significantly worse than that of the other drugs; therefore, it is prescribed less often than previously.

Guidelines for treatment of several fungal diseases can be found on the Web site of the Infectious Diseases Society of America (www.idsociety.org) (click on "Practice Guidelines").

KEY POINT

- Currently, azole resistance appears to be more common than polyene and echinocandin resistance in patients with fungal infections.

Bibliography

Cortez KJ, Roilides E, Quiroz-Telles F, et al. Infections caused by Scedosporium spp. Clin Microbiol Rev. 2008;21(1):157-197. [PMID: 18202441]

Durkin MM, Connolly PA, Wheat LJ. Comparison of radioimmunoassay and enzyme-linked immunoassay methods for detection of Histoplasma capsulatum var. capsulatum antigen. J Clin Microbiol. 1997;35(9):2252-2255. [PMID: 9276396]

Nucci M, Anaissie E. Fusarium infections in immunocompromised patients. Clin Microbiol Rev. 2007;20(4):695-704. [PMID: 17934079]

Pukkila-Worley R, Mylonakis E. Epidemiology and management of cryptococcal meningitis: developments and challenges. Expert Opin Pharmacother. 2008;9(4):551-560. [PMID: 18312157]

Rickerts V, Mousset S, Lambrecht E, et al. Comparison of histopathological analysis, culture, and polymerase chain reaction assays to detect invasive mold infections from biopsy specimens. Clin Infect Dis. 2007;44(8):1078-1083. [PMID: 17366453]

Spinello IM, Munoz A, Johnson RH. Pulmonary coccidioidomycosis. Semin Respir Crit Care Med. 2008;29(2):166-173. [PMID: 18365998]

Upton A, Kirby KA, Carpenter P, Boeckh M, Marr KA. Invasive aspergillosis following hematopoietic cell transplantation: outcomes and prognostic factors associated with mortality. Clin Infect Dis. 2007;44(4):531-540. [PMID: 17243056]

Walsh TJ, Anaissie EJ, Denning DW, et al; Infectious Diseases Society of America. Treatment of aspergillosis: clinical practice guidelines of the Infectious Diseases Society of America. Clin Infect Dis. 2008;46(3):327-360. [PMID: 18177225]

Sexually Transmitted Infections

Introduction

Sexually transmitted diseases (STDs) can cause inflammatory discharge, genital ulcers, and anogenital warts. Discussion of these infections and their associated syndromes are discussed below and in **Table 23**.

STDs Characterized by Inflammatory Discharge

Chlamydia

Chlamydial infection (caused by *Chlamydia trachomatis*) is the most commonly diagnosed sexually transmitted bacterial

TABLE 23 Summary of Common Sexually Transmitted Disease–related Syndromes

Genital ulcer disease

  Syphilis (*Treponema pallidum*)

  Genital herpes (herpes simplex virus)

  Chancroid (*Haemophilus ducreyi*)

  Granuloma inguinale (donovanosis [*Klebsiella granulomatis*])

  Lymphogranuloma venereum (*Chlamydia trachomatis*)

Urethritis/cervicitis

  Gonorrhea (*Neisseria gonorrhoeae*)

  Chlamydia trachomatis

Vaginal discharge

  Trichomonas vaginalis

  Bacterial vaginosis

  Vulvovaginal candidiasis

Pelvic inflammatory disease/epididymitis

Genital warts

  Human papillomavirus

Ectoparasites

  Pediculosis pubis

  Scabies

infection in the United States, with prevalence highest in sexually active teenagers and young adults (age ≤25 years). Because patients with *Chlamydia* are frequently asymptomatic and untreated infections can cause severe sequelae in women (pelvic inflammatory disease, infertility, ectopic pregnancy, and chronic pelvic pain), annual screening is recommended for sexually active women 25 years of age or younger. Men with chlamydial disease may have urethral discharge or may be asymptomatic, but their long-term health consequences are minimal compared with those in women, and screening and treatment in heterosexual men primarily benefit their female sexual partners. Chlamydial infection can also cause proctitis in men and women who are the receptive partners in anal intercourse. Conjunctivitis can also occur, either due to self-inoculation from a genitourinary focus or from untreated maternal infection in newborn infants.

Antibiotic therapy for sexual partners of patients with chlamydial infection is recommended. Recommended chlamydial infection therapy is presented in **Table 24**.

Gonorrhea

The clinical syndromes of *C. trachomatis* and *Neisseria gonorrhoeae* both cause cervicitis, urethritis, and proctitis, but gonorrheal infection is characterized by a more exudative polymorphonuclear immune response and, consequently, a more visibly purulent discharge than is chlamydial infection; however, diagnosis cannot reliably be based on clinical findings. The diagnosis of gonorrhea is suggested by clinical evidence of inflammation in a susceptible anatomic site (urethra, cervix) in a sexually active patient. The results of nonspecific laboratory testing that may be readily available in some office settings, such as reactive leukocyte esterase on urine dipstick testing, may also support a presumptive diagnosis. The results of more specific laboratory testing, such as the presence of gram-negative intracellular diplococci on Gram stain of purulent secretions or the identification of *Neisseria gonorrhoeae* in culture or nucleic acid amplification testing, will confirm the diagnosis.

Untreated infection of mucosal sites can result in bacteremia and disseminated gonococcal infection characterized by fever, papular and pustular skin lesions on the distal extremities, tenosynovitis, and less commonly, septic arthritis (**Figure 7**). Perihepatitis (Fitz-Hugh–Curtis syndrome) and peritonitis may also occur with intraperitoneal extension of untreated pelvic infection in women.

Antibiotic therapy for sexual partners is recommended in patients with gonorrheal infection. Because of the high rate of concurrent chlamydial infection in patients with gonorrhea, co-treatment for both infections should be given in patients with gonorrhea unless *Chlamydia* has been definitively ruled out. Fluoroquinolones, such as ciprofloxacin, are no longer recommended in treating gonorrhea owing to high rates of resistance in recent years.

Complications of Chlamydial and Gonorrheal Infections

Pelvic inflammatory disease

Pelvic inflammatory disease (PID) is a serious complication of untreated gonorrhea or chlamydial infection in women and develops when infection ascends to sites above the cervix. PID includes a spectrum of disorders of the female upper genital tract, including endometritis, salpingitis, tubo-ovarian abscess, and pelvic peritonitis. Diagnosis is established clinically, and presumptive therapy is recommended in sexually active women with suggestive findings, including cervical motion tenderness, uterine tenderness, or adnexal tenderness on pelvic examination. The disorder is usually polymicrobial in etiology, and treatment targeting gonorrhea and *Chlamydia*, as well as gram-negative bacilli, anaerobes, and gram-positive bacteria, is recommended (see Table 24).

Epididymitis

Infection of the epididymal glands may occur in men with untreated gonorrheal infection–related or chlamydial infection–related urethritis. Presumptive treatment for these pathogens is recommended in sexually active men 35 years of age or younger with epididymal tenderness and swelling on scrotal examination.

TABLE 24 Summary of Recommended Treatment for Common Sexually Transmitted Infections

Disease	Recommended Treatment	Alternatives
Syphilis		
Primary, secondary, or early latent (<1 year)	Benzathine penicillin G, 2.4 MU IM, in a single dose	Doxycycline, 100 mg orally BID for 14 days; ceftriaxone, 1 g/d IV or 1 g/d IM for 8-10 days
Late latent (>1 year) or latent of unknown duration	Benzathine penicillin G, 2.4 MU, 1 weekly dose IM for 3 doses, 1 week apart (total, 7.2 MU)	Doxycycline, 100 mg orally BID for 28 days
Neurosyphilis	Aqueous crystalline penicillin G, 18 to 24 MU/d, administered as 3 to 4 MU IV every 4 hours; or continuous infusion for 10-14 days	Procaine penicillin, 2.4 MU IM once daily, plus probenecid 500 mg orally QID, both for 10 to 14 days
HIV infection	For primary, secondary, and early latent syphilis, treat as above. Some specialists recommend three doses. For late latent syphilis or latent syphilis of unknown duration, perform CSF examination before treatment	Alternatives to standard penicillin in HIV-infected persons have not been well studied
Pregnancy	Penicillin is the only recommended treatment for syphilis during pregnancy. Women who report allergies should be desensitized, then treated with penicillin	
Gonococcal Infections[a]		
Cervix, urethra, rectum	Ceftriaxone, 125 mg IM in a single dose; or cefixime, 400 mg orally in a single dose	Spectinomycin, 2 g IM in a single dose; fluoroquinolones are no longer recommended for GC treatment.
Chlamydial Infections		
Adult/adolescents	Azithromycin, 1 g orally in a single dose; or doxycycline, 100 mg orally BID for 7 days	Erythromycin base, 500 mg orally QID for 7 days; or erythromycin ethylsuccinate, 800 mg orally QID for 7 days; or ofloxacin, 300 mg orally BID for 7 days; or levofloxacin, 500 mg orally once daily for 7 days
Pregnancy	Azithromycin, 1 g orally in a single dose; or amoxicillin, 500 mg orally TID for 7 days	Erythromycin base, 500 mg orally QID for 7 days; or erythromycin, 250 mg orally QID for 14 days; or erythromycin ethylsuccinate, 800 mg orally QID for 7 days; or erythromycin ethylsuccinate, 400 mg orally QID for 14 days
Nongonococcal urethritis	Azithromycin, 1 g orally in a single dose; or doxycycline, 100 mg orally BID for 7 days	Erythromycin base, 500 mg orally QID for 7 days; or erythromycin ethylsuccinate, 800 mg orally QID for 7 days; or ofloxacin, 300 mg orally BID for 7 days; or levofloxacin, 500 mg orally once daily for 7 days
Pelvic inflammatory disease (outpatient management)[b]	Ceftriaxone, 250 mg IM in a single dose; or ceftriaxone, 2 g IM once plus probenecid, 1 g orally once; or another third-generation cephalosporin plus doxycycline, 100 mg orally BID for 14 days	If gonorrhea ruled out in process: levofloxacin, 500 mg orally once daily for 14 days; or ofloxacin, 400 mg BID for 14 days
Herpes Simplex Virus		
First clinical episode of genital herpes	Acyclovir, 400 mg orally TID for 7-10 days; or acyclovir, 200 mg orally 5 times daily for 7-10 days; or famciclovir, 250 mg orally TID for 7-10 days; or valacyclovir, 1 g orally BID for 7-10 days	

BID = twice daily; CSF = cerebrospinal fluid; GC = gonococcal infection; IM = intramuscularly; MU = million units; QID = four times daily; TID = three times daily.

[a]Treat also for chlamydial infection if not ruled out by a sensitive test (nucleic acid amplification test).

[b]These regimens may be administered with or without metronidazole, 500 mg orally BID for 14 days.

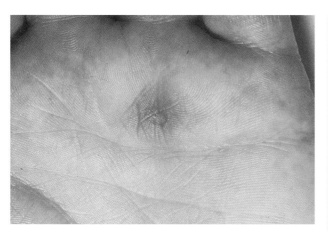

FIGURE 7.
Pustular skin lesion characteristic of disseminated gonococcal infection.

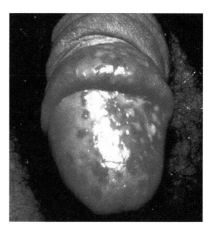

FIGURE 8.
Painful grouped erosions, with or without vesicles, are characteristic of genital herpes.

KEY POINTS

- Because patients with *Chlamydia* are frequently asymptomatic and untreated infections can cause severe sequelae in women (pelvic inflammatory disease, infertility, ectopic pregnancy, and chronic pelvic pain), annual screening is recommended for sexually active women 25 years of age or younger.

- The clinical syndromes of *Chlamydia trachomatis* and *Neisseria gonorrhoeae* both cause cervicitis, urethritis, and proctitis, but gonorrheal infection is characterized by a more exudative polymorphonuclear immune response and, consequently, a more visibly purulent discharge than is chlamydial infection; however, diagnosis cannot be reliably based on clinical findings.

- Pelvic inflammatory disease is a serious complication of untreated gonorrhea or chlamydial infection in women, develops when infection ascends to sites above the cervix, and includes endometritis, salpingitis, tubo-ovarian abscess, and pelvic peritonitis.

- Infection of the epididymal glands may occur in men with untreated gonorrheal infection–related or chlamydial infection–related urethritis.

Genital Ulcer Infection

Herpes

The most common cause of genital ulcers is herpes simplex virus. More than 21% of adults in the United States are chronically infected with herpes simplex virus type 2 (HSV-2), the most common cause of genital herpes, and most are unaware of their infection.

Grouped vesicles on an erythematous base constitute the classic clinical presentation (**Figure 8**). These lesions begin to ulcerate when the vesicles rupture. Burning, tingling, and erythema are less typical manifestations of genital herpes and can appear without vesicular or ulcerative lesions. As many as 15% of primary herpes episodes may be caused by HSV-1, which is clinically indistinguishable from HSV-2–related episodes. Diagnosis of genital herpes is often made clinically, but confirmation requires viral culture or polymerase chain reaction (PCR) assay of genital lesions; type-specific serologic testing can identify HSV-2 infection but cannot determine the cause of an ulcerative genital lesion (see Viral Infections). The Tzanck test (showing multinucleated giant cells) is not recommended owing to lack of sensitivity. Herpes simplex treatment is discussed in **Table 24**.

Syphilis

Syphilis is characterized by progressive stages of disease, including primary-stage, secondary-stage, latent, and tertiary or late syphilis. The primary stage of syphilis is caused by *Treponema pallidum* and is characterized by genital ulceration. The lesion classically appears 2 to 3 weeks after exposure and is frequently firm, indurated, and painless, with a clean, smooth base. Treponemal infection is usually widely disseminated when ulceration appears. The lesion may resolve without specific antibiotic therapy owing to an effective host immune response.

Signs and symptoms of secondary-stage syphilis typically appear weeks to months after the onset of primary-stage disease, although signs of secondary-stage disease may coincide with genital ulceration. The most characteristic features are a maculopapular rash involving the palms of the hands and soles of the feet (**Figure 9**), which develops in approximately 60% of all patients; generalized lymphadenopathy, fever, malaise, and fatigue may also occur.

Signs and symptoms of inflammation in other organs can also develop during secondary-stage syphilis, including hepatitis, glomerulonephritis, and aseptic meningitis.

Diagnosis of primary- and secondary-stage mucocutaneous lesions can be established by darkfield microscopy

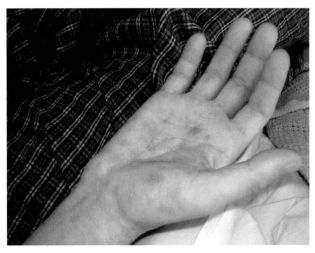

FIGURE 9.
Characteristic maculopapular lesions of secondary syphilis on the palm.

visualization of motile *T. pallidum* in exudative fluid from the lesions. A presumptive diagnosis can be based on reactive syphilis serology in a patient with suggestive clinical findings. The risk for infectious transmission to sexual partners is highest during the primary and secondary stages of syphilis. Providing prophylactic treatment to persons exposed to syphilis infection at these early stages helps to prevent disease dissemination throughout the community.

Infection confirmed by reactive syphilis serology in the absence of clinical findings constitutes latent syphilis. Early latent syphilis is defined as infection of less than 1 year's duration, and patients may relapse, with development of mucocutaneous lesions characteristic of earlier stages. Late latent syphilis is defined as infection of longer than 1 year's duration. It is frequently impossible to document that the infection was acquired within the past year because the results of previous serologic tests are unavailable, and most patients are therefore categorized as having "syphilis of unknown duration." Tertiary or late syphilis occurs years to decades after initial infection.

Clinical features vary depending on the level of organ involvement. Any visceral organ in patients with tertiary syphilis can be eroded by gummas (inflammatory tumors). Other classic clinical syndromes of tertiary syphilis include brain and spinal cord nerve destruction (also known as general paresis and tabes dorsalis) and cardiovascular syphilis. Because central nervous system invasion may also occur early in infection, concurrent neurosyphilis can develop during any stage of syphilis.

The preferred therapy for syphilis at all stages is parenteral penicillin, and this agent is the only acceptable therapy for pregnant patients. Treatment for syphilis by stage is summarized in **Table 24**. All patients diagnosed with syphilis should be offered serologic testing for HIV.

Chancroid

Chancroid, caused by the organism *Haemophilus ducreyi*, is characterized by painful genital ulceration, typically with irregular borders. Although chancroid is found primarily in underdeveloped countries and is not widespread in the United States, it is believed to be substantially underdiagnosed and underreported. Chancroid epidemics occur only sporadically in the United States, usually in association with prostitution and drug use. This organism is difficult to isolate; therefore, a diagnosis is difficult to establish in the laboratory. Most cases of chancroid are identified based on the characteristic genital ulcerative lesion that persists despite treatment for other genital ulcerative disease causes and after laboratory testing has eliminated other etiologies of genital ulceration such as syphilis and herpes.

Lymphogranuloma Venereum

Lymphogranuloma venereum (LGV) is a systemic STD that occurs rarely in the United States. However, since 2003, the Netherlands and other European countries have reported increases in LGV proctitis among men who have sex with men, and LGV cases in this group have also been identified in the United States and Canada. LGV is caused by *C. trachomatis*, but by a distinctly different set of serovars than those that cause other sexually transmitted genitourinary chlamydial infections. When LGV is characterized by a genital ulcer, it is classically associated with lymphadenitis. Factors associated with LGV-related proctocolitis include concurrent HIV infection, visible ulcerations on anoscopy, and purulent discharge from the ulcer's base.

KEY POINTS

- Grouped vesicles on an erythematous base constitute the classic clinical presentation of genital herpes; these lesions begin to ulcerate when the vesicles rupture.
- The lesion in syphilis classically appears 2 to 3 weeks after exposure and is frequently firm, indurated, and painless, with a clean, smooth base.
- The most characteristic features of secondary syphilis are a maculopapular rash involving the palms of the hands and soles of the feet, generalized lymphadenopathy, and, possibly, fever, malaise, and fatigue.
- The preferred therapy for syphilis at all stages is parenteral penicillin, and this agent is the only acceptable therapy for pregnant patients.

Ectoparasites and External Genital Warts

Pubic lice (*Phthirus pubis*) are transmitted by intimate contact, including between sexual partners. Infestation is usually characterized by itching, although patients may also be asymptomatic (see MKSAP 15 Dermatology).

Anogenital warts are caused by multiple subtypes of human papillomavirus (HPV). Certain subtypes of HPV are strongly associated with development of cervical cancer, although these subtypes tend to differ from those that cause anogenital warts. Most sexually active people are exposed to human papillomavirus. A vaccine highly protective against the development of high-grade cervical lesions is available in the United States and is recommended for use in all young women, ages 9 through 26 years (see MKSAP 15 General Internal Medicine). There are various provider- and patient-applied genital wart therapies, most of which destroy the HPV-infected skin.

KEY POINTS

- Pubic lice are transmitted by intimate contact, including between sexual partners.
- Certain subtypes of human papillomavirus are strongly associated with development of cervical cancer, although these subtypes tend to differ from those that cause anogenital warts.

Bibliography

Centers for Disease Control and Prevention, Workowski KA, Berman SM. Sexually transmitted diseases treatment guidelines, 2006 [erratum in MMWR Recomm Rep. 2006;55(36):997]. MMWR Recomm Rep. 2006;55(RR-11):1-94. [PMID: 16888612]

Fife KH, Warren TJ, Ferrera RD, et al. Effect of valacyclovir on viral shedding in immunocompetent patients with recurrent herpes simplex virus 2 genital herpes: a US-based randomized, double-blind, placebo-controlled clinical trial. Mayo Clin Proc. 2006;81(10):1321-1327. [PMID: 17036557]

U.S. Preventive Services Task Force. Screening for chlamydial infection: U.S. Preventive Services Task Force recommendation statement. Ann Intern Med. 2007;147(2):128-134. [PMID: 17576996]

Van der Bij AK, Spaargaren J, Morré SA, et al. Diagnostic and clinical implications of anorectal lymphogranuloma venereum in men who have sex with men: a retrospective case-control study. Clin Infect Dis. 2006;42(2):186-194. [PMID: 16355328]

Wang SA, Harvey AB, Conner SM, et al. Antimicrobial resistance for Neisseria gonorrhoeae in the United States, 1988 to 2003: the spread of fluoroquinolone resistance. Ann Intern Med. 2007;147(2):81-88. [PMID: 17638718]

Xu F, Sternberg MR, Kottiri BJ, et al. Trends in herpes simplex virus type 1 and type 2 seroprevalence in the United States. JAMA. 2006;296(8):964-973. [PMID: 16926356]

Osteomyelitis

Introduction

Osteomyelitis is characterized by an intense suppurative inflammatory reaction in bone associated with edema and thrombosis. This condition compromises the vascular supply to the bone, and, with time, can lead to areas of dead bone known as *sequestra*. Infection can erode through the bone into the adjacent soft tissues and skin and may manifest externally as a sinus tract. As the bone reforms, new bone forms around the sequestra (termed *involucrum*).

Osteomyelitis can be characterized by the duration of illness (acute or chronic), mechanism of infection (hematogenous, extension from a contiguous focus, direct contamination), affected bone, the host's physiologic status, and the presence of orthopedic hardware. The clinical presentation and treatment vary depending on the type of osteomyelitis.

In adults, hematogenous spread is responsible for less than 20% of all cases, occurring in patients at risk for bloodstream infections, including those on hemodialysis with tunneled intravascular catheters and those with long-term intravascular catheters or in patients with high-grade bacteremia, endocarditis, or sickle cell disease. In adults, the intervertebral disk space and two adjacent vertebrae are the most common sites of hematogenous osteomyelitis. Only one microorganism is usually isolated in patients with hematogenous osteomyelitis; 40% to 60% of cases are caused by *Staphylococcus aureus*.

In adults, contiguously disseminated infection from surrounding tissues occurs more commonly than hematogenously spread infection and is usually caused by soft tissue infection such as that in patients with diabetic foot ulcers. Patients with osteomyelitis from contiguous spread usually have a polymicrobial infection. Contiguously spread osteomyelitis may be due to direct bone contamination from a puncture wound, open fracture, or prosthetic material or hardware in the bone that may have been used to stabilize a fracture or in joint replacement.

KEY POINTS

- Patients at increased risk for hematogenously spread osteomyelitis include those on hemodialysis with tunneled intravascular catheters and with long-term intravascular catheters or those with high-grade bacteremia, endocarditis, or sickle cell disease.
- In adults, the intervertebral disk space and two adjacent vertebrae are the most common sites of hematogenous osteomyelitis.
- Patients with osteomyelitis from contiguous spread usually have a polymicrobial infection.

Diagnosis

The clinical hallmarks of acute osteomyelitis are local pain and fever, particularly in patients with acute hematogenous osteomyelitis, but these may be absent in chronic and contiguous osteomyelitis. The presence of a sinus tract overlying a bone structure and palpation of bone by a sterile, blunt, stainless steel probe in the depth of a foot ulcer are almost always associated with osteomyelitis. Patients who have undergone total joint arthroplasty and have had joint pain since surgery are more likely to have a prosthetic joint infection compared with pain-free patients. Prosthetic loosening in the first 2 years after arthroplasty raises the index of suspicion for a prosthetic joint infection.

Given the limitations of physical examination in the diagnosis of osteomyelitis, radiologic studies are frequently used. However, radiographs may be negative early in the course of illness because it can take 2 weeks or more for evidence of acute infection to manifest, and radiography lacks both sensitivity (60%) and specificity (60%) in the diagnosis of osteomyelitis. In patients in whom radiographic results are negative but clinical suspicion for osteomyelitis remains high, MRI is indicated. MRI scans show changes of acute osteomyelitis within days of infection and are superior to and more sensitive (90%) and specific (80%) than plain films and CT scans; can detect soft tissue abscesses and epidural, paravertebral, or psoas abscesses possibly requiring surgical drainage; and can delineate anatomy before surgery. Nonetheless, false-positive MRI results may occur in patients with noninfectious conditions such as fractures, tumors, and healed osteomyelitis. In patients with a pacemaker or metal hardware precluding MRI or in those in whom MRI results are inconclusive, nuclear studies may be used alternatively to MRI.

KEY POINT

- The presence of a sinus tract overlying a bone structure and palpation of bone by a sterile, blunt, stainless steel probe in the depth of a foot ulcer are almost always associated with osteomyelitis.

Evaluation and Management of Diabetes Mellitus–Associated Osteomyelitis

Superficial diabetic foot infections can cause cellulitis, and contiguously disseminated foot infection can affect deep soft tissues, causing abscesses or even necrotizing fasciitis; bone infection can also occur (see MKSAP 15 Endocrinology and Metabolism and MKSAP 15 Dermatology). The clinical appearance of a diabetic foot infection is often not helpful in predicting the presence of underlying osteomyelitis.

Physical examination findings suggestive of osteomyelitis include visible bone in an ulcer base or contact with bone on insertion of a metal probe at the ulcer base, the latter of which has a positive predictive value of approximately 90% and a negative predictive value of approximately 60% for diagnosing osteomyelitis. Ulcers larger than 2 × 2 cm, the presence of an ulcer for more than 2 weeks, and an erythrocyte sedimentation rate greater than 70 mm/h are also associated with the presence of underlying osteomyelitis and require diagnostic confirmation by deep tissue culture. Except for the finding in superficial cultures of *S. aureus*, cultures obtained from a sinus tract or from an ulcer base in patients with diabetic foot infections usually do not correlate with the deep

pathogens causing bone infection. In addition to isolating *S. aureus*, swabs of sinus tracts or deep ulcers may also be useful for identifying resistant organisms such as methicillin-resistant *S. aureus* (MRSA) or vancomycin-resistant enterococci (VRE), allowing for implementation of appropriate infection-control measures.

Bone biopsy is the gold standard diagnostic test and the only definitive way to confirm osteomyelitis. Bone biopsy not only provides histopathologic evidence but also may identify the infecting organism and susceptibilities for guiding antibiotic therapy.

Bone biopsy can be done percutaneously (typically CT-guided) or by open biopsy. Open biopsy facilitates procurement of a larger piece of bone than that obtained through percutaneous biopsy, thereby increasing the diagnostic yield and facilitating debridement of the bone and surrounding tissues if necessary. Bone biopsy may not be needed for patients with suspected osteomyelitis and a supportive imaging study in the setting of positive blood cultures. Open bone biopsy is not always feasible in patients with diabetes or vascular disease, who may have wound-healing problems. In such patients, CT-guided percutaneous bone biopsy is a reasonable alternative but can result in sampling errors.

In stable patients, it is important to attempt to establish a pathologic and microbiologic diagnosis rather than simply treat empirically to avoid complications associated with long antibiotic courses, such as catheter-associated bacteremia and deep venous thrombosis; drug reactions; and *Clostridium difficile* or fungal infections. In addition, empiric antibiotic regimens may not cover all of the pathogens involved in these often polymicrobial infections.

Deep cultures obtained at surgery often include aerobic gram-positive cocci such as *S. aureus* (including MRSA) and coagulase-negative staphylococci. Other organisms may also be found, including aerobic gram-negative rods such as *Pseudomonas* (also associated with puncture wounds through sneakers in nondiabetic patients), and anaerobes.

Choice of antibiotic therapy should be based on culture and susceptibility results. Multiple antibiotic regimens, including piperacillin/tazobactam, ampicillin/sulbactam, and ticarcillin/clavulanic acid, are used to treat osteomyelitis of the foot in diabetic patients, and these agents have good gram-negative and anaerobic activity. Alternatively, a third- or fourth-generation cephalosporin can be combined with metronidazole in these patients. Clindamycin and a fluoroquinolone such as ciprofloxacin or levofloxacin are appropriate in patients with penicillin allergy. Vancomycin, linezolid, or daptomycin may be added to any of these regimens in patients in whom concern or proof of MRSA exists or in ill patients for whom no cultures are available to guide therapy.

In patients who are not ill and in whom no evidence of extensive concurrent soft tissue infection or cellulitis exists, antibiotics should be withheld prior to obtaining a bone biopsy to increase the diagnostic yield. In ill patients or those with extensive cellulitis or soft tissue infection, empiric antibiotics with any of the above regimens are warranted.

Generally, antibiotics are given intravenously for 4 to 6 weeks through a peripherally inserted central-line catheter based on culture and susceptibility results. Oral antibiotics can be used but usually only after an initial induction with intravenous antibiotics in patients with susceptible organisms and in those in whom compliance with an oral regimen can be assured.

An open surgical procedure, as well as antibiotics, is often required in patients with osteomyelitis of the foot to débride devitalized tissue and remove necrotic bone. The goal of surgery is to remove as much of the infected tissue as possible while trying to maintain foot functionality. Shorter courses of antibiotics are appropriate for patients in whom all of the devitalized tissue and bone is removed. Alternatively, in patients in whom potentially infected bone has been left to allow for preservation of foot function, longer courses of antibiotics may be required.

KEY POINTS

- Physical examination findings suggestive of osteomyelitis include visible bone in an ulcer base or contact with bone on insertion of a metal probe at the ulcer base.

- Bone biopsy is the gold standard diagnostic test and the only definitive way to confirm osteomyelitis.

- Piperacillin/tazobactam, ampicillin/sulbactam, and ticarcillin/clavulanic acid are among the regimens used to treat osteomyelitis of the foot in diabetic patients; alternatively, a third- or fourth-generation cephalosporin can be combined with metronidazole in these patients.

Evaluation and Management of Vertebral Osteomyelitis

Vertebral osteomyelitis is most often disseminated hematogenously. Segmental arteries supply blood to the vertebrae, with bifurcating arteries supplying blood to the inferior margin of one end plate and the superior margin of the adjacent end plate. Consequently, when infection occurs, it generally follows this vascular pattern involving bone in two adjacent vertebral bodies with invasion into their intervertebral disk. This pattern of vertebral involvement can help distinguish osteomyelitis from a compression fracture or tumor, which can be difficult to differentiate based on radiographic findings alone. Potential sources of hematogenous osteomyelitis include skin (injection drug users), urinary tract, or respiratory tract infection; endocarditis; or intravascular catheter–related infection.

The most common organism found in vertebral osteomyelitis is *S. aureus* (including MRSA); coagulase-negative staphylococci are also common. Other organisms, including gram-negative rods and *Candida* species, occur less frequently.

Most patients with vertebral osteomyelitis have back or neck pain that gradually worsens over weeks or months, with fever present in only 50%. Tenderness to palpation over the involved portion of the spine is also common. Because these findings are nonspecific, a high degree of suspicion is needed to establish a diagnosis.

Laboratory values typically include a normal leukocyte count, a markedly increased erythrocyte sedimentation rate (often greater that 100 mm/h), and an elevated serum C-reactive protein level. Because blood cultures are positive in up to 75% of patients with vertebral osteomyelitis, they should be obtained in all patients in whom this condition is suspected. Diagnostic bone biopsy may not be needed in patients with a compatible clinical scenario and in whom an organism such as *S. aureus* is identified. Endocarditis should be ruled out with echocardiography in patients with positive blood cultures and no other sources of infection.

Patients with imaging studies suggestive of vertebral osteomyelitis but blood cultures revealing no pathogen should undergo a CT-guided percutaneous needle biopsy. Patients in whom results of the first needle biopsy are nondiagnostic may require a repeat biopsy. Empiric antibiotic treatment may be given if an etiologic agent is not identified to guide specific therapy. Any empiric regimen in patients with suspected vertebral osteomyelitis requires coverage for *S. aureus*, including MRSA coagulase–negative staphylococci, and enteric gram-negative rods. Vancomycin plus an antipseudomonal third- (ceftazidime) or fourth-generation cephalosporin (cefepime) or an extended-spectrum β-lactam antibiotic are appropriate choices. If no clinical improvement occurs within several weeks after an empiric regimen is instituted, repeat percutaneous or open biopsy is indicated.

Most patients with vertebral osteomyelitis respond to antibiotic therapy. Surgery is rarely needed for uncomplicated vertebral osteomyelitis but is frequently necessary for epidural or paravertebral abscesses or spinal instability. Antibiotics are chosen based on the isolated pathogen and susceptibilities and are usually given intravenously for 6 to 8 weeks, but longer courses may be necessary depending on disease course and response.

KEY POINTS

- Blood cultures should be obtained in all patients in whom vertebral osteomyelitis is suspected.

- Patients who have imaging studies suggestive of vertebral osteomyelitis but blood cultures revealing no pathogen should undergo a CT-guided percutaneous needle biopsy.

- Patients with vertebral osteomyelitis are usually given antibiotics intravenously for 6 to 8 weeks but may require longer therapy depending on disease course and response to therapy.

Bibliography

Dagirmanjian A, Schils J, McHenry M, Modic MT. MR imaging of vertebral osteomyelitis revisited. AJR Am J Roentgenol. 1996;167(6): 1539-1543. [PMID: 8956593]

Kapoor A, Page S, Lavalleu M, Gale DR, Felson DT. Magnetic resonance imaging for diagnosing foot osteomyelitis: a meta-analysis. Arch Intern Med. 2007; 167(2):125-132 [PMID: 17242312]

Kowalski TJ, Berbari EF, Huddleston PM, Steckelberg JM, Osmon DR. Do follow-up imaging examinations provide useful prognostic information in patients with spine infection? Clin Infect Dis. 2006;43(2):172-179. [PMID: 16779743]

Lew DP, Waldvogel FA. Osteomyelitis. Lancet. 2004;364(9431):369-379. [PMID: 15276398]

Lipsky BA, Berendt AR, Deery HG, et al; Infectious Diseases Society of America.. Diagnosis and treatment of diabetic foot infections. Clin Infect Dis 2004;39(7):885-910. [PMID: 15472838]

Senneville E, Mellie H, Beltrand E, et al. Culture of percutaneous bone biopsy specimens for diagnosis of diabetic foot osteomyelitis: concordance with ulcer swab cultures. Clin Infect Dis. 2006;42(1):57-62. [PMID: 16323092]

Fever of Unknown Origin

Introduction

Fever commonly accompanies many infectious and noninfectious illnesses. Most febrile illnesses resolve before a diagnosis is made or before the illness develops other distinguishing features. Fever may also be a manifestation of a serious illness that can be readily diagnosed and treated. In a subgroup of patients, the source of the fever cannot be found. Patients who have a high fever (greater than 38.3 °C [101.0 °F]) persisting for more than 3 weeks with no diagnosis despite a complete history, physical examination, and negative routine laboratory and diagnostic studies have fever of unknown origin (FUO).

Causes of Fever of Unknown Origin

FUO usually falls into one of three major categories: infectious illness, rheumatic disease, or malignancy. In recent years, infection and malignancy have been less commonly associated with FUO, whereas rheumatic illnesses and undiagnosed causes are more commonly implicated. The specific causes and diagnostic workup differ based on patient population. In the normal host, common infectious causes include tuberculosis or intraabdominal or pelvic abscess. Osteomyelitis, and, in particular, vertebral osteomyelitis, occasionally is characterized by FUO without localizing back pain or symptoms. Endocarditis, a once common cause of FUO, is less often found to be implicated because of the availability of better blood culture techniques and the widespread use of antibiotics. When endocarditis causes FUO, it is usually associated with culture-negative organisms, such as *Coxiella burnetii* (Q fever), *Bartonella quintana*, or the HACEK organisms (*Haemophilus aphrophilus*, *Actinobacillus actinomycetemcomitans*, *Cardiobacterium hominis*, *Eikenella corrodens*, and *Kingella kingae*).

One of the more common vasculitides is temporal arteritis, which can present as FUO in adults older than 50 years, even in the absence of the classic symptoms of headache, jaw claudication, or polymyalgia rheumatica. Other vasculitides, such as Wegener granulomatosis and diseases such as systemic lupus erythematosus and adult-onset Still disease, should also be considered.

The most common FUO-associated malignancy is non-Hodgkin lymphoma. Renal cell carcinoma, any malignancy that metastasizes to the liver, and leukemia are other common causes.

A fourth category of miscellaneous causes includes drug fever, factitious fever, subacute thyroiditis, a large hematoma, pheochromocytoma, familial Mediterranean fever, deep venous thrombosis, and thromboembolic diseases.

KEY POINT

- In recent years, infection and malignancy are less commonly associated with fever of unknown origin, whereas the association with rheumatic illnesses and undiagnosed causes has increased.

Evaluation

A thorough history and physical examination are the most important components of the evaluation of a patient with FUO. Because affected patients may have an evolving illness with new and changing signs and symptoms, repeated examinations are essential. Travel history, animal exposures, sick contacts, environmental toxin exposures, recent antibiotic use, new medications, and risks for immune suppression are all important historical clues.

Febrile illnesses are often associated with rash. Some are nondescript, such as the exanthems of enteroviral infections, whereas others have more distinctive patterns, such as the erythema migrans rash of Lyme disease (see Tick-borne Disease).

The rash's distribution (extremity vs. trunk), presence on the palms and the soles, chronicity relative to fever, and characteristics (vesicular vs. petechial) are also important in determining a potential cause. Some fever-associated skin lesions suggest serious underlying illnesses, such as Janeway lesions, Osler nodes, or subconjunctival petechiae occurring in infective endocarditis.

Initial laboratory data and radiographic evaluation in patients with FUO include a complete blood count, complete metabolic profile with liver chemistry studies, urinalysis, and blood cultures. Lactate dehydrogenase measurement, serum protein electrophoresis, HIV serology, tuberculin skin testing, Epstein-Barr virus serologies, heterophile antibody testing, cytomegalovirus serologies, rapid plasma reagin measurement, rheumatoid factor measurement, antinuclear antibody measurement, erythrocyte sedimentation rate, C-reactive protein measurement, and, possibly, CT imaging of the chest, abdomen, and pelvis, might also be considered in the appropriate setting. Abnormalities detected on these studies or new findings in the history or on repeat physical examinations should guide further evaluation.

Despite an extensive workup, one third to one half of patients may not receive a specific diagnosis. These patients generally have a good prognosis, with resolution of fever in several months. Despite the temptation to provide treatment, perhaps because of urging from patients or family, clinicians should not prescribe empiric courses of antibiotics and corticosteroids to these patients.

KEY POINTS

- Because patients with fever of unknown origin may have evolving illness with new and changing signs and symptoms, repeated examinations are essential.

- Some fever-associated skin lesions, such as Janeway lesions, Osler nodes, or subconjunctival petechiae, suggest serious underlying illnesses.

- Patients with fever of unknown origin in whom no specific diagnosis is found despite an extensive workup generally have a good prognosis, with resolution of the fever in several months.

Bibliography

McKinnon HD, Howard T. Evaluating the febrile patient with a rash [erratum in Am Fam Physician. 2001;64(2):220]. Am Family Phys. 2000;62:804-816. [PMID: 10969859]

Mourad O, Palda V, Detsky AS. A comprehensive evidence-based approach to fever of unknown origin. Arch Intern Med. 2003;163(5):545-551. [PMID: 12622601]

Zenone T. Fever of unknown origin in adults: evaluation of 144 cases in a non-university hospital. Scand J Infect Dis. 2006;38(8):632-638. [PMID: 16857607]

Repeated Infections

Introduction

Even though they are not common, primary or acquired immunodeficiency syndromes should be considered in the differential diagnosis of patients with multiple or recurrent infections. Primary deficiencies are most commonly found in children but are increasingly being recognized in adults. Acquired immunodeficiencies are recognized more often than primary deficiencies because they are more common and typically present with characteristic findings suggestive of the correct diagnosis.

Congenital IgA Deficiency

The most common primary immunodeficiency is congenital IgA deficiency. Studies of blood from blood banks suggest an incidence of 1 in 300 to 1 in 500 in North America. Most patients with this disorder are asymptomatic; therefore, the deficiency often goes undetected or is discovered serendipitously. Patients with an IgA deficiency accompanied by low levels of one or more IgG subtypes may experience multiple sinopulmonary bacterial infections. Patients with IgA deficiency are also prone to gastrointestinal infections (particularly *Giardia lamblia*) and have an increased risk for autoimmune disorders including rheumatoid arthritis and systemic lupus erythematosus.

KEY POINT

- Patients with an IgA deficiency accompanied by low levels of one or more IgG subtypes may experience multiple sinopulmonary bacterial infections; gastrointestinal infections and autoimmune disorders may also occur.

Common Variable Immunodeficiency

Common variable immunodeficiency (CVI) is comprised of a group of acquired disorders most often characterized by low levels of one or more immunoglobulin classes or subclasses.

The male-to-female ratio is 1 to 1.3, with a marked predominance in whites of European descent. Various forms of cellular immune defects may also occur with or without the immunoglobulin defects. Although, by definition, these are not congenital disorders, some have been shown to have a genetic component as demonstrated by the significant prevalence of similar disorders in relatives and the several specific genetic mutations delineated in the families of some patients with CVI. Diagnosis of CVI is often delayed by years because of its variability in presentation.

CVI is characterized by repeated sinopulmonary infections occurring over several years, with repeated episodes of bronchitis and sinusitis occurring in 67% or more of these patients. Bronchiectasis is found in 33% or more of this population, often presenting or progressing during treatment of the CVI with intravenous immune globulin. More than 50% of patients with CVI have had at least one episode of bacterial or nonbacterial pneumonia. Gastrointestinal infections characterized by the same array of pathogens as encountered in the general population occur in 25% or more of patients with CVI, but *Giardia lamblia* is the single most commonly encountered enteric pathogen in some reports. Bacterial and nonbacterial meningitis develops more frequently in patients with CVI than in persons without CVI. Patients with markedly low levels of immunoglobulins may have severe and sustained central nervous system enteroviral infections that may lead to permanent neurologic impairment or death.

A few patients with CVI and no evidence of HIV infection develop opportunistic infections with *Pneumocystis* species or other fungi and are found to have T-cell defects similar to those in patients with late-stage HIV infection. For unknown reasons, many patients with CVI also develop autoimmune disorders, most commonly autoimmune hemolytic anemia and thrombocytopenia, rheumatoid arthritis, and pernicious anemia.

KEY POINT

- The most common presentation of common variable immunodeficiency is repeated sinopulmonary infections.

Abnormalities in the Complement System

Inherited deficiencies in any of the terminal complement components C5, C6, C7, C8, or C9 (the "attack complex" of complement) are associated with enhanced susceptibility to recurrent infection with *Neisseria meningitidis* or *N. gonorrhoeae*. Defects in components of the alternative pathway of complement activation and the lectin pathway may also be associated with neisserial infections. Inherited deficiency of factors P (properdin) or D of the alternative pathway is associated with a higher incidence of neisserial infections. Mannose-binding lectin (MBL) functional defects may occur in up to 5% of the general population, and variant alleles causing reduced levels of MBL may be found in up to 33%. Neisserial infections occur in patients with MBL functional defects, and MBL defects are associated with poorer prognosis when accompanied by other defects in host defense, such as cystic fibrosis or other complement defects.

Homozygosity for C3 deficiency is rare but is associated with multiple pyogenic infections similar to those occurring in patients with immunoglobulin deficiency. Because factor I is pivotal in the inactivation of C3b, patients with homozygous deficiency of factor I constantly consume C3 and B, and consequently, are more susceptible to pyogenic infections.

The appropriate screening test for deficiencies in classic complement components C1 through C8 is the total hemolytic complement assay or CH_{50}. As performed in most laboratories, this test will not detect C9 deficiency or deficiencies in the alternative or lectin pathways. Screening for these defects should be pursued in more specialized laboratories. When screening test results are abnormal, specific tests for individual complement components should be done.

KEY POINT

- Increased susceptibility to neisserial infections occurs in patients with deficiencies of C5 through C9 of "the attack complex," P and D of the alternative pathway, and mannose-binding lectin of the lectin pathway of the complement system.

Bibliography

Manuel O, Tarr PE, Venetz JP, Trendelenburg M, Meylan PR, Pascual M. Meningococcal disease in a kidney transplant recipient with mannose-binding lectin deficiency. Transpl Infect Dis. 2007;9(3):214-218. [PMID: 17692067]

Oksenhendler E, Gérard L, Fieschi C, et al; DEFI Study Group. Infections in 252 patients with common variable immunodeficiency. Clin Infect Dis. 2008;46(10):1547-1554. [PMID: 18419489]

Bioterrorism

Introduction

Bioterrorism refers to the intentional release of infectious agents to cause direct harm and stimulate fear in a community. Infectious agents identified by public health experts as most likely to be used by bioterrorists in an attack, for their lethal potential or ease of dissemination, or because they have been developed for these purposes or used before, are designated as Class A agents. Early recognition of bioterrorism cases with prompt reporting to public health officials is essential to minimize mass casualties in a large-scale attack. Clinical and epidemiologic features of Class A agents and their recommended countermeasures are summarized in **Table 25**.

Anthrax

Bacillus anthracis is a gram-positive aerobic rod that forms extremely hardy spores. Although naturally occurring cases occur, particularly with livestock exposure, they are extremely uncommon in the United States. Inhalational anthrax is the most rapidly lethal form of clinical illness and the likely presentation should anthrax spores be intentionally released to produce mass casualties. Inhalational anthrax presents as a nonspecific flu-like illness with cough, dyspnea, and chest pain with progression to rapid deterioration, shock, and death. Initial findings on chest imaging may include mediastinal widening, pleural effusions, and, possibly, infiltrates.

Cutaneous anthrax is the most common clinical syndrome in naturally occurring infection and develops after nonintact skin is exposed to spores. Clinical signs of cutaneous anthrax include a painless edematous papule, which is often pruritic, with possible hemorrhagic and necrotic progression (**Figure 10, page 48**).

Gastrointestinal anthrax is an uncommon presentation of naturally occurring infection. It occurs following ingestion of contaminated meat and may be a presenting syndrome in a bioterrorism attack should the agent be intentionally dispersed in the food supply.

KEY POINTS

- Inhalational anthrax presents as a nonspecific flu-like illness with cough, dyspnea, and chest pain with progression to rapid deterioration, shock, and death.

TABLE 25 Summary of Key Features of Class A Bioterrorism Agents

Disease and Agent Type	Incubation period	Clinical Signs and Symptoms	Treatment	Isolation required	Prophylaxis	Vaccine
Anthrax	1 to 60 days	Inhalational: febrile flu-like illness followed by severe respiratory distress; cutaneous: edematous necrotic lesion; gastrointestinal, oropharyngeal exudates, abdominal pain, and distention	Ciprofloxacin; doxycycline	No	Ciprofloxacin or other fluoroquinolone; doxycycline	Live vaccine targeting toxins, available on limited basis
Smallpox	7 to 17 days	High fevers and prostration followed by rash; skin lesions most dense on face/extremities	Supportive care	Yes	Vaccine if exposure in the last 7 days	Vaccinia live viral vaccine; use limited
Plague	1 to 6 days	Fulminating pneumonia followed by sepsis	Streptomycin, doxycycline, or ciprofloxacin	Yes (pneumonic form) during first 48 hours of antibiotic therapy	Doxycycline or ciprofloxacin	None
Botulism	2 hours to 8 days	Normal sensorium with bulbar nerve palsies; descending flaccid paralysis	Antibotulinum immune globulin (antitoxin); supportive care	No	Passive immunization (antitoxin)	Antitoxin in short supply
Tularemia	3 to 5 days	Febrile, flu-like symptoms, respiratory symptoms, sepsis	Streptomycin, doxycycline, or ciprofloxacin	No	Doxycycline or ciprofloxacin	Not highly effective; limited availability
Viral hemorrhagic fever	Variable	Multiorgan system failure, hemorrhage	Supportive care	Yes, depending on agent	None	None

- Initial findings of inhalational anthrax on chest imaging may include mediastinal widening, pleural effusions, and, possibly, infiltrates.
- Clinical signs of cutaneous anthrax include a painless, often pruritic, edematous papule, with possible hemorrhagic and necrotic progression.

Smallpox (Variola Major)

Smallpox is caused by a DNA virus. Naturally occurring smallpox was eradicated from the world in 1977, but the virus still exists in laboratory repositories. It is highly contagious through person-to-person dissemination and is associated with a 30% mortality rate. Most of the world's population is not immune to this virus because routine childhood vaccination was discontinued with smallpox eradication.

Smallpox presents initially with high fever and malaise followed by a vesicular/papular/pustular rash. Typically, the rash develops on the face and extremities and then spreads to the trunk. Skin lesions in any one region of the body appear in synchronous stages of development (all papules, vesicles, or pustules) contrary to chickenpox (**Figure 11, page 48**).

No specific antiviral agents are effective in treating smallpox, but vaccination up to 4 to 7 days following exposure is effective in preventing disease. Therefore, patient isolation and mass vaccination constitute the appropriate public heath response to a smallpox epidemic.

KEY POINTS

- Smallpox presents initially with high fever and malaise followed by a vesicular/papular/pustular rash first on the face and extremities and then on the trunk, with lesions appearing on the body in synchronous stages of development.
- Patient isolation and mass vaccination constitute the appropriate public heath response to a smallpox epidemic.

Plague

Plague is a systemic infection caused by the gram-negative bacillus (or coccobacillus) *Yersinia pestis* that can be spread by aerosolization of the bacteria or by inoculation from flea bites. Plague typically consists of three clinical syndromes:

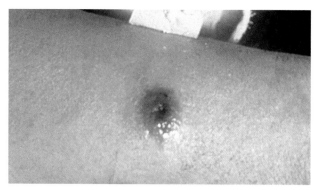

FIGURE 10.
Papule characteristic of cutaneous anthrax.
If this disease remains untreated, disseminated infection and sepsis can follow.

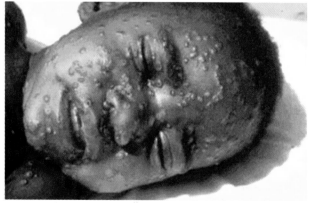

FIGURE 11.
Dense pustules involving the face and trunk are characteristic of smallpox.

(1) pneumonic plague, occurring with inhalation of bacteria (likely presentation with intentional release); (2) bubonic plague, characterized by purulent lymphadenitis near the inoculation site (more common in the naturally occurring zoonotic form of infection); and (3) septicemic plague, a septic presentation that can arise from either of the other syndromes.

Person-to-person spread of plague is possible with pneumonic plague. Streptomycin (or gentamicin), doxycycline, and ciprofloxacin are recommended therapy. Antibiotics and patient isolation for the first 48 hours of therapy are recommended to prevent secondary spread of pneumonic plague.

KEY POINT

- Antibiotics and patient isolation for the first 48 hours of therapy are recommended to prevent secondary spread of pneumonic plague.

Botulism

Botulism is caused by toxins produced by the anaerobic gram-positive bacillus *Clostridium botulinum*. Naturally occurring botulism develops when food becomes contaminated with the bacteria during processing, particularly in canning or pickling. Use of botulism as a bioweapon would likely involve the intentional release of large amounts of aerosolized toxin or inoculation of toxin into food.

In the classic clinical triad of botulism, patients are afebrile with a clear sensorium, but with bulbar palsies and a flaccid descending paralysis. Long-term mechanical ventilation may be required in patients with ventilatory failure. Supportive therapy and botulinum antitoxin administration are recommended.

KEY POINTS

- The use of botulism as a bioweapon would likely involve the intentional release of large amounts of aerosolized toxin or inoculation of toxin into food.
- In the classic clinical triad of botulism, patients are afebrile with a clear sensorium, but with bulbar palsies and a flaccid descending paralysis.

Tularemia

Tularemia is a naturally occurring bacterial zoonosis with clinical features similar to those associated with plague. It is caused by a gram-negative coccobacillus, *Francisella tularensis*. Because inhalation would be the likely exposure route in a bioterrorism attack, an acute pneumonia-like syndrome would be the expected presentation. In naturally occurring infections, exposure can occur through ingestion of contaminated food (oropharyngeal tularemia) or through insect-vector bites (oculoglandular fever). There is no person-to-person transmission. Recommended treatment is streptomycin (or gentamicin), doxycycline, or ciprofloxacin.

KEY POINT

- In a bioterrorism attack, an acute pneumonia-like syndrome resulting from inhalation would be the most likely presentation of tularemia.

Viral Hemorrhagic Fever

Viral hemorrhagic fever refers to a group of illnesses (for example, Marburg fever or Ebola fever) caused by several distinct families of RNA viruses residing in animal reservoirs. In all patients, severe multisystem failure, coagulopathy, and hemorrhage develop. Treatment is supportive. An effective public health response would require recognition of a cluster of cases, specialized diagnostic testing in public health laboratories, and isolation of patients with suspected disease to avoid person-to-person dissemination.

KEY POINTS

- Viral hemorrhagic fever is characterized by severe multisystem failure, coagulopathy, and hemorrhage.

- An effective public health response to suspected viral hemorrhagic fever is recognition of a cluster of cases, specialized diagnostic testing, and isolation of patients with suspected infection.

Bibliography

Arnon S, Schechter R, Inglesby TV, et al; Working Group on Civilian Biodefense. Botulinum Toxin as a Biological Weapon. Medical and Public Health Management. JAMA. 2001;285(8):1059-1070. [PMID: 11209178]

Borio L, Inglesby T, Peters CJ, et al; Working Group on Civilian Biodefense. Hemorrhagic Fever Viruses as Biological Weapons. Medical and Public Health Management. JAMA. 2002;287(18): 2391-2405. [PMID: 11988060]

Dennis DT, Inglesby TV, Henderson DA, et al; Working Group on Civilian Biodefense. Tularemia as a Biological Weapon: Medical and Public Health Management. JAMA. 2001;285(21):2763-2773. [PMID: 11386933]

Henderson DA, Inglesby TV, Bartlett JG, et al; Working Group on Civilian Biodefense. Smallpox as a Biological Weapon: Medical and Public Health Management. JAMA. 1999;281(22):2127-2137. [PMID: 10367824]

Inglesby TV, Dennis DT, Henderson DA, et al; Working Group on Civilian Biodefense. Plague as a Biological Weapon Medical and Public Health Management. JAMA. 2000;283(17):2281-2290. [PMID: 10807389]

Inglesby TV, O'Toole T, Henderson DA, et al; Working Group on Civilian Biodefense. Anthrax as a Biological Weapon, 2002 Updated Recommendations for Management. JAMA. 2002;287(17):2236-2252. [PMID: 11980524]

Kuehnert MJ, Doyle TJ, Hill HA, et al. Clinical features that discriminate inhalational anthrax from other acute respiratory illnesses. Clin Infect Dis. 2003;36(3):328-336. [PMID: 12539075]

Kyriacou DN, Yarnold PR, Stein AC, et al. Discriminating inhalational anthrax from community-acquired pneumonia using chest radiograph findings and a clinical algorithm. Chest. 2007;131(2):489-496. [PMID: 17296652]

Travel Medicine

Introduction

The evaluation of an ill returning traveler often seems formidable because of the many diseases in the developing parts of the world with which Western physicians lack familiarity. However, most patients are likely to have one of only a few diagnoses (**Table 26**).

Malaria

Malaria is largely preventable through mosquito avoidance and chemoprophylaxis. Mosquito avoidance includes staying in screened areas from dusk to dawn when the female *Anopheline* mosquito does most of its biting; sleeping with bed netting, preferably permethrin treated; and using effective insect repellents. Insect repellents containing about 30% DEET (N,N-diethyl-3-methylbenzamide) are considered the most effective. **Table 27** lists types of malaria chemoprophylaxis.

TABLE 26 Most Common Diagnoses in the Febrile Traveler Returning from a Developing Country
Short Incubation Period[a,b]
Malaria
Typhoid fever
Dengue
Rickettsial disease
Hepatitis A
Long Incubation Period[a,c]
Malaria
Tuberculosis

[a]It is not always possible to estimate the incubation period in a person who has been abroad for an extended period.

[b]Two weeks or less.

[c]Greater than 4 weeks.

Although its incubation period can be as short as 10 days, malaria in 5% of patients can present after 1 year, and in rare cases, may not become evident for many years after return from travel. Any traveler returning from a malaria-endemic area in the past year with febrile illness should undergo malaria evaluation.

Most travelers do not have malaria's characteristic cyclical fevers, are not anemic, and do not have splenomegaly or other suggestive physical findings, but up to 25% have prominent gastrointestinal symptoms. Thick and thin peripheral blood smear for malaria parasites continues to be the most common way to diagnose and speciate malaria. Six to eight negative smears obtained over 48 hours effectively exclude the diagnosis.

Once a diagnosis of malaria is established, determining whether the infecting organism is *Plasmodium falciparum* or one of the other three main species (*Plasmodium vivax*, *Plasmodium ovale*, and *Plasmodium malariae*) that infect humans is appropriate. This step is important because infections with *P. falciparum* are potentially fatal and are always considered emergencies. Clues to diagnosing *P. falciparum* are listed in **Table 28**. *Plasmodium knowlesi*, the malaria of the macaque monkeys in Southeast Asia, has recently been shown to infect humans. Peripheral blood smear findings of *P. knowlesi* and *P. malariae* are similar, but *P. knowlesi* is associated with a much more virulent course than is *P. malariae*.

KEY POINTS

- Malaria prevention includes staying in screened areas from dusk to dawn; sleeping with bed netting, preferably permethrin treated; using effective insect repellents; and chemoprophylaxis when traveling to endemic areas.

- Malarial infection with *Plasmodium falciparum* species is potentially fatal and is always considered an emergency.

TABLE 27 Chemoprophylaxis for Malaria			
Travel to Areas of the World Where There Is No Resistant _Plasmodium falciparum_[a,b]			
Drug	**Dosing Information**	**Side Effects**	**Notes**
Chloroquine phosphate (500 mg daily) or hydroxychloroquine sulfate (400 mg daily)	Begin therapy the week before travel; take weekly and for 4 weeks after leaving a malaria-endemic area	Minimal toxicity when taken for malaria prophylaxis includes gastrointestinal upset and pruritus	
Travel to Areas of the World Where There Is Known Resistant _Plasmodium falciparum_[b,c]			
Drug	**Dosing Information**	**Side Effects**	**Notes**
Mefloquine (250 mg daily)	Begin 2 weeks prior to departure; take weekly and for 4 weeks after leaving a malaria-endemic area	Potential concerns regarding neuropsychiatric side effects, including seizures and sleep disturbances (although, when studied, these seem to be no more common than with chloroquine). Prolongs QT intervals and should not be used in persons with known cardiac conduction abnormalities[d]	Moderately expensive; mefloquine resistance has been reported in Africa and at the border between Thailand and Cambodia
Doxycycline (100 mg daily)	Begin 1 day prior to departure; take daily and for 1 month after leaving a malaria-endemic area	Gastrointestinal side effects, photosensitivity rash, vaginitis	Least-expensive antimalarial agent; contraindicated in pregnancy
Atovaquone and proguanil in a fixed-dose combination	Begin 1 day prior to departure; take daily and for 1 week after return	Gastrointestinal side effects and rash	Most expensive antimalarial agent

[a]Areas of the world that are still considered to have chloroquine-sensitive _P. falciparum_ include the Dominican Republic, Haiti, Mexico, Central America west of the Panama Canal Zone, and the Middle East.

[b]These drugs are not predictably active against the hypnozoites in the liver of _P. vivax_ and _P. ovale_. Terminal prophylaxis with primaquine should be considered. Alternatively, one could wait and only treat if clinical disease develops.

[c]Travelers to the Thailand-Cambodian border region should take doxycycline or atovaquone and proguanil owing to mefloquine resistance in that region of the world.

[d]Although not proven riskier than other options, the manufacturer has added a warning to avoid use in persons with active or a history of severe psychiatric disturbances or seizures or with known cardiac conduction abnormalities.

Typhoid Fever

Patients with typhoid fever typically present with a nonspecific syndrome of fever and constitutional symptoms 1 to 3 weeks after ingestion of contaminated food or water. Abdominal pain, cough, and chills may also occur. Diarrhea is not common initially but often develops with disease progression. The diagnosis is established by identifying the organism in blood, urine, stool, or, occasionally, bone marrow. Treatment may include a third-generation cephalosporin, a fluoroquinolone antibiotic, or azithromycin. Resistance to the fluoroquinolones is increasing. Relapses may occur 2 to 3 weeks after treatment in up to 5% of patients.

KEY POINTS

- Typhoid fever is characterized by fever, constitutional symptoms, and, possibly, abdominal pain, cough, and chills, 1 to 3 weeks after ingestion of contaminated food or water; diarrhea often occurs with disease progression.

- Treatment of typhoid fever may include a third-generation cephalosporin, a fluoroquinolone antibiotic, or azithromycin; however, fluoroquinolone resistance is increasing.

Traveler's Diarrhea

Traveler's diarrhea occurs in about 50% of persons traveling to developing parts of the world. It is generally mild but can result in several days of unpleasant symptoms. Patients can decrease the risk of developing traveler's diarrhea through careful attention to food and drink consumption, water purification, and medications. Unpeeled fresh fruits and vegetables should be avoided. Ice made with local water should be avoided. Adding alcohol to local water will not result in a high enough concentration of alcohol to render the water safe. Carbonated water is safe as are drinks prepared with boiled water. For travelers to very remote areas, local water can be made bacteria safe by adding sodium hypochlorite (2

TABLE 28 Clues to the Diagnosis of *Plasmodium falciparum* Infection

Epidemiology

   If malaria is acquired in Africa, the likelihood that it is *Plasmodium falciparum* is at least 3:1

   P. falciparum infections have a clinical onset beyond 2 months after exposure in only 5% of cases; therefore, patients with symptoms lasting beyond 2 months after return from travel are unlikely to have *P. falciparum* infection

Peripheral Blood Smear Findings Likely for *P. falciparum* Infection

   Level of parasitemia is >2%

   Only ring forms are present

   Banana-shaped gametocytes are seen

   Erythrocytes of all sizes are infected

   Numerous multiply infected erythrocytes are seen

   Erythrocytes contain no Schüffner granules

TABLE 29 Agents for the Treatment of Traveler's Diarrhea

Drug	Dosage
Ciprofloxacin	500 mg, twice daily for 3 days[a]
Norfloxacin	400 mg, twice daily for 3 days[a]
Levofloxacin	500 mg, once daily for 3 days[a]
Azithromycin	1000 mg as a single dose
Rifaximin	200 mg, three times daily for 3 days

[a]A single dose may be effective, and treatment can be stopped if symptoms have resolved in 24 hours.

drops/1.89 L [2 quarts]) or tincture of iodine (5 drops/0.95 L [1 quart]) to the water and then waiting for 30 minutes before consumption. However, protozoan parasites, such as *Giardia* and *Cryptosporidium*, are relatively resistant to halogens; they can be removed with the use of any commercially available water filter.

Prophylactic medications for traveler's diarrhea generally are not recommended. However, prophylactic medications including trimethoprim-sulfamethoxazole, doxycycline, the fluoroquinolones, and rifaximin may be considered for patients in high-risk settings such as those with underlying inflammatory bowel syndrome; bismuth subsalicylate in large doses may also have some benefit. Probiotic agents are not recommended. **Table 29** lists antibiotics used in the treatment of traveler's diarrhea. Antimotility agents can decrease symptoms but should be used with caution in patients with high fever and blood or mucus in the stool because they may exacerbate disease caused by the more invasive pathogens. Untreated traveler's diarrhea usually resolves in 3 to 5 days, but treatment can improve symptoms and shorten the course.

KEY POINTS

- To avoid traveler's diarrhea, travelers should ensure unpeeled fresh fruits and vegetables are avoided, and ice made with local water is avoided.
- Untreated traveler's diarrhea usually resolves in 3 to 5 days, but treatment can improve symptoms and shorten the course.

Dengue Virus Infection

Four serotypes of a flavivirus cause dengue. The primary vector is the *Aedes* mosquito, which is found in much of the world. Most affected patients experience a self-limited febrile illness. Symptoms of fever, severe myalgia, and retro-orbital pain are characteristic of, but not specific for, dengue fever. Dengue shock syndrome and dengue hemorrhagic fever occur in patients in whom a second infection develops in a person who was previously infected with a different serotype.

The *Aedes* mosquito is active during the daytime; consequently, bed netting is of limited value. There is no effective vaccine for dengue; therefore, mosquito avoidance with insect repellent and use of screens is the primary preventive approach. There is no specific treatment for dengue.

KEY POINTS

- Fever, severe myalgia, and retro-orbital pain are characteristic of, but not specific for, dengue fever.
- Mosquito avoidance with insect repellent and use of screens is the primary preventive approach for dengue.

Hepatitis A Virus Infection

Hepatitis A virus infection occurs throughout the world, but the risks of acquiring it are increased in developing countries. This infection is transmitted through fecal contamination of food and drink. Any traveler who has not had hepatitis A virus infection or hepatitis A immunization is at risk for acquiring this disease. At-risk travelers should be immunized at least 2 to 4 weeks before traveling to an endemic area. A single dose of vaccine results in virtually 100% protection by 4 weeks after inoculation; immune globulin is no longer recommended for travelers. A second dose administered at least 6 months after the initial dose results in antibody titers likely to last many decades. The treatment for hepatitis A virus infection is supportive; no antiviral medication is available.

KEY POINT

- Any traveler who has not had hepatitis A virus infection should be immunized at least 2 to 4 weeks before traveling to an endemic area.

Rickettsial Diseases

Rickettsial diseases are tick transmitted, occur throughout the world, and are typically named for the geographic region. For example, African tick bite fever occurs in sub-Saharan Africa, and Mediterranean tick bite fever occurs in northern Africa and the Middle East. All are characterized by headache, fever, myalgia, and often, a truncal maculopapular or vesicular rash. The clinical clue is the presence of an eschar that occurs at the site of the tick bite. This illness is self-limited, but treatment with doxycycline is recommended.

KEY POINT

- Rickettsial diseases can be distinguished from illnesses with similar presentations by the presence of the eschar and the rash.

Fungal Infections

The association of coccidioidomycosis with travel to the arid areas of the Southwest United States is well known. However, this organism is also endemic to other arid areas in the Western hemisphere, particularly Mexico and parts of South America. Similarly, histoplasmosis occurs in the Ohio River valley, but endemicity of this fungus in Mexico and Central America is also a consideration for travelers returning from those destinations. *Penicillium marneffei* is endemic to Southeast Asia, parts of China, Hong Kong, and Taiwan. Disseminated infection with this organism is occurring increasingly in immunosuppressed patients, especially those infected with AIDS.

KEY POINT

- *Penicillium marneffei* is a cause of disease in AIDS-infected patients in Southeast Asia.

Risks of Commercial Travel–Related Infection

The risks associated with commercial travel remain low. Owing to environmental control measures on commercial aircraft, risk for dissemination of infectious disease is minimal to persons other than those sitting close to an index patient. The World Health Organization reviewed information on 35 flights on which a patient with symptomatic severe acute respiratory syndrome (SARS) had been onboard. Only four cases appeared to be associated with possible transmission.

Aircraft transmission of tuberculosis may occur, but, like SARS, the risk for transmission is very small and is related to proximity to the index patient.

Aircraft have been a great concern as a potential vector for the global spread of influenza. However, the actual transmission of influenza infection during flight is much less of a health concern.

Cruise ships have also been associated with outbreaks of diseases, particularly Legionnaires disease and norovirus. As with land-related outbreaks, those occurring aboard ship have also been associated with contaminated water sources. Owing

to prolonged exposure on cruises, it is not surprising that influenza outbreaks also occur in this setting.

KEY POINT

- The risk of acquiring infection on commercial transportation is very low.

Bibliography

Adach JA, DuPont HL. Rifaximin: a novel nonabsorbed rifamycin for gastrointestinal disorders. Clin Infect Dis. 2006;42(4):541-547. [PMID: 16421799]

Azara A, Piana A, Sotgiu G, et al. Prevalence study of Legionella spp. Contamination n cruise ships. BMC Public Health. 2006;6:100. [PMID: 16620388]

Hill DR, Ericsson CD, Pearson RD, et al. The practice of travel medicine: guidelines by the Infectious Diseases Society of America. Clin Infect Dis. 2006;43(12):1499-1539. [PMID: 17109284]

Mangili A, Gendreau M. Transmission of infectious disease during commercial air travel. Lancet 2005;365(9463):989-996. [PMID: 15767002]

Mootsikapun P, Srikulbutr S. Histoplasmosis and penicilliosis: Comparison of clinical features, laboratory findings and outcome. Int J Infect Dis. 2006;10(1):66-71. [PMID: 16242368]

Patra S, Kumar A, Trivedi SS, Puri M, Sarin SK. Maternal and fetal outcomes in pregnant women with acute hepatitis E virus infection. Ann Intern Med. 2007;147(1):28-33. [PMID: 17606958]

Sohail MR, Fischer PR. Health risks to air travelers. Infect Dis Clin N Am. 2005;19(1):67-84. [PMID: 15701547]

Thwing J, Skarbinski J, Newman RD, et al; Centers for Disease Control and Prevention. Malaria surveillance - United States, 2005. MMWR Surveill Summ. 2007;56(6):23-40. [PMID: 17557074]

World Health Organization. FAQ on tuberculosis. www.who.int/tb/xdr/faqs/en/. Published in 2007. Accessed on July 24, 2009.

Infectious Diarrhea

Introduction

Diarrhea is an important cause of morbidity and mortality in the United States and worldwide. Infections are usually due to bacteria, viruses, or parasites (see MKSAP 15 Gastroenterology and Hepatology).

Campylobacter Infection

Campylobacter species are small gram-negative bacteria that are a major cause of acute infectious diarrhea. *Campylobacter jejuni* and *Campylobacter coli* are the two most common species involved in human disease and are often resistant to fluoroquinolone antibiotics.

Human infection usually results from eating raw or undercooked poultry, drinking infected raw milk, or ingesting any food contaminated with these organisms.

Diagnosis

Campylobacter infection is indistinguishable from many other bacterial causes of diarrhea. Most patients develop abdominal pain and diarrhea 3 to 7 days after becoming infected, and some have a brief febrile prodrome. The diarrhea is watery, can be bloody, and may cause 10 to 14 bowel movements per day. Diagnosis is established by stool culture.

A reactive arthritis or Guillain-Barré syndrome may occur after *Campylobacter* infection.

Treatment and Prevention

Campylobacter infection usually resolves in less than 1 week without treatment. Antibiotics should be considered for patients who are severely ill, immunocompromised, pregnant, or elderly. Macrolide agents such as erythromycin are considered first-line therapy in the United States.

Proper cooking of chicken and other meat products is the most effective prevention. Avoiding cross-contamination of cutting boards and knives when handling chicken and other foods is also very important.

KEY POINTS

- *Campylobacter* infection usually results from eating raw or undercooked poultry, drinking infected raw milk, or ingesting any food contaminated with these bacteria.
- Most patients with *Campylobacter* infection recover without treatment.
- Reactive arthritis and Guillain-Barré syndrome may develop after *Campylobacter* infections.

Escherichia coli Infection

Enteropathogenic *Escherichia coli* (EPEC) causes diarrheal outbreaks in neonatal nurseries. Enteroinvasive *E. coli* (EIEC) induces an illness very similar to *Shigella* infection. Enterotoxigenic *E. coli* (ETEC) and enteroaggregative *E. coli* (EAEC) are common pathogens associated with traveler's diarrhea (see Travel Medicine) and can cause chronic diarrhea in children in developing countries. Entero-hemorrhagic *E. coli* (EHEC), also known as Shiga toxin–producing *E. coli* (STEC), causes a hemorrhagic colitis and is associated with the hemolytic uremic syndrome (HUS) (see MKSAP 15 Nephrology and Hematology and Oncology). In the United States, most STEC infections are due to the *E. coli* O157:H7 strain.

E. coli O157:H7 colonizes the gut of cattle. Beef becomes contaminated during slaughtering and processing. Several outbreaks have been associated with prewashed and bagged lettuce, unpasteurized apple juice and milk, lakes and wading pools, and petting zoos. *E. coli* O157:H7 is a low-dose pathogen (<100 organisms are needed to cause an infection).

Diagnosis

STEC infection must be considered in the differential diagnosis of bloody diarrhea but is often difficult to distinguish from other causes (**Table 30**).

Once the diagnosis is suspected, the microbiology laboratory must be notified to test stool culture samples on sorbitol-MacConkey agar.

Treatment and Prevention

Treatment is supportive. Antimotility agents should be avoided. Antibiotics are generally not needed. A randomized, prospective, controlled trial did not substantiate an association between antibiotic use and subsequent development of HUS or a decrease in duration of gastrointestinal symptoms, contrary to earlier studies.

Proper cooking of food is critical to prevent disease dissemination. Prevention also includes regulatory standards to decrease fecal soilage of meat at slaughter houses as well as earlier recognition of outbreaks.

KEY POINTS

- Enterohemorrhagic *Escherichia coli*, also known as Shiga toxin–producing *E. coli*, causes a hemorrhagic colitis.
- In the United States, most Shiga toxin–producing *Escherichia coli* infections are due to the *E. coli* O157:H7 strain.
- Treatment of Shiga toxin–producing *Escherichia coli* infections is generally supportive.
- Hemolytic uremic syndrome is an occasional complication of Shiga toxin–producing *Escherichia coli* infection.

Shigella Infection

Shigella causes illness characterized by fever; abdominal cramping; and small-volume, mucoid, bloody diarrhea. Signs and symptoms usually develop several days after exposure. In the United States, the disease develops mostly in children, particularly those in day-care centers. In developing countries, *Shigella* infection occurs in areas of overcrowding and poor sanitation. Because only a few organisms are needed to cause disease, *Shigella* is easily transmitted from person to person.

Diagnosis

The diagnosis should be considered in anyone presenting with the signs and symptoms described above. Once suspected, the diagnosis is readily established by routine stool culture. Local and systemic complications are rare but may include HUS syndrome.

Treatment and Prevention

Shigella infection usually lasts about 1 week and is self-limited in most patients. However, treatment is recommended for all patients to decrease transmission risk. In adults, empiric antibiotic therapy is started with a fluoroquinolone for 5 days.

TABLE 30 Differential Diagnosis of Bloody Diarrhea

Disease or Organism	Comments
Shigella species and *Campylobacter* species	Two most common causes of bloody diarrhea in the United States
	Usually occur in adults
	Usually occur as isolated cases rather than outbreaks
	Usually associated with fever
Shiga toxin–producing *Escherichia coli* O157:H7	Usually occurs in children
	Usually occurs as outbreaks rather than isolated cases
	Not associated with fever
Entamoeba histolytica	Causes abdominal pain, diarrhea, and bloody stools
	Occurs in travelers to endemic areas
Vibrio parahaemolyticus	Caused by consumption of raw or undercooked shellfish and oysters
	Organisms most common in coastal waters of the Gulf Coast or Southeast Asia
	Causes bloody diarrhea in 15% of patients
Aeromonas species	Organisms found in fresh and brackish water
	Occasionally causes bloody diarrhea
Clostridium difficile	Often hospital associated
	Often follows course of antibiotics
	Typically presents with watery diarrhea, occult colonic bleeding, abdominal pain, low-grade fever, and leukocytosis
Inflammatory bowel disease	Can cause chronic bloody diarrhea and abdominal pain
	May cause fistula formation
	Associated with extraintestinal manifestations
	May present as a fever of unknown origin

When needed, oral rehydration is usually sufficient, but intravenous hydration may be required.

Strict hand washing is essential to limit disease spread. In the hospital environment, contact precautions for all enteric infections are required.

KEY POINTS

- In the United States, *Shigella* infection causes a classic dysentery syndrome mostly in children, particularly in day-care centers.
- Although *Shigella* infection is self-limited in most patients, treatment for all patients is recommended to decrease the risk of spread to others.

Salmonella Infection

Salmonella typhi and *Salmonella paratyphi* are the causative agents of typhoid fever, which is a worldwide health problem. The disease rarely occurs in the United States except in travelers returning from endemic areas. In contrast, nontyphoidal salmonellae are frequent causes of gastroenteritis in the United States. These organisms are associated with animal reservoirs, particularly poultry and eggs, that cause foodborne outbreaks. Transmission may also occur in children who handle pet reptiles, such as turtles, snakes, lizards, and iguanas.

Diagnosis

Salmonella gastroenteritis is clinically indistinguishable from gastroenteritis caused by other pathogens. Characteristic findings are nausea, vomiting, diarrhea, and cramping abdominal pain beginning 8 to 72 hours after exposure. Diagnosis is made by routine stool culture, although samples can take up to 72 hours to become positive.

Approximately 5% of patients with *Salmonella* gastroenteritis may develop invasive disease and extraintestinal manifestations, such as bacteremia, endovascular infections, endocarditis, and osteomyelitis. Blood cultures are usually positive in these patients. Infants younger than 1 year of age and the elderly are at greatest risk for complications. Salmonellae also have a predilection for aortic plaque, other endovascular foci, and bone prostheses and can cause infection at these sites.

Treatment and Prevention

The decision to treat a patient with nontyphoidal *Salmonella* gastroenteritis is based on several factors. Because the disease is usually self-limited and resolves in less than 1 week, antibiotic treatment is not required for most healthy persons between 2 and 50 years of age.

Treatment is indicated for (1) immunocompetent patients younger than 2 years or older than 50 years because of the increased incidence of complications in these age groups; (2) immunocompetent patients of any age with severe infection requiring hospitalization; (3) immunocompetent patients of any age with known or suspected atherosclerotic plaques and endovascular or bone prostheses because of possible seeding of these areas during a bloodstream infection; and (4) immunocompromised patients of any age, such as patients with HIV infection or those receiving corticosteroids or other immunosuppressive agents.

Immunocompetent patients who require treatment should receive antibiotics for 7 to 10 days because of the possibility of a bloodstream infection.

The duration of therapy for immunocompromised patients is usually a minimum of 2 weeks and frequently ranges from 4 to 6 weeks because of the higher incidence of relapse in this population.

Oral fluoroquinolones are first-line therapy. Susceptibility testing should be performed and the choice of antibiotics modified if necessary. Because asymptomatic shedding of salmonellae occurs in the stool for several weeks, even after appropriate antibiotic therapy, follow-up stool cultures are not recommended for most immunocompetent patients.

Infected food handlers and health care workers should remain at home until they are asymptomatic. Negative stool cultures are often required for these individuals. Good general hygiene and meticulous hand washing are essential to decrease disease spread.

KEY POINTS

- Salmonellae are associated with animal reservoirs, especially poultry and eggs, but have also been transmitted to children following handling of pet reptiles.
- *Salmonella* gastroenteritis is clinically indistinguishable from gastroenteritis caused by other pathogens.
- No antibiotic treatment is required for most healthy persons between 2 and 50 years of age who develop *Salmonella* gastroenteritis.
- Fluoroquinolones are first-line agents for patients with *Salmonella* gastroenteritis who require treatment.

Viral Gastroenteritis

Acute gastroenteritis is very common, and viruses are the most frequent cause. Rotavirus is the most serious cause of viral gastroenteritis in infants and young children, followed by enteric adenovirus and astrovirus.

Norovirus affects all age groups. It is the most common cause of pathogen-induced gastroenteritis. Norovirus is transmitted by the fecal-oral route. Because only 10 to 100 organisms are required to cause infection, norovirus is highly contagious and has been associated with epidemic outbreaks in numerous settings. Most food-related illnesses are due to norovirus.

Diagnosis

Characteristic findings include the abrupt onset of vomiting and diarrhea. Vomiting is usually the predominant symptom and is frequently associated with fever, abdominal discomfort, and headache. Symptoms typically begin 24 hours after exposure and can last 48 to 72 hours. The diagnosis is usually presumptive and is based on clinical findings and stool cultures that are negative for bacteria. If needed, the diagnosis can be confirmed by polymerase chain reaction.

Treatment and Prevention

No specific antiviral therapy is needed because recovery usually occurs within 72 hours. However, immunity is short lived, and reinfection may develop. Preventive measures include meticulous hand washing; careful disposal of items contaminated with viral-impregnated feces, such as soiled diapers; and identification of contaminated food and water supplies.

KEY POINT

- No specific treatment is needed for norovirus gastroenteritis because recovery usually occurs within 72 hours.

Giardiasis

In the United States, the two most common infectious causes of chronic diarrhea are the parasites *Giardia* and *Cryptosporidium*. Giardiasis is caused by *Giardia lamblia*, which exists in two forms: an infectious cyst that lives in the environment and a trophozoite that attaches to the small bowel and is responsible for the symptoms. Most infections occur in children and develop most often in day-care centers where child hygiene is poor. In addition, waterborne transmission is a major cause of the epidemic spread of the disease. Cysts can live in lakes, streams, and municipal water supplies and are relatively resistant to chlorination.

Diagnosis

Less than 50% of infected patients develop symptoms, which are generally acute and self-limited and include foul-smelling, fatty stools; abdominal cramps; and nausea. Symptoms often last 2 to 4 weeks, and up to one third of patients will develop a chronic infection. Malabsorption may also occur and result in significant weight loss. The protracted illness and weight loss help distinguish giardiasis from other causes of gastroenteritis. Lactose deficiency is also very common and can persist for months after an acute infection and may be confused with disease relapse or failure of the infection to clear after appropriate antibiotic therapy.

The diagnosis is established by finding *Giardia* ova and parasites in the stool. Several stool samples are needed because the organism is excreted only intermittently. Immune assays of stool are greater than 90% sensitive and 95% specific for detecting *Giardia*.

Treatment and Prevention

All symptomatic patients should be treated. Treatment may also be indicated for asymptomatic patients, especially children in day-care centers, to decrease the spread of infection to others and decrease the risk of reinfection. Several treatment regimens are available. Metronidazole for 5 days is most often used for adults.

In travelers to endemic areas, disease can be prevented by boiling water or using iodine-treated water or water filtration systems. Hand washing is essential to decrease person-to-person spread.

KEY POINTS

- In the United States, the parasites *Giardia* and *Cryptosporidium* are the two most common infectious entities causing chronic diarrhea.

- Up to 30% of patients with acute symptomatic giardiasis develop a chronic infection associated with malabsorption and significant weight loss.

- Metronidazole is most commonly used to treat adults with giardiasis.

Cryptosporidiosis

Infection is spread from person to person or from a contaminated water source. Numerous community outbreaks have been associated with drinking water, swimming pools, and water parks. The organisms are resistant to chlorine disinfectants and are not effectively removed by many water filtration systems.

Diagnosis

An immunocompetent person who develops cryptosporidiosis typically experiences diarrhea, malaise, anorexia, and crampy abdominal pain that can last up to 2 weeks. Immunocompromised hosts, such as those with HIV infection and a CD4 cell count less than 100/μL, may have prolonged diarrhea lasting more than 1 month that is often associated with significant weight loss and wasting. Biliary disease, including acalculous cholecystitis and sclerosing cholangitis, may develop in patients with HIV infection and concomitant cryptosporidiosis. Chronic cryptosporidiosis is associated with decreased survival in this patient population.

Routine stool examination for ova and parasites does not detect *Cryptosporidium* spores. The microbiology laboratory should therefore be notified of the suspected diagnosis so that acid-fast stains can be performed. Enzyme-linked immunosorbent assays of stool using monoclonal antibodies against the oocyst are extremely sensitive and specific for *Cryptosporidium*.

Treatment and Prevention

Treatment depends on the immune status of the host. Immunocompetent patients generally require no specific therapy because the disease is self-limited. If symptoms persist beyond several weeks, a course of nitazoxanide can be tried because it has been shown to hasten symptom resolution and clear oocysts from the stool. Immunocompromised patients, such as those with HIV infection, respond poorly to nitazoxanide, paromomycin, trimethoprim-sulfamethoxazole, and metronidazole. For these patients, initiation of highly active antiretroviral therapy to induce immune reconstitution is critical for controlling the cysts.

Proper hygiene is essential to decrease person-to-person spread of *Cryptosporidium*. Boiling or filtering of tap water may decrease the incidence of infection in immunocompromised hosts but is not routinely recommended. Persons who are immunocompromised should also limit time in public swimming pools, water parks, and lakes.

KEY POINTS

- Immunocompetent patients with cryptosporidiosis typically develop diarrhea, malaise, anorexia, and crampy abdominal pain that can last up to 2 weeks, whereas immunocompromised hosts may have prolonged diarrhea lasting more than 1 month that is often associated with significant weight loss and wasting.

- Immunocompetent patients with cryptosporidiosis generally do not require treatment; immunocompromised patients with HIV infection require initiation of highly active antiretroviral therapy to induce immune reconstitution.

Clostridium difficile Infection

Clostridium difficile infection is an inflammatory condition of the colon caused by the ingestion of this spore-forming, anaerobic, gram-positive bacillus. The inflammatory response is secondary to toxin-induced cytokines (toxins A and B) in the colon. Findings can range from watery diarrhea to ileus and life-threatening conditions such as toxic megacolon, perforation, or sepsis. *C. difficile* infection has recently been associated with increased mortality.

Epidemiology

C. difficile is the most common cause of acute care hospital-acquired diarrhea and accounts for 15% to 30% of all cases of antibiotic-associated diarrhea. The organism is ubiquitous in the general environment, but hospitals are the major reservoir for this pathogen. Spores can survive for months on hospital surfaces, and typical hospital cleaning products do not have sporicidal activity.

The reported incidence of *C. difficile* infection has increased over the past 8 years. This increase closely parallels the emergence of a virulent *C. difficile* strain, identified as BI, NAP1, and toxinotype III and ribotype 027 by various typing methods. Recent epidemic BI/NAP1 isolates have been found to hyperproduce toxins A and B in vitro. These isolates are also more likely to be resistant to fluoroquinolones.

> **KEY POINT**
>
> - *Clostridium difficile* is a spore-forming bacillus that is the most common cause of acute care hospital-acquired diarrhea, accounting for 15% to 30% of all cases of antibiotic-associated diarrhea.

Risk Factors

The most widely recognized risk factor for development of *C. difficile* infection is disruption of predominantly anaerobic intestinal flora by antibiotics, which can occur weeks to months after antibiotic exposure. Almost all classes of antibiotics have been associated with infection, including the fluoroquinolones.

The likelihood that hospitalized patients will ingest *C. difficile* spores is increased by proximity to an infected roommate and a prolonged hospital stay. Elderly and immunocompromised patients are more likely to develop infection. In patients of all ages, additional risk factors include disruption of intestinal mucosa due to chemotherapy, decreased gastric acidity caused by proton pump inhibitors and H_2 blockers, repeated enemas, prolonged nasogastric tube insertion, and gastrointestinal surgery.

> **KEY POINT**
>
> - The most widely recognized risk factor for development of *Clostridium difficile* infection is disruption of predominantly anaerobic intestinal flora by antibiotics, which can occur weeks to months after antibiotic exposure.

Diagnosis

Several clinical features are consistent with *C. difficile* infection, including frequent watery stools and abdominal cramping. Systemic findings, such as fever and leukocytosis, are usually absent in patients with mild disease. Colitis may develop and is associated with fever, cramps, leukocytosis, and fecal leukocytes. Colitis is documented by colonoscopy (showing pseudomembranes) or CT (showing colonic-wall thickening). Severe disease may cause paralytic ileus with cessation of diarrhea and development of toxic megacolon. Renal failure and shock may also occur.

A definitive diagnosis requires laboratory identification of *C. difficile* toxin in a stool sample or visualization of pseudomembranes. Several diagnostic methods are available to detect the toxin (**Table 31**).

Laboratory testing is recommended for patients older than 1 year who have symptoms consistent with *C. difficile* infection and a recent history of antibiotic use. The method used will likely depend on the availability of tests in a given laboratory. If the test is associated with low sensitivity or long turnaround time, empiric treatment is recommended for patients with clinical findings consistent with *C. difficile* infection.

TABLE 31 Stool Tests for Diagnosis of *Clostridium difficile* Infection

Test	Detects	Advantages	Disadvantages
Cytotoxin assay	Primarily toxin B	Standard; highly sensitive and specific	Requires tissue culture facility; labor intensive; results take 24-48 h
Toxin enzyme immunoassay	Toxin A or A and B	Fast (2-6 h); easy to perform; high specificity	Not as sensitive as the cytotoxin assay
Glutamate dehydrogenase enzyme immunoassay	Bacterial enzyme (glutamate dehydrogenase)	Fast (<1 h); inexpensive; easy to perform; very sensitive	Poor specificity; toxin testing required to verify diagnosis
Culture	Toxigenic and nontoxigenic *C. difficile*	Most sensitive; allows strain typing in epidemics	Requires anaerobic culture; labor intensive; not specific for toxin-producing bacteria; results take 2-5 days
Batched real-time (RT) PCR	*tcdB* (toxin)	Good sensitivity and specificity	Labor intensive; typically run in batches (1 daily); expensive; not yet commercially available
On-demand real-time (RT) PCR	*tcdB*, (toxin), *tcdC* deletion, and binary toxin (outbreak strain)	Rapid (<1 h); requires less than 2 min of preparation; highly sensitive and specific	Expensive; not yet commercially available

PCR = polymerase chain reaction.

Reprinted with permission from Kelly CP, LaMont JT. *Clostridium difficile* infection. Annu Rev Med. 1998;49:375-390. [PMID: 9509270] Copyright 1998, Annual Reviews Inc.

- Laboratory studies for detection of *Clostridium difficile* organisms include enzyme-linked immunosorbent assay for toxins, stool culture, cell cytotoxicity assays, and polymerase chain reaction.

Treatment

The first step in treating *C. difficile* infection is to discontinue the offending antibiotic if possible. Before 2000, metronidazole and vancomycin were considered to have comparable efficacy and relapse rates. Given the higher cost of oral vancomycin and the theoretical concern about the development of vancomycin-resistant enterococci after exposure to enteral vancomycin, oral (or intravenous) metronidazole was generally the preferred initial agent for patients with mild or moderate *C. difficile* infection. Newer evidence suggests that vancomycin may be more effective than metronidazole, and this difference is most important in patients with severe disease. Metronidazole is now used in patients with mild to moderate *C. difficile* infection and in those who cannot receive enteral treatment. It is contraindicated in pregnancy. About 20% of patients with *C. difficile* infection develop a relapse after initial treatment, which is a function of ecologic derangement of colon flora and not resistance to either of these agents. Of these, 45% have a single recurrence, and up to 55% experience two or more repeat episodes. Antibiotic resistance does not appear to be associated with recurrent infection (**Table 32**).

A first recurrence is treated in the same way as the initial episode, based on disease severity. Metronidazole should be limited to treatment of a first recurrence and for a maximum of 28 days over two treatment courses. Prolonged courses of vancomycin with tapering or pulse doses at the end of treatment can be used for treating second and later recurrences. Although study populations were small, studies reported that a 10- to 14-day course of vancomycin followed by tapering or pulse doses of this agent over a 4- to 6-week period was associated with significant reductions in multiple relapses.

Limited, and mostly discouraging, data exist on the available alternative agents, including intravenous immune globulin, probiotics such as *Saccharomyces boulardii* and *Lactobacillus rhamnosus GG*, rifaximin, nitazoxanide, and tolevamer, and rifampin resistance has already been detected. A novel alternative therapy is fecal instillation of donor specimens of stool to restore bacterial homeostasis.

- Newer evidence suggests that vancomycin may be more effective than metronidazole in treating *Clostridium difficile* infection, and this difference is most important in patients with severe disease.

TABLE 32 Treatment for CDI[a]				
	Initial Treatment		**Recurrence**	
Mild	**Severe/Normal Bowel Function**	**Severe/Ileus**	**First Recurrence**	**Subsequent Recurrences (≥2)**
Metronidazole, 500 mg orally TID for 10-14 d	Vancomycin (effective in enteral [oral or rectal] form only), 125 mg enterally QID for 10-14 d	Vancomycin (effective in enteral [oral or rectal] form only), 125 mg enterally QID for 10-14 d plus intravenous metronidazole	Treatment with the same drug used to treat the first episode is recommended	Vancomycin[b] (effective in enteral [oral or rectal] form only), 125 mg enterally QID for 10-14 d, followed by pulse dose over 4-6 weeks
Vancomycin[c], 125 mg orally QID for 10-14 d	Patients with severe infection who do not respond to medical treatment might require emergent colectomy	Patients with severe infection who do not respond to medical treatment might require emergent colectomy		Sequential vancomycin followed by rifaximin
				Concomitant vancomycin with rifampin (resistance already described)
				Intravenous immune globulin
				Infuse donor stool

CDI = *Clostridium difficile* infection. TID = three times daily; QID = four times daily.

[a]A systematic review of probiotic efficacy indicated that findings from the current literature do not support their use for *Clostridium difficile* infection. Moreover, the literature is evolving to demonstrate that the so-called nonpathogenic strains of the various fungi and bacteria used in the currently marketed probiotics have caused numerous cases of *Lactobacillus* bacteremia and *Saccharomyces boulardii* fungemia in immunocompetent and immunocompromised hosts.

[b]Vancomycin alone rather than with metronidazole, in part because of the adverse effects (e.g., peripheral neuropathy) resulting from long-term exposure to metronidazole.

[c]Vancomycin is typically reserved for patients with severe disease, those who cannot tolerate or fail to respond to metronidazole, and pregnant patients (in whom metronidazole is contraindicated). Also associated with increased cost and concern about vancomycin resistance.

- A first recurrence of *Clostridium difficile* infection is treated in the same way as the initial episode, based on disease severity.
- Prolonged courses of vancomycin with tapering or pulse doses at the end of treatment can be used for treating second and later recurrences of *Clostridium difficile* infection.

Control of *Clostridium difficile* Infection

Environmental and Health Care Worker Contamination

Control of *C. difficile* infection depends on measures to reduce or eliminate environmental contamination and effective hygiene to prevent transmission by health care workers (see Health Care–Associated Infections for a complete discussion of control of nosocomial infections). *C. difficile* spores are found in 34% to 58% of sites in hospital wards, including on toilets, bathtubs, and bed frames. The heaviest contamination is on floors and carpets. Other sources of contamination include nurses' uniforms and other clothing, blood pressure cuffs, thermometers, telephones, call buttons, scales, and feeding tube equipment. Only chlorine-based disinfectants and high-concentration vaporized hydrogen peroxide are sporicidal. Environmental cleaning with sodium hypochlorite (bleach) solutions decreases levels of *C. difficile* surface contamination and is associated with a significant reduction in these organisms.

Proper hand washing is the most effective prevention. Alcohol-based hand hygiene products do not kill spores and are not effective in removing *C. difficile* from the hands. However, hand washing (30 seconds to 2 minutes with soap and water followed by proper hand drying with disposable paper towels) is effective for spore removal.

Patient Contamination

Recent studies have found that patients with documented *C. difficile* infection or asymptomatic carriage have high rates of skin contamination (61% to 78%). Even the approximately 19% of patients who are noncarriers have skin contamination. Use of chlorhexidine-saturated cloths for patient cleansing has been shown to reduce *C. difficile* spores on patients' skin and subsequent transmission to health care workers' hands.

Other Infection Control Measures

Preventive measures for control of *C. difficile* infection include barrier precautions (gloves and gown), the use of dedicated equipment, single-use rectal thermometers, and endoscope disinfection. Risks to patients can also be decreased by avoiding unnecessary antibiotics and other agents that alter intestinal flora (for example, agents that suppress gastric acid).

Bundles (a group of practices that when performed collectively are more effective than when performed individually) have been shown to reduce various hospital-acquired infections. The use of a comprehensive *C. difficile* bundle, consisting of education, increased/early case-finding methodologies, expanded infection control measures, a *C. difficile* management team, and targeted antimicrobial management, was associated with rapid and sustainable *C. difficile* control.

KEY POINTS

- Environmental cleaning with sodium hypochlorite (bleach) solutions decreases *Clostridium difficile* surface contamination and is associated with a significant reduction in these organisms.
- Hand washing is the most effective way to remove *Clostridium difficile* spores from health care workers' hands.

Bibliography

Aas J, Gessert CE, Bakken JS. Recurrent Clostridium difficile Colitis: Case Series Involving 18 Patients Treated with Donor Stool Administered via a Nasogastric Tube. 2003;36(5):580-585. [PMID: 12594638]

Barlett, JG. The Case for Vancomycin as the Preferred Drug for Treatment of Clostridium difficile Infection. Clin Infect Dis. 2008;49(10):1489-1492. [PMID: 18419480]

Bartlett JG, Gerding DN. Clinical Recognition and Diagnosis of Clostridium difficile Infection. Clin Infect Dis. 2008;46(Suppl 1):S12-S18. [PMID: 18177217]

Bartlett JG. Antibiotic-associated diarrhea. Clin Infect Dis. 1992;15(4):573-581. [PMID: 1420669]

Centers for Disease Control and Prevention. Clostridium difficile: information for healthcare providers. www.cdc.gov/ncidod/hip/gastro/ClostridiumDifficileHCP_print.htm. Published July 22, 2005. Accesed on July 27, 2009.

Curry SR, Marsh JW, Shutt KA, et al. High Frequency of Rifampin Resistance Identified in an Epidemic C. difficile Clone from a Large Teaching Hospital. Clin Infect Dis. 2008;48(4):425-429. [PMID: 19140738]

Gerding DN, Muto CA, Owens RC. Measures to Control and Prevent Clostridium difficile Infection. Clin Infect Dis. 2008;46(Suppl 1):S43-S49. [PMID: 18177221]

Gerding DN, Muto CA, Owens RC. Treatment of Clostridium difficile Infection. Clin Infect Dis. 2008;46(Suppl 1):S32-S42. [PMID: 18177219]

Musher DM, Musher BL. Contagious acute gastrointestinal infections. N Engl J Med. 2004;351(23):2417-2427. [PMID: 15575058]

Muto CA, Blank MK, Marsh JW, et al. Control of an Outbreak of Infection with the Hypervirulent Clostridium difficile BI Strain in a University Hospital Using a Comprehensive "Bundle" Approach. Clin Infect Dis. 2007;45(10):1266-1273. [PMID: 17968819]

Muto CA, Pokrywka M, Shutt K, et al. A large outbreak of Clostridium difficile-associated disease with an unexpected proportion of deaths and colectomies at a teaching hospital following increased fluoroquinolone use. Infect Control Hosp Epidemiol. 2005;26(3):273-280. [PMID: 15796280]

Owens RC, Donskey CJ, Gaynes RP, Loo VG, Muto CA. Antimicrobial-Associated Risk Factors for Clostridium difficile Infection. Clin Infect Dis. 2008;46(Suppl 1):S19-S31. [PMID: 18177218]

Riggs MM, Sethi AK, Zabarsky TF, Eckstein EC, Jump RLP, Donskey CJ. Asymptomatic Carriers Are a Potential Source for Transmission of Epidemic and Nonepidemic Clostridium difficile Strains among Long-Term Care Facility Residents. 2007;45(8):992-998. [PMID: 17879913]

Ruiz-Palacios GM. The health burden of campylobacter infection and the impact of antimicrobial resistance: playing chicken. Clin Infect Dis. 2007;44(5):701-703. [PMID: 17278063]

Safdar N, Said A, Gangnon RE, Maki DG. Risk of hemolytic uremic syndrome after antibiotic treatment of Escherichia coli 0157:H7 enteritis: a meta analysis. JAMA. 2002;288(8):996-1001. [PMID: 12190370]

Turcios RM, Widdowson MA, Mead PS, Glass RI. Reevaluation of epidemiologic criteria for identifying outbreaks of acute gastroenteritis due to norovirus: United States, 1998-2000. Clin Infect Dis. 2006;42(7):964-969. [PMID: 16511760]

Varma JK, Molbak K, Barrett T, et al. Antimicrobial resistant non-typhoidal salmonella is associated with excess blood stream infections and hospitalizations. J Infect Dis. 2005;191(4):554-561. [PMID: 15655779]

Infections in Transplant Recipients

Introduction

Solid organ transplants include those of the kidney, pancreas, liver, heart, lung, and intestine. Hematopoietic cells derived from bone marrow, peripheral blood, or umbilical cords are also used in transplantation to treat hematologic malignancies, inherited and acquired immune deficiencies, aplastic anemia, and inherited erythrocyte dyscrasias such as sickle cell anemia.

Transplantation Antirejection Drugs

See **Table 33** for a listing of the most commonly used transplantation antirejection medications. Generally, transplantation antirejection drugs block lymphocyte functions in various ways, blunting the ability of the host to recognize and reject the transplanted organ or cells, while simultaneously interfering with normal host defenses against infection. Rejection, infection, and adverse drug effects are the three predominant complications of transplantation.

Important antirejection drug interactions are listed in **Table 34**. These interactions may alter blood levels or otherwise change the effects of the antirejection drugs or may change the absorption, clinical effectiveness, or potential toxicities of the additional medications. Because antirejection drug effects are so broad, physicians should prescribe new medications for transplant recipients with caution. Antibiotics, in particular, are frequently used to treat opportunistic and other infections in transplant recipients, and many of these agents have profound effects on the antirejection drugs and vice versa. For example, the azoles, the antifungal activity of which is mediated through their effects on fungal cytochrome P-450 enzymes, also affect mammalian cytochrome P-450 enzymes and increase the levels of cyclosporine and other medications. This concept has been used to advantage by

TABLE 33 The Most Commonly Used Transplantation Antirejection Medications

Calcineurin inhibitors (cyclosporine and tacrolimus)

Inhibitors of mammalian targets of rapamycin (mTOR) (sirolimus [rapamycin] and everolimus)

Inhibitors of nucleotide synthesis (mycophenolate mofetil, mizoribine, and leflunomide)

Antimetabolites (azathioprine)

Antibodies
  Polyclonal antithymocyte globulin
  Mouse anti-CD3 monoclonal antibody (muromonab CD3)
  Humanized anti-CD52 monoclonal antibody (alemtuzumab)
  Anti-CD20 monoclonal antibody (rituximab)
  Anti-CD25 monoclonal antibody (daclizumab and basiliximab)
  Intravenous immune globulin

Corticosteroids (prednisone, methylprednisolone, and others)

mTOR = mammalian target of rapamycin.

some transplant groups to facilitate smaller doses of the more costly cyclosporine by including the less expensive ketoconazole in treatment regimens.

Several pretransplantation preventive measures minimize the risk of posttransplant infection, including immunizations and screening for evidence of various infectious organisms. Immunization for influenza, pneumococci, tetanus, diphtheria, and others are all recommended (**Table 35**). Tests to identify dormant infection with cytomegalovirus, toxoplasmosis, tuberculosis, histoplasmosis, *Strongyloides*, and other latent infections, especially in endemic areas, are also appropriate. After transplantation, many other prophylactic measures may be considered.

KEY POINTS

- Because antirejection drug effects are so broad, physicians should prescribe new medications for transplant recipients with caution.

- Immunizations for influenza, pneumococci, measles, tetanus, diphtheria, and pertussis are all recommended prior to transplantation.

- Tests to identify past infection with cytomegalovirus, toxoplasmosis, tuberculosis, histoplasmosis, *Strongyloides*, and other latent infections are appropriate before transplantation.

Posttransplantation Infections in the Immediate Postoperative Period

Within the first 4 weeks postoperatively, the most common infections in transplant recipients are the same as those that develop postoperatively in patients who have undergone nontransplant-related surgery. Bacterial wound infections caused by staphylococci (coagulase-negative and *Staphylococcus aureus*), hemolytic streptococci, or enteric bacteria (often mixed infections) are common. *Clostridium difficile*–associated diarrhea, central line–associated bloodstream infections, catheter-associated urinary tract infections, and health care–related pneumonias also occur in the immediate post-transplantation period, often during inpatient care. Transplant recipients may also become infected with microorganisms harbored within the transplanted tissues, including bacteria, West Nile virus, or tuberculosis. Many of these donor tissue–associated infections are more critical in later posttransplantation periods.

KEY POINT

- Within the first 4 weeks postoperatively, the most common infections in transplant recipients are the same as those that develop postoperatively in patients who have undergone nontransplant-related surgery.

Posttransplantation Infections in the Later Postoperative Period

Viruses

There is an important difference between cytomegalovirus (CMV) infection and disease. Infection is defined by the presence of a positive culture, polymerase chain reaction assay, CMV antigen, or serology, whereas disease requires the presence of infection plus typical findings, such as fever, leukopenia, hepatitis, pneumonitis, pancreatitis, colitis, and meningoencephalitis. CMV disease frequently occurs after the first month of transplantation but occurs less commonly 6 to 12 months after transplantation. CMV infection occurs most often in the setting of a CMV-negative transplant recipient with an organ from a CMV-positive donor. When donor and recipient are serologically negative for CMV, CMV posttransplantation infections infrequently occur. Almost any organ system may be infected with CMV, and often, the manifestations of CMV disease are different from those occurring when CMV causes disease in immunocompetent patients. CMV disease may cause serious consequences in transplant recipients, including an increased risk for renal graft failure. Perforations and significant bleeding are potential complications in patients with gastrointestinal CMV involvement. CMV-related pneumonia can be especially severe, leading to acute respiratory failure, the need for mechanical ventilation, and other complications.

Prophylaxis with ganciclovir, valganciclovir, or high-dose acyclovir is appropriate for transplant recipients at risk for or with known CMV infection. These antiviral agents are effective in preventing CMV disease and generally are well tolerated. Valganciclovir is available as an oral agent and is often preferred.

Some transplant programs also regularly monitor their patients for evidence of CMV activation by measuring the amount of circulating CMV antigen with immunofluorescence or viral DNA by polymerase chain reaction. In

TABLE 34 Selected Drug Interactions of Transplantation Antirejection Medications

Anti-Rejection Drug	Additional Medication	Effect of Combination
Cyclosporine	Azoles	Increased levels of cyclosporine
	Ofloxacin	Increased levels of cyclosporine
	Erythromycin	Increased levels of cyclosporine
	Aminoglycosides	Increased nephrotoxicity
	Sulfonamides	Decreased levels of cyclosporine and increased nephrotoxicity
	Statins	Increased levels of the statin
	Diltiazem	Increased levels of cyclosporine
	Rifampin	Decreased levels of cyclosporine
	Amphotericin B	Increased nephrotoxicity
	St. John's Wort	Decreased levels of cyclosporine
Sirolimus	Azoles	Increased levels of sirolimus
	Cyclosporine	Increased levels of sirolimus
Mycophenolate mofetil	Cholestyramine	Decreased levels of mycophenolic acid (active metabolite of mycophenolate mofetil)
	Iron and antacids	Decreased levels of mycophenolic acid
Azathioprine	Warfarin	Decreased activity of warfarin
	Allopurinol	Decreased 6-MP activity

TABLE 35 Recommended Vaccinations for Adult Solid Organ Transplant Candidates and Recipients

Vaccine	Inactivated/Live Attenuated (I/LA)	Recommended Before Transplant[a]	Recommended After Transplant	Monitor Vaccine Titers
Influenza, injected	I	Yes	Yes	No
Hepatitis B[b]	I	Yes	Yes	Yes
Hepatitis A	I	Yes	Yes	Yes
Tetanus	I	Yes	Yes	No
Polio, inactivated	I	Yes	Yes	No
Streptococcus pneumoniae[c] (polysaccharide vaccine [Pneumovax®])	I/I	Yes	Yes	Yes
Neisseria meningitidis[d]	I	Yes	Yes	No
Rabies[e]	I	Yes	Yes	No
Varicella	LA	Yes	No	Yes
BCG[f]	LA	Yes	No	No
Smallpox[g]	LA	No	No	No
Anthrax	I	No	No	No

BCG = bacille Calmette-Guérin.

[a]Whenever possible, the complete complement of vaccines should be administered before transplantation. Vaccines noted to be safe for administration after transplantation may not be sufficiently immunogenic after transplantation. Some vaccines, such as the 23-valent pneumococcal polysaccharide vaccine (Pneumovax®), should be repeated regularly (every 3-5 years) after transplantation.

[b]Routine vaccine schedule recommended prior to transplant and as early as possible in the course of disease; vaccine poorly immunogenic after transplantation, and accelerated schedules may be less immunogenic.

[c]Pneumococcal 23-valent polysaccharide vaccine (Pneumovax®) should be administered before transplantation and repeated every 3 to 5 years after initial vaccination.

[d]Certain patients (members of the military, travelers to high-risk areas, properdin deficient, terminal complement component deficient, those with functional or anatomic asplenia, college freshmen living on campus) are candidates for the meningococcal vaccine.

[e]Not routinely administered. Recommended for exposures or potential exposures due to vocation or avocation.

[f]The indications for BCG administration in the United States are limited to instances in which exposure to tuberculosis is unavoidable and where measures to prevent its spread have failed or are not possible.

[g]Transplant recipients who are face-to-face contacts of a patient with smallpox should be vaccinated; vaccinia immune globulin may be administered concurrently if available. Those who are less intimate contacts should not be vaccinated.

Reproduced with permission from Guidelines for vaccination of solid organ transplant candidates and recipients. Am J Transplant. 2004;4(Suppl 10):160-163. [PMID: 15504229] Copyright, 2004 John Wiley & Sons.

patients with increasing CMV levels, even without signs of disease, many transplant programs will begin treatment with ganciclovir.

Ganciclovir or valganciclovir prophylaxis is not only associated with markedly fewer cases of CMV disease and less serious disease, but it is also associated with a significantly reduced incidence of bacterial (including bacterial sepsis), herpes simplex virus, and fungal infections; bronchiolitis obliterans in lung transplant recipients; posttransplantation lymphoproliferative disease; and graft rejection. These findings suggest that CMV augments infections of many kinds and interferes with host defense mechanisms, perhaps locally and systemically. CMV often develops in organs concurrently with various other pathogens such as with bacterial pneumonia or polyomavirus BK in the kidneys.

Viruses other than CMV may also develop in transplant recipients. Epstein-Barr virus (EBV) is a common viral pathogen, especially in hematopoietic cell transplant patients. EBV may cause a self-limited infectious mononucleosis in these patients, and it presents similarly to classic mononucleosis in normal hosts. EBV is found in almost all patients with posttransplantation lymphoproliferative disease (PTLD), and it is believed to be pathogenic, especially considering its universal involvement in X-linked lymphoproliferative disease, which has many similarities to PTLD.

There is no specific antiviral treatment for EBV infection. Management of PTLD consists of decreasing or discontinuing immunosuppressive therapy and often leads to organ or graft failure. Coinfection with CMV and EBV occurs commonly in transplant recipients, and patients who receive effective anti-CMV prophylaxis have a reduced risk for developing PTLD.

Patients generally acquire polyomavirus BK virus (also referred to as BK virus) in early childhood, and it remains dormant for the life of the individual. However, in immuno-suppressed individuals, the virus may reactivate and cause symptomatic disease. Kidney transplant patients with BK virus infection may develop BK-related nephropathy, organ rejection, or ureteral strictures. Hematopoietic cell transplant recipients may develop reactivation of BK virus infection, usually manifested as hemorrhagic cystitis. Transplant patients with BK-related nephropathy have decoy cells in the urine (cells with intranuclear inclusions) and BK viremia. CMV infection and BK virus infection often occur simultaneously. Patients receiving adequate anti-CMV prophylaxis have a lower incidence of BK virus reactivation.

Although no approved treatment for the BK virus exists, several drugs, including leflunomide, cidofovir, and the fluoroquinolones, are being used experimentally with early promising results. Reversing immunosuppressive therapy may help to mitigate BK viral infection, but this approach may also lead to graft rejection.

Patients also acquire polyomavirus JC virus asymptomatically in childhood, and it remains dormant for the life of the individual. This virus may also reactivate in transplant recipients, causing progressive multifocal leukoencephalopathy, a uniformly progressive, and ultimately fatal, central nervous system disease. The only known effective treatment for polyomavirus JC virus infection is to reverse immunosuppressive therapy.

KEY POINTS

- Cytomegalovirus (CMV) infection occurs most commonly in the setting of a CMV-negative transplant recipient with an organ from a CMV-positive donor.

- Prophylaxis with ganciclovir, valganciclovir, or high-dose acyclovir is appropriate for transplant recipients at risk for cytomegalovirus infection.

- Epstein-Barr virus infection occurs frequently in transplant recipients and is thought to be pathogenic in posttransplantation lymphoproliferative disease.

- Cytomegalovirus prophylaxis can reduce the risk for posttransplantation lymphoproliferative disease.

- Polyomavirus BK virus infection in kidney transplant recipients may cause BK virus–related nephropathy, organ rejection, or ureteral strictures.

Fungi

Pneumocystis jirovecii is a common cause of pneumonia in the posttransplantation period as it is in most other settings of immunosuppression. *Pneumocystis* pneumonia in transplant recipients is potentially fatal if left untreated; however, therapy with trimethoprim-sulfamethoxazole is usually effective when the infection is diagnosed and treated early, especially in patients with no additional life-threatening complications. Patients who are allergic to sulfonamides may be treated with pentamidine, clindamycin plus primaquine, atovaquone, or trimetrexate plus leucovorin with or without dapsone. Trimethoprim-sulfamethoxazole is commonly given as prophylaxis to patients in the immediate posttransplantation period, at least until the immunosuppressive therapy is significantly tapered, and it is effective in preventing toxoplasmosis, nocardial, and listerial infections.

Candida albicans and non-*albicans* species often colonize the upper airways; therefore, determining whether antifungal treatment is required in transplant recipients in whom these organisms are identified can be challenging. *Candida* rarely causes a primary pneumonia, but in immunosuppressed patients, it may be found secondarily in bronchial secretions from patients infected with other organisms. Patients with *Candida* species in pulmonary secretions after recent lung transplantation are often treated. When a *Candida* species is identified in a culture specimen obtained from a nonsterile body site, it is difficult to determine whether antifungal treatment is necessary. However, if there are other culture sites from which *Candida* is grown concurrently, treatment should be more seriously considered. When *Candida* is grown in the urine culture of patients with an indwelling catheter, removal of the catheter and replacement with a fresh catheter are prudent if a catheter is still felt to be necessary. A repeat urine culture should be performed after removal of the initial catheter, especially if signs or symptoms persist. Often, the urine will become sterile on repeat culture, and no treatment will be required. However, if repeat urine cultures continue to grow the fungus, treatment should be more strongly considered. *Candida* species growing in the urine of a kidney transplant recipient should warrant further investigation for organ infection; treatment is required when there is pyuria, dysuria, systemic signs and symptoms of infection such as fever or leukocytosis, or signs of decreased renal function. When *Candida* species is grown in blood cultures, treatment should always be prescribed, and all vascular lines should be removed.

Fluconazole is usually effective for the treatment of posttransplantation candidal infection in most hospitals except when *Candida glabrata*, *Candida krusei*, or other resistant fungi are the cause. One of the newer triazoles such as voriconazole, an echinocandin such as caspofungin, or one of the amphotericin B preparations may be used in affected patients.

Aspergillus is a common pathogen in transplant recipients, associated with a high mortality rate (>50% in many studies), especially when not treated early and aggressively (see Fungal Infections). Voriconazole is the first-line empiric treatment when *Aspergillus* infection is suspected.

- *Pneumocystis* pneumonia in transplant recipients is potentially fatal if left untreated; however, therapy with trimethoprim-sulfamethoxazole is usually effective when the infection is diagnosed and treated early, especially in the absence of other life-threatening complications.

- *Candida* grown in the urine culture of a kidney transplant recipient should warrant further evaluation for organ infection; treatment is required in these patients.

- Fluconazole is usually effective for the treatment of posttransplantation candidal infection in most hospitals except when *Candida glabrata*, *Candida krusei*, or other resistant fungi are the cause.

- *Aspergillus* is a common pathogen in transplant recipients, associated with a high mortality rate (>50% in many studies), especially when not treated early and aggressively.

Parasites

Immunosuppressive therapy with antirejection drugs may exacerbate various parasitic diseases, and one of the most important of these is strongyloidiasis. *Strongyloides stercoralis* is a small roundworm with an autoinfectious cycle in humans, and it may be dormant for 30 or more years. It is found most commonly in tropical and subtropical areas but may also be found in temperate climates. Evaluation for *Strongyloides* should be done before transplantation because a state of hyperinfestation associated with an extremely high mortality rate (the *Strongyloides* hyperinfection syndrome) may occur during immunosuppression. This syndrome should be considered in transplant patients with signs of bacterial sepsis or pulmonary, gastrointestinal, or central nervous system disease, including meningitis. Ideally, *Strongyloides* carriers should be identified by pretransplantation stool examination or serology and then treated with thiabendazole or albendazole for preemptive eradication of this organism.

- Evaluation for *Strongyloides* should be done before transplantation because a state of hyperinfestation (the *Strongyloides* hyperinfection syndrome) may occur during immunosuppression, and this syndrome is associated with an extremely high mortality rate.

- *Strongyloides* carriers should be identified by pretransplantation stool examination or serology and are treated with thiabendazole or albendazole for preemptive eradication of this organism.

Bibliography

Bollée G, Sarfati C, Thiéry G, et al. Clinical picture of Pneumocystis jiroveci pneumonia in cancer patients. Chest. 2007 Oct;132(4):1305-1310. [PMID: 17934116]

Fishman JA. Infection in solid-organ transplant recipients. N Engl J Med. 2007;357(25):2601-2614. [PMID: 18094380]

Lewin KJ. Post-transplant lymphoproliferative disorders. Pathol Oncol Res. 1997;3(3):177-82. [PMID: 18470727]

Page RL 2nd, Miller GG, Lindenfeld J. Drug therapy in the heart transplant recipient: part IV: drug-drug interactions. Circulation. 2005;111(2):230-239. [PMID: 15657387]

Health Care–Associated Infections

Epidemiology

Health care–associated infections (HAIs) are infections that develop in hospitalized patients that were neither present nor incubating on hospital admission. In 2002, the Centers for Disease Control and Prevention (CDC) estimated that 1.7 million HAIs occurred (9.3 infections per 1000 patient days or 4.5 infections per 100 admissions). More than 98,000 deaths were attributed to HAIs. Of these, most deaths were due to pneumonia; other causes of death in order of decreasing frequency were bloodstream infections, urinary tract infections, and surgical site infections. Based on CDC estimates, the cost for treating HAIs in the United States is estimated to be $4.5 billion to $29 billion annually. The major types of HAIs are related to invasive or surgical procedures. Infection types and frequencies are shown in **Table 36**.

Prevention

HAIs are 1 of the 10 leading causes of death in the United States, accounting for 50% of all major complications of hospitalization. National and state agencies have recently instituted measures to monitor and prevent these infections. Many states have enacted legislation mandating public reporting of HAIs. The Centers for Medicare and Medicaid Services will not reimburse inpatient charges for care of selected preventable infections that were not present on hospital admission. These include urinary catheter–associated infections, vascular catheter–associated infections, and deep-chest surgical site infections (mediastinitis) after cardiac surgery. Ventilator-associated pneumonia, *Clostridium difficile* infections, and several others may soon be added.

Although quantification is not yet possible, many HAIs can be prevented. Hand hygiene is the single most important measure to reduce infection risk. All caregivers should clean their hands before and after contact with patients and their environment. Alcohol-based hand cleansers and soap and water are very effective for killing or removing most bacteria (although alcohol-based cleansers do not remove *C. difficile* spores). The patient-care environment must undergo extensive daily and post-discharge cleaning so that pathogens will not be passed from one patient to another. In addition,

TABLE 36 Hospital-Acquired Infections – Percentage and Common Pathogens

Infection	Percentage	Common Pathogens
Urinary tract infections	36	*Escherichia coli* and other gram-negative rods; enterococci[a]; yeast
Surgical site infections	20	*Staphylococcus aureus*[b]; coagulase-negative staphylococci; gram-negative rods
Primary bloodstream infections (BSIs), including catheter line–associated BSIs	11	*Staphylococcus aureus*; coagulase-negative staphylococci; gram-negative rods; yeast
Pneumonia	11	*Staphylococcus aureus*[b]; *Pseudomonas* species, *Acinetobacter* species, and other gram-negative rods[c]

Others
  Colitis
  Gastroenteritis
  Peritonitis
  Sinusitis
  Meningitis
  Decubitus ulcers
	22	*Clostridium difficile*; *Staphylococcus aureus*[b]; coagulase-negative staphylococci; gram-negative rods; enteric flora

[a]Often vancomycin-resistant enterococci.

[b]Often methicillin-resistant *Staphylococcus aureus*.

[c]Other causes: *Legionella pneumophila*.

appropriate immunizations of health care workers can prevent infection in both workers and patients.

Transmission-based precautions are required in certain situations. Patients who are colonized or infected with certain organisms can serve as vectors for transmission to others. Examples of multidrug-resistant organisms requiring transmission-based precautions include methicillin-resistant *Staphylococcus aureus*, vancomycin-resistant enterococci, *Acinetobacter* species, and *C. difficile*. Use of barriers such as gowns, gloves, and masks are necessary to prevent cross-contamination of these pathogens. Equipment can also become contaminated. Therefore, dedicated equipment should be used for patients with pathogens requiring transmission-based precautions, or equipment should be thoroughly cleaned before being reused. Devices such as indwelling urinary catheters, endotracheal tubes, and central-line vascular catheters should be used only when necessary and removed as soon as possible.

Colonization with multidrug-resistant organisms may go unrecognized in some patients. Surveillance testing can identify these patients so that transmission-based precautions can be initiated. Such testing has been associated with a significant reduction in HAIs due to multidrug-resistant organisms.

Specific infection types have known risk factors, and interventions can be coupled or bundled together to reduce risk. Devices such as indwelling catheters, endotracheal tubes, and central-line catheters should be used only when necessary and removed as soon as possible.

Specific Health Care–Associated Infections

Urinary Tract Infections

Urinary tract infections (UTIs) are the most common HAIs. Most are caused by indwelling urinary catheters. Approximately 1 million infections occur annually. Bacteriuria occurs in 3% to 10% of catheterized patients daily, and incidence is directly related to the duration of catheterization. The treatment cost for each hospital-acquired UTI is approximately $675, with an increase to $2836 when bacteremia develops. Overall costs to the health care system exceed $400 million annually.

UTIs are generally considered unavoidable in patients requiring indwelling catheters for more than 4 days, primarily because of the ubiquity of bacterial colonization over time. An estimated 5% of patients will become colonized for each day of catheterization beyond 2 days, and 10% to 25% of these patients will develop symptomatic UTIs. Secondary bacteremia occurs in approximately 3% of patients and is associated with an increased risk of death (13% to 30% mortality rate). Common pathogens include *Escherichia coli*, other gram-negative rods, and entero-cocci. These pathogens previously had predicted drug suscepti-bilities and were usually treated with fluoroquinolones or trimethoprim-sulfamethoxazole. However, increased drug resist-ance is now being reported.

Prevention

The most effective way to prevent UTIs is to decrease catheter use. Devices should be used for specific indications. Examples include (1) to diagnose pathologic findings in the lower urinary tract or the cause of urinary retention, (2) to monitor fluid status in acutely ill patients when this directly impacts medical treatment, and (3) to manage patients with stage 3 or 4 pressure ulcers on the buttocks. However, urinary catheters often are used for convenience, which significantly increases the risk of UTIs. If the catheter is needed, measures are required to decrease the risk of bacteriuria and subsequent infection. These include hand washing, using an aseptic tech-nique and sterile equipment for catheter insertion and care, securing the catheter properly, maintaining unobstructed urine flow and closed sterile drainage, and considering use of antibacterial-coated catheters.

Surgical Site Infections

Surgical site infections (SSIs) are the second most common cause of hospital-acquired infections, accounting for approx-imately 20% of cases. These infections are increasing because the number of surgical procedures performed in the United States is increasing annually. SSIs are associated with increased costs and poorer outcomes in hospitalized patients. They prolong hospital stays by an average of 7.4 days and increase costs by $400 to $2600. Costs and out-comes secondary to these infections vary by surgery type. SSIs following cardiac surgery are associated with signifi-cantly higher costs, ranging from $8200 to $42,000.

The risk of infection is influenced by complex interac-tions, including (1) patient-related factors such as extremes of age, host immunity, nutritional status, and the presence of diabetes mellitus; (2) procedure-related factors, such as place-ment of a foreign body, duration of surgery, skin antisepsis, and the magnitude of tissue trauma; (3) microbial factors that mediate tissue adherence and invasion or that enable bacteria to survive the host immune response and concurrent colo-nization or infection; and (4) factors related to perioperative antimicrobial prophylaxis.

Additional risks for SSIs include corticosteroid ther-apy, smoking, body mass index (BMI) greater than 30, a low preoperative serum albumin level or malnutrition, remote infection at the time of surgery, the need for peri-operative transfusions, preoperative colonization of the nares, and hypoxemia.

Prevention

Approximately 40% to 60% of SSIs can be prevented by implementing the following four components of care, which are supported by the Centers for Medicare and Medicaid Services, the Hospital Quality Alliance, the Institute for Healthcare Improvement, and many other groups.

Antimicrobial Prophylaxis

A short course of preoperative antimicrobial prophylaxis has been shown to reduce the risk of SSIs. The goal of prophy-laxis is to decrease the number of organisms that can con-taminate the surgical site to a level that cannot overwhelm host defenses. Optimal surgical prophylaxis requires ade-quate concentrations of antimicrobial agents in the serum, tissues, and wound during the entire time that the incision is open and at risk for bacterial contamination. Prophylaxis begins preoperatively. The first antimicrobial dose should be given within 60 minutes before the incision is made (120 minutes if a fluoroquinolone or vancomycin is indicated), be active against all potential contaminants, be safe and inex-pensive, and have the least effect on normal body flora. Antimicrobial prophylaxis should generally be discontinued within 24 hours postoperatively. This recommendation is supported by the published literature and is endorsed by the Centers for Medicare and Medicaid Services Surgical Infection Prevention Project.

Other variables such as use of surgical scrub by operat-ing room personnel, preoperative skin preparation, and the operating room environment can also influence surgical site infection risk.

Preoperative Hair Removal

Numerous studies have shown that razor shaving is associated with decreased skin integrity caused by nicks and cuts on the skin surface. If hair is removed, this should be done immedi-ately before surgery and preferably using electric hair clippers.

Glucose Control during Cardiac Surgery

Prospective randomized studies have shown that patients with diabetes who are undergoing cardiac surgery have a reduced risk of infection if perioperative glucose control is provided. This is done by using a continuous intravenous insulin infu-sion to maintain serum glucose at a level of less than 200 mg/dL (11.1 mmol/L).

Avoidance of Hypothermia

Hypothermia causes numerous perioperative adverse out-comes, including myocardial events, coagulopathy with increased blood loss and transfusion requirements, post-operative wound infections, and prolonged hospitaliza-tions. Recent data suggest that better intraoperative and postoperative temperature control of the patient may reduce these risks.

- The most effective way to decrease hospital-acquired urinary tract infections is to avoid unnecessary catheterization.

- Short courses of preoperative antimicrobial prophylaxis can reduce the risk of surgical site infections as can appropriate preoperative hair removal, body temperature control during surgery, and use of glucose control in patients with diabetes mellitus who are undergoing cardiac surgery.

Primary Bloodstream Infections

Primary bloodstream infections (BSIs) occur without a recognizable focus of infection at another anatomic site. The increased use of intravascular catheters is believed to contribute to the large increase in BSIs.

BSIs typically are caused by microbes from the skin that migrate along the external surface of catheters. Approximately 50,000 catheter line–associated BSIs occur in the United States annually. Reported case fatality rates have ranged from 14% to 40%.

Patients surviving a hospital-acquired BSI require an additional 7 to 24 days of hospitalization. The longer stays and additional costs of antibiotics and diagnostic tests significantly add to health care costs, and overall excess costs are reported to range from $3517 to $33,268 per patient.

Prevention

In 2004, the CDC reported the median rate for catheter line–associated BSIs in ICUs of all types ranged from 1.8 to 5.2 infections per 1000 catheter days. Hospitals have always compared their rates with the CDC mean. If their rates were at or below the mean, little was done to try to reduce the rate of infections even more. In 2001, a regional initiative involving 32 hospitals in western Pennsylvania was begun with the goal of eliminating these infections in ICUs. The intervention was multifaceted and followed published CDC guidelines. It consisted of five components:

1. Promotion of targeted, evidence-based catheter insertion practices (that is, use of maximum sterile barrier precautions during catheter insertion, use of chlorhexidine for skin disinfection before insertion, avoidance of femoral artery insertion sites, use of recommended insertion site dressing-care practices, and removal of catheters when no longer indicated).

2. Promotion of an educational module about central line–associated BSIs and strategies for preventing these infections.

3. Promotion of standardized recording tools for documenting adherence to recommended catheter insertion practices.

4. Promotion of a standardized list of contents for catheter insertion kits that included all supplies required to adhere to recommended insertion practices.

5. Provision of feedback of individual unit-specific rates and aggregate regional catheter line–associated BSI rates.

Over 4 years, the pooled infection rate decreased by 68%, from 4.31 to 1.36 per 1000 catheter days ($P < 0.001$) from April 2001 through March 2005. Many of the participating hospitals subsequently achieved even lower infection rates and have sustained these reductions. Many other facilities and regions have successfully implemented this bundled approach to reducing central line–associated BSIs. Such bundles are now widely used and are endorsed by the Institute for Healthcare Improvement.

- The increased use of intravascular catheters is believed to contribute to the large increase in bloodstream infections.

- Health care bundles to prevent catheter insertion–associated bloodstream infections, including evidence-based practices, education modules, standardized recording tools, standardized catheter-insertion kits, and provisions for providing feedback, are now widely used in hospitals.

Hospital-Acquired Pneumonia

Hospital-acquired pneumonia (HAP) is defined as pneumonia that develops at least 48 hours after hospitalization and includes ventilator-associated pneumonia, non–ventilator-associated pneumonia, and postoperative pneumonia. Approximately 300,000 cases of HAP occur annually in the United States, and mortality rates range from 30% to 70%. HAP increases the hospital stay by 7 to 9 days and is associated with higher costs of medical care.

The most common cause of HAP is microaspiration of bacteria that colonize the oropharynx and upper airways in seriously ill patients. Gram-negative bacilli and *Staphylococcus aureus* are the most common pathogens, and the number of drug-resistant organisms continues to escalate. Endotracheal intubation with mechanical ventilation poses the greatest overall risk (**Table 37**). Endotracheal intubation breaches airway defenses, impairs cough and mucociliary clearance, and facilitates microaspiration of bacteria-laden secretions that pool above the inflated endotracheal tube cuff. Consequently, 85% of all cases of HAP occur in ventilated patients. Major risk factors for postoperative pneumonia are age older than 70 years, abdominal or thoracic surgery, and dependent functional status.

The diagnosis is based on clinical presentation, leukocytosis, and new or changing chest radiographic findings. Bronchoscopic samplings from the lower respiratory tract and/or blood cultures can help identify the pathogen.

TABLE 37 Risk Factors for Hospital-Acquired Pneumonia

Host related	Advanced age
	Severity of illness
	Trauma or head injury
	Poor nutritional status
	Coma
	Impaired airway reflexes
	Chronic obstructive pulmonary disease
	Neuromuscular disease
Device related	Endotracheal tube
	Nasogastric tube
	Bronchoscopy
Drug related	Immunosuppressive therapy
	Peptic ulcer medications
Miscellaneous	Thoracic or upper abdominal surgery
	Duration of surgery
	Duration of hospitalization
	Large-volume aspiration

Patients requiring mechanically assisted ventilation may also have worsening oxygenation and increased tracheal secretions. However, no single symptom, sign, or radiographic finding is sensitive or specific enough to enable a diagnosis, and several clinical variables must be considered.

Prevention

Removing the endotracheal tube as quickly as possible will reduce the risk for infection. Patients should have daily "sedation vacations" and be assessed for extubation readiness. While intubated, patients should be in a semi-upright or upright position. Mouth care may also reduce the risk of infection. Continuous aspiration of subglottic secretions using a specially designed endotracheal tube attached to a suction device may reduce the risk for aspiration, but data about this procedure are inconclusive. Selective decontamination of the oropharynx (using topical gentamicin, colistin, or vancomycin) or of the entire gastrointestinal tract is controversial and not uniformly recommended.

KEY POINT

- The most effective way to reduce hospital-acquired pneumonia is to remove endotracheal tubes as quickly as possible, maintain the patient in an upright or semi-upright position, and perform subglottic suctioning.

Bibliography

Centers for Disease Control and Prevention. Guideline for Isolation Precautions: Preventing Transmission of Infectious Agents in Healthcare Settings. www.cdc.gov/ncidod/dhqp/gl_isolation.html. Published June, 2007. Accessed on July 27, 2009.

Centers for Disease Control and Prevention. Guidelines for prevention of nosocomial pneumonia. MMWR Morb Mortal Wkly Rep. MMWR Recomm Rep. 1997;46(RR-1):1-79. [PMID: 9036304]

Furnary A, Zerr K, Grunkemeier G, Starr A. Continuous intravenous insulin infusion reduces the incidence of deep sternal wound infection in diabetic patients after cardiac surgical procedures. Ann Thorac Surg. 1999;67(2):352-360 . [PMID: 10197653]

Institute for Healthcare Improvement (IHI). Prevent Central Line-Associated Bloodstream Infections. www.ihi.org/IHI/Programs/Campaign/CentralLineInfection.htm. Accessed on July 27, 2009.

Kurz A, Sessler D, Lenhardt R. Perioperative normothermia to reduce the incidence of surgical-wound infection and shorten hospitalization. Study of Wound Infection and Temperature Group. New Engl J Med. 1996;334(19):1209-1215. [PMID: 8606715]

Mangram AJ, Horan TC, Pearson ML, Silver LC, Jarvis WR, et al; The Hospital Infection Control Practices Advisory Committee. Guideline for Prevention of Surgical Site Infection, 1999. Infect Control Hosp Epidemiol. 1999; 20(4):247-278. [PMID: 10219875]

Muto CA, Jernigan JA, Ostrowksy BE, et al. Guideline for preventing nosocomial transmission of multidrug-resistant strains of Staphylococcus aureus and Enterococcus. Infect Control Hosp Epidemiol. 2003;24(5):362-386. [PMID: 12785411]

O'Grady NP, Alexander M, Dellinger EP, et al. Guidelines for the prevention of intravascular catheter-related infections. MMWR Recomm Rep. 2002;51(RR-10):1-29. [PMID: 12233868]

Pronovost P, Needham D, Berenholtz S, et al. An intervention to decrease catheter-related bloodstream infections in the ICU [erratum in N Engl J Med. 2007;356(25):2660]. N Engl J Med. 2006; 355(26):2725-2732. [PMID: 17192537]

Wong ES. Guideline for prevention of catheter-associated urinary tract infections. Am J Infect Control. 1983;11(1):28-33. [PMID: 6551151]

HIV/AIDS

Since the first case of HIV infection was reported more than 25 years ago, much has been learned about its epidemiology and treatment. In industrialized countries where highly active antiretroviral therapy (HAART) is readily available, HIV/AIDS has evolved from a once fatal illness to a more chronic, manageable disease. In resource-deprived countries, HIV/AIDS continues to have devastating effects on individuals, family units, and the general community owing to its associated high morbidity and mortality rates.

Epidemiology

HIV/AIDS refers to all cases of HIV infection, whether or not the infection has progressed to AIDS. The diagnosis of AIDS is based on surveillance case definitions established by the Centers for Disease Control and Prevention (CDC), which are the same for adults, adolescents, and children (**Table 38**).

At the end of 2003, an estimated 1,039,000 to 1,185,000 people in the United States were living with HIV/AIDS. In 2005, 37,163 cases of HIV/AIDS in adults, adolescents, and children were diagnosed. The largest

TABLE 38 Diagnosis of AIDS – Centers for Disease Control and Prevention

Definitive AIDS Diagnosis (with or without laboratory evidence of HIV infection)

1. Candidiasis of esophagus, trachea, bronchi, or lungs

2. Cryptococcosis, extrapulmonary

3. Cryptosporidiosis with diarrhea persisting for >1 month

4. Cytomegalovirus infection of an organ other than the liver, spleen, or lymph nodes

5. Herpes simplex virus infection causing a mucocutaneous ulcer that persists >1 month, or bronchitis, pneumonia, or esophagitis of any duration

6. Kaposi sarcoma in a patient <60 years

7. Lymphoma of the brain (primary) in a patient <60 years

8. *Mycobacterium avium* complex or *Mycobacterium kansasii* infection, disseminated (at a site other than or in addition to the lungs, skin, or cervical or hilar lymph nodes)

9. *Pneumocystis jirovecii* pneumonia

10. Progressive multifocal leukoencephalopathy

11. Toxoplasmosis of the brain

Definitive AIDS Diagnosis (with laboratory evidence of HIV infection)

1. Coccidioidomycosis, disseminated (at a site other than or in addition to the lungs or cervical or hilar lymph nodes)

2. HIV encephalopathy

3. Histoplasmosis, disseminated (at a site other than or in addition to the lungs or cervical or hilar lymph nodes)

4. Isosporiasis with diarrhea persisting >1 month

5. Kaposi sarcoma at any age

6. Lymphoma of the brain (primary) at any age

7. Other non-Hodgkin lymphoma of B-cell or unknown immunologic phenotype

8. Any mycobacterial disease caused by mycobacteria other than *Mycobacterium tuberculosis*, disseminated (at a site other than or in addition to the lungs, skin, or cervical or hilar lymph nodes)

9. Disease caused by extrapulmonary *M. tuberculosis*

10. *Salmonella* (nontyphoid) septicemia, recurrent

11. HIV wasting syndrome

12. CD4 cell count <200/μL or a CD4 lymphocyte percentage below 14%

13. Pulmonary tuberculosis

14. Recurrent pneumonia

15. Invasive cervical cancer

Presumptive AIDS Diagnosis (with laboratory evidence of HIV infection)

1. Candidiasis of esophagus: (a) recent onset of retrosternal pain on swallowing, and (b) oral candidiasis

2. Cytomegalovirus retinitis: characteristic appearance on serial ophthalmoscopic examinations

3. Mycobacteriosis: specimen from stool or normally sterile body fluids or tissue from a site other than the lungs, skin, or cervical or hilar lymph nodes showing acid-fast bacilli of a species not identified by culture

4. Kaposi sarcoma: erythematous or violaceous plaque-like lesion on skin or mucous membrane

5. *Pneumocystis jirovecii* pneumonia: (a) a history of dyspnea on exertion or nonproductive cough of recent onset (within the past 3 months); and (b) chest radiographic evidence of diffuse bilateral interstitial infiltrates or gallium scan evidence of diffuse bilateral pulmonary disease; and (c) arterial blood gas analysis showing an arterial P_{O_2} <70 mm Hg or a low respiratory diffusing capacity of carbon monoxide (DLCO) of <80% of predicted value or an increase in the alveolar-arterial oxygen tension gradient; and (d) no evidence of bacterial pneumonia

6. Toxoplasmosis of the brain: (a) recent onset of a focal neurologic abnormality consistent with intracranial disease or a reduced level of consciousness; and (b) brain imaging evidence of a lesion having a mass effect or the radiographic appearance of which is enhanced by injection of contrast medium; and (c) serum antibody to toxoplasmosis or successful response to therapy for toxoplasmosis

7. Recurrent pneumonia: (a) more than one episode in a 1-year period; and (b) acute pneumonia (new symptoms, signs, or radiographic evidence not presented earlier) diagnosed on clinical or radiographic grounds by the patient's physician

8. Pulmonary tuberculosis: (a) apical or miliary infiltrate; and (b) radiographic and clinical response to antituberculosis therapy

estimated proportion of HIV/AIDS diagnoses were among men who have sex with men, followed by adults and adolescents infected through heterosexual contact. The CDC has developed a new and innovative system designed to estimate the number of new HIV infections (or incidence) in the United States in a given year. Using this new technology, the CDC estimates that 56,300 new HIV infections occurred in the United States in 2006.

Surveillance data on HIV infections provide a more complete picture of the HIV/AIDS epidemic and the need for prevention and care services than does the picture provided by AIDS data alone. As of April 2008, all 50 states, the District of Columbia, and 5 dependent areas—American Samoa, Guam, the Northern Mariana Islands, Puerto Rico, and the U.S. Virgin Islands—use the same confidential name-based reporting system to collect HIV and AIDS data.

HIV transmission patterns have changed over time. Heterosexual transmission accounts for a growing number of new AIDS cases, increasing from 3% in 1985 to 31% in 2005. Over the same period, the proportion of cases occurring in men who have sex with men has decreased from 65% to 43%. In 1985, injection drug use accounted for 19% of the cases, peaking at 39% in 1997, and finally dropping to 28% in 2005.

The proportion of women with newly diagnosed AIDS has increased from 8% in 1985 to 27% in 2005. Based on CDC prevalence estimates, approximately 300,000 women in the United States are living with HIV/AIDS. Black women accounted for 66% of new cases in 2005, whereas Hispanic and white women each accounted for 16%.

In the United States, the HIV/AIDS epidemic has disproportionately affected black persons compared with persons of other races and ethnicities. According to the 2005 U.S. Census figures, black persons constituted 12% of the general population, but by the end of 2005, black persons accounted for 49% of the estimated 37,163 newly diagnosed HIV/AIDS cases in this country.

The epidemiology of HIV/AIDS worldwide is quite different. According to the Joint United Nations Program on AIDS/HIV (UNAIDS), an estimated 33.2 million people were living with HIV/AIDS by the end of 2007, and an estimated 2.5 million people were newly infected with the virus in 2007. Sub-Saharan Africa remains the most seriously affected region with an estimated 22.5 million cases, constituting a prevalence of 12.5%.

KEY POINTS

- HIV/AIDS refers to all cases of HIV infection, whether or not the infection has progressed to AIDS.

- Approximately 1.2 million people in the United States are living with HIV/AIDS.

- The largest estimated proportion of HIV/AIDS diagnoses is among men who have sex with men, followed by adults and adolescents infected through heterosexual contact.

Pathophysiology and Natural History

HIV belongs to a family of retroviruses. There are three subfamilies of retroviruses, two of which (oncoviruses and lentiviruses) cause human disease and a third (spumavirus) that is not known to be associated with human disease. HIV is a member of the lentiviruses or slow viruses, which have long incubation periods and may take years to replicate and present clinically in infected patients.

The HIV genome consists of three structural genes: *gag*, *pol*, and *env*. The *gag* gene codes for viral capsid proteins p15, p17, and p24; *env* encodes for viral envelope proteins gp120 and gp41; and *pol* encodes for proteins responsible for viral replication and reverse transcriptase.

The most common mode of transmission involves deposition of HIV on genital or rectal mucosal surfaces or direct inoculation of HIV into the bloodstream by injection drug use. Envelope protein 120 (gp120) has a high affinity for the CD4 molecule on helper T lymphocytes. After initial binding, HIV must bind to a specific co-receptor (CCR5 or CXCR4) followed by fusion of HIV and the host cell membrane. After fusion, viral DNA is inserted into the cytoplasm of the host cell, allowing reverse transcriptase to convert it to proviral DNA. At this point, incorporation of the viral DNA is facilitated by the viral enzyme integrase. Once the viral gene products are transcribed and assembled, HIV protease cleaves the precursor proteins for release to resume the cycle.

About 40% to 90% of persons with primary HIV infection develop an acute mononucleosis-like syndrome that usually occurs within 2 to 6 weeks following the initial infection. This has also been called the acute retroviral syndrome and is associated with signs and symptoms resulting from initial HIV infection and dissemination (**Table 39**). The duration of illness is usually less than 2 weeks. Health care providers should consider a diagnosis of acute retroviral syndrome in patients presenting with a compatible history and obtain measurement of the plasma HIV RNA viral load and an assay for HIV antibodies. Acute infection is defined by detectable HIV RNA in the plasma and a negative or indeterminate HIV antibody assay.

Over time, persons infected with HIV have a progressive loss of CD4 lymphocytes. Although the average time from initial infection with HIV to development of AIDS is approximately 10 years, the rate of disease progression varies considerably among infected persons. Numerous factors contribute to the rate of disease progression, including the plasma HIV RNA viral load, CD4 cell count, age, socioeconomic status, and host genetics. On average, an infected person loses 50 to 80 CD4 cells/μL per year. Some persons have rapid progression, and others are considered to have long-term nonprogression or to be elite controllers (persons who are infected with HIV but who maintain a plasma HIV

TABLE 39 Signs and Symptoms Suggestive of Acute Retroviral Syndrome

Signs and Symptoms	Frequency (%)
Fever	96
Lymphadenopathy	74
Exudative pharyngitis	70
Rash	70
Myalgia or arthralgia	54
Diarrhea	32
Headache	32
Nausea and vomiting	27
Hepatosplenomegaly	14
Weight loss	13
Thrush	12
Neurologic symptoms	12
Meningoencephalitis	
Peripheral neuropathy	
Facial palsy	
Guillain-Barré syndrome	
Brachial neuritis	
Cognitive impairment or psychosis	

RNA viral load of less than 50 copies/mL without antiretroviral therapy).

KEY POINTS

- About 40% to 90% of persons with primary HIV infection develop acute retroviral syndrome, which is a mononucleosis-like syndrome that usually occurs within 2 to 6 weeks following the initial infection.

- Patients with acute retroviral syndrome have a detectable plasma HIV RNA viral load and a negative or indeterminate HIV antibody assay.

- Elite controllers are persons who are seropositive for HIV but maintain a plasma HIV RNA viral load of less than 50 copies/mL without antiretroviral therapy.

Screening and Diagnosis of HIV Infection

The CDC has recently broadened its recommendations for HIV testing and now recommends routine HIV testing in all health care settings (including emergency departments) for any patient aged 13 to 64 years. Patients must be told that such a test will be performed and may decline testing (opt-out screening). Separate written consent is not required. General consent for medical care is considered sufficient to include consent for HIV testing, and prevention counseling is not required as part of HIV diagnostic testing or screening programs in health care settings.

All patients beginning treatment for tuberculosis should also be screened routinely for HIV infection (see *Mycobacterium tuberculosis* Infection). Additionally, all patients being treated for sexually transmitted diseases (STDs), including those attending STD clinics, should be screened routinely for HIV during each visit for a new sign or symptom, regardless of whether or not the patient is known or suspected to have specific risk behaviors for HIV infection.

Persons engaged in high-risk behavior should be tested annually. Those likely to be at high risk include injection drug users and their sex partners, persons who exchange sex for money or drugs, sex partners of HIV-infected persons, and men who have sex with men or heterosexual persons who themselves or whose sex partners have had more than one sex partner since their most recent HIV test.

These CDC testing guidelines were revised because of the many persons who have undiagnosed HIV infection or who are diagnosed late in the course of infection. Persons who are infected but are not aware of their condition are unable to receive treatment that can keep them healthy and extend their lives and are also unable to protect their sex partners or drug-use partners from becoming infected.

In clinical practice, the standard screening procedure is an enzyme-linked immunosorbent assay (ELISA) followed by a confirmatory Western blot assay if the initial ELISA is positive. The ELISA is approximately 99% specific and 98.5% sensitive; the Western blot assay is nearly 100% sensitive and 100% specific in diagnosing chronically infected persons. The Western blot detects antibodies to HIV proteins, including core (p17, p24, p55), polymerase (p31, p51, p66), and envelope (gp41, gp120, gp160) proteins. Specific criteria are used to interpret a Western blot assay (**Table 40**). HIV antibodies generally appear in the circulation 2 to 12 weeks following initial infection. During this period between initial infection and the development of antibodies (the "window period") of up to 2 to 3 months, serologic test results are negative. Therefore, recently exposed persons whose initial ELISA is negative should have repeat testing at 6 weeks and 3 months.

The development of rapid serologic tests has made HIV testing easier. These tests all provide results in 20 minutes or less and have sensitivities and specificities that exceed 99.5%.

TABLE 40 Interpretation of Western Blot Assay

Result	Pattern
Positive	Reactivity to gp120 plus either gp41 or p24
Negative	Nonreactive
Indeterminate	Presence of any other band pattern not meeting criteria for a positive result

gp = glycoprotein.

A negative test is considered a definitive negative result unless the person is in the "window period," and a positive test is considered a preliminary positive result and should be confirmed with a Western blot assay.

KEY POINTS

- The Centers for Disease Control and Prevention now recommends routine HIV testing in all health care settings (including emergency departments) for any patient aged 13 to 64 years after the patient is notified that testing will be performed.
- Separate written consent for HIV testing is not required.
- Standard HIV screening is done by an enzyme-linked immunosorbent assay (ELISA) followed by a confirmatory Western blot assay if the initial ELISA is positive.
- Rapid serologic HIV tests with high sensitivities and specificities are available that provide results in 20 minutes or less.

Management

Initiation of Care

Ideally, the initial encounter occurs in the outpatient setting with an asymptomatic person who has been electively tested and found positive for HIV. However, the first encounter often occurs in the office or hospital following the development of signs and symptoms of immune compromise or opportunistic infection. In this setting, some patients may not be aware of their HIV status.

The first step in establishing care is to determine or confirm the patient's HIV status. Pretest counseling should include an assessment of risk behaviors, a discussion of methods to avoid the transmission of HIV, an explanation of HIV and the tests performed to detect HIV antibodies, a clarification of the differences between HIV infection and AIDS, and a discussion of the confidentiality of test results. The initial test is an ELISA, and if it is positive, a Western blot assay is done before the results are shared with the patient.

The initial evaluation includes a complete history and physical examination. The patient's social support system should be evaluated, and the reaction to learning about HIV infection should be explored, because anxiety, depression, and adjustment disorders commonly occur early in the course of infection. If the patient has a previously established diagnosis of HIV/AIDS, a complete antiretroviral treatment history should be obtained. The patient should be educated about precautions needed to avoid virus transmission as well as the indications and goals of antiretroviral therapy and the need for preventive care. Ideally, patients should have some knowledge of resistance mechanisms and understand the importance of

adhering to the treatment regimen. Providing appropriate counseling and education generally requires several visits.

Laboratory Testing

Baseline Laboratory Studies

Laboratory testing is performed to assess immune status and rule out concomitant diseases or exposure to previous infections possibly requiring treatment, prophylaxis, or immunization. Assessment of liver, bone marrow, and kidney function is important. Serum lipid levels should be measured before beginning antiretroviral therapy because hyperlipidemia can be a complication of HIV infection or antiretroviral therapy. Required laboratory studies are listed in **Table 41**.

HIV RNA Viral Load Testing

Viral load testing measures the amount of HIV-1 RNA present in the plasma. The plasma HIV RNA viral load is the best predictor of prognosis and the rate of decline of CD4 lymphocytes. Higher HIV RNA concentrations are associated with greater amounts of viral replication, more rapid decreases in CD4 lymphocytes, and increased chances of developing

TABLE 41 Laboratory Tests for Patients with HIV Infection	
Test	**Frequency**[a]
HIV antibody testing	Baseline
CD4 cell count	Every 3-4 months
HIV RNA viral load (polymerase chain reaction)	Baseline $\times 2$, every 3-4 months, and 1 month after change in therapy
Complete blood count, differential, platelet count	Baseline, then every 6 months
Aminotransferases, glucose, and creatinine	Baseline, then every 6 months
Fasting lipid profile	Baseline, then every 6-12 months if on therapy
Hepatitis B surface antigen (HBsAg) and antibody to hepatitis B surface antigen (anti-HBs)	Baseline
Hepatitis C virus antibody (anti-HCV)	Baseline
Toxoplasma IgG antibody	Baseline
Cytomegalovirus IgG antibody	Baseline
Tuberculin skin test using purified protein derivative	Baseline, then annually
Rapid plasma reagin	Baseline, then annually
Pap smear	Baseline, then every 6 months $\times 2$, then annually if normal
Glucose-6-phosphate dehydrogenase	Baseline
Genotype or phenotype resistance tests	Baseline

[a]Frequency may vary depending on individual patient.

AIDS or dying. The viral load is used to assess and monitor the efficacy of antiretroviral medications and to guide ongoing treatment decisions.

Several factors can influence the viral load. Improper handling of specimens may cause erroneously low values. Immune stimulation as a result of opportunistic infections, blood transfusions, herpesvirus outbreaks, and immunizations may transiently increase HIV RNA levels. Therefore, the viral load should not be measured for 4 weeks after any of these events.

A change in viral load is not considered significant unless it is at least a 0.5-log change, that is, a threefold difference in the number of copies/mL. An "undetectable" viral load refers to a result that is below the lower threshold of the test. The most common test currently used can measure HIV RNA of less than 50 copies/mL. These ultrasensitive assays are best suited for monitoring viral loads in patients on antiretroviral therapy. The viral load should be checked 4 weeks after antiretroviral therapy is initiated or changed. A 90% to 99% reduction in the plasma HIV RNA load usually occurs within the first 2 weeks of initiating effective therapy. Subsequent decreases are more gradual, reflecting the clearance of chronically infected T cells or macrophages. Current recommendations target a viral load of less than 50 copies/mL as the goal of antiretroviral therapy, because this level appears to be associated with more durable viral suppression. This value should be achieved within 6 months of beginning effective therapy.

Once the viral load is undetectable, it should be monitored every 3 to 4 months using an ultrasensitive assay. The viral load should also be measured every 3 to 4 months in patients who are not on antiretroviral therapy. An undetectable viral load does not mean that the virus is no longer present in the body or that cure has been achieved. Individuals with undetectable viral loads are still considered infectious.

Preventive Care

A number of preventive measures contribute to disease avoidance for patients with HIV infection. These include routine immunizations, cervical cancer screening, and medications for primary and secondary prophylaxis of opportunistic diseases. Routine immunizations include pneumococcal vaccine every 5 years and influenza vaccine annually. Hepatitis A and B vaccines should be administered unless the presence of protective antibodies is documented. Some clinicians defer immunizations in patients with CD4 cell counts below 200/μL because an immunologic response to vaccines may be blunted.

A tuberculin skin test using purified protein derivative should be performed annually. In patients with HIV infection, a tuberculin skin test resulting in 5 or more mm of induration is considered positive. Treatment for latent tuberculosis infection is indicated for all patients who have a positive tuberculin skin test or have had recent contact with a person with tuberculosis once active tuberculosis has been excluded by clinical evaluation and chest radiography (see *Mycobacterium tuberculosis* Infection).

Women with HIV infection have a higher incidence of cervical dysplasia and invasive cervical carcinoma, and many experts therefore suggest more frequent Pap smear screenings in these patients. One approach is to obtain two Pap smears 6 months apart and then annually if results are normal. Patients with abnormalities should be referred for colposcopy. Suppressive therapy for herpes simplex virus is recommended for both men and women with HIV infection who have frequent outbreaks of anogenital herpes simplex virus infection.

Several drugs have been shown to provide effective prophylaxis against opportunistic infections in patients with HIV infection and to prolong life in some patients. The CD4 cell count is an indicator of immune competence. Recommendations regarding when to initiate prophylaxis are based on CD4 cell count levels below which these infections are likely to occur (**Table 42**). Many patients who receive highly active antiretroviral therapy (HAART) have marked increases in their CD4 cell counts, which appear to reflect immune reconstitution with initial return of memory cells, and, later, of naïve CD4 lymphocytes. Recent guidelines recommend discontinuing primary and secondary prophylaxis for certain opportunistic infections when a sustained (3- to 6-month) rise in the CD4 cell count occurs above the threshold for prophylaxis initiation. Data support the withdrawal of primary and secondary prophylaxis for *Pneumocystis jirovecii* pneumonia, *Mycobacterium avium* complex infection, and toxoplasmosis. Data also support the withdrawal of secondary prophylaxis for cytomegalovirus infection after the CD4 cell count increases to 100 to 150/μL. If the count subsequently falls below the threshold for initiating prophylaxis, prophylactic therapy should be resumed.

Because of the improved longevity in patients with HIV infection, it is important to perform standard health maintenance measures, including screening for breast cancer, colorectal cancer, and hyperlipidemia.

KEY POINTS

- All patients with newly diagnosed HIV infection require a complete history and physical examination; laboratory studies to evaluate liver, kidney, and bone marrow function; and a lipid profile.

- In patients with newly diagnosed HIV infection, the plasma HIV RNA viral load is the best predictor of prognosis and of rate of decline of CD4 lymphocytes.

- Patients with HIV with undetectable HIV RNA viral loads are still infectious.

- A tuberculin skin test using purified protein derivative should be performed annually in patients with HIV infection.

- Preventive measures in patients with HIV infection include routine immunizations and breast, cervical, and colorectal cancer screening.

Complications of HIV Infection in the HAART Era

Metabolic Disorders

The use of HAART has resulted in tremendous improvements in morbidity and mortality in patients with HIV infection. However, use of these agents is also associated with morphologic body changes, including fat accumulation (lipohypertrophy) in the abdomen and breasts; fat loss (lipoatrophy) in the face, buttocks, and extremities; or a combination of both.

The cause of these abnormalities is not well understood but is thought to be related to HIV and/or the direct and indirect effects of antiretroviral agents.

Cardiovascular Disease

Soon after the introduction of HAART, there were several reports of cardiovascular events occurring in relatively young patients taking these agents. Several observational studies yielded conflicting results. A large prospective trial, the Data Collection on Adverse Events of Anti-HIV Drugs (D:A:D) study, is an international collaboration of 11 cohorts of

TABLE 42 Prophylaxis for Opportunistic Infections in Patients with HIV Infection

Pneumocystis jirovecii pneumonia (PCP): CD4 cell count <200/μL CD4% <14, Recurrent Candidiasis, Persistent Fever, Previous PCP			
Drug	Dose	Side Effects	Comments
TMP-SMX	1 DS tab daily; or 1 SS tab daily; or 1 DS tab 3 times weekly	Nausea, vomiting, pruritus, rash, cytopenia, fever, elevated aminotransferases, high incidence of allergy	Drug of choice; many clinicians advocate desensitization for allergy; requires concomitant toxoplasmosis and bacterial prophylaxis (Streptococcus pneumoniae, Shigella, Staphylococcus aureus); avoid in patients with G6PD deficiency
Dapsone	100 mg/d	Rash, pruritus, hepatitis, anemia, neutropenia, hemolytic anemia with or without G6PD deficiency	Requires concomitant toxoplasmosis prophylaxis with pyrimethamine, 50 mg/wk, and folinic acid, 25 mg/wk; check for G6PD deficiency before use
Atovaquone	750 mg BID	Rash, GI intolerance, diarrhea	Take with food
Pentamidine, aerosolized	300 mg by mouth using Respiguard II® nebulizer	Cough, wheezing, chest pain, laryngitis, dyspnea	Associated with greater failure rate
Toxoplasmosis: CD4 cell count <100/μL positive Toxoplasma IgG antibody titer			
Drug(s)	Dose	Side Effects	Comments
TMP-SMX	1 DS tab daily; or 1 SS tab daily	See PCP prophylaxis above	Drug of choice; requires concomitant PCP prophylaxis
Dapsone	50 mg/d	Bone marrow suppression, GI intolerance	Requires concomitant PCP prophylaxis
Pyrimethamine	50 mg weekly		
Leucovorin	25 mg weekly		
Dapsone	200 mg weekly	See PCP prophylaxis above	
Pyrimethamine	75 mg weekly		
Leucovorin	25 mg weekly		
Mycobacterium avium complex infection: CD4 cell count <50/μL (0.05 × 10⁹/L)			
Drug	Dose	Side Effects	Comments
Azithromycin	1200 mg weekly	GI intolerance, diarrhea	Most cost-effective regimen. Breakthrough infections with resistance to macrolides
Clarithromycin	500 mg BID	GI intolerance, headache, elevated aminotransferases	Breakthrough infections with resistance to macrolides
Rifabutin	300 mg/d	Orange urine, rash, GI intolerance, neutropenia, dose-related uveitis	Dosage must be adjusted if used with protease inhibitors or non-nucleoside reverse transcriptase inhibitors

BID = twice daily; DS tab = double-strength tablet; GI = gastrointestinal; G6PD = glucose-6-phosphate dehydrogenase; SS tab = single-strength tablet; TMP-SMX = trimethoprim-sulfamethoxazole.

investigators that followed 23,437 patients with HIV infection in the United States, Europe, and Australia. Investigators found that increased exposure to protease inhibitors, but not non-nucleoside reverse transcriptase inhibitors, is associated with an increased risk of myocardial infarction, which is partly explained by dyslipidemia.

Another major observation of the D:A:D study was the importance of traditional risk factors for cardiovascular disease in this patient population. Based on a multivariate analysis, significant predictors of increased cardiovascular risk in patients taking HAART were older age, male sex, history of previous cardiovascular events, family history of heart disease, and smoking. Clinicians treating patients with HIV infection must therefore identify and aggressively treat conditions that are risk factors for cardiovascular disease, especially smoking, hypertension, diabetes mellitus, obesity, and dyslipidemia.

Immune Reconstitution Inflammatory Syndrome

HAART suppresses HIV viral replication, which prevents further clinical deterioration and allows the immune system to regenerate. An abrupt transition to a pathologic inflammatory state occurs in a small subset of patients taking HAART, which results in clinical deterioration despite immunologic and virologic control. This inflammatory response has been given many names, including immune reconstitution inflammatory syndrome (IRIS), HAART attacks, immune restoration/recovery state, and immune rebound illness. IRIS is the term most often used.

There are two forms of IRIS: unmasking and paradoxical. Both develop more often in patients with advanced HIV infection who are just beginning HAART. Unmasking IRIS occurs in patients with an occult subclinical infection in whom HAART causes improvement of immune function with the ability to mount an effective response against pathogens. Paradoxical IRIS is a clinical recurrence of a previously successfully treated infection and is primarily due to the presence of persistent antigens.

The timing of IRIS after initiation of HAART varies from as little as 3 days to as long as 5 years. Management is conservative. Occasional use of corticosteroids is needed for severe reactions.

Opportunistic Infections

Opportunistic infections remain a significant cause of morbidity and mortality in patients with HIV/AIDS. These infections result from an imbalance in cell-mediated immunity. The immune system is no longer able to maintain control in patients with HIV infection, which allows fungi, bacteria, and viruses to invade impaired hosts and cause disease. In healthy persons, infections with these pathogens may result in a mild illness followed by recovery. In patients infected with HIV, severe illness may occur because the immune system is impaired. This discussion will be limited to the major AIDS-defining opportunistic infections.

Cryptococcal Infections

Cryptococcal meningitis is the most common form of meningitis in patients with AIDS, who typically present with symptoms such as headache, irritability, and nausea that can mimic other disorders. Most patients have a CD4 cell count of less than $100/\mu L$. The diagnosis is based on detection of cryptococcal antigen in the cerebrospinal fluid (CSF) or culture of *Cryptococcus neoformans* in the CSF. Treatment is divided into three phases (induction, consolidation, and maintenance). The usual induction therapy is amphotericin B, with or without flucytosine, for 14 days followed by fluconazole for 8 weeks during the consolidation phase. Therapy during the maintenance phase is continuous fluconazole until the patient has successfully completed a course of initial therapy, has no signs and symptoms of cryptococcosis, and has a documented sustained increase in the CD4 cell count ($>200/\mu L$ for >6 months).

Cytomegalovirus Infection

Cytomegalovirus is a common pathogen that occurs in late stages of HIV infection, usually in patients with a CD4 cell count of less than $50/\mu L$. It can be associated with either disseminated or localized end-organ disease. Many organs may be involved, including the retina, gastrointestinal tract, and nervous system. Cytomegalovirus only rarely invades the lungs in patients with HIV infection. Treatment involves the use of ganciclovir induction followed by maintenance therapy with this agent. Other agents that have been used in patients who are intolerant to ganciclovir or have dose-limiting toxicity are foscarnet and cidofovir. The length and type of treatment depends on the specific organ system involved.

Mycobacterium avium complex Infection

Disseminated *Mycobacterium avium* complex infection is common in patients with advanced-stage HIV infection and a CD4 cell count of less than $50/\mu L$. Symptoms include fever, weight loss, hepatosplenomegaly, malaise, and abdominal pain. The diagnosis is generally confirmed by recovering the pathogen from sterile tissue (usually blood). Treatment consists of a combination of a macrolide and ethambutol with or without rifampin.

Pneumocystis jirovecii Pneumonia

Pneumocystis jirovecii pneumonia remains the most common AIDS-defining illness and cause of death in patients with AIDS. The diagnosis should be considered in any patient with a CD4 cell count of less than $200/\mu L$ who presents with fever, dry cough, and dyspnea developing over several days or weeks. The chest radiograph typically shows bilateral interstitial infiltrates, but findings can vary from a normal film to consolidation or a pneumothorax. The diagnosis is established by silver stain examination of induced sputum or a bronchoscopic sample showing characteristic cysts. A 3-week course of trimethoprim-sulfamethoxazole is the standard treatment. Corticosteroids are required for patients with evidence of hypoxia (arterial Po_2 <70 mm Hg or an alveolar-arterial gradient >35 mm Hg) and should be continued for the entire course of treatment.

Toxoplasmosis

Toxoplasmosis almost always presents as reactivation disease in patients with HIV infection and typically occurs when the CD4 cell count is less than 100/µL. Additional findings are fever, neurologic deficits, and an MRI showing ring-enhancing lesions (**Figure 12**). Sulfadiazine plus pyrimethamine and folinic acid are given initially. Follow-up MRI is critical to assess treatment response. If there is no therapeutic response after 14 days, stereotactic brain biopsy is recommended to rule out other causes, especially a primary central nervous system lymphoma.

KEY POINTS

- The risk of cardiovascular disease is increased in patients being treated with highly active antiretroviral therapy.
- In patients with HIV infection, aggressive risk factor reduction for cardiovascular disease should be implemented.
- The immune reconstitution inflammatory syndrome, which is a sudden deterioration in a patient's clinical condition despite immunologic and virologic control, occurs in a small subset of patients being treated with highly active antiretroviral therapy.
- The major AIDS-defining opportunistic infections are cryptococcal infection, cytomegalovirus infection, *Pneumocystis jirovecii* pneumonia, *Mycobacterium avium* complex infection, and toxoplasmosis.

Treatment of HIV Infection

The U.S. Department of Health and Human Services (DHHS) (http://aidsinfo.nih.gov/Guidelines/Default.aspx?MenuItem=Guidelines&Search=On) and the International AIDS Society–USA (IAS-USA) (www.iasusa.org/guidelines/index.html) frequently update guidelines for use of antiretroviral therapy in patients with HIV infection. Current guidelines review the goals of therapy, when to begin treatment, and how to use available antiretroviral agents.

The goals of antiretroviral therapy are to prolong life, avoid destruction or allow reconstitution of the immune system, prevent opportunistic infections, and provide improved quality of life by reducing HIV-related symptoms. Effective therapy aims to lower the HIV RNA viral load to less than 50 copies/mL in all patients, whether treatment naïve or treatment experienced. Such dramatic reductions in viral load improve prognosis, minimize the development of resistance, and prolong the duration of the antiretroviral response.

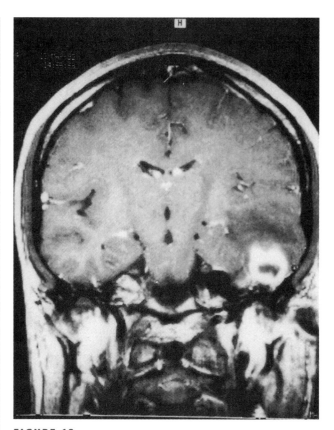

FIGURE 12.
Imaging studies of toxoplasmosis encephalitis.
T1-weighted MRI scan with contrast enhancement demonstrating ring enhancement.

When to Initiate Treatment

The most appropriate time to begin treating patients with HIV infection is not known and is an issue of great debate. Current guidelines recommend initiating antiretroviral therapy in patients with a history of an AIDS-defining illness or a CD4 cell count of less than 350/µL. In addition, strong evidence from clinical trials suggests that treating patients with an AIDS-defining illness and a CD4 cell count of less than 200/µL improves survival and reduces disease progression. **Table 43** lists the indications for starting antiretroviral therapy in treatment-naïve patients.

The guidelines have recently been changed to include the recommendation to treat all patients with HIV infection, regardless of their CD4 cell count, who have evidence of HIV nephropathy or hepatitis B co-infection that requires treatment or women who are pregnant.

Antiretroviral Agents

Twenty-five antiretroviral agents are currently approved for treating HIV infection (**Table 44**). Six different antiretroviral drug classes are licensed. These are nucleoside/nucleotide reverse transcriptase inhibitors (NRTIs), non-nucleoside

TABLE 43 Indications for Beginning Antiretroviral Therapy in Patients with HIV Infection

Patients with a history of an AIDS-defining illness

Patients with a CD4 cell count <350/µL

Patients with HIV-associated nephropathy

Patients with co-infection with chronic hepatitis B that requires treatment

Patients who are pregnant

The optimal time to initiate therapy in asymptomatic patients with a CD4 cell count >350/µL who do not meet any of the above criteria is not well defined. Patient scenarios and comorbidities should be taken into consideration.

TABLE 44 Antiretroviral Agents Approved by the U.S. Food and Drug Administration - 2008

Nucleoside/Nucleotide Reverse Transcriptase Inhibitors

Abacavir (Ziagen®)

Didanosine (Videx®)

Emtricitabine (Emtriva®)

Lamivudine (Epivir®)

Stavudine (Zerit®)

Tenofovir (Viread®)

Zalcitabine (Hivid®)

Zidovudine (Retrovir®)

Non-Nucleoside Reverse Transcriptase Inhibitors

Delavirdine (Rescriptor®)

Efavirenz (Sustiva®)

Etravirine (Intelence®)

Nevirapine (Viramune®)

Protease Inhibitors

Atazanavir (Reyataz®)

Darunavir (Prezista®)

Fosamprenavir (Lexiva®)

Indinavir (Crixivan®)

Lopinavir/ritonavir (Kaletra®)

Nelfinavir (Viracept®)

Ritonavir (Norvir®)

Saquinavir HGC (Invirase®)

Saquinavir SGC (Fortovase®)

Tipranavir (Aptivus®)

Fusion Inhibitors

Enfuvirtide (Fuzeon®)

Co-receptor Antagonists

Maraviroc (Selzentry®)

Integrase Inhibitors

Raltegravir (Isentress®)

HGC = hard gel capsule; SGC = soft gel capsule.

reverse transcriptase inhibitors (NNRTIs), protease inhibitors, fusion inhibitors, integrase inhibitors, and co-receptor antagonists. The NRTIs are nucleoside/nucleotide analogues and act as chain terminators that impair the transcription of viral RNA into DNA. The NNRTIs inhibit reverse transcriptase by binding to the enzyme. Protease inhibitors impair the packaging of viral particles into a mature virus capable of budding from the cell and productively infecting additional lymphocytes. The fusion inhibitors impair membrane fusion of HIV to T cells, thus preventing one of the key steps in entry. Co-receptor antagonists block a second major step in entry by binding to the chemokine receptors (CCR5 or CXCR4), and integrase inhibitors prevent incorporation of viral DNA into the host cell genome.

Recommended first-line regimens include two NRTIs plus either a NNRTI or a protease inhibitor. The DHHS guidelines currently indicate that the preferred NRTI is a fixed-dose formulation of emtricitabine/tenofovir, the NNRTI-containing agent is efavirenz, and the protease inhibitors are lopinavir/ritonavir, fosamprenavir/ritonavir, darunavir/ritonavir, or atazanavir/ritonavir. Efavirenz is contraindicated in women of child-bearing age because of its teratogenic effects (pregnancy risk category D). The protease inhibitors are frequently prescribed in combination with low-dose ritonavir (100 mg daily or twice daily), a technique known as boosting. Ritonavir is a potent inhibitor of the cytochrome P-450 system, specifically the CYP3A4 isoenzyme. All protease inhibitors are a substrate of this enzyme. This inhibition increases the trough level and prolongs the half-life of these drugs.

Common side effects and toxicities of antiretroviral agents are listed in **Table 45**.

Resistance Testing

Two types of resistance tests, genotype and phenotype, are used in clinical practice. Genotype testing identifies mutations present to reverse transcriptase and protease genes. Because such tests typically measure only dominant species when the assay is performed, resistant strains that account for less than 20% of the total viral populations are not detected. Genotype

results are generally available in 1 to 2 weeks. Phenotype testing measures the ability of HIV to grow in the presence of varying concentrations of antiretroviral drugs. This procedure involves recombining the patient's gene sequences with a laboratory HIV clone and measuring the replication of the virus in different drug concentrations. The concentrations that inhibit 50% (IC_{50}) and 90% (IC_{90}) of the virus are compared with a reference strain of HIV. Reporting of phenotype results can take 2 to 3 weeks.

Resistance testing is recommended for patients who develop acute HIV infection (within 6 to 12 months of virus transmission), compliant patients who fail to benefit from adequate therapy, and treatment-naïve patients with chronic HIV infection.

There are several caveats to resistance testing:

1. Resistance testing measures only dominant species (>20% of the viral population) when the test is performed.

2. An HIV RNA viral load of greater than 500 copies/mL must be present to perform the test.

3. Genotype mutations may be difficult to interpret because of the multiple mutations that are required for drug resistance and cross-resistance.

4. Consultation with an HIV expert improves results.

HIV Vaccine

Historically, a vaccine has been one of the most effective means of combating and controlling infectious diseases. Extensive efforts have been made to develop an effective vaccine to combat HIV infection. Despite several clinical trials evaluating therapeutic and preventive vaccines, none has been found to be effective. An HIV vaccine is generally considered as the most likely and perhaps only way to halt the AIDS pandemic. However, after more than 20 years of research, HIV remains a difficult target for a vaccine, and, currently, no vaccines appear close to development.

KEY POINTS

- Current guidelines recommend beginning treatment for patients with HIV infection who have an AIDS-defining illness or a CD4 cell count less than 350/μL or for all patients with HIV infection regardless of CD4 cell count who have HIV nephropathy, hepatitis B co-infection, or are pregnant.

- The first-line regimen for treatment of HIV infection is two nucleoside/nucleotide reverse transcriptase inhibitors plus one non-nucleoside reverse transcriptase inhibitor or one protease inhibitor.

- Efavirenz is contraindicated in women of child-bearing age because of its teratogenic effects (pregnancy risk category D).

- Resistance testing is recommended for patients who develop acute HIV infection (within 6 to 12 months of virus transmission), compliant patients who fail to benefit from adequate therapy, and treatment-naïve patients with chronic HIV infection.

- To date, no vaccine against HIV appears to be effective.

Bibliography

Aberg JA, Gallant JE, Anderson J, et al; HIV Medicine Association of the Infectious Diseases Society of America. Primary care Guidelines for the management of persons infected with human immunodeficiency virus: recommendations of the HIV Medicine Association of the Infectious Diseases Society of America. Clin Infect Dis. 2004;39(5):609-629. [PMID: 15356773]

Branson BM, Handsfield HH, Lampe MA, Janssen RS, Taylor AW, Lyss SB, Clark JE. Revised recommendations for HIV testing of adults, adolescents, and pregnant women in health care settings. MMWR Recomm Rep. 2006;55(RR14):1-17. [PMID: 16988643]

Centers for Disease Control and Prevention. HIV/AIDS epidemic update. www.cdc.gov/hiv/topics/surveillance/basic.htm. Accessed on July 27, 2009.

Friis-Moller N, Sabin CA, Weber R, et al; The Data Collection on Adverse Events of Anti-HIV Drugs(DAD)Study group. Combination antiretroviral therapy and the risk of myocardial infarction. New Engl J Med. 2003;349(21):1993-2003. [PMID: 14627784]

Guidelines for the use of antiretroviral agents in HIV-1 infected adults and adolescents. www.aidsinfo.nih.gov./Guidelines/GuidelineDetail .aspx?MenuItem=Guidelines&Search=Off&GuidelineID=7&Class ID=1. Published November 3, 2008. Accessed on July 27, 2009.

Hammer SM. Management of newly diagnosed HIV Infection. N Engl J Med. 2005;353(16):1702-1710. [PMID: 16236741]

Kaplan JE, Benson CA, Holmes KK, Brooks JI, Pau A, Masur H. Guidelines for Prevention and Treatment of Opportunistic Infections in HIV infected adults and adolescents. Recommendations from CDC, the National Institutes of Health, and the HIV Medicine Association of the Infectious Diseases Society of America. www.cdc .gov/mmwr/pdf/rr/rr5804.pdf. Published April 10, 2009. Accessed on July 27, 2009.

World Health organization. AIDS Epidemic Update. www.unaids .org/en. Published December, 2008. Accessed on July 27, 2009.

TABLE 45 Common Side Effects and Toxicities of Antiretroviral Therapy

Side Effect/Toxicity	Antiretroviral Agent
Anemia	Zidovudine
Leukopenia	Zidovudine
Pancreatitis	Didanosine
Peripheral neuropathy	Didanosine, stavudine, zalcitabine
Rash	Non-nucleoside reverse transcriptase inhibitors
Teratogenic	Efavirenz (pregnancy risk category D)
Indirect hyperbilirubinemia	Atazanavir, indinavir
Hepatitis	Nevirapine, tipranavir
Nephrolithiasis	Atazanavir, indinavir
Hypersensitivity	Abacavir
Central nervous system symptoms (dizziness, vivid dreams)	Efavirenz
Diarrhea	Lopinavir/ritonavir, nelfinavir

Viral Infections

Influenza Viruses

Influenza viruses belong to the family Orthomyxoviridae and are classified into three distinct types, influenza A, B, and C, based on major antigenic differences. Influenza A and B viruses are responsible for most seasonal influenza epidemics each year. Hemagglutinin (H) and neuraminidase (N) are proteins found in influenza A viruses that are used to further define these virus subtypes (for example, H1N1, H3N2). Different types and subtypes of viruses can circulate over the course of an influenza season. In addition, influenza viruses are constantly changing by a process called "antigenic drift."

Influenza is the most frequent cause of death from a vaccine-preventable disease in the United States. Each year, approximately 5% to 20% of the U.S. population develops influenza, resulting in about 200,000 hospitalizations and 36,000 influenza-associated pulmonary and circulatory deaths annually. Attack rates during outbreaks may be as high as 10% to 40%. In the Northern Hemisphere, most disease occurs from November to as late as May.

Influenza is an acute contagious illness that attacks the respiratory tract in humans. The incubation period is typically 1 to 4 days after exposure. Signs and symptoms may include fever (usually high), headache, extreme fatigue, nonproductive cough, sore throat, nasal congestion, rhinorrhea, and myalgia. Gastrointestinal symptoms (nausea, vomiting, and diarrhea) may also occur but are more common in children.

Prevention and Treatment

The current strategy for influenza control includes primary prevention with vaccination targeting persons at high risk for complications. High-risk persons may also be protected from exposure to influenza virus by immunizing persons with whom they have frequent, close contact. Protection of caregivers from influenza may reduce interruptions in care during influenza epidemics and reduce potential exposure to patients. Antiviral chemoprophylaxis provides immediate protection (unlike vaccine) and may be useful in persons who have not been vaccinated or who are not expected to respond to a vaccine or until vaccine-induced immunity becomes effective (about 2 weeks after vaccination); however, antiviral chemoprophylaxis is expensive and can be associated with side effects. Persons who are candidates for chemoprophylaxis include residents in an assisted-living facility during an influenza outbreak, persons who are at higher risk for influenza-related complications and have had recent household or other close contact with a person with laboratory-confirmed influenza, and health care workers who have had recent close contact with a person with laboratory-confirmed influenza.

Two classes of antiviral agents, neuraminidase inhibitors and adamantanes, have efficacy against some strains of influenza virus (**Table 46**).

Neuraminidase inhibitors (oseltamivir and zanamivir) are typically active against influenza A and influenza B viruses. Oseltamivir is given orally, and zanamivir is only available as an inhaled powder. These antiviral agents are most effective when therapy is started within the first 24 hours of symptom development but are not found to confer benefit when begun 48 or more hours after symptom development.

TABLE 46 Antiviral Agents for Influenza				
Characteristics	**Amantadine[a]**	**Rimantadine[a]**	**Zanamivir**	**Oseltamivir**
Protein target	M2 inhibitor	M2 inhibitor	Inhibition of the influenza neuraminidase enzyme	Inhibition of the influenza neuraminidase enzyme
Activity	Influenza A only	Influenza A only	Influenza A and B	Influenza A and B
Side effects	CNS (13%), GI (3%)	CNS (6%), GI (3%)	Bronchospasm	GI (9%)
Metabolism	None	Multiple (hepatic)	None	Hepatic
Excretion	Renal	Primarily renal	Renal	Renal (tubular secretion)
Drug interactions	Antihistamines, anticholinergic agents	None	None	Probenecid (increased levels of oseltamivir)
Dose adjustments needed	Patients ≥65 years; CrCl <50 mL/min	Patients ≥65 years; CrCl <10 mL/min	None	CrCl <30 mL/min; severe liver dysfunction
Contraindications	Acute-angle glaucoma	Severe liver dysfunction	Underlying airways disease	
FDA-Approved Indications				
Therapy	Adults and children ≥1 year	Adults only	Adults and children ≥7 years	Adults and children ≥1 year
Prophylaxis	Yes	Yes	No	Adults and children ≥13 years

CNS = central nervous system; CrCl = creatinine clearance; FDA = U.S. Food and Drug Administration; GI = gastrointestinal.

[a]Currently not recommended as general empiric therapy but can be used when oseltamivir resistance is suspected in patients with seasonal influenza A (H1N1) virus.

Reprinted with permission from Mandell GL, Bennett JE, Dolin R. Principles and Practice of Infectious Diseases. 6th ed. London, England: Churchill Livingstone; 2002:Table 162-5. Copyright 2004, Elsevier.

The adamantanes (amantadine and rimantadine) are only active against some types of influenza A virus. However, because of the emergence of influenza A virus resistance to adamantanes, the Centers for Disease Control and Prevention (CDC) and the U.S. Advisory Committee on Immunization Practices (ACIP) recommend that these agents not currently be used for the treatment or chemoprophylaxis of influenza A in the United States.

Drug-Resistant Influenza Viruses

Adamantane resistance among circulating influenza A viruses has increased rapidly worldwide over the past several years, increasing from 0.4% during the 1994-1995 influenza season to 12.3% during the 2003-2004 season. In 2005-2006 in the United States, a rate of adamantane resistance of 92% was reported in influenza A H3N2 strains, but susceptibility to neuraminidase inhibitors was retained and these trends were sustained in the 2006-2007 season. Influenza A viral resistance to the adamantanes can emerge rapidly and confer cross-resistance to amantadine and rimantadine; therefore, the CDC and ACIP continue to recommend against using adamantanes for the treatment or chemoprophylaxis of influenza A in the United States until susceptibility has been reestablished among circulating influenza A viruses.

Historically, neuraminidase inhibitor resistance was uncommon (<1%). However, in 2008-2009, resistance to oseltamavir increased significantly. Consequently, treatment guidelines are now based on the predominant circulating strain (**Table 47**).

Emergence of New Influenza Viruses

Influenza A viruses can infect humans, birds, pigs, horses, seals, whales, and other animals, but wild birds are the natural hosts for these viruses. Birds are only infected with influenza A viruses, which circulate among birds worldwide. Although wild birds usually do not become ill when infected with these viruses, domestic poultry, such as turkeys and chickens, can become very ill and die. Infected birds shed virus in saliva, nasal secretions, and feces, and the virus spreads among susceptible birds that have contact with contaminated excretions.

Avian influenza virus (H5N1), or "bird flu," is an influenza A virus that does not typically infect humans. In 1997, however, the first cases of direct bird-to-human spread were documented during an outbreak of avian influenza virus infection among poultry in Hong Kong. The virus caused severe respiratory illness in 18 patients, and 6 died. Other human cases have subsequently been reported. Although most patients became ill after contact with infected poultry or contaminated surfaces, a few cases of human-to-human spread of H5N1 virus may have occurred. Human infection has primarily been reported in Asia and parts of Europe and Africa. Because influenza viruses are able to mutate, there is concern that the H5N1 virus could easily spread from person to person. Because humans have had minimal exposure to this virus, there is little or no immune protection in the human population, and an influenza pandemic could possibly occur if the virus becomes readily communicable.

Novel H1N1 virus ("swine flu") is an emerging influenza A virus. It was first detected in humans in the United States in April 2009. Since then, all of the United States and more than 70 countries have confirmed cases. Symptoms (cough, fever, and runny nose) are similar to those occurring in seasonal influenza as is the mode of spread, including person-to-person transmission. This virus is susceptible to neuraminidase inhibitors but resistant to the adamantanes.

TABLE 47 Interim Recommendations for the Selection of Influenza Antiviral Treatment Using Laboratory Test Results and Viral Surveillance Data, United States, 2008-2009 Season[a]

Rapid Antigen or Other Laboratory Test	Predominant Influenza Virus(es) in Community	Preferred Medication(s)	Alternative (Combination Antiviral Treatment)
Not done or negative, but clinical suspicion for influenza	H1N1 or unknown	Zanamivir	Oseltamivir plus rimantadine[b]
Not done or negative, but clinical suspicion for influenza	H3N2 or B	Oseltamivir or zanamivir	None
Positive A	H1N1 or unknown	Zanamivir	Oseltamivir plus rimantadine[b]
Positive A	H3N2 or B	Oseltamivir or zanamivir	None
Positive B	Any	Oseltamivir or zanamivir	None
Positive A+B[c]	H1N1 or unknown	Zanamivir	Oseltamivir plus rimantadine[b]
Positive A+B[c]	H3N2 or B	Oseltamivir or zanamivir	None

[a]Influenza antiviral medications used for treatment are most beneficial when initiated within the first 2 days of illness. Clinicians should consult the package insert of each antiviral medication for specific dosing information, approved indications and ages, contraindications/warnings/precautions, and adverse effects.

[b]Amantadine can be substituted for rimantadine but is associated with an increased risk of adverse events. Human data are lacking to support the benefits of combination antiviral treatment of influenza; however, these interim recommendations are intended to assist clinicians treating patients who might be infected with oseltamivir-resistant influenza A (H1N1) virus.

[c]Positive A+B indicates a rapid antigen test that cannot distinguish between influenza and influenza B viruses.

Reprinted from the Centers for Disease Control and Prevention. http://www2a.cdc.gov/HAN/ArchiveSys/ViewMsgV.asp?AlertNum=00279. Published December 19, 2008. Accessed on July 31, 2009.

Pigs can be infected with human, avian, and swine influenza viruses; consequently, they potentially may be infected with influenza viruses from different species (for example, ducks and humans) simultaneously. If this happens, genetic reassortment is possible, creating a new and potentially more communicable and/or virulent virus. Symptoms in infected pigs are similar to those in humans.

KEY POINTS

- Influenza viruses are classified into three types, influenza A, B, and C, but only influenza A and B viruses are communicable in humans.

- Typically, the adamantanes (amantadine and rimantadine) are effective against influenza A virus, whereas neuraminidase inhibitors (oseltamivir and zanamivir) are effective against both influenza A and B viruses, but because of emergence of resistance, treatment guidelines are now based on the predominant circulating strain and its expected susceptibility.

- Avian influenza virus (H5N1) or "bird flu" and a novel H1N1 virus ("swine flu") are subtypes of influenza A virus that have recently developed in humans, who have little or no immune protection to these viruses.

Herpes Simplex Viruses

Herpes simplex viruses (HSV) types 1 and 2 are enveloped DNA viruses that cause chronic latent infection in sensory nerve ganglia. Primary infection with either virus may be clinically evident or may go unrecognized. Both HSV-1 and HSV-2 reactivate after a latent period to cause recurrent signs and symptoms. Both predominantly affect the mouth (herpes labialis) or the genitals (genital herpes), depending on the exposure. However, HSV-1 is much more common in the mouth, and HSV-2 is more common in the anogenital region.

Primary HSV-1 infection occurs following exposure to the secretions (usually saliva) of infected persons while they are shedding the virus. Signs and symptoms include shallow ulcerations of the oral mucosa, tongue, and gingiva that may be accompanied by fever. Reactivation and clinical recurrences may be spontaneous or triggered by various factors such as trauma or immune suppression. Recurrences of HSV-1 infection may appear similar to primary infection but are usually clinically less severe. In immunocompromised patients, primary HSV-1 infection and reactivation may be severe and life-threatening.

Relatively common extraoral manifestations of HSV-1 infection in immunocompetent adults include lesions of the eyes (HSV keratitis), central nervous system (HSV encephalitis), and hands (herpetic whitlow) (**Figure 13**).

Encephalitis presents with fever, seizures, and altered mental status. CT or MRI of the brain shows evidence of

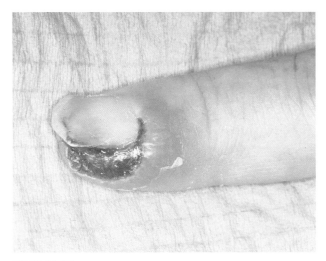

FIGURE 13.
Painful erosion on the distal finger characteristic of herpetic whitlow. This lesion was preceded by grouped, confluent vesicles on an erythematous base.

temporal-parietal lesions. Focal seizure activity in the temporal-parietal area is typically evident on electroencephalograms.

Patients with primary HSV-2 infection who have clinically evident symptoms present with painful ulcerations on the mucosal and cutaneous surfaces of the genital area (see Sexually Transmitted Diseases and MKSAP 15 Dermatology). Fever, malaise, and headache may also occur. Rarely, headache and neck stiffness develop, suggesting meningitis. Patients with recurrent genital herpes may present with burning, erythema, and dysuria as well as classic herpetic lesions. The average patient has four recurrences yearly that are likely to be clinically milder than the initial episode but vary in severity.

A clinical diagnosis of HSV-1 or HSV-2 lesions is easily made when viral infection has previously been confirmed and when recurrent lesions appear characteristic. When the diagnosis is less certain, HSV may be detected by viral culture or polymerase chain reaction (PCR) assay of fluid from a lesion. If HSV encephalitis is suspected, PCR assay of cerebrospinal fluid is highly sensitive for detecting the virus. Type-specific serologic testing is available and is useful for diagnosing chronic infection but not for identifying the cause of mucocutaneous or central nervous system lesions.

Treatment

Various antiviral agents are effective against HSV-1 and HSV-2. Acyclovir is the prototypical drug in this group. It is activated by viral thymidine kinase and then inhibits viral DNA polymerase to inhibit viral DNA synthesis. Valacyclovir (the acyclovir prodrug), penciclovir, and famciclovir have similar mechanisms of action. Foscarnet acts by inhibiting viral polymerases and does not require phosphorylation by viral thymidine kinase. Trifluridine and vidarabine are available as topical agents for the treatment of herpes keratoconjunctivitis.

Systemic therapy with acyclovir, valacyclovir, or famciclovir alleviates symptoms of primary and recurrent HSV-1 and HSV-2 infections and reduces subsequent outbreaks and viral shedding. The choice of whether to use oral or intravenous therapy for treatment of an infection due to HSV-1 or HSV-2 should be based on the patient's ability to tolerate oral medication and the severity of the clinical presentation. Chronic suppressive antiviral therapy prevents outbreaks of genital herpes. Topical application of acyclovir has shown little clinical benefit in the treatment of HSV infections, and its use should be discouraged.

In patients with possible herpes encephalitis or other clinically severe HSV infections, presumptive treatment with parenteral acyclovir is warranted while the diagnostic evaluation is being completed.

Drug-Resistant Herpes Simplex Viruses

Viral mutation in the thymidine kinase gene is the usual cause of acyclovir resistance, which has been described in immunocompromised patients. Acyclovir-resistant HSV infection should therefore be suspected in an immunocompromised patient who has herpetic lesions that are clinically unresponsive to acyclovir or related antiviral agents. Foscarnet is the drug of choice for clinically severe infection due to acyclovir-resistant HSV. Valacyclovir, penciclovir, and famciclovir should not be used in this setting.

KEY POINTS

- Herpes simplex virus type 1 more commonly affects the mouth (herpes labialis), whereas herpes simplex virus type 2 is much more common in the anogenital region (genital herpes).

- Polymerase chain reaction assay of cerebrospinal fluid is a highly sensitive test for detecting herpes simplex virus encephalitis.

- Systemic therapy with acyclovir, valacyclovir, or famciclovir alleviates symptoms of primary and recurrent herpes simplex virus type 1 and 2 infections and reduces subsequent outbreaks and viral shedding.

- In patients with possible herpes simplex virus encephalitis or other clinically severe herpes virus infections, presumptive treatment with parenteral acyclovir is warranted while the diagnostic workup is being completed.

Varicella-Zoster Virus

Varicella-zoster is a human herpesvirus that causes both varicella (chickenpox) and herpes zoster (shingles). Varicella is a primary infection that occurs mostly in children. Following infection, the varicella-zoster virus remains latent in the sensory dorsal root ganglia. Reactivation causes herpes zoster.

Varicella (Chickenpox)

In the United States, more than 90% of adults have serologic evidence of varicella immunity. The infection is highly contagious and is transmitted by aerosolized droplets from respiratory secretions or by direct contact with the fluid from vesicular skin lesions. The incubation period is 10 to 21 days.

Varicella causes a febrile illness associated with a diffuse vesicular rash. The vesicles appear in crops in various stages of development, are intensely pruritic, and generally crust and heal within 1 week (**Figure 14**). Because the lesions are so pruritic, scratching can lead to secondary bacterial skin infections. Other serious complications include invasive group A streptococcal infections (toxic shock syndrome and necrotizing fasciitis), cerebellar ataxia, severe encephalitis, and pneumonia. Varicella is more likely to disseminate and cause complications in immunocompromised patients. However, varicella pneumonia can occur in immunocompetent persons. It occurs more often in adults than in children, develops with increased frequency in cigarette smokers and pregnant women, and is associated with high mortality rates.

Treatment

Acyclovir is currently the only antiviral agent recommended for treating varicella. No specific treatment is needed for most children younger than 12 years of age, who generally have uncomplicated disease. Therapy is required for those at high risk for developing complications, including children older than 12 years of age, otherwise healthy adults, immunocompromised patients, and patients with pre-existing skin disorders or cardiopulmonary disease.

Oral acyclovir should be given within the first 24 hours of the appearance of the rash. Immunocompromised patients or patients with complications such as pneumonia or encephalopathy should be given intravenous acyclovir.

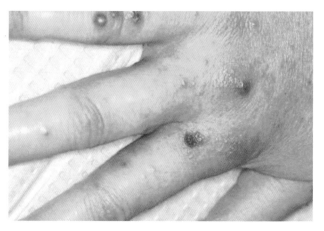

FIGURE 14.
Vesicular lesions on an erythematous base are characteristic of varicella infection.
The lesions occur in crops and are present in various stages on the same region of the skin.

Prevention

The varicella vaccine is available as a single vaccine or in a combined form for immunization against mumps, measles, rubella, and varicella. The ACIP has recently updated its recommendations regarding use of this vaccine. All children should receive two doses—the first at 12 to 15 months of age and the second at 4 to 6 years of age. All susceptible adults should receive two doses at 4- to 8-week intervals. The varicella vaccine is a live virus vaccine and is therefore relatively contraindicated in immunocompromised patients. However, because varicella infection is associated with high morbidity rates in this patient population and because of the excellent efficacy of the vaccine, it is used in select groups of immunocompromised patients, such as susceptible persons with leukemia who are in remission. It is also used in susceptible HIV-positive adults with a CD4 cell count greater than $200/\mu L$ or in susceptible HIV-positive children with a CD4 cell count greater than 15%.

Although most adults in the United States have serologic immunity to varicella, those who are susceptible and experience a close-contact exposure to the virus and are at high risk for developing complications of varicella should be considered for postexposure prophylaxis with varicella-zoster immune globulin, varicella vaccine, or acyclovir. Susceptible persons who are immunocompromised or pregnant should receive varicella-zoster immune globulin within 96 hours of exposure. For healthy nonpregnant adults, varicella vaccine given within 3 to 5 days of exposure will prevent or lessen the severity of the infection. Alternatively, healthy adults can receive early treatment with acyclovir at the first sign of skin lesions.

Herpes Zoster (Shingles)

After primary infection with varicella-zoster virus, the virus remains latent in the sensory dorsal root ganglia. Latency is maintained by the host's cell-mediated immunity. This immunity diminishes with age or because of medical conditions such as malignancy or immunosuppressive therapy. Reactivation of the latent virus results in a painful vesicular eruption known as herpes zoster (shingles) (see MKSAP 15 Dermatology). The vesicular rash is usually preceded by pruritus and pain that is frequently described as deep, throbbing, or stabbing. The thoracic dermatomes are most often involved. However, reactivation of the virus within the trigeminal nerve ganglia may cause herpes zoster ophthalmicus, and, possibly, blindness, if not treated appropriately (**Figure 15**).

Reactivation within the geniculate ganglion that affects the eighth cranial nerve may cause herpes zoster oticus (Ramsay Hunt syndrome). Immunocompromised patients are at high risk for developing disseminated herpes zoster (both cutaneous and visceral disease), which can be associated with high morbidity and mortality rates.

In most immunocompetent patients, the lesions begin to crust within 7 to 10 days, and the acute pain syndrome

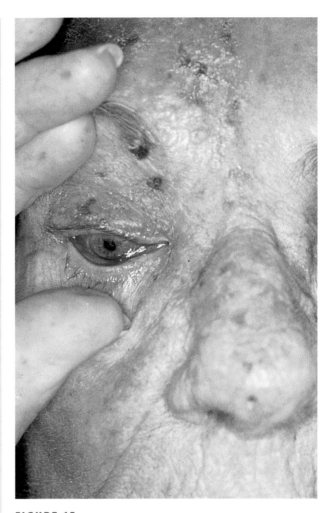

FIGURE 15.
Herpes zoster ophthalmicus.
Involvement of the nasociliary branch of the trigeminal nerve manifests as vesicles on the tip of the nose and is a clue to corneal involvement. If not appropriately treated, this can lead to blindness.

resolves. If the pain persists, development of postherpetic neuralgia is likely. Risk factors include age older than 60 years at the onset of herpes zoster and having an acute episode of herpes zoster with severe pain and an extensive vesicular rash.

Treatment

The cornerstone of therapy for herpes zoster is antiviral agents and opiate analgesics. Corticosteroids may have a role in specific patients. When given within 72 hours of rash onset, the antiviral agents acyclovir, valacyclovir, and famciclovir have been shown to decrease the severity and duration of pain, promote more rapid healing of lesions, and possibly decrease the incidence and severity of postherpetic neuralgia. These benefits appear to be greatest in patients older than 50 years of age. Oral valacyclovir and famciclovir have improved bioavailability compared with oral acyclovir, which is poorly absorbed and requires a high pill burden.

Although the benefits of antiviral therapy are well established, the benefits of corticosteroids plus acyclovir are less clear; in addition, no studies have been done regarding use of corticosteroids plus valacyclovir or famciclovir. Corticosteroids may help accelerate lesion healing, decrease the time to acute pain resolution, decrease insomnia incidence, facilitate quicker return to normal daily activities, and decrease the need for analgesic pain medicine. Unfortunately, they do not appear to reduce the incidence of postherpetic neuralgia. Because the benefits are modest, corticosteroids should probably be used only in patients with severe acute herpes zoster who have no contraindications to these agents. For patients at risk for postherpetic neuralgia, early adjuvant therapy with a tricyclic antidepressant (for example, amitriptyline) or an anticonvulsant (for example, gabapentin) should also be considered, although side effects often limit their usefulness.

Prevention of Herpes Zoster and Postherpetic Neuralgia
In May 2006, the U.S. Food and Drug Administration approved the use of a live attenuated herpes zoster vaccine for persons older than 60 years. The vaccine can decrease the incidence of herpes zoster by approximately 50% and shorten pain duration for those patients who develop herpes zoster. It can also decrease postherpetic neuralgia incidence by approximately 67%. The vaccine is well tolerated, and a mild injection site reaction is one of the few side effects. Because it is a live virus vaccine, it is generally not recommended for pregnant women, patients with hematologic malignancies or HIV infection, or patients receiving immunosuppressive therapy. The herpes zoster vaccine is contraindicated in anyone with a history of anaphylaxis to any of its components, including neomycin and gelatin. It can be given to persons who have had a previous episode of herpes zoster and to those who are not certain if they have had chickenpox in the past (although up to 98% of adults in the United States are seropositive for varicella). There is no need to perform serologic testing for varicella immunity before giving the vaccine. To date, the ACIP has not made any specific recommendations about follow-up or booster vaccinations.

KEY POINTS

- Varicella (chickenpox) causes a diffuse, intensely pruritic, vesicular rash; the vesicles appear in crops in various stages of development.

- Acyclovir is currently the only antiviral agent recommended for treating varicella.

- Varicella vaccine given within 3 to 5 days of exposure will prevent or lessen the severity of infection in otherwise healthy, nonpregnant, susceptible adults.

- Antiviral therapy can lessen acute herpes zoster pain severity, speed lesion healing, and decrease postherpetic neuralgia incidence and severity.

- Administration of a live attenuated herpes zoster vaccine to persons older than 60 years can decrease postherpetic neuralgia incidence and decrease pain duration in patients who develop this disorder.

Bibliography

Centers for Disease Control and Prevention (CDC). A new product (VariZIG) for post exposure prophylaxis of varicella available under investigational new drug application expanded access protocol. MMWR Rep. 2006;55(8):209-210. [PMID: 16511443]

Centers for Disease Control and Prevention (CDC). Update: Novel Influenza A (H1N1) Virus Infection — Mexico, March—May, 2009. Morbidity and Mortality Weekly Report (MMWR). 2009;58(21): 585-589. [PMID: 19498336]

Centers for Disease Control and Prevention. H1N1 Swine Flu. www.cdc.gov/h1n1flu/. Accessed at on July 31, 2009.

Gilbert SC. Suppressive therapy versus episodic therapy with oral valacyclovir for recurrent herpes labialis: efficacy and tolerability in an open-label, crossover study. J Drugs Dermatol. 2007;6(4):400-405. [PMID: 17668537]

Gupta R, Warren T, Wald A. Genital herpes. Lancet. 2007;370(9605): 2127-2137. [PMID: 18156035]

Harper SA, Bradley JS, Englund JA, et al. Seasonal influenza in adults and children—diagnosis, treatment, chemoprophylaxis, and institutional outbreak management: clinical practice guidelines of the Infectious Diseases Society of America. Clin Infect Dis. 2009;48(8): 1003-1032. [PMID: 19281331]

Hayden FG, Pavia AT. Antiviral Management of Seasonal and Pandemic Influenza. J Infect Dis. 2006;194(Suppl 2):S119-S26. [PMID: 17163384]

Kimberlan DW, Whitley RJ. Varicella Zoster vaccine for the prevention of Herpes zoster. N Engl J Med. 2007;356(13):1338-1343. [PMID: 17392303]

Marin M, Güris D, Chaves SS, Schmid S, Seward JF; Advisory Committee on Immunization Practices, Centers for Disease Control and Prevention (CDC). Prevention of Varicella: Recommendations of the Advisory Committee on Immunization Practices(ACIP). MMWR Recomm Rep. 2007;56(RR-4):1-40. [PMID: 17585291]

Martinez V, Caumes E, Chosidow O. Treatment to prevent recurrent genital herpes. Curr Opin Infect Dis. 2008;21(1):42-48. [PMID: 18192785]

Wallace MR, Bowler WA, Murray NB, Brodine SL, Oldfield EC 3rd. Treatment of Adult Varicella with oral Acyclovir. A randomized placebo controlled trial. Ann Intern Med. 1992;117(5):358-363. [PMID: 1323943]

Whitley RJ, Weiss H, Gnann JW, et al; The National Institute of Allergy and Infectious Disease Collaborative antiviral study group. Acyclovir with and without prednisone for the treatment of Herpes zoster. A randomized placebo controlled trial. Ann Intern Med. 1996;125(5):376-383. [PMID: 8702088]

Whitley RJ. Herpes simplex encephalitis: adolescents and adults. Antiviral Res. 2006;71(2-3):141-148. [PMID: 16675036]

New Principles in Antibiotics

Introduction

Despite a significant recent reduction in the development of new drugs, several novel concepts in the use of antibiotics have emerged. These include (1) expanding the use of new drugs, (2) finding new uses for older drugs, (3) improving drug dosing, and (4) establishing stewardship programs for more effective utilization of drugs.

New Antibacterial Drugs

The most recent antibacterial agents approved by the U.S. Food and Drug Administration are primarily new members of older antibiotic classes. Doripenem and ceftobiprole are both β-lactams, and tigecycline is a glycylcycline, which is related to the tetracyclines. However, what makes any new drug worthwhile is not its class but its potential to provide greater effectiveness than older agents. Although these three drugs are effective, early experience has not shown them to be clinically superior to other available antibiotics.

Another newer drug, daptomycin, appears promising for treating staphylococcal bacteremia and right-sided endocarditis in addition to its known effectiveness for treating skin and skin structure infections. The pivotal study of daptomycin for treatment of bacteremia showed that it was equally effective for methicillin-susceptible *Staphylococcus aureus* (MSSA) and methicillin-resistant *S. aureus* (MRSA) infections. Although daptomycin was no more effective than β-lactams for treating MSSA infections, it may be a useful alternative to vancomycin for treating MRSA infections in patients with fluctuating renal function or patients who require a relatively high (≥2 μg/mL) vancomycin minimal inhibitory concentration (MIC).

New evidence suggests that vancomycin MIC cutoffs have been too liberal, and there has been a downward adjustment for the MIC breakpoint for vancomycin-susceptible and vancomycin-intermediate *S. aureus*. This means that more *S. aureus* strains will be classified as intermediate and require broader use of alternative agents.

New Uses for Older Antibacterial Drugs

Two relatively older drugs, linezolid and ertapenem, have been shown to be effective for treating diabetic foot infections without osteomyelitis. However, treatment should be limited to a 10- to 14-day course because of cost and the potential risks of long-term therapy (mitochondrial toxicity for linezolid and need for intravenous infusion for ertapenem).

Several older drugs that were formerly prescribed less often because of potential toxicity or unprofitability are now being used more often. There is good evidence that oral vancomycin is superior to metronidazole for treating severe *Clostridium difficile* colitis. Although patients with severe colitis have a 10% to 20% relapse rate with either drug, those given vancomycin have a higher response rate and more rapid improvement. Earlier concerns about an association between

oral vancomycin and an increased risk for vancomycin-resistant enterococcal infections have decreased, and vancomycin is no longer considered more likely to cause resistance than metronidazole or other agents that also disrupt the normal colonic flora (see Infectious Diarrhea).

Several gram-negative pathogens have become more widespread and have developed new mechanisms of resistance. *Acinetobacter baumannii* is becoming more common and more resistant in patients hospitalized in the United States and in wounded soldiers returning from combat in Asia. The increase in the number of cephalosporin-resistant strains (especially *Klebsiella* species and *Escherichia coli*) is alarming because these strains are usually widely resistant to other classes of drugs as well. The enzyme responsible for this resistance, extended-spectrum β-lactamase (ESBL), has become more widespread. Furthermore, several of these strains have also become carbapenem resistant. Because of increased carbapenem resistance, use of colistin and the polymyxins, which were formerly prescribed infrequently because of neural and renal toxicity, has become more common. These drugs have a unique spectrum for multidrug-resistant *A. baumannii*, *Pseudomonas* species, and ESBL-producing *E. coli* and *Klebsiella pneumoniae*. Neurotoxicity is now less of a concern, although reversible renal toxicity can be dose limiting. Although colistin and the polymyxins do have clinical efficacy, they are only indicated for critically ill patients. Therefore, cure rates for these agents are somewhat disappointing.

Tigecycline has in vitro activity against *A. baumannii* and many ESBL-producing pathogens. However, it is not indicated for treatment of hospital-acquired pneumonia or bacteremia and does not have activity against *Pseudomonas aeruginosa*. Published data are inconclusive about off-label use of tigecycline for treating highly resistant bacterial infections.

Antibiotic Dosing

Although randomized clinical trials are the best method to study drug efficacy, they are inefficient for determining optimal dosing. Pharmacodynamics proposes hypotheses and provides experimental data for optimizing outcomes based on the interaction of drugs and organisms (drug-bug interactions). Some drugs work best as long as they sustain concentrations above those needed to suppress the pathogen for a substantial part of the day and confer no further benefit at higher doses (time dependent), and others work better when they achieve high levels for even a short time (concentration dependent). These drugs can impair the ability of bacteria to recover after exposure even if the drug is no longer present. Vancomycin and the β-lactams are time dependent, and the fluoroquinolones and aminoglycosides are concentration dependent.

Most dosing decisions are based on an absolute or weight-based schedule; sometimes this is modified by an algorithm to account for reduced kidney or liver function. The only practical way for clinicians to monitor drug levels is the serum assay, which is widely available only for vancomycin and the aminoglycosides. Use of vancomycin peak levels is not helpful because they do not predict toxicity or efficacy, whereas trough levels between 10 and 20 μg/mL are considered reasonable for treating most infections (aiming for trough levels of 15-25 μg/mL for more severe infections and those caused by bacteria with higher vancomycin MICs). Vancomycin trough levels do not need to be checked for patients with mild to moderate infections and stable renal function or those requiring treatment for only 1 or 2 days.

The peak levels of aminoglycosides vary by drug and indication. Once-daily dosing is considered reasonable and safe for gram-negative infections, whereas two or three daily doses are recommended when aminoglycosides are used as synergistic agents for gram-positive infections.

Stewardship

Stewardship refers to programs instituted by hospitals to reduce the use of unnecessary antibiotics. Because of the many drugs available and an increased need to treat infections in critically ill patients, there is a temptation to overuse antibiotics. In addition to potential harm to individual patients, antibiotic overuse can influence the selection of hospital flora towards more resistant and difficult-to-treat bacteria. Some hospitals have instituted programs to promote rational use of antibiotics to minimize this selection pressure, adhere more closely to evidence-based treatment guidelines, and ascertain that dosing is individualized for patients. These programs often save money by decreasing excessively long treatment courses and reducing redundant antibiotic coverage.

In some stewardship programs, approval is sought "up front" before initiating select antibiotics. Other programs look for ways to reduce the use of broad-spectrum drugs after several days of therapy and establish an appropriate duration of treatment once a diagnosis is established. For example, patients with ventilator-associated pneumonia who respond well to treatment have similar outcomes with 8 versus 15 days of therapy. In addition, shorter courses of antibiotic therapy were associated with fewer superinfections and lower total drug toxicity.

KEY POINTS

- Despite their sometimes significant morbidity, older antibiotics are being used more often for treating highly resistant pathogens.

- Determining the correct antibiotic dose is more strongly influenced by improved understanding of drug-organism interaction than by reliance on serum drug levels; exceptions are vancomycin and the aminoglycosides.

- Antibiotic stewardship programs aim to reduce unnecessary use of antibiotics, with particular attention to those drugs that are most likely to change the hospital ecology to favor more resistant bacteria.

Bibliography

Fishman N. Antimicrobial stewardship. Am J Infect Control. 2006;34(5 Suppl 1):S55-63. [PMID: 16813983]

Fowler VG, Boucher HW, Corey GR, et al; S. aureus Endocarditis and Bacteremia Study Group. Daptomycin versus Standard Therapy for Bacteremia and Endocarditis Caused by Staphylococcus aureus. N Engl J Med. 2006;355(7):653-665. [PMID: 16914701]

Zar FA, Bakkanagari SR, Moorthi KM, Davis MB. A comparison of vancomycin and metronidazole for the treatment of Clostridium difficile–associated diarrhea, stratified by disease severity. Clin Infect Dis. 2007;45(3):302-307. [PMID: 17599306]

Self-Assessment Test

This self-assessment test contains one-best-answer multiple-choice questions. Please read these directions carefully before answering the questions. Answers, critiques, and bibliographies immediately follow these multiple-choice questions. The American College of Physicians is accredited by the Accreditation Council for Continuing Medical Education (ACCME) to provide continuing medical education for physicians.

The American College of Physicians designates MKSAP 15 Infectious Disease for a maximum of 16 *AMA PRA Category 1 Credits*™. Physicians should only claim credit commensurate with the extent of their participation in the activity. Separate answer sheets are provided for each book of the MKSAP program. Please use one of these answer sheets to complete the Infectious Disease self-assessment test. Indicate in Section H on the answer sheet the actual number of credits you earned, up to the maximum of 16, in ¼-credit increments. (One credit equals one hour of time spent on this educational activity.)

Use the self-addressed envelope provided with your program to mail your completed answer sheet(s) to the MKSAP Processing Center for scoring. Remember to provide your MKSAP 15 order and ACP ID numbers in the appropriate spaces on the answer sheet. The order and ACP ID numbers are printed on your mailing label. If you have *not* received these numbers with your MKSAP 15 purchase, you will need to acquire them to earn CME credits. E-mail ACP's customer service center at custserv@acponline.org. In the subject line, write "MKSAP 15 order/ACP ID numbers." In the body of the e-mail, make sure you include your e-mail address as well as your full name, address, city, state, ZIP code, country, and telephone number. Also identify where you have made your MKSAP 15 purchase. You will receive your MKSAP 15 order and ACP ID numbers by e-mail within 72 business hours.

CME credit is available from the publication date of July 31, 2009, until July 31, 2012. You may submit your answer sheets at any time during this period.

Self-Scoring Instructions:

Infectious Disease

Compute your percent correct score as follows:

Step 1: Give yourself 1 point for each correct response to a question.

Step 2: Divide your total points by the total number of questions: 118.

The result, expressed as a percentage, is your percent correct score.

	Example	Your Calculations
Step 1	100	
Step 2	100 ÷ 118	÷ 118
% Correct	85%	%

Directions

*Each of the numbered items is followed by lettered answers. Select the **ONE** lettered answer that is **BEST** in each case.*

Item 1

A 55-year-old man is evaluated in the hospital for a 2-day history of fever and erythema at the site of a peripherally inserted central catheter. The patient was recently diagnosed with acute myeloid leukemia for which he received chemotherapy 11 days ago. Medical history is also significant for the vancomycin IgE-mediated hypersensitivity reaction characterized by urticaria, bronchospasm, and hypotension.

On physical examination, temperature is 39.1 °C (102.5 °F), blood pressure is 100/70 mm Hg, pulse rate is 110/min, and respiration rate is 22/min. BMI is 25. Erythema and tenderness are noted at the catheter insertion site in the left antecubital fossa. A new grade 3/6 holosystolic murmur that increases with inspiration is heard at the left lower sternal border.

Laboratory studies:

Hemoglobin	7.0 g/dL (70 g/L)
Leukocyte count	1000/µL (1.0×10^9/L), with 5% neutrophils
Platelet count	20,000 (20×10^9/L)

Multiple blood cultures reveal growth of methicillin-resistant *Staphylococcus aureus.*

A chest radiograph and electrocardiogram are unremarkable. A transthoracic echocardiogram reveals moderate tricuspid insufficiency and a vegetation on the tricuspid valve.

In addition to catheter removal, which of the following is the most appropriate treatment?

(A) Cefazolin
(B) Clindamycin
(C) Daptomycin
(D) Nafcillin

Item 2

A 32-year-old female physician is beginning a postgraduate fellowship at a university hospital and must undergo tuberculin skin testing. This is the first time she will have undergone such testing. She is healthy. She grew up in Africa and completed medical school and residency training in London. She received the bacille Calmette-Guérin (BCG) vaccine as a child.

Tuberculin skin testing results indicate a 16-mm area of induration at the tuberculin skin testing site.

Physical examination is normal.

Which of the following is the most appropriate next step in the management of this patient?

(A) Chest radiograph
(B) Isoniazid, rifampin, pyrazinamide, and ethambutol
(C) Repeat tuberculin skin testing in 2 weeks
(D) No additional therapy or evaluation

Item 3

A 52-year-old man is hospitalized because of cough, fever, and pleuritic chest pain that developed 2 days after he attended a football game. Family members report that four friends who attended the game with the patient but live in another state have also been hospitalized with pneumonia; one of the friends died yesterday.

On physical examination, the patient appears acutely ill. Temperature is 38.9 °C (102.0 °F), blood pressure is 102/62 mm Hg, pulse rate is 114/min, and respiration rate is 28/min. Auscultation reveals egophony of the right side of the chest.

The leukocyte count is 16,000/µL (16×10^9/L), with 80% polymorphonuclear cells and 12% band forms. A chest radiograph shows a dense infiltrate in the right middle and right lower lobes with air bronchograms. Blood culture specimens show no growth after 24 hours.

Which of the following is the most likely diagnosis?

(A) Inhalational anthrax
(B) Mycoplasmal pneumonia
(C) Staphylococcal pneumonia
(D) Tularemia

Item 4

A 57-year-old woman is evaluated for the acute onset of dyspnea and dry cough that have rapidly worsened over the past 3 days. The patient underwent liver transplantation 15 months ago. The patient's current therapy consists of sirolimus, azathioprine, prednisone, and inhaled pentamidine. She is allergic to sulfonamides.

On physical examination, temperature is 38.4 °C (101.1 °F), blood pressure is 140/80 mm Hg, pulse rate is 110/min, and respiration rate is 23/min. Arterial oxygen saturation is 83% on ambient air. Pulmonary examination reveals scattered fine crackles bilaterally. Complete blood count, blood urea nitrogen level, serum creatinine level, and urinalysis are all normal.

A chest radiograph shows slight, diffuse, increased opacities bilaterally. A CT scan of the chest reveals bilateral diffuse, fine alveolar and interstitial infiltrates. A sputum sample cannot be obtained.

Which of the following is the most likely cause of this patient's findings?

(A) *Aspergillus fumigatus*
(B) *Candida glabrata*
(C) *Pneumocystis jirovecii*
(D) *Staphylococcus aureus*
(E) *Streptococcus pneumoniae*

Item 5

A 30-year-old man with a 6-year history of AIDS is hospitalized for gradually increasing confusion, decreased vision, dysarthria, and right hemiparesis of 8 weeks' duration. He has not visited his internist for more than 2 years. His CD4 cell count was 35/μL when last checked 2 years ago. There is no indication that he is currently taking any HIV-related medications.

On physical examination, he has evidence of wasting syndrome. Vital signs are normal. Funduscopic examination is normal. Neurologic examination discloses right hemiparesis and right hemianopia. He scores 18 of 30 on the Mini–Mental State Examination (normal >24/30). The remainder of the examination is normal.

Laboratory studies:

Hematocrit	33%
Leukocyte count	1400/μL (1.4×10^9/L) with 81% neutrophils, 4% band forms, and 15% lymphocytes
Platelet count	120,000/μL (120×10^9/L)
Creatinine	0.6 mg/dL (53 μmol/L)

MRI of the brain with contrast shows five bilateral, hypodense, nonenhancing lesions in the white matter of the periventricular parieto-occipital region with no mass effect.

Which of the following is the most likely diagnosis?

(A) Cytomegalovirus encephalitis
(B) Primary central nervous system lymphoma
(C) Progressive multifocal leukoencephalopathy
(D) Toxoplasmosis

Item 6

A 49-year-old man is evaluated for a 5-day history of pain and redness around a small ulcer on the heel of the right foot. He has a history of diabetes mellitus but no prior diabetic foot infection. Current medications are metformin and glipizide. He is up-to-date on all immunizations, including tetanus.

On physical examination, temperature is 37.2 °C (99.0 °F), blood pressure is 130/75 mm Hg, pulse rate is 83/min, and respiration rate is 16/min; BMI is 27.

A small amount of erythema extending about 1 cm around a 3- × 3-mm ulcer is noted at the right heel. The area involved is tender, warm, and limited to superficial skin and subcutaneous tissues. There is no necrosis, purulent discharge, or evidence of maceration between the toes. Lymphangitis and lymphadenopathy are absent. The remainder of the physical examination is normal.

Laboratory studies, including a complete blood count, metabolic panel, and urinalysis, are normal except for a leukocyte count of 12,000/μL (12×10^9/L).

A radiograph of the foot shows no evidence of bone involvement and a minimal amount of edema.

Antibiotic therapy against which of the following pathogens is most appropriate in this patient?

(A) Aerobic gram-negative bacilli
(B) Aerobic gram-positive cocci
(C) Aerobic gram-positive cocci and anaerobic organisms
(D) Anaerobic organisms

Item 7

An 18-year-old woman is evaluated in the emergency department because of a 3-day history of lower abdominal pain. She does not have urinary frequency, dysuria, flank pain, nausea, or vomiting. Her only medication is an oral contraceptive agent.

On physical examination, temperature is 38.3 °C (101.0 °F), blood pressure is 118/68 mm Hg, pulse rate is 104/min, and respiration rate is 16/min. Abdominal examination is normal. There is no flank tenderness. Pelvic examination shows cervical motion tenderness, fundal tenderness, and bilateral adnexal tenderness on bimanual examination.

The leukocyte count and urinalysis are normal. Urine and serum pregnancy tests are negative.

Which of the following is the most appropriate treatment?

(A) Ampicillin and gentamicin, intravenously
(B) Azithromycin, orally
(C) Cefoxitin, intramuscularly
(D) Ceftriaxone, intramuscularly, and doxycycline, orally
(E) Metronidazole, orally

Item 8

A 75-year-old man with type 2 diabetes mellitus is evaluated in the emergency department for a draining chronic ulcer on the left foot, erythema, and fever. Drainage initially began 3 weeks ago. Current medications include metformin and glyburide.

On physical examination, he is not ill appearing. Temperature is 37.9 °C (100.2 °F); other vital signs are normal. The left foot is slightly warm and erythematous. A plantar ulcer that is draining purulent material is present over the fourth metatarsal joint. A metal probe makes contact with bone. The remainder of the examination is normal.

The leukocyte count is normal, and an erythrocyte sedimentation rate is 70 mm/h. A plain radiograph of the foot is normal.

Gram stain of the purulent drainage at the ulcer base shows numerous leukocytes, gram-positive cocci in clusters, and gram-negative rods.

Which of the following is the most appropriate management now?

(A) Begin imipenem
(B) Begin vancomycin and ceftazidime
(C) Begin vancomycin and metronidazole
(D) Perform bone biopsy

Item 9

A 57-year-old man is evaluated for progressive dementia of 4 months' duration. The patient was in excellent health until his family noticed that he was becoming more forgetful, particularly over the past 2 months, with increasing disorientation, clumsiness, and episodes of spontaneous limb jerking. In the past 2 weeks, he has also become aphasic.

Medical history includes bilateral corneal transplant for keratoconus at age 25 years.

Physical examination, including vital signs, is normal. The patient is obtunded. On neurologic examination, the patient responds with purposeful movement to sternal rub. Myoclonus is elicited by a loud hand clap.

Routine laboratory studies are normal.

Cerebrospinal fluid analysis:

Leukocyte count	2/μL (2 × 10⁶/L)
Erythrocyte count	1/μL (1 × 10⁶/L)
Protein	41 mg/dL (410 mg/L)
Glucose	84 mg/dL (4.7 mmol/L)
HIV serology	Negative

A CT of the head is normal. An electroencephalogram shows periodic sharp waves.

Which of the following is the most likely diagnosis?

(A) Creutzfeldt-Jakob disease
(B) HIV/AIDS encephalopathy
(C) Lyme disease
(D) West Nile virus encephalitis

Item 10

A 29-year-old woman is evaluated in the emergency department for blurred vision, diplopia, slurred speech, nasal regurgitation of fluids, and bilateral upper extremity weakness. The vision disturbances developed yesterday, and the slurred speech and upper extremity weakness began earlier today. Two other patients with similar symptoms are also being evaluated in the emergency department.

On physical examination, the patient is alert, awake, and fully oriented. Speech is fluid but slurred. Temperature is 37.0 °C (98.6 °F), blood pressure is 90/60 mm Hg, pulse rate is 50/min, and respiration rate is 12/min. The pupils are dilated, and extraocular movements show bilateral deficits in cranial nerve IV. She cannot abduct her arms against resistance.

Complete blood count and routine blood chemistry studies are normal. CT scan of the head is normal. Lumbar puncture is performed; cerebrospinal fluid examination is unremarkable.

Which of the following is the most likely diagnosis?

(A) Botulism
(B) Guillain-Barré syndrome
(C) Myasthenia gravis
(D) Poliomyelitis

Item 11

A 28-year-old man is evaluated at a community health center for a 10-day history of sore throat, headache, fever, anorexia, and muscle aches. Two days ago, a rash developed on his trunk and abdomen. He had been previously healthy and has not had any contact with ill persons. He has had multiple male and female sexual partners and infrequently uses condoms. He has been tested for HIV infection several times, most recently 8 months ago; all results were negative.

On physical examination, temperature is 38.6 °C (101.4 °F). There are several small ulcers on the tongue and buccal mucosa and cervical and supraclavicular lymphadenopathy. A faint maculopapular rash is present on the trunk and abdomen.

A rapid plasma reagin test is ordered.

Which of the following diagnostic studies should also be done at this time?

(A) CD4 cell count measurement
(B) Epstein-Barr virus IgM measurement
(C) HIV RNA viral load measurement
(D) Skin biopsy

Item 12

A 24-year-old woman is evaluated for new-onset severe headache. The headache began acutely 3 days ago and is constant and localized to the right temporal area of the head. She has taken ibuprofen and acetaminophen without relief. She also reports swelling along the right side of her jaw that began about 2 weeks ago.

On physical examination, temperature is 37.1 °C (98.8 °F); the remaining vital signs are normal. The face is swollen and erythematous along the right mandible, with no evidence of drainage. The rest of the physical examination findings, including the neurologic examination, is normal.

The peripheral leukocyte count is normal. A contrast-enhanced CT scan of the head and face shows a soft-tissue mass surrounding the right mandible, with extension through the mandible and erosion of the base of the skull. There is a 3-cm ring-enhancing lesion in the right temporal lobe of the brain. The patient undergoes CT-guided stereotactic aspiration of the lesion.

Pending culture results of the lesion, which of the following empiric antimicrobial regimens should be initiated?

(A) Clindamycin plus ceftriaxone
(B) Penicillin G
(C) Penicillin G plus metronidazole
(D) Trimethoprim-sulfamethoxazole
(E) Vancomycin plus gentamicin

Item 13

A 75-year-old man has a 2-month history of gradually increasing, nontrauma-related, severe low back pain. The patient often feels warm and diaphoretic. He has no urine or stool incontinence. Ten weeks ago, he was discharged from the hospital after a prolonged intensive care unit stay for the treatment of community-acquired pneumonia–associated sepsis. During his stay, he required mechanical ventilation, enteral nutrition, and prolonged central venous access.

On physical examination, temperature is 38.1 °C (100.5 °F); other vital signs are normal. There is mild tenderness to palpation over the low back with no definitive point of maximum tenderness. Neurologic examination is normal.

Complete blood count and urinalysis are normal. Erythrocyte sedimentation rate is 90 mm/h. Blood cultures are drawn.

Which of the following is the optimal diagnostic evaluation?

(A) CT scan of the lumbar spine
(B) MRI of the lumbar spine
(C) Plain radiograph of the lumbar spine
(D) Three-phase bone scintigraphy

Item 14

A 28-year-old man with long-standing HIV infection is evaluated in the office for a 1-week history of dysphagia and mild odynophagia and a 2.3-kg (5-lb) weight loss. He has not had fever or hematemesis. History is significant for *Pneumocystis jirovecii* pneumonia. The patient is nonadherent to his highly active antiretroviral therapy (HAART) regimen but does take trimethoprim-sulfamethoxazole prophylaxis.

Physical examination is normal except for white plaques on the tongue and soft palate. His most recent CD4 cell count was 68/µL.

He is counseled regarding the importance of adhering to his HAART regimen.

Which of the following is the most appropriate treatment for this patient's dysphagia and odynophagia?

(A) Amphotericin B
(B) Fluconazole
(C) Omeprazole
(D) Prednisone
(E) Valganciclovir

Item 15

A 42-year-old woman is evaluated for a postoperative wound infection. Eight weeks ago, the patient underwent bilateral augmentation mammoplasty. Six weeks after surgery, she developed violaceous draining nodules at the surgical closure site of the right breast. After 7 days of dicloxacillin, the wound had enlarged. Wound cultures grew normal skin flora. The patient was hospitalized, and intravenous vancomycin plus cefepime was added but without clinical benefit. A second set of wound cultures grew a few colonies of *Candida albicans.*

Medical history is otherwise unremarkable.

On physical examination, temperature is 38.0 °C (100.4 °F), blood pressure is 105/75 mm Hg, pulse rate is 84/min, and respiration rate is 16/min. Her left breast surgical scar is well healed, and the right breast surgical wound is partially opened and packed along the medial half. The lateral half of the wound is erythematous, with two sinus tracts draining purulent material.

Which of the following is the most likely causative agent for her wound infection?

(A) Fluconazole-resistant *Candida albicans*
(B) Methicillin-resistant *Staphylococcus aureus*
(C) *Mycobacterium abscessus*

(D) *Mycobacterium tuberculosis*
(E) *Nocardia asteroides*

Item 16

A 45-year-old man is evaluated in the emergency department for low-grade fever, obtundation, and personality changes of 5 days' duration, with progressively declining mental status.

On physical examination, temperature is 37.3 °C (99.2 °F), and the remaining vital signs are normal. The Glasgow Coma Scale score is 6. There are no focal neurologic findings.

MRI of the brain shows bilateral swelling and enhancement of the temporal lobes. Cerebrospinal fluid (CSF) analysis indicates lymphocytic meningitis, and CSF polymerase chain reaction (PCR) results are positive for herpes simplex virus type 1. Intravenous acyclovir is initiated, and the patient is admitted to the hospital. Two weeks into therapy, the patient remains obtunded, with only minimal improvement since admission. A repeat MRI of the brain is unchanged, and CSF PCR testing continues to be positive for herpes simplex virus type 1.

Which of the following is the most appropriate management?

(A) Add dexamethasone
(B) Brain biopsy
(C) Change to ganciclovir
(D) Change to foscarnet
(E) Continue acyclovir

Item 17

A 45-year-old-man is evaluated in late August for fever, erythema, and painful swelling of the left hand 2 days after he went swimming in the Gulf of Mexico. While he was swimming, he cut the palm of his left hand on a shell. He has a history of injection drug use, which he discontinued 15 years ago, and chronic hepatitis C for which he has declined treatment. Immunization history is unknown. His takes no medications.

On physical examination, temperature is 39.1 °C (102.4 °F), blood pressure is 90/60 mm Hg, pulse rate is 120/min, and respiration rate is 24/min. The left hand is shown on page 93.

The cardiopulmonary examination is normal. The abdomen is distended with ascites, and the liver and spleen are not palpable.

Which of the following is the most likely cause of this patient's hand infection?

(A) *Clostridium tetani*
(B) *Pasteurella multocida*
(C) *Rickettsia rickettsii*
(D) *Vibrio vulnificus*

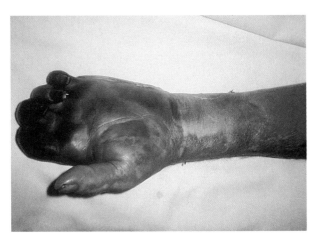

Item 18

A 27-year-old previously healthy woman is diagnosed with community-acquired pneumonia for which she receives ceftriaxone therapy. Medical history is otherwise noncontributory.

Routine and mycobacterial sputum cultures are performed. The patient recovers uneventfully over the subsequent 2 weeks, and a follow-up chest radiograph shows improvement. The routine sputum cultures reveal only normal flora; however, after 3 weeks, the mycobacterial culture grows two colonies of *Mycobacterium avium* complex.

Which of the following is the most appropriate next step in management?

(A) Initiate clarithromycin, rifampin, and ethambutol

(B) Initiate isoniazid

(C) Initiate isoniazid, rifampin, pyrazinamide, and ethambutol

(D) No further treatment

Item 19

A 42-year-old woman is evaluated for a 2-day history of an increasing cough productive of small amounts of green–brown sputum and fever that began today. Medical history is significant for acute myelomonocytic leukemia diagnosed 5 weeks ago for which she is receiving consolidation chemotherapy.

On physical examination, temperature is 38.6 °C (101.5 °F), blood pressure is 110/90 mm Hg, pulse rate is 100/min, and respiration rate is 24/min. She appears acutely ill. Pulmonary examination reveals crackles in the right upper posterior thorax.

Chest radiograph discloses a 2- × 2-cm cavitating right upper lobe lesion. Bronchoscopy results are unremarkable. Histologic results of a CT-guided lung needle biopsy show slender mycelia demonstrating acute angle branching. Results of polymerase chain reaction testing for *Aspergillus* species are negative. Culture results are pending.

Which of the following is the most appropriate empiric therapy pending culture results?

(A) Amphotericin B deoxycholate

(B) Amphotericin B lipid complex

(C) Flucytosine

(D) Liposomal amphotericin B

(E) Voriconazole

Item 20

A 35-year-old male customs inspector is brought to the emergency department because of a 2-day history of fever, shortness of breath, and chest pain. He has had no recent known contact with ill persons.

On physical examination, the patient is diaphoretic and appears acutely ill. He is oriented only to person. Temperature is 38.0 °C (100.4 °F), blood pressure is 88/60 mm Hg, pulse rate is 110/min, and respiration rate is 28/min. Coarse bronchial breath sounds are heard.

The leukocyte count is 15,000/µL (15 × 10^9/L). A chest radiograph shows a widened mediastinum and bilateral pleural effusions.

A buffy coat Gram stain of a peripheral blood smear shows box car–shaped gram-positive bacilli.

Which of the following is the most appropriate treatment?

(A) Ciprofloxacin, rifampin, and vancomycin

(B) Erythromycin, clindamycin, and rifampin

(C) Erythromycin, vancomycin, and rifampin

(D) Penicillin, rifampin, and vancomycin

Item 21

A 63-year-old woman is evaluated for fever and hypotension 4 days after kidney-pancreas transplantation surgery. She was treated with cyclosporine, prednisolone, and mycophenolate mofetil. The incisional pain has not increased, and, except for slightly increased erythema surrounding the incision, there are no localizing signs or symptoms. Medical history is significant for type 1 diabetes mellitus since the age of 12 years. Until the onset of her current symptoms, she had been doing well after surgery.

On physical examination, temperature is 39.4 °C (102.9 °F), blood pressure is 88/52 mm Hg, pulse rate is 100/min, and respiration rate is 20/min. Cardiopulmonary examination is normal. On abdominal examination, there is erythema surrounding the surgical right lower quadrant incision and moderate tenderness to palpation of the surgical wound. The remainder of the examination is normal.

Laboratory studies:

Hemoglobin	12.1 g/dL (121 g/L)
Leukocyte count	13,400/µL (13.4 × 10^9/L)
Creatinine	1.9 mg/dL (168 µmol/L)
Urinalysis	7 leukocytes/hpf, 25 erythrocytes/hpf, and trace protein

The patient and organ donor are serologically positive for cytomegalovirus infection.

A chest radiograph reveals no infiltrates. Abdominal radiographs show only a small amount of free peritoneal gas. CT scans of the chest and abdomen reveal only some peri-incisional fluid.

Which of the following is the most likely cause of this patient's current symptoms and findings?

(A) Candidal wound infection
(B) Cytomegalovirus infection
(C) *Pneumocystis jirovecii* pneumonia
(D) Staphylococcal wound infection

Item 22

A 25-year-old man is evaluated for a 2-week history of left-sided facial pain. Medical history is unremarkable. A diagnosis of sinusitis is established, and the patient receives therapy with azithromycin, which partially resolves his pain. One week after initiation of therapy, he is admitted to the emergency department with headache and a tonic-clonic seizure.

On physical examination, temperature is normal, and he is drowsy. There are no focal neurologic deficits. Laboratory studies are normal. An MRI shows a 3.5-cm ring-enhancing lesion in the left frontoparietal region. Aspiration of the lesion reveals purulent material. Empiric therapy with vancomycin, metronidazole, and ceftriaxone is initiated. Culture of the aspirate grows only *Escherichia coli*.

Which of the following is the most appropriate treatment?

(A) Change antimicrobial therapy to imipenem
(B) Change antimicrobial therapy to levofloxacin
(C) Continue ceftriaxone only
(D) Continue metronidazole and ceftriaxone only
(E) Continue vancomycin, metronidazole, and ceftriaxone

Item 23

A 25-year-old pregnant woman at 25 weeks' gestation undergoes a new-patient evaluation. She has recently diagnosed HIV infection and has never taken antiretroviral therapy. Her current CD4 cell count is 550/μL, and her HIV RNA viral load is 20,000 copies/mL. She takes no medications except for a daily prenatal vitamin.

Physical examination, including vital signs, is normal.

Which of the following is the most appropriate management of this patient?

(A) Initiate antiretroviral therapy when CD4 cell count is <500/μL
(B) Initiate zidovudine-lamivudine and efavirenz now
(C) Initiate zidovudine, lamivudine, and lopinavir-ritonavir now
(D) Initiate zidovudine therapy at delivery

Item 24

A 28-year-old man is evaluated for a new lesion on his left leg that he noticed 2 weeks ago. The patient was diagnosed with HIV infection 1 month ago. He is asymptomatic and does not take antiretroviral therapy or any other medications.

On physical examination, the patient appears well; vital signs are normal. There is a small, raised, nontender, violaceous lesion on the left lower extremity.

The remainder of the examination is normal. A stool specimen is negative for occult blood.

Laboratory studies:

Complete blood count	Normal
Liver chemistry panel	Normal
Renal function studies	Normal
CD4 cell count	409/μL
HIV RNA viral load	15,000 copies/mL

A chest radiograph is normal. A biopsy of the lesion is obtained, results of which confirm a diagnosis of Kaposi sarcoma.

Which of the following is the most appropriate treatment at this time?

(A) Begin chemotherapy
(B) Begin highly active antiretroviral therapy
(C) Begin intralesional vinblastine injections
(D) Begin topical alitretinoin (9-*cis*-retinoic acid)
(E) Continue to monitor CD4 cell count and HIV RNA viral load

Item 25

A 40-year-old man is evaluated for the acute onset of fever, headache, nausea, and lethargy. He has a history of obstructive hydrocephalus for which he underwent ventriculo-peritoneal shunt placement approximately 6 months ago, and the shunt has been functioning well.

On physical examination, temperature is 38.0 °C (100.4 °F), blood pressure is 110/70 mm Hg, pulse rate is 90/min, and respiration rate is 14/min. Examination of the head reveals the presence of the shunt catheter without evidence of skin breakdown or tenderness along the site. He is oriented only to person and place and needs to be aroused to answer questions. The remainder of the physical examination, including funduscopic and neurologic examinations, is normal.

Laboratory studies indicate a leukocyte count of 11,000/μL (11×10^9/L) with a normal differential. Cerebrospinal fluid, obtained after tapping of the shunt, reveals a leukocyte count of 200/μL (200×10^6/L) with 90% neutrophils, a glucose concentration of 40 mg/dL (2.22 mmol/L), and a protein level of 100 mg/dL (1000 mg/L). Gram stain results are negative.

Pending culture results, which of the following antimicrobial regimens should be initiated in this patient?

(A) Trimethoprim-sulfamethoxazole
(B) Trimethoprim-sulfamethoxazole plus rifampin
(C) Vancomycin
(D) Vancomycin, ampicillin, plus ceftriaxone
(E) Vancomycin plus cefepime

Item 26

A previously well 60-year-old man presents in August with the acute onset of altered mental status.

On physical examination, temperature is 38.6 °C (101.5 °F). The remaining vital signs are normal. Neurologic examination reveals bilateral tremors and myoclonus of the extremities and cogwheel rigidity.

MRI of the brain shows hypodense lesions on T1-weighted images in the thalamus and basal ganglia, which are hyperintense on T2-weighted images. Cerebrospinal fluid analysis indicates a leukocyte count of $120/\mu L$ ($120 \times 10^6/L$) (90% lymphocytes) with normal glucose and elevated protein levels.

Which of the following is the most likely cause of the patient's findings?

(A) *Listeria monocytogenes*
(B) *Toxoplasma gondii*
(C) *Tropheryma whippelii*
(D) Varicella zoster virus
(E) West Nile virus

Item 27

A 25-year-old woman has a 1-week history of a rash and hair loss. The patient uses crack cocaine and recently entered a drug rehabilitation program. Results of an HIV test were negative on admission to the program. The patient has an allergy to penicillin characterized by extensive formation of hives, wheezing, and dyspnea that required emergency treatment. She has no history of sexually transmitted diseases.

Physical examination discloses patchy hair loss and a maculopapular eruption on the chest and trunk.

The results of a confirmatory serologic treponemal antigen assay and a rapid plasma reagin test are positive for syphilis. A pregnancy test is negative.

Which of the following is the most appropriate treatment?

(A) Benzathine penicillin G
(B) Benzathine penicillin G plus methylprednisolone
(C) Ceftriaxone
(D) Doxycycline
(E) Erythromycin

Item 28

A 38-year-old man is evaluated for a 3-week history of progressive right-sided weakness of the upper and lower extremities, difficulty with balance, and slurred speech. Medical history includes syphilis 12 years ago that was treated with benzathine penicillin G and recurrent herpes simplex proctitis treated with acyclovir. The patient has no history of illicit drug use.

The patient has not had routine medical care in the past 5 years and has never been tested for HIV infection. On physical examination, temperature is 37.2 °C (99.0 °F), blood pressure is 115/80 mm Hg, pulse rate is 80/min, and respiration rate is 14/min. The Mini–Mental State Examination score is 22 (normal >24/30). Speech is dysarthric. There is moderate right-sided hemiparesis with increased muscle tone on the right.

Laboratory studies:

Hematocrit	37%
Leukocyte count	$4500/\mu L$ ($4.5 \times 10^9/L$)
Platelet count	$240,000/\mu L$ ($240 \times 10^9/L$)
Serologic testing for HIV antibodies	Positive

MRI of the brain reveals numerous ring-enhancing lesions in the basal ganglia and the corticomedullary junction, predominantly on the left side with no mass effect or edema.

Which of the following is the most appropriate next management step?

(A) Begin corticosteroids
(B) Begin empiric treatment with sulfadiazine, pyrimethamine, and folinic acid
(C) Obtain CT scan of the head with contrast
(D) Obtain stereotactic brain biopsy
(E) Obtain thallium-201 SPECT scan

Item 29

A 75-year-old woman is evaluated for a 1-day history of fever and altered mental status. She was recently diagnosed with autoimmune hemolytic anemia for which she has been taking high-dose prednisone therapy for the past 3 weeks. She also has a 6-month history of chronic lymphocytic leukemia.

On physical examination, she is difficult to arouse. Temperature is 38.4 °C (101.2 °F), blood pressure is 110/70 mm Hg, pulse rate is 100/min, and respiration rate is 16/min. There is resistance to neck flexion.

A non-contrast–enhanced CT scan of the head is normal. Cerebrospinal fluid (CSF) analysis indicates a leukocyte count of $1200/\mu L$ ($1200 \times 10^6/L$) with 50% neutrophils and 50% lymphocytes, a glucose concentration of 30 mg/dL (1.7 mmol/L) (serum glucose, 110 mg/dL [6.1 mmol/L]), and a protein level of 200 mg/dL (2000 mg/L). CSF Gram stain results are negative, and empiric therapy with dexamethasone, vancomycin, ampicillin, and ceftriaxone is initiated. Blood and CSF cultures grow *Listeria monocytogenes*.

Which of the following antimicrobial regimens should now be administered?

(A) Ampicillin plus gentamicin
(B) Ceftriaxone
(C) Chloramphenicol
(D) Vancomycin plus gentamicin

Item 30

A 39-year-old man with pancreatic cancer is evaluated for profound neutropenia occurring with each of several rounds of chemotherapy. His absolute neutrophil count has been less than $100/\mu L$ ($0.10 \times 10^9/L$) for the past 15 days. He also has a cough productive of blood-tinged brown sputum and has had temperatures to 40.1 °C (104.1 °F) for 3 days. Empiric treatment with piperacillin/tazobactam is started. Chest radiographs reveal several cavitary lesions in both lungs.

On physical examination, temperature is 39.1 °C (102.3 °F), blood pressure is 98/62 mm Hg, pulse rate is 118/min, and respiration rate is 24/min. Pulmonary examination discloses bilateral crackles and occasional wheezes.

Laboratory studies:

Hemoglobin	8.3 g/dL (83 g/L)
Leukocyte count	<100/µL (0.1 × 10⁹/L)
Platelet count	<10,000/µL (10 × 10⁹/L)
Creatinine	1.2 mg/dL (106 µmol/L)

Nasopharyngeal swab and expectorated sputum cultures both grow *Aspergillus fumigatus.*

Which of the following is the most appropriate addition to his treatment?

(A) Amphotericin B deoxycholate

(B) Fluconazole

(C) Ketoconazole

(D) Liposomal amphotericin B

(E) Voriconazole

Item 31

A 70-year-old man has a 1-day history of a painful rash on his chest. Three days before the rash became apparent, he developed severe pain and paresthesias in the same area.

Skin examination findings of the left side of the chest are shown.

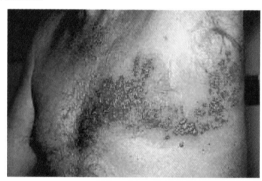

The remainder of the examination is unremarkable.

In addition to appropriate analgesic agents, which of the following should be given at this time?

(A) Corticosteroids

(B) Oral famciclovir

(C) Intravenous acyclovir

(D) Topical penciclovir

Item 32

A 61-year-old homeless man is hospitalized after being "found unconscious" in an alley on a cold morning in March. On physical examination, the patient is barely arousable. Temperature is 33.0 °C (91.5 °F), blood pressure is 90/50 mm Hg, pulse rate is 50/min, and respiration rate is 10/min. Numerous draining skin lesions are noted.

Active internal rewarming is undertaken, and intravenous fluid resuscitation is initiated. The chest radiograph is normal. Urine and blood culture specimens are obtained, and cefepime and vancomycin are begun. Blood cultures and aspirates of deep soft tissue lesions grow methicillin-susceptible *Staphylococcus aureus.* All other culture results are negative.

His clinical course improves by hospital day 3, and the antibiotic stewardship team recommends changing cefepime and vancomycin to nafcillin alone.

Which of the following is the most important reason for making this recommendation?

(A) Cost-saving

(B) Need for fewer daily infusions

(C) Reduced risk of nephrotoxicity

(D) Reduction of selection for resistant colonizing organisms

Item 33

A 32-year-old woman is evaluated for a 2-day history of fever, urinary frequency, left-sided flank pain, and nausea without vomiting. She also has diet-controlled type 2 diabetes mellitus.

On physical examination, temperature is 38.3 °C (100.9 °F), blood pressure is 122/82 mm Hg, pulse rate is 102/min, and respiration rate is 18/min. Left-sided costovertebral angle tenderness is present. Abdominal and pelvic examinations are normal.

Laboratory studies:

Leukocyte count	14,000/µL (14 × 10⁹/L) with 82% polymorphonuclear cells and 8% band forms
Blood urea nitrogen	14 mg/dL (5.0 mmol/L)
Creatinine	1.1 mg/dL (97.2 µmol/L)
Urinalysis	Positive for leukocyte esterase and nitrites
Pregnancy test	Negative

Which of the following is the most appropriate empiric treatment?

(A) Ampicillin

(B) Levofloxacin

(C) Nitrofurantoin

(D) Trimethoprim-sulfamethoxazole

Item 34

A 24-year-old man is evaluated in the emergency department for fever, nausea, vomiting, and severe headache of 4 hours' duration. This is the third such episode in 6 years, with the other two episodes resulting in a diagnosis of meningococcal meningitis. During the second episode, the patient's total hemolytic complement (CH₅₀) level was normal, and he was given the meningococcal vaccine.

On physical examination, temperature is 39.2 °C (102.5 °F), blood pressure is 98/62 mm Hg, pulse rate is regular at 108/min, and respiration rate is 24/min. There is marked nuchal rigidity.

Lumbar puncture is performed, and cerebrospinal fluid (CSF) results are compatible with bacterial meningitis. CSF culture grows *Neisseria meningitidis.* CH_{50} complement level is 73 (normal, 43 to 105).

Which of the following additional tests would be appropriate to determine the cause of this patient's multiple episodes of meningococcal meningitis?

(A) C9 and alternative and lectin pathway component measurement

(B) Lymphocyte subset panel

(C) MRI of the brain and spinal cord

(D) Quantitative immunoglobulin and immunoglobulin subset panel

(E) Repeat CH_{50} measurement

Item 35

A 19-year-old male college student has a 2-day history of a urethral discharge and a burning sensation on urination. He has had three female sexual partners in the past month.

Physical examination discloses a scant mucoid discharge from the urethral orifice. No rashes or other lesions are seen.

Gram stain of the urethral secretions shows greater than 12 polymorphonuclear cells/hpf. No intra- or extracellular organisms are seen.

Which of the following is the most appropriate treatment?

(A) Acyclovir orally

(B) Azithromycin orally

(C) Benzathine penicillin G, intramuscularly

(D) Cefixime orally

(E) Metronidazole orally

Item 36

A 72-year-old man is evaluated for a chronic nonproductive cough of 4 weeks' duration. He denies pain, weight loss, fever, chills, or night sweats. He does not smoke. He is a farmer who keeps cattle and chickens. He takes no medications.

On physical examination, vital signs are normal. The lungs are clear to auscultation. The remainder of the physical examination is normal.

A chest radiograph shows multiple small nodular infiltrates throughout both lungs. The CT scan reveals several dozen of these lesions scattered throughout both lungs as well as three small pulmonary, one mediastinal, and several small splenic calcifications but no cavitation.

Laboratory studies indicate a hemoglobin level of 14.8 g/dL (148 g/L) and a leukocyte count of 4900/μL (4.9×10^9/L).

Which of the following tests will most likely confirm the diagnosis?

(A) Fungal blood cultures

(B) *Histoplasma* serology

(C) *Histoplasma* urinary antigen detection

(D) Sputum culture

Item 37

A 23-year-old preschool teacher calls the nurse for assessment of a 3-year-old child with fever and a progressive disseminated vesicular rash. The child has not had any vaccinations because of autism fears. The teacher does not recall having had chickenpox or a personal varicella vaccination.

Which of the following is the most appropriate action for the teacher at this time?

(A) Immediate acyclovir therapy

(B) Intramuscular immune globulin

(C) Serologic testing for varicella virus antibodies

(D) Varicella-zoster immune globulin (VZIG)

(E) Zoster immunization

Item 38

A 32-year-old man has a 1-day history of dysuria and a urethral discharge. He is in a monogamous sexual relationship. The patient has no drug allergies.

Physical examination discloses a urethral discharge. No rashes or other lesions are seen. Gram stain results are shown.

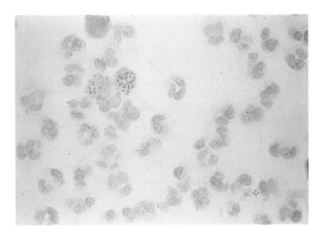

In addition to screening for other sexually transmitted diseases, which of the following is the most appropriate treatment?

(A) Azithromycin, single dose orally

(B) Benzathine penicillin, single dose intramuscularly

(C) Ceftriaxone and doxycycline

(D) Ciprofloxacin and doxycycline

Item 39

A 54-year-old woman is hospitalized for recurrent pneumonia, the present episode of which began 3 days ago. She has been hospitalized twice over the past 2 months for pneumonia that was treated with 2-week regimens of amoxicillin plus clavulanic acid and clarithromycin plus ceftriaxone, respectively, with improvement within 1 to 3 days of therapy. Each episode was characterized by the sudden onset of fever, chest tightness, dyspnea, nonproductive cough, and diffuse interstitial pulmonary infiltrates on chest radiograph.

Medical history is otherwise unremarkable. For the past 2 months, she has been house-sitting for a friend who has a hot tub that she uses occasionally.

On physical examination, she is mildly dyspneic. Temperature is 37.7 °C (99.9 °F), blood pressure is 135/80 mm Hg, pulse rate is 90/min, and respiration rate is 22/min. Arterial oxygen saturation is 90% on ambient air. Diffuse fine crackles are heard throughout both lung fields. The leukocyte count is 7600/µL (7.6 × 10⁹/L), and the serum lactate dehydrogenase level is 450 U/L.

A chest radiograph shows an interstitial micronodular pattern most prominent in the lower and mid-lung zones. HIV serology and bronchoscopic lavage results of routine cultures and rapid testing for influenza; parainfluenza 1, 2, and 3; adenovirus; respiratory syncytial virus; *Chlamydophila pneumoniae*; and *Mycoplasma pneumoniae* are negative. The results of a mycobacterial smear are negative, and cultures are pending.

Which of the following is the most appropriate treatment?

(A) Ceftriaxone and azithromycin
(B) Corticosteroids
(C) Doxycycline
(D) Ethambutol and clarithromycin
(E) Piperacillin-tazobactam

Item 40

A 29-year-old woman with two children in day care is evaluated in the office for loose stools of 3 days' duration. She has HIV-1 infection, with a CD4 cell count of 395/µL and an undetectable HIV RNA viral load. Her children are HIV negative and are currently recovering from their own bouts of diarrhea. They are being evaluated by the public health department for cryptosporidiosis.

On physical examination, she appears comfortable and is at her baseline weight of 80 kg (176 lb). Temperature is normal. The blood pressure is 118/72 mm Hg, and the pulse rate is 74/min, neither of which changes on standing. The remainder of the examination is normal.

Stool is brown and negative for blood.

Which of the following is the most appropriate next step in management?

(A) Order a bacterial stool culture
(B) Treat patient only with trimethoprim-sulfamethoxazole
(C) Treat whole family with paromomycin
(D) Reassure and re-evaluate in 1 week

Item 41

A 35-year-old man is evaluated in the emergency department 72 hours after initiation of clindamycin and quinine therapy for peripheral blood smear–confirmed babesiosis. The patient showed improvement the first 48 hours after treatment, but his condition has now begun to deteriorate. Recent travel history includes a 1-month trip to Cape Cod, Massachusetts, from which he returned to his home in New York City 1 week ago.

On physical examination, temperature is 40.0 °C (104.0 °F), blood pressure is 90/60 mm Hg, and pulse rate is 110/min. There is conjunctival icterus. Lymphadenopathy is absent, and the neck is supple. Cardiopulmonary examination is normal. Abdominal examination reveals a tender right upper quadrant with hepatomegaly.

Repeat laboratory studies:

Hemoglobin	9.2 g/dL (92 g/L)
Platelet count	40,000/µL (40 × 10⁹/L)
Leukocyte count	2700/µL (2.7 × 10⁹/L)
Alanine aminotransferase	874 U/L
Blood cultures from 72 hours ago	Negative × 2
Bilirubin	7.4 mg/dL (126.5 µmol/L)

A chest radiograph is normal.

Which of the following is the most appropriate treatment at this time?

(A) Begin cefepime and vancomycin
(B) Begin corticosteroids
(C) Begin doxycycline
(D) Switch to atovaquone and azithromycin

Item 42

A 55-year-old man is evaluated for fever and increasing erythema and swelling of the right lower extremity. The patient noticed these symptoms after cutting his leg on a piece of concrete while walking through flood waters following a tsunami 2 days ago in Thailand. The symptoms first appeared just above the ankle but have now spread to just above the knee. The patient has a 25-year history of heavy alcohol use. He received a tetanus immunization within the past 5 years.

On physical examination, temperature is 38.9 °C (102.1 °F), pulse rate is 115/min, and respiration rate is 23/min; BMI is 25. The right leg is edematous and very tender to touch, with diffuse erythema and hemorrhagic bullae and ecchymoses spreading from the right ankle to just above the right knee.

Laboratory studies:

Leukocyte count	17,000/µL (17 × 10⁹/L)
Creatinine	1.5 mg/dL (132.6 µmol/L)
Alanine aminotransferase	60 U/L
Aspartate aminotransferase	100 U/L
Albumin	2.4 g/dL (24 g/L)
Prothrombin time	16 s
Activated partial thromboplastin time	45 s

Gram stain of bullous fluid reveals gram-negative bacilli. Blood cultures are positive for gram-negative bacilli.

Which of the following is the most likely cause of this patient's infection?

(A) *Aeromonas hydrophila*
(B) *Capnocytophaga canimorsus*
(C) *Pasteurella multocida*
(D) *Vibrio cholerae*

Item 43

A 70-year-old man is evaluated in the emergency department for the acute onset of fever, cough productive of yellow sputum, right-sided pleuritic chest pain, and dizziness. He has a history of diabetes mellitus and hypertension treated with hydrochlorothiazide, lisinopril, glyburide, and metformin.

On physical examination, temperature is 35.0 °C (95.0 °F), blood pressure is 110/70 mm Hg, pulse rate is 120/min, and respiration rate is 36/min. He appears to be in acute respiratory distress. Pulmonary examination reveals dullness to percussion, increased fremitus, and crackles at the right lung base. He is oriented only to person.

Laboratory studies:

Hematocrit	42%
Leukocyte count	23,000/μL (23×10^9/L) with 40% band forms
Platelet count	150,000/μL (150×10^9/L)
Blood urea nitrogen	46 mg/dL (16.4 mmol/L)
Creatinine	1.4 mg/dL (123.8 μmol/L)

Arterial blood gas studies (ambient air):

P_{O_2}	50 mm Hg
P_{CO_2}	30 mm Hg
pH	7.48

Chest radiograph shows a right lower lobe infiltrate.

Which of the following is the most appropriate management of this patient?

(A) Admit to general medical floor
(B) Admit to the intensive care unit
(C) Observe in the emergency department for 12 hours
(D) Treat as an outpatient

Item 44

A 55-year-old man with a history of coronary artery disease and diabetes mellitus will undergo elective coronary artery bypass graft surgery. His last hemoglobin A_{1c} value was 7.8%, and his plasma glucose level 2 hours prior to scheduled surgery was 238 mg/dL (13.2 mmol/L). Hemoglobin is 11.9 g/dL (119 g/L).

His current medications include glipizide, metformin, and pioglitazone. He has no allergies.

Prior to surgery, hair is clipped from his anterior chest in the area of the anticipated surgical incision. He is scheduled to receive preoperative cefazolin with a second dose if the surgery duration is longer than 4 hours.

The addition of which of the following interventions will most likely contribute to a decreased risk of surgical site infection for this patient?

(A) Blood transfusion
(B) Maintenance of operative hypothermia
(C) Mupirocin nasal ointment at the time of anesthesia
(D) Perioperative intravenous insulin therapy

Item 45

A 20-year-old male college student is evaluated for a 3-day history of intermittent fever and rigors as well as vomiting, diarrhea, and severe headache. Two weeks ago, he returned from a 20-day African safari in Kenya and Tanzania. He sought no medical advice about immunizations or other prophylaxis prior to the trip.

On physical examination, the patient is not ill appearing. Temperature is 39.0 °C (102.2 °F), blood pressure is 105/70 mm Hg, pulse rate is 100/min, and respiration rate is 22/min. The remainder of the examination is normal.

Laboratory studies:

Hemoglobin	14.5 g/dL (145 g/L)
Leukocyte count	3700/μL (3.7×10^9/L)
Platelet count	95,000/μL (95×10^9/L)
Glucose	85 mg/dL (4.7 mmol/L)

A malaria smear shows greater than 5% parasitemia with only ring forms present.

Which of the following is the most appropriate treatment?

(A) Chloroquine
(B) Pyrimethamine-sulfadoxine
(C) Quinine and doxycycline
(D) Quinine and doxycycline followed by primaquine

Item 46

A 64-year-old woman with a 10-year history of type 2 diabetes mellitus is hospitalized because of a nonpainful draining ulcer on the plantar aspect of the left foot. The ulcer is chronic and nonhealing but over the past 3 days has enlarged and begun draining foul-smelling material. Yesterday, the patient developed fever, and the area around the ulcer became erythematous. Medications include metformin and pioglitazone.

On physical examination, she does not appear ill. Temperature is 38.3 °C (101.0 °F); other vital signs are normal. A 3- × 2-cm deep plantar ulcer that is draining a purulent green exudate is present at the base of the fourth metatarsal. The entire foot is warm, erythematous, and edematous. Pulses in the foot are palpable. No bone is visible or detected with a metal probe. A plain radiograph of the foot is normal.

Which of the following imaging studies of the foot should be done next?

(A) CT scan
(B) Indium-labeled leukocyte scan

(C) MRI

(D) Triple-phase technetium bone scan

Item 47

A 52-year-old woman is evaluated for a 6-week history of generalized malaise and fatigue. She received a kidney transplant 15 years ago for hypertension-related renal failure. Her current medications include cyclosporine and azathioprine.

The vital signs and general physical examination are normal.

Complete blood count is normal. The blood urea nitrogen level is 56 mg/dL (20 mmol/L), and the serum creatinine level is 3.0 mg/dL (265.2 μmol/L) compared with a value 2 months ago of 1.7 mg/dL (150.3 μmol/L). Urinalysis is significant for 19 leukocytes/hpf, no erythrocytes, 2+ protein, and many squamous and renal tubular epithelial cells, some of which have intranuclear inclusions.

Infection with which of following is the most likely cause of this patient's worsening kidney function?

(A) Cytomegalovirus

(B) Epstein-Barr virus

(C) Human herpesvirus-8

(D) Polyomavirus BK virus

(E) Polyomavirus JC virus

Item 48

A 48-year-old man undergoes emergency department evaluation for a painful, swollen right thigh following a recent fall at home. The patient has multiple sclerosis and is taking a tapering course of corticosteroids. He also has long-standing type 2 diabetes mellitus complicated by peripheral sensory neuropathy and recurrent gastroparesis. Current medications are prednisone and insulin glargine and insulin lispro.

On physical examination, temperature is 38.4 °C (101.2 °F). BMI is 17.5. The right thigh has a fluctuant, erythematous, tender mass surrounded by an area of skin thickening and erythema extending 7 cm beyond the bulging area. Neurologic examination findings are consistent with multiple sclerosis as well as areflexia and lack of sensation and proprioception in the feet.

While in the emergency department, the patient vomits twice and is given intravenous fluids. In the operating room, the surgeons incise and drain the thigh lesion, and cultures are obtained. Imipenem, vancomycin, and intravenous fluids are begun, and the patient is hospitalized.

Laboratory studies immediately following surgery:

Leukocyte count	24,000/μL (24 × 10⁹/L) with a left shift
Gram stain of surgical drainage fluid	Many leukocytes and occasional gram-negative rods
Creatinine	0.4 mg/dL (35.4 μmol/L)

On hospital day 2, his condition has stabilized and he is no longer vomiting. The culture of the drained fluid shows *Klebsiella oxytoca* that is resistant to ampicillin and cefazolin but susceptible to all carbapenems, trimethoprim-sulfamethoxazole, and colistin. The patient asks to be discharged for home care by his wife.

Which of the following is the most appropriate therapy?

(A) Colistin

(B) Ertapenem

(C) Imipenem and vancomycin

(D) Linezolid

Item 49

A 35-year-old woman is evaluated for chronic, nonhealing, painful erosive genital lesions. The lesions have been treated with intravenous acyclovir, 15 μg/kg three times daily, for 14 days. The patient has AIDS with a CD4 cell count of 55/μL. She recently began taking highly active antiretroviral therapy and trimethoprim-sulfamethoxazole, one double-strength tablet daily.

Physical examination discloses multiple 2- × 3-cm erosive lesions surrounding the vaginal introitus and on the right labia.

Viral culture is positive for herpes simplex virus type 2 that is resistant to acyclovir.

Which of the following is the most appropriate treatment?

(A) Famciclovir

(B) Foscarnet

(C) Penciclovir

(D) Valacyclovir

Item 50

A 69-year-old man is evaluated for a 3-month history of malaise and intermittent low-grade headache of gradually worsening intensity and a 2-month history of intermittent fevers and night sweats. He takes no medications.

On physical examination, temperature is 38.2 °C (100.7 °F), pulse rate is 88/min, and respiration rate is 16/min. He is oriented to person and place but not time or date. The neck is stiff and painful on flexion. Cardiopulmonary and abdominal examinations are normal. There are no skin lesions.

Results of a tuberculin skin test are normal.

A CT scan of the head shows no lesions.

A lumbar puncture is performed; cerebrospinal fluid (CSF) analysis is as follows:

Leukocyte count	440/μL (440 × 10⁶/L) with 22% neutrophils, 64% lymphocytes, and 14% mononuclear cells
Protein	266 mg/dL (2660 mg/L)
Glucose	34 mg/dL (1.9 mmol/L)
Opening pressure	320 mm H₂O
VDRL	Negative
Rapid plasma reagin	Negative
Fluorescent treponemal antibody absorption (FTA-ABS)	Negative

Gram stains, acid-fast bacilli testing, and fungal stains are negative. Cultures for bacteria, fungi, and mycobacteria are pending.

Which of the following tests should be done next?

(A) CSF cryptococcal polysaccharide antigen assay

(B) CSF polymerase chain reaction (PCR) for *Neisseria meningitidis*

(C) CSF PCR for *Streptococcus pneumoniae*

(D) Serum antibody assay for *Histoplasma capsulatum*

Item 51

A 62-year-old man is evaluated in July for a 24-hour history of fever, myalgia, and a frontal headache. He is otherwise healthy and takes no medications.

Recent travel includes a 2-week camping trip to the Blue Ridge Mountains of Virginia 11 days ago. The patient does not recall a specific insect or tick bite.

On physical examination, the patient appears mildly ill. Temperature is 38.7 °C (101.6 °F), blood pressure is 125/65 mm Hg, pulse rate is 90/min, and respiration rate is 18/min. There is no lymphadenopathy or rash. Cardiopulmonary and abdominal examinations are normal.

Laboratory studies:

Hemoglobin	15.2 g/dL (152 g/L)
Leukocyte count	3700/µL (3.7 × 10⁹/L)
Platelet count	110,000/µL (110 × 10⁹/L)
Aspartate amino-transferase	94 U/L
Alanine aminotransferase	92 U/L
Sodium	130 meq/L (130 mmol/L)

Chest radiograph and blood cultures are pending.

Which of the following is the most appropriate next step in management?

(A) Doxycycline

(B) Oseltamivir

(C) Postpone treatment pending diagnostic test results

(D) Vancomycin and ceftriaxone

Item 52

An otherwise healthy 28-year-old woman has had two episodes of acute cystitis within the past 6 months. The patient is sexually active and has intercourse with her husband on average 2 times per week and says her cystitis does not seem to be intercourse related. Each time, symptoms remit after a single course of trimethoprim-sulfamethoxazole. The patient is currently asymptomatic but will be traveling abroad for the next 2 months and is concerned about recurrent infections. Her only medication is an oral contraceptive for birth control. She reports no allergies.

Which of the following is the most appropriate management?

(A) Ciprofloxacin after intercourse

(B) Ciprofloxacin for 10 days when symptoms develop

(C) Trimethoprim chronic suppressive therapy

(D) Trimethoprim-sulfamethoxazole for 3 days when symptoms develop

Item 53

A 74-year-old woman is evaluated in the emergency department with a 2-day history of diarrhea characterized by 10 bowel movements daily, with worsening abdominal pain and fever. Today she has had no bowel movements but does have an increasingly distended abdomen. Five weeks ago, the patient was hospitalized with necrotizing fasciitis of the right thigh for which she underwent debridement, received nafcillin and clindamycin therapy, and was discharged after 2 weeks. On discharge, she was prescribed a 2-week course of nafcillin, which she completed 1 week ago.

On physical examination, the patient is awake but disoriented. Temperature is 38.6 °C (101.5 °F), blood pressure is 90/55 mm Hg, pulse rate is 122/min, and respiration rate is 24/min. The abdomen is distended and tender to palpation, and bowel sounds are absent.

Laboratory studies indicate a leukocyte count of 32,500/µL (32.5 × 10⁹/L), serum albumin level of 2.5 g/dL (25 g/L), and a serum creatinine level of 2.5 mg/dL (221 µmol/L). Stool, blood, and urine samples are obtained for culture, and she is admitted to the intensive care unit.

Which of the following is the most appropriate treatment?

(A) Intravenous metronidazole and oral vancomycin

(B) Intravenous vancomycin

(C) Oral metronidazole

(D) Oral metronidazole and oral vancomycin

(E) Oral vancomycin

Item 54

A 20-year-old female college student is evaluated in December because of a 12-hour history of fever, myalgia, headache, and a rash. Her only medication is an oral contraceptive agent.

On physical examination, the patient appears ill. Temperature is 38.8 °C (101.8 °F), blood pressure is 90/45 mm Hg, pulse rate is 112/min, and respiration rate is 24/min. A petechial rash most prominent on the lower extremities is present. Passive neck flexion causes discomfort.

Laboratory studies:

Leukocyte count	10,500/µL (10.5 × 10⁹/L) with 80% polymorphonuclear cells (PMNs) and 20% band forms
Platelet count	105,000/µL (105 × 10⁹/L)
Blood urea nitrogen	30 mg/dL (10.7 mmol/L)
Creatinine	2.5 mg/dL (221 µmol/L)
Bicarbonate	15 meq/L (15 mmol/L)

Lumbar puncture is performed. Opening pressure is 300 mm H₂O. Cerebrospinal fluid leukocyte count is 1250/µL (1250 × 10⁶/L) with 95% PMNs. Protein is 100 mg/dL (1000 mg/L). Gram stain shows numerous PMNs; no organisms are seen.

Which of the following is the most likely diagnosis?

(A) *Listeria monocytogenes* meningitis

(B) *Neisseria meningitidis* meningitis

(C) Rocky Mountain spotted fever

(D) Viral meningitis

Item 55

A 21-year-old man is evaluated in August for a 2-day history of fever, diffuse myalgia, and a mild frontal headache. Recent travel history includes a 2-month hike on the Appalachian Trail completed 10 days prior to presentation.

On physical examination, the patient is not ill appearing. Vital signs are normal except for a temperature of 37.9 °C (100.2 °F). Skin examination findings of the lower extremity are shown.

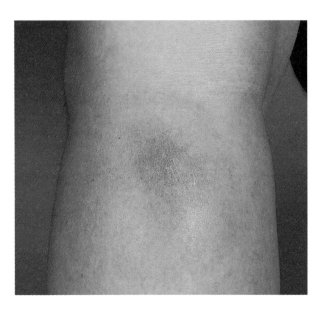

A 21-day course of oral doxycycline is initiated, and after 2 days, the rash resolves and the patient is asymptomatic.

One week after completing therapy, the patient undergoes follow-up evaluation for generalized malaise, diffuse aching, and a mild sore throat. The rash and the fever have not returned.

Physical examination is normal.

Laboratory studies:

Leukocyte count	7600/µL (7.6 × 10⁹/L)
Hemoglobin	16.4 g/dL (164 g/L)
Erythrocyte sedimentation rate	14 mm/h
Alanine aminotransferase	34 U/L
Serologic test for *Borrelia burgdorferi*	Positive

Which of the following is the most appropriate next step in treatment?

(A) Intravenous ceftriaxone for 4 weeks

(B) Oral amoxicillin for 4 weeks

(C) Oral atovaquone for 4 weeks

(D) Oral azithromycin for 4 weeks

(E) No additional antibiotic or antimicrobial therapy

Item 56

A 49-year-old man underwent a kidney transplant for polycystic kidney disease 18 months ago. His current immunosuppressive therapeutic regimen consists of cyclosporine and mycophenolate mofetil. After a 2-week febrile illness with a productive cough, he was found to have right upper pulmonary lobe cavitary lesions growing *Aspergillus fumigatus*, and treatment with voriconazole was begun.

Six days after voriconazole initiation, he develops severe anorexia and experiences nausea and vomiting. He is afebrile. A tremor develops, and his blood pressure rises from 130/70 mm Hg to 160/98 mm Hg.

Laboratory studies:

Hemoglobin	9.9 g/dL (99 g/L)
Leukocyte count	3400/µL (3.4 × 10⁹/L)
Platelet count	122,000/µL (122 × 10⁹/L)
Blood urea nitrogen	41 mg/dL (14.6 mmol/L)
Creatinine	3.2 mg/dL (282.8 µmol/L) (compared with a previous value of 1.1 mg/dL [97.2 µmol/L] 3 weeks ago)

Which of the following laboratory studies is most likely to explain the cause of this patient's deteriorating condition?

(A) Blood cultures for bacteria

(B) Blood cultures for fungi

(C) Measurement of cyclosporine blood levels

(D) Measurement of voriconazole blood levels

Item 57

A 70-year-old man is admitted to the hospital with the acute onset of personality change; the patient is accompanied by his family. Family members noticed the change in personality a few days earlier, when the patient, who is usually able to perform his activities of daily living, became suddenly unable to care for himself and recognize family members. Medical history is otherwise not significant.

On physical examination, temperature is 38.3 °C (101.0 °F), blood pressure is 140/82 mm Hg, pulse rate is 90/min, and respiration rate is 18/min. The patient is obtunded. A non–contrast-enhanced CT scan of the head is normal. Cerebrospinal fluid (CSF) analysis reveals a leukocyte count of 80/µL (80 × 10⁶/L) (90% lymphocytes), an erythrocyte count of 50/µL (50 × 10⁶/L), a glucose concentration of 80 mg/dL (4.4 mmol/L) (serum glucose of 120 mg/dL [6.7 mmol/L]), and a protein level of 90 mg/dL (900 mg/L). CSF Gram stain results are negative.

In addition to immediate empiric therapy, which of the following studies should be done next?

(A) Brain biopsy

(B) CSF antibody studies

(C) CSF polymerase chain reaction assay

(D) Electroencephalography

(E) MRI of the brain

Item 58

A 24-year-old man is evaluated 1 day after being bitten on the right hand while trying to break up a fight between two patrons at a local bar. The puncture wound has no evidence of infection, and no underlying soft tissue or tendon/bone is visible. Vaccination history includes tetanus toxoid, diphtheria toxoid, and acellular pertussis 1 year ago.

On physical examination, vital signs are normal. Examination of the dorsum of the right hand reveals several tiny punctures and tears and minimal erythema without tenderness, edema, or increased warmth. There is no axillary or epitrochlear lymphadenopathy.

Radiographs of the right hand show no gas or foreign body.

Which of the following is the most appropriate treatment?

(A) Amoxicillin-clavulanate
(B) Clindamycin
(C) Tetanus immunization
(D) Observation

Item 59

A 32-year-old man with AIDS and a recent CD4 cell count of 6/µL is admitted to the hospital with a 2-week history of fever and chills, a nonproductive cough, and gradually worsening dyspnea at rest and on exertion. He has been unable to tolerate highly active antiretroviral therapy and has taken no medications for the past 3 years.

On physical examination, temperature is 38.3 °C (101.0 °F), blood pressure is 100/68 mm Hg, pulse rate is 110/min, and respiration rate is 18/min. Cardiopulmonary examination discloses tachycardia with no murmur and diffuse crackles throughout all lung fields. The alveolar-arterial oxygen gradient is 50 mm Hg.

A chest radiograph shows bilateral interstitial pulmonary infiltrates. An induced sputum sample shows few leukocytes and no predominant organism. Bronchoscopy is scheduled.

Which of the following is the most appropriate empiric treatment for this patient?

(A) Ceftriaxone and azithromycin
(B) Isoniazid, rifampin, pyrazinamide, and ethambutol
(C) Trimethoprim-sulfamethoxazole
(D) Trimethoprim-sulfamethoxazole and prednisone

Item 60

A 27-year-old man is evaluated for concerns noted by his wife of a marked change in overall behavior over the past 6 months, including deterioration in his general hygiene and episodes of talking to imaginary people. His employer has also raised concerns about his work performance. The patient has also noted intermittent tingling in the hands and feet. Most recent travel includes 2 years in Oxford, England, between 1995 and 1997. Family history is unremarkable.

On physical examination, vital signs are normal. The patient is fully alert, but oriented only to place and person. His gait is ataxic. He scores 14 of 30 (normal >24/30) on the Mini-Mental State Examination. The remainder of the examination is normal.

Routine laboratory studies are normal. Results of urine drug screen, HIV antibody testing, and the rapid plasma reagin test for syphilis are negative. No abnormalities are noted on CT scan of the head, and electroencephalography shows only nonspecific slowing.

Which of the following is the most appropriate next step in management?

(A) Brain biopsy
(B) Corneal biopsy
(C) Intravenous acyclovir
(D) Intravenous dexamethasone
(E) Tonsillar biopsy

Item 61

A 71-year-old man with chronic obstructive pulmonary disease (COPD) is evaluated in the emergency department for a 3-day history of watery diarrhea alternating with constipation. He has maintained his usual regimen of COPD treatment with an inhaled corticosteroid and a β-agonist. He now reports having 10 to 15 bowel movements daily, with no blood in the stool. Fifteen days ago, the patient was started on amoxicillin for acute bronchitis.

He also has increasing abdominal distension, worsening abdominal pain with cramping, sweating, and increased diarrhea. Two days ago, he was evaluated in an urgent care center for his diarrhea. Stool testing for enteric pathogens and ova and parasites was negative as were results of an enzyme-linked immunosorbent assay for *Clostridium difficile* toxin. Gram stain of the stool revealed many fecal leukocytes.

On physical examination, temperature is 38.2 °C (100.9 °F), blood pressure is 130/80 mm Hg, and pulse rate is 90/min. The abdomen is distended and tender to palpation.

Which of the following is the most appropriate treatment?

(A) Ciprofloxacin
(B) Loperamide
(C) Metronidazole
(D) No treatment

Item 62

An 18-year-old woman is evaluated in the emergency department for a 3-day history of fever and rash accompanied by joint pain and swelling that initially involved only the left elbow before progressing to the left wrist. Medical history is unremarkable. She takes a depot medroxyprogesterone acetate injection every 12 weeks for contraception.

On physical examination, temperature is 38.1 °C (100.6 °C); other vital signs are normal. The left wrist is erythematous and swollen, and pain is induced with active range of motion. The left elbow is also swollen and painful. Scattered lesions are present on the left hand and both feet. Skin examination findings of the left hand are shown.

Appropriate cultures are taken.

Which of the following is the most appropriate treatment?

(A) Acyclovir
(B) Ceftriaxone
(C) Ciprofloxacin
(D) Gentamicin

Item 63

A 55-year-old man is evaluated for a 7-day history of intermittent fever and rigors, vomiting, diarrhea, and severe headache and confusion. Four weeks ago, he returned from a 15-day eco-adventure in southern Africa. He did not consistently take his malaria prophylaxis during the trip.

On physical examination, the patient appears very ill. Temperature is 39.0 °C (102.2 °F), blood pressure is 105/70 mm Hg, pulse rate is 100/min, and respiration rate is 22/min. He is confused. There is scleral icterus. Cardiopulmonary examination is normal. There is a palpable spleen tip.

Laboratory studies:

Hemoglobin	10.5 g/dL (105 g/L)
Leukocyte count	3700/µL (3.7 × 10⁹/L)
Platelet count	75,000/µL (75 × 10⁹/L)
Plasma glucose	75 mg/dL (4.2 mmol/L)
Creatinine	1.3 mg/dL (114.9 µmol/L)

A malaria smear shows 20% parasitemia with only ring forms present.

Infection with which of the following is the most likely diagnosis?

(A) *Plasmodium falciparum*
(B) *Plasmodium knowlesi*
(C) *Plasmodium malariae*
(D) *Plasmodium ovale*
(E) *Plasmodium vivax*

Item 64

A 63-year-old woman is evaluated in December 2008 for a 1-day history of severe myalgia and fatigue, fever, and a nonproductive cough.

On physical examination, temperature is 39.1 °C (102.5 °F), blood pressure is 140/85 mm Hg, pulse rate is 112/min, and respiration rate is 24/min. Cardiopulmonary examination is normal. Influenza illness is suspected, but test results (including strain type) will not be available until tomorrow.

Which of the following is the most appropriate treatment for this patient?

(A) Amantadine
(B) Oseltamivir
(C) Rimantadine
(D) Zanamivir

Item 65

A 70-year-old man is evaluated in January for a 2-day history of fever and cough productive of yellow sputum. He was well until 10 days ago when he developed headache, myalgia, and coryza. He seemed to be improving by day 8 of his illness, but he then developed his current symptoms. Medical history is significant for hypertension and chronic obstructive pulmonary disease treated with hydrochlorothiazide, albuterol, and tiotropium.

On physical examination, temperature is 38.9 °C (102.0 °F), blood pressure is 110/70 mm Hg, pulse rate is 100/min, and respiration rate is 22/min. Pulmonary examination reveals crackles at the left lung base.

Laboratory studies indicate a leukocyte count of 15,000/µL (15 × 10⁹/L) with 20% band forms. Chest radiograph reveals a left lower lobe infiltrate.

Which of the following empiric antimicrobial regimens should be initiated?

(A) Azithromycin plus ceftriaxone
(B) Clindamycin plus levofloxacin
(C) Piperacillin-tazobactam
(D) Vancomycin plus levofloxacin

Item 66

A 44-year-old female veterinarian is evaluated in the emergency department after sustaining a cat bite 2 days ago that has resulted in a tender, red, and warm right calf wound. The patient is up-to-date on her rabies and tetanus immunizations. Medical history is significant for an anaphylactic IgE-mediated reaction to penicillin.

On physical examination, temperature is 39.2 °C (102.6 °F), blood pressure is 100/70 mm Hg, pulse rate is 110/min, and respiration rate is 18/min; BMI is 25. There is a necrotic-appearing puncture wound with significant erythema, warmth, and tenderness to touch over the right calf. There is no inguinal lymphadenopathy. The remainder of the physical examination is unremarkable.

Laboratory studies:

Hemoglobin	13.5 g/dL (135 g/L)
Leukocyte count	18,000/μL (18 × 10^9/L), with 84% neutrophils, 2% band forms, 10% lymphocytes, 4% monocytes
Platelet count	225,000/μL (225 × 10^9/L)

Two sets of blood cultures are drawn.

Radiographs of the distal right lower extremity show no gas or foreign body.

In addition to wound irrigation and debridement of necrotic tissue, which of the following is the most appropriate treatment?

(A) Ampicillin-sulbactam

(B) Cefoxitin

(C) Ciprofloxacin and clindamycin

(D) Erythromycin

(E) Imipenem

Item 67

A 32-year-old woman has a 3-day history of vaginal odor and discharge. She has no history of sexually transmitted diseases or allergies and takes no medications except for an oral contraceptive agent.

On physical examination, vital signs are normal. Pelvic examination discloses a gray discharge with a fishy odor. The cervix appears normal, and there is no uterine or adnexal tenderness.

Vaginal fluid pH is 7.0. A wet mount of the fluid shows vaginal epithelial cells studded with adherent bacteria and no motile organisms.

Which of the following is the most appropriate treatment?

(A) Azithromycin, orally, in a single dose

(B) Metronidazole, orally for 7 days

(C) Metronidazole, orally, in a single dose

(D) Topical miconazole

Item 68

A 45-year-old man is evaluated in a clinic in Vietnam while on a mission trip for the acute onset of fever, headache, stiff neck, and altered mental status.

On physical examination, temperature is 39.4 °C (103.0 °F), blood pressure is 100/60 mm Hg, pulse rate is 110/min, and respiration rate is 22/min. The patient has meningismus and is oriented only to person.

Laboratory studies indicate a leukocyte count of 25,000/μL (25 × 10^9/L) with 20% band forms and a platelet count of 90,000/μL (90 × 10^9/L). Cerebrospinal fluid analysis shows a leukocyte count of 2000/μL (2000 × 10^6/L) with 99% neutrophils, a glucose concentration of 20 mg/dL (1.11 mmol/L), and a protein level of 200 mg/dL (2000 mg/L). Gram stain reveals gram-positive cocci in chains.

Which of the following regimens should be initiated?

(A) Ampicillin, ceftriaxone, plus dexamethasone

(B) Vancomycin

(C) Vancomycin plus ceftriaxone

(D) Vancomycin, ceftriaxone, plus dexamethasone

(E) Vancomycin, ceftriaxone, plus rifampin

Item 69

A 65-year-old man recently migrated to the United States from Africa. He is evaluated in the emergency department for a 3-week history of cough and dyspnea, now with hemoptysis. He has also had fevers, night sweats, and a 13.6-kg (30-lb) weight loss over the past 3 months.

On physical examination, he is thin and coughs frequently. Temperature is 38.3 °C (101.0 °F), blood pressure is 100/60 mm Hg, pulse rate is 101/min, and respiration rate is 30/min. Pulmonary examination reveals crackles over the right upper lung field.

Which of the following is the most important initial infection-control option in this setting?

(A) Chest radiograph

(B) Institution of airborne precautions

(C) Sputum for acid-fast bacilli stain and culture

(D) Tuberculin skin testing

Item 70

A 31-year-old man is evaluated for a 12-day history of low-grade fever, pleuritic chest pain, and a nonproductive cough. Two weeks ago, the patient traveled to Phoenix, Arizona, for 3 days to play in a golf tournament. He lives in central Pennsylvania. Medical history is noncontributory, and he takes no medications.

On physical examination, temperature is 37.7 °C (100.0 °F). The remaining vital signs are normal. Chest examination reveals occasional bibasilar crackles.

The leukocyte count is 7400/μL (7.4 × 10^9/L) with 52% neutrophils, 32% lymphocytes, 10% monocytes, and 6% eosinophils. Chest radiographs show bilateral small, scattered infiltrates and bilateral pleural effusions.

Thoracentesis is performed and yields 300 mL of amber-colored turbid fluid with a leukocyte count of 1200/μL (1.2 × 10^9/L) with 88% lymphocytes and 12% neutrophils. Gram stain and acid-fast bacilli stain show no organisms.

Which of the following is the most likely cause of this patient's illness?

(A) *Blastomyces dermatitidis*

(B) *Coccidioides immitis*

(C) *Cryptococcus neoformans*

(D) *Fusarium oxysporum*

(E) *Histoplasma capsulatum*

Item 71

An 80-year-old woman is evaluated for diarrhea characterized by six to eight bowel movements per day with abdominal pain. She was hospitalized 2 months ago for pneumonia complicated by a *Clostridium difficile* infection (CDI) treated with a course of metronidazole. One month after discharge, she developed a urinary tract infection and was given ciprofloxacin; CDI was again diagnosed 5 days later and treated with a course of metronidazole.

On physical examination, the patient is afebrile, blood pressure is 130/78 mm Hg, and pulse rate is 90/min. Abdominal examination reveals hyperactive bowel sounds with mild diffuse tenderness.

The leukocyte count is 18,900/µL (18.9×10^9/L). *C. difficile* toxin assay is positive.

A course of which of the following is the most appropriate treatment?

(A) Intravenous vancomycin
(B) Oral metronidazole followed by tapering doses of metronidazole
(C) Oral vancomycin followed by tapering doses of metronidazole
(D) Oral vancomycin followed by tapering doses of vancomycin

Item 72

A 38-year-old man is admitted to the hospital for a 12-hour history of bilateral lower-extremity paralysis. The patient is an injection drug user. Over the past week, he developed lower back pain, which progressed to pain and numbness radiating down both lower extremities. On the day of admission, he was unable to walk but continued to use injection drugs.

On physical examination, vital signs, including temperature, are normal. Cardiac examination reveals a regular rhythm and a grade 2/6 holosystolic murmur heard at the apex and radiating to the axilla. Neurologic examination demonstrates 0/5 strength in both lower extremities and absent sensation in both legs.

Emergent MRI of the spine shows evidence of osteomyelitis of the L1 and L2 vertebrae, diskitis of the L1-L2 disk space, and an epidural fluid collection compressing the spinal cord. Three blood cultures are drawn, and empiric therapy with vancomycin and ceftazidime is initiated.

In addition to continuing antimicrobial therapy, which of the following is the most appropriate management?

(A) CT-guided aspiration of the epidural fluid collection
(B) Electromyography of the lower extremities
(C) Emergent laminectomy
(D) Lumbar puncture

Item 73

A previously healthy 39-year-old woman is evaluated for the acute onset of fever and obtundation. Temperature is 38.3 °C (101.0 °F). The remaining vital signs are normal. There is no evidence of nuchal rigidity, and the neurologic examination reveals no focal findings.

Cerebrospinal fluid analysis shows 10 leukocytes/µL (10×10^6/L) (90% lymphocytes), an elevated protein level, and a normal glucose concentration. An MRI of the brain with gadolinium reveals swelling and enhancement of both temporal lobes. Intravenous acyclovir is initiated, but results of the cerebrospinal fluid polymerase chain reaction (PCR) assay for herpes simplex viruses (HSV) 1 and 2 are negative.

Which of the following is the most appropriate management?

(A) Add ganciclovir
(B) Discontinue acyclovir
(C) Perform a brain biopsy of the right temporal lobe
(D) Repeat HSV PCR on a new specimen

Item 74

A 65-year-old man is evaluated in the emergency department for a 3-day history of gradually worsening low back pain and fever. He was evaluated by his internist 4 weeks ago for these symptoms, but his condition has recently worsened.

On physical examination, temperature is 38.0 °C (100.4 °F); other vital signs are normal. General examination, including neurologic examination, is normal. MRI of the spine shows enhancement of the L3-L4 end plates and inflammation of the disk space. No epidural enhancement or paravertebral collections are seen. The patient is hospitalized. Blood cultures are negative. The patient's pain has worsened.

Which of the following is the most appropriate next management step?

(A) Begin ceftriaxone
(B) Begin nafcillin
(C) Obtain CT-guided percutaneous needle biopsy
(D) Repeat the blood cultures

Item 75

A 25-year-old man is brought to the emergency department because of a 1-day history of fever and progressive delirium.

On physical examination, temperature is 38.5 °C (101.3 °F), blood pressure is 86/58 mm Hg, pulse rate is 122/min, and respiration rate is 34/min. The patient is oriented only to person. On pulmonary examination, he demonstrates increased work of breathing. There is no lymphadenitis. Abdominal examination is normal.

The leukocyte count is 32,000/µL (32×10^9/L). A chest radiograph shows bilateral diffuse alveolar infiltrates. An initial blood smear shows small gram-negative coccobacilli, and special stains show bacteria that look like safety pins.

Infection with which of the following organisms is most likely?

(A) *Francisella tularensis*
(B) *Salmonella enterica*
(C) *Staphylococcus aureus*
(D) *Streptococcus pneumoniae*
(E) *Yersinia pestis*

Item 76

A 51-year-old man is hospitalized for fever, shaking, chills, and worsening abdominal discomfort and pain over the past week. The patient underwent cardiac transplantation 5 months ago because of ischemic cardio-myopathy. His post-transplantation regimen consists of cyclosporine, mycophenolate mofetil, prednisone, trimethoprim-sulfamethoxazole, and acyclovir.

On physical examination, temperature is 38.4 °C (101.1 °F), blood pressure is 100/70 mm Hg, pulse rate is 70/min, and respiration rate is 18/min. The cardiopulmonary examination is normal. On abdominal examination, bowel sounds are absent, and there are rigidity and tenderness to palpation with diffuse rebound tenderness. The remainder of the physical examination is unremarkable.

Abdominal radiograph shows free gas and signs of ileus. The patient undergoes immediate exploratory laparotomy, and a small jejunal perforation is found.

Infection with which of the following is the most likely cause of this patient's bowel perforation?

(A) Cytomegalovirus
(B) *Escherichia coli O127*
(C) *Giardia lamblia*
(D) Herpes simplex virus
(E) *Strongyloides stercoralis*

Item 77

An 18-year-old woman has a 3-day history of fever, headache, and painful sores in the genital area. The patient has no previous history of genital lesions. Medical history is unremarkable, and her only medication is an oral contraceptive agent. She does not use condoms.

On physical examination, temperature is 38.1 °C (100.6 °F); other vital signs are normal. There are no signs of meningismus. Tender ulcerative lesions with a yellow crusted roof cover the labia bilaterally and the vaginal introitus.

Which of the following is the most likely diagnosis?

(A) Chancroid
(B) Genital herpes simplex virus infection
(C) Primary syphilis
(D) Vulvovaginal candidiasis

Item 78

A 68-year-old man is diagnosed with *Clostridium difficile* infection 5 days after elective hip replacement surgery. This hospital has recently reported a high incidence of *C. difficile* infections. The patient was in a two-bed hospital room.

In addition to bleach for enhanced room cleaning, which of the following "bundled" measures would be most effective in preventing the spread of *C. difficile* in this hospital setting?

(A) Airborne precautions and alcohol hand sanitizer
(B) Airborne precautions and soap and water for hand hygiene
(C) Barrier precautions and alcohol hand sanitizer
(D) Barrier precautions and soap and water for hand hygiene
(E) Droplet precautions and soap and water for hand hygiene

Item 79

A 34-year-old man undergoes follow-up evaluation in the HIV clinic for early-stage HIV-1 infection and new-onset lower extremity edema. His CD4 cell counts have consistently been greater than 350/µL, and he has never taken antiretroviral agents. The most recent laboratory studies from 1 month earlier show a CD4 cell count of 360/µL and an HIV RNA viral load of 150,000 copies/mL.

On physical examination, temperature is normal, blood pressure is 120/60 mm Hg, pulse rate is 70/min, and respiration rate is 14/min. Funduscopic, cardiopulmonary, and abdominal examinations are normal. There is pitting edema to just below the knees and in the sacral area.

Laboratory studies:

Creatinine	1.9 mg/dL (168 µmol/L)
Blood urea nitrogen	28 mg/dL (10 mmol/L)
Albumin	3 g/dL (30 g/L)
Urinalysis	4+ protein; 2 to 3 erythrocytes/hpf; 1 to 2 leukocytes/hpf
Urine protein-creatinine ratio	4.5 mg/mg

Renal ultrasound shows enlarged echogenic kidneys with no evidence of hydronephrosis.

Which of the following is the most likely diagnosis?

(A) Acute interstitial nephritis
(B) HIV-associated nephropathy
(C) IgA nephropathy
(D) Postinfectious glomerulonephritis

Item 80

A 25-year-old man is evaluated in the emergency department for a 3-day history of scrotal pain without fever. Medical history is unremarkable, and he takes no medications. The patient is frequently sexually active with women and never has sex with men.

On physical examination, vital signs, including temperature, are normal. Genitourinary examination discloses a purulent urethral discharge and right-sided scrotal swelling and tenderness, especially superior to the right testis.

Duplex Doppler ultrasonography of the scrotum shows normal-sized testes and a swollen right epididymis with normal blood flow.

Which of the following is the most appropriate treatment?

(A) Ampicillin and gentamicin
(B) Azithromycin
(C) Ceftriaxone and doxycycline
(D) Ofloxacin

Item 81

A 30-year-old man is evaluated for the rapid onset of headache, fever, nausea, vomiting, and alteration in consciousness. He has a history of maxillary sinusitis.

On physical examination, he appears acutely ill, with a temperature of 38.9 °C (102.0 °F). The patient undergoes an emergent non-contrast–enhanced CT scan of the head, which reveals evidence of right maxillary sinusitis and mass effect with a shift of midline structures to the left. MRI with gadolinium demonstrates a crescentic, elliptically shaped density over the convexity of the right cerebrum, with shift of the brain to the left and an elliptically shaped density in the interhemispheric fissure.

In addition to appropriate antimicrobial therapy, which of the following is the most appropriate management?

(A) Craniotomy fluid drainage
(B) CT-guided needle aspiration
(C) Lumbar puncture
(D) Mannitol

Item 82

A 32-year-old man is evaluated for a fever 4 weeks after receiving a new diagnosis of pulmonary tuberculosis and late-stage HIV infection (CD4 cell count of 10/μL and an HIV RNA viral load of 700,000 copies/mL). A four-drug antituberculosis regimen consisting of isoniazid, rifabutin, pyrazinamide, and ethambutol and an antiretroviral regimen consisting of tenofovir, emtricitabine, and lopinavir/ritonavir are initiated.

On physical examination, temperature is 38.3 °C (101.0 °F); the remaining vital signs are normal. There is an enlarged, fluctuant, and tender right cervical lymph node that was not present 4 weeks ago. The skin, mucosal, and cardiopulmonary examinations are normal, and there is no evidence of hepatosplenomegaly.

A repeat CD4 cell count at today's visit is 130/μL, and the HIV RNA viral load is 2000 copies/mL.

A chest radiograph is normal.

Which of the following is the most likely diagnosis?

(A) Hodgkin lymphoma
(B) Immune reconstitution inflammatory syndrome
(C) Kaposi sarcoma
(D) Non-Hodgkin lymphoma

Item 83

An 18-year-old woman undergoes evaluation in the emergency department for increasing muscle pain in the left biceps area, nausea, light-headedness, and fever of 3 days' duration. She was recently diagnosed with varicella virus infection. She admits to having vigorously scratched a lesion in that area and in other areas several days earlier. Vaccinations except for the varicella vaccine are up-to-date. Her only medication has been ibuprofen as needed.

On physical examination, temperature is 38.7 °C (101.8 °F), blood pressure is 85/55 mm Hg, pulse rate is 120/min, and respiration rate is 20/min. Skin examination reveals healing varicella lesions. The left biceps area is notable for tenderness, warmth, and "woody" induration to palpation.

Laboratory studies:

Hemoglobin	11.0 g/dL (110 g/L)
Leukocyte count	20,000/μL (20 × 10⁹/L)
Platelet count	75,000 (75 × 10⁹/L)
Creatinine	2.0 mg/dL (176.8 μmol/L)
Alanine aminotransferase	95 U/L
Aspartate aminotransferase	100 U/L

Urinalysis is normal. MRI shows evidence of superficial fascial necrosis between the skin and the biceps muscle.

The patient had a single dose of vancomycin and piperacillin-tazobactam before undergoing emergency surgical debridement. Gram stain of the surgically obtained tissue and fluid reveals only gram-positive cocci in short chains.

Which of the following treatment regimens should be given now?

(A) Intravenous immune globulin
(B) Metronidazole and ciprofloxacin
(C) Penicillin and clindamycin
(D) Vancomycin plus cefepime and metronidazole

Item 84

A 35-year-old man seeks disease-prevention advice prior to taking a 6-week African safari trip to Tanzania and Kenya, where he will spend time camping in tents. He is generally healthy and takes no medications. All of his basic immunizations are up-to-date.

Immunizations for hepatitis A, typhoid, and yellow fever are recommended; prescriptions for traveler's diarrhea treatment and malaria prophylaxis are provided; risks of travel-related automobile injury are discussed; and information about careful contact with dogs is provided.

In addition to the steps taken above, which of the following is the most appropriate advice to provide to this patient for his upcoming travel?

(A) Avoid carbonated water (soda)
(B) Avoid locally made hot tea
(C) Sleep under bed netting
(D) Use citronella-based insect repellents
(E) Wear a facemask on the airplane

Item 85

A 21-year-old woman has a 3-day history of an abnormal vaginal discharge. Medical history is unremarkable, and her only medication is an oral contraceptive agent.

Physical examination, including pelvic examination, is normal except for a yellow-green vaginal discharge. Findings of a wet mount preparation are shown on page 109.

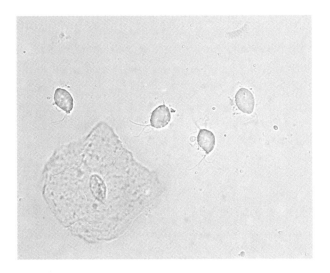

Which of the following is the most appropriate treatment?

(A) Doxycycline, twice daily for 7 days
(B) Metronidazole gel, four times daily for 5 days
(C) Single-dose fluconazole
(D) Single-dose metronidazole

Item 86

A 45-year-old woman is evaluated for fever, diminished appetite, weight loss, and cough productive of foul-smelling sputum of 2 weeks' duration. She has a history of chronic alcoholism and frequent hospital admissions for alcohol-withdrawal seizures, with the most recent episode occurring 3 weeks ago.

On physical examination, temperature is 38.3 °C (101.0 °F), blood pressure is 130/84 mm Hg, pulse rate is 80/min, and respiration rate is 18/min. Her breath is foul smelling and dentition is poor. Pulmonary examination reveals some crackles and rhonchi in the right anterior chest.

Laboratory studies indicate a leukocyte count of 12,500/µL (12.5 × 10⁹/L) with 8% band forms. The chest radiograph is shown.

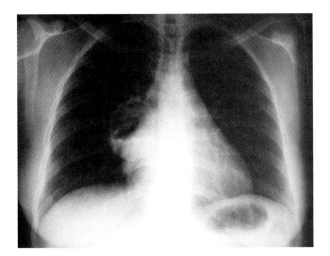

Sputum Gram stain results indicate gram-positive cocci in chains, gram-negative bacilli, and gram-positive bacilli.

Which of the following empiric antimicrobial regimens should be initiated?

(A) Ampicillin-sulbactam
(B) Aztreonam
(C) Ceftriaxone
(D) Levofloxacin
(E) Metronidazole

Item 87

A 35-year-old man is evaluated in the emergency department for a 1-month history of chronic cough productive of blood-tinged sputum. He admits to frequent encounters with commercial sex-workers while visiting Russia, India, and Thailand.

On physical examination, temperature is 38.8 °C (100.9 °F), blood pressure is 90/50 mm Hg, pulse rate is 95/min, and respiration rate is 30/min. Thrush is noted on oral examination. Crackles are heard over the upper lung fields.

Bilateral upper lobe cavitary lesions are present on a chest radiograph. Acid-fast bacillus is found on the direct sputum smear.

Which of the following is the best treatment option?

(A) Ciprofloxacin, pyrazinamide, ethambutol, ethionamide, and cycloserine
(B) Isoniazid
(C) Isoniazid and rifampin
(D) Isoniazid, rifampin, pyrazinamide, and ethambutol

Item 88

A 26-year-old man with a history of HIV infection/AIDS is evaluated for a sudden widespread eruption of skin lesions. His last office visit was 1 year ago when his CD4 cell count was 50/µL. At that time, trimethoprim-sulfamethoxazole, azithromycin, and highly active antiretroviral therapy were initiated, but the patient discontinued them owing to persistent nausea and vomiting and did not return for follow-up care until today.

On physical examination, he appears cachectic. Temperature is 38.3 °C (101.0 °F). Skin findings, which are widely disseminated but concentrated on the face, scalp, and neck, consist of 2- to 5-mm umbilicated papules with surrounding erythema.

The remainder of the physical examination is normal.

Which of the following is the most likely diagnosis?

(A) Cytomegalovirus infection
(B) Disseminated cryptococcal infection
(C) Herpes simplex virus infection
(D) *Mycobacterium avium* complex

Item 89

A 70-year-old man is evaluated in the emergency department with the acute onset of fever, rigors, and productive cough. The patient has a history of diabetes mellitus and chronic obstructive pulmonary disease treated with glyburide, metformin, albuterol, and tiotropium and a severe penicillin allergy that leads to anaphylaxis.

On physical examination, the patient appears confused. The temperature is 40.0 °C (104.0 °F), blood pressure is 90/60 mm Hg, pulse rate is 120/min, and respiration rate is 34/min. Pulmonary examination reveals diffuse rhonchi in both lung fields.

Laboratory studies:

Leukocyte count	3000/µL (3×10^9/L) with 50% band forms
Platelet count	80,000/µL (80×10^9/L)
Blood urea nitrogen	40 mg/dL (14.3 mmol/L)
Creatinine	2.1 mg/dL (185.6 µmol/L)

A chest radiograph reveals right lower lobe and left lingular infiltrates. The patient is admitted to the intensive care unit.

Which of the following empiric antimicrobial regimens should be initiated?

(A) Azithromycin plus cefotaxime
(B) Levofloxacin plus aztreonam
(C) Trimethoprim-sulfamethoxazole
(D) Vancomycin plus gentamicin

Item 90

A 39-year-old woman is evaluated in the emergency department for fever, myalgia, and malaise 2 days after her pet dog bit her on the left lower extremity. Medical history is significant for a splenectomy 5 years ago following a motor vehicle accident. She has received tetanus, pneumococcal, meningococcal, and *Haemophilus influenzae* type B vaccines, and her dog's immunizations are up-to-date. There are no allergies, and the remainder of the medical history is noncontributory.

On physical examination, temperature is 38.7 °C (101.7 °F), blood pressure is 90/60 mm Hg, pulse rate is 110/min, and respiration rate is 26/min; BMI is 26. There is erythema and tenderness at site of the puncture wound on the left thigh. An abdominal laparotomy scar is noted. There is no inguinal lymphadenopathy. The remainder of the physical examination is normal.

Laboratory studies:

Hemoglobin	10.0 g/dL (100 g/L)
Leukocyte count	16,600/µL (16.6×10^9/L) with 56% neutrophils, 33% band forms, 10% lymphocytes, and 1% monocytes
Platelet count	17,500/µL (17.5×10^9/L)
Peripheral blood smear	Many Howell-Jolly bodies
Blood urea nitrogen	40 mg/dL (14.3 mmol/L)
Creatinine	2.4 mg/dL (212.2 µmol/L)
Alanine aminotransferase	500 U/L
Aspartate aminotransferase	450 U/L

Multiple blood cultures reveal growth of gram-negative rods/bacilli. The urinalysis is normal. Radiographs of the left femur show no gas or foreign body.

Which of the following is the most likely cause of this patient's septic presentation?

(A) *Capnocytophaga canimorsus*
(B) *Escherichia coli*
(C) *Salmonella* species
(D) *Staphylococcus aureus*
(E) *Streptococcus pyogenes*

Item 91

A 25-year-old man is admitted to the hospital with fever, stiff neck, and headache 10 days after experiencing a closed head injury resulting from a motor vehicle accident. Immediately after the accident, he experienced a 15-minute loss of consciousness but then awakened with return of his mental status to normal. Three days later, he noted drainage of a clear fluid from his left nostril.

On physical examination, temperature is 38.9 °C (102.0 °F). Laboratory studies reveal a leukocyte count of 17,000/µL (17×10^9/L) with 15% band forms. A non-contrast–enhanced CT scan of the head is normal. Cerebrospinal fluid analysis reveals a leukocyte count of 700/µL (700×10^6/L) with 85% neutrophils, glucose concentration of 40 mg/dL (2.22 mmol/L), and a protein level of 120 mg/dL (1200 g/L). Results of Gram stain are negative.

Which of the following empiric regimens should be initiated?

(A) Meropenem plus dexamethasone
(B) Vancomycin
(C) Vancomycin, ceftriaxone, plus dexamethasone
(D) Vancomycin plus ceftriaxone

Item 92

A 34-year-old man is brought to the emergency department by his wife, who reports that he has had a headache and fever for 2 days and developed "odd behavior" earlier today. While in the emergency department, the patient has a generalized seizure. Medical history is unremarkable, and he takes no medications.

On physical examination, he is lethargic and disoriented but is aroused by a sternal rub. Temperature is 38.9 °C (102.0 °F), blood pressure is 112/78 mm Hg, pulse rate is 96/min, and respiration rate is 22/min. He is able to move all extremities. Deep tendon reflexes are 2+ bilaterally.

Results of a complete blood count and routine blood chemistry studies are normal. CT scan of the head shows focal low-density lesions in the temporoparietal region. There is no evidence of hemorrhage. Lumbar puncture is performed. Cerebrospinal fluid (CSF) findings indicate a leukocyte count of 18/µL (18×10^6/L) with 90% mononuclear cells, an erythrocyte count of 29/µL (29×10^6/L), a glucose concentration of 60 mg/dL (3.3 mmol/L), and a protein level of 70 mg/dL (700 mg/L). CSF Gram stain results are negative.

Which of the following is the most appropriate initial treatment?

(A) Acyclovir, intravenously

(B) Ceftriaxone, ampicillin, plus vancomycin intravenously

(C) Cidofovir, intravenously

(D) Levofloxacin, intravenously

(E) Penicillin G, intravenously

Item 93

A 65-year-old woman is evaluated because a screening urine culture for an insurance policy grows greater than 10^5 colony-forming units/mL of *Escherichia coli*. She does not have fever, dysuria, urinary frequency, or other symptoms. Medical history is unremarkable. She has no allergies and takes no medications. Physical examination findings are normal.

Which of the following is the most appropriate treatment?

(A) Amoxicillin

(B) Ciprofloxacin

(C) Trimethoprim-sulfamethoxazole

(D) No treatment

Item 94

A 62-year-old woman is evaluated for a 6-month history of cough of increasing intensity productive of up to one-half cup of yellow–green sputum per day. She has also had a 13.6-kg (30-lb) weight loss over the past year. Medical history is significant for home oxygen–dependent chronic obstructive pulmonary disease (COPD). Current medications include inhaled tiotropium, salmeterol, and albuterol.

On physical examination, temperature is 38.1 °C (100.5 °F), blood pressure is 104/78 mm Hg, pulse rate is 92/min, and respiration rate is 24/min. Pulmonary examination reveals scattered crackles bilaterally. Cardiac auscultation discloses distant heart sounds.

Chest radiograph shows emphysematous changes and a dense infiltrate in the right middle lobe. A CT scan of the chest localizes a 4-cm infiltrate to the subpleural surface. Bronchoscopy fails to procure the lesion. Bronchoalveolar lavage fluid shows a few hyphal forms suggestive of aspergillosis.

Which of the following diagnostic tests should be done next?

(A) Blood cultures

(B) CT-guided needle biopsy with polymerase chain reaction test

(C) Galactomannan antigen detection serum assay

(D) Repeat bronchoscopy with bronchoalveolar lavage

Item 95

A 29-year-old man is evaluated in the emergency department for the acute onset of fever, headache, stiff neck, and confusion. Medical records indicate that he was diagnosed with meningococcal meningitis 9 months ago, at which time he received appropriate antibiotic therapy and quickly recovered without any complications. The patient has no other medical problems and does not take any medications or illicit substances or abuse alcohol.

On physical examination, the patient appears confused. Temperature is 38.9 °C (102.0 °F) and blood pressure is 100/50 mm Hg. Lumbar puncture is performed, and cerebrospinal fluid (CSF) analysis shows neutrophilic pleocytosis, a low glucose concentration, and an elevated protein level. CSF Gram stain reveals gram-negative diplococci. Intravenous ceftriaxone is initiated, and the patient's condition rapidly improves. CSF cultures grow *Neisseria meningitidis*.

Which of the following tests should be performed to determine the most likely reason for this patient's recurrent meningitis?

(A) Metrizamide cisternography

(B) MRI of the brain with gadolinium

(C) Nitroblue tetrazolium reduction test

(D) Quantitative immunoglobulin measurement

(E) Total hemolytic complement (CH_{50}) measurement

Item 96

A 68-year-old man is evaluated in the hospital for daily fevers, with temperatures as high as 39.6 °C (103.2 °F) for the past 3 days, and a 2-day history of cough productive of thick tan sputum that was not responsive to vancomycin and cefepime therapy. He also has acute myeloid leukemia for which he has been receiving induction chemotherapy. His absolute neutrophil count has been less than $100/\mu L$ $(0.10 \times 10^9/L)$ for 12 days.

Chest radiographs reveal a dense right upper lobe infiltrate. CT scan of the chest shows cavitation and three other small densities in the right middle and lower lobes. Bronchoscopy with bronchoalveolar lavage yields washings with mostly lymphocytes and macrophages and no organisms on Gram stain, acid-fast bacilli testing, and fungal stains. Empiric therapy with voriconazole is initiated. After several days, the fungal cultures appear to be growing a mold.

Which of the following organisms is the most likely cause of this patient's pulmonary lesions?

(A) *Aspergillus fumigatus*

(B) *Candida lusitaniae*

(C) *Histoplasma capsulatum*

(D) *Nocardia asteroides*

(E) *Pseudallescheria boydii*

Item 97

A 60-year-old woman is evaluated for the acute onset of fever, chills, nonproductive cough, diarrhea, and altered mental status after returning from a cruise. She is the third person on the cruise who has presented with these symptoms within the past several days. Medical history is significant for a 10-year history of diabetes mellitus controlled with diet and metformin therapy.

On physical examination, temperature is 39.4 °C (103.0 °F), blood pressure is 100/56 mm Hg, pulse rate is 100/min, and respiration rate is 32/min. Crackles are heard at the left lung base. On neurologic examination, the patient is oriented only to person.

Laboratory studies indicate a hematocrit of 34%, a leukocyte count of 18,000/µL (18 × 10⁹/L), a platelet count of 149,000/µL (149 × 10⁹/L), and a serum sodium concentration of 125 meq/L (125 mmol/L). Chest radiograph reveals an alveolar infiltrate in the left lower lobe and a small left pleural effusion.

Which of the following studies is most likely to be helpful in determining the cause of pneumonia in this patient?

(A) Acid-fast bacilli sputum smear
(B) Blood culture
(C) *Legionella* urinary antigen test
(D) Nasal swab for influenza virus
(E) Thoracentesis

Item 98

A 75-year-old man is hospitalized with a 1-day history of fever, painful rash, and confusion. The patient has Crohn disease treated with prednisone and 6-mercaptopurine. The corticosteroid dose was recently escalated and then tapered for treatment of a disease flare.

On physical examination, the patient appears ill and confused. Temperature is 37.9 °C (100.3 °F), blood pressure is 120/70 mm Hg, pulse rate is 110/min, and respirations are 28/min and shallow. Arterial oxygen saturation is 90% on ambient air. A prominent vesicular rash is present on the chest in a dermatomal pattern, and multiple vesicular lesions of a similar nature are scattered on the trunk, arms, and legs. Examination of the lungs discloses scattered crackles.

Laboratory studies:

Leukocyte count	5200/µL (5.2 × 10⁹/L) with a normal differential
Blood urea nitrogen	34 mg/dL (12.1 mmol/L)
Creatinine	2.3 mg/dL (203.3 µmol/L)
Alanine aminotransferase	95 U/L
Aspartate aminotransferase	98 U/L

A chest radiograph shows bilateral interstitial infiltrates. Lumbar puncture is performed. The cerebrospinal fluid (CSF) leukocyte count is 48/µL (48 × 10⁶/L) with 10% polymorphonuclear cells, 70% lymphocytes, and 20% monocytes; protein is 90 mg/dL (900 mg/L), and glucose is 70 mg/dL (3.9 mmol/L) (plasma glucose is 110 mg/dL [6.1 mmol/L]). Gram stain and culture of the CSF and blood and urine cultures are negative.

In addition to replacement of corticosteroids in stress doses, which of the following is the most appropriate treatment?

(A) Acyclovir, intravenously
(B) Foscarnet

(C) Herpes zoster vaccine
(D) Valganciclovir

Item 99

A 24-year-old woman is evaluated for a 6-day history of progressively worsening generalized malaise, myalgia, frontal headache, and fever in addition to a small papule on the back of her left thigh. She returned 4 days ago from a 4-month trip to Botswana. Prior to the trip, she was immunized for hepatitis A. She has also been taking mefloquine as prophylaxis for malaria.

On physical examination, temperature is 38.7 °C (101.6 °F), blood pressure is 110/70 mm Hg, and pulse rate is 66/min. She has a faint, maculopapular erythematous eruption on her trunk and a 1/2-cm × 1/2-cm, mildly tender, ulcerating papule on the left anterior thigh that is surrounded by a halo of erythema.

Several ipsilateral femoral lymph nodes are enlarged.

Laboratory studies:

Hemoglobin	12.1 g/dL (121 g/L)
Leukocyte count	4300/µL (4.3 × 10⁹/L)
Creatinine	0.9 mg/dL (79.6 µmol/L)
Alanine aminotransferase	92 U/L
Aspartate aminotransferase	94 U/L

Which of the following is the most likely cause of this patient's illness?

(A) Dengue virus
(B) *Leishmania major*
(C) *Mycobacterium marinum*
(D) *Rickettsia africae*
(E) *Vibrio vulnificus*

Item 100

A 46-year-old man undergoes a routine evaluation. Medical history is significant for HIV infection for which he has taken emtricitabine, tenofovir, and atazanavir boosted with ritonavir for the past 3 years. He has tolerated his antiretroviral therapy without difficulty and is currently asymptomatic.

Physical examination and vital signs are normal except for scleral icterus.

Laboratory studies:

Hemoglobin	14.4 g/dL (144 g/L)
Reticulocyte count	1% of erythrocytes
Total bilirubin	4.5 mg/dL (76.9 µmol/L)
Direct bilirubin	1.2 mg/dL (20.5 µmol/L)
Alanine aminotransferase	24 U/L
Aspartate aminotransferase	20 U/L
Hepatitis B surface antigen	Nonreactive
Anti-hepatitis B surface antigen	Reactive
Hepatitis C antibody	Nonreactive
CD4 cell count	520/µL
HIV RNA viral load	<48 copies/mL

Which of the following is the most likely cause of this patient's hyperbilirubinemia?

(A) AIDS cholangiopathy
(B) Atazanavir

(C) Autoimmune hemolytic anemia

(D) Common bile duct stone

(E) Hepatitis B

Item 101

A 31-year-old female physician collects blood for a blood culture. As she attempts to transfer the blood to the blood culture bottle, she sticks her left index finger with the needle and sustains a deep injury. She immediately washes the area with soap and water and reports to the employee health department. The source of the blood is seropositive for HIV and hepatitis C virus infection. The source patient has HIV infection but has never taken antiretroviral therapy. Six months ago, his HIV viral RNA load was 26,000 copies/mL. There are no available data on his hepatitis C viral load or hepatitis B viral status.

The physician is not pregnant. She has been immunized against hepatitis B.

Results of the physician's baseline HIV and hepatitis B and C virus serologies and pregnancy test are pending. Also pending are the source patient's HIV and hepatitis C viral loads and hepatitis B serologies.

In addition to counseling, which of the following would be the most appropriate next step in management?

(A) Immediately begin interferon alfa-2b and ribavirin

(B) Immediately begin interferon alfa-2b, ribavirin, and three antiretroviral agents

(C) Immediately begin three antiretroviral agents

(D) Immediately begin zidovudine

(E) No additional measures are required

Item 102

A 22-year-old woman is evaluated in September for the acute onset of fever, myalgia, arthralgia, and nonproductive cough. Medical history is noncontributory.

On physical examination, the patient is not ill-appearing. Temperature is 38.0 °C (100.5 °F), blood pressure is 114/62 mm Hg, pulse rate is 90/min, and respiration rate is 18/min. A few crackles are heard at the right lung base.

The leukocyte count is 12,000/µL (12 × 10⁹/L), and the remaining laboratory studies are normal. Chest radiograph reveals a right middle lobe infiltrate.

Which of the following oral antimicrobial agents should be initiated?

(A) Azithromycin

(B) Moxifloxacin

(C) Oseltamivir

(D) Penicillin

Item 103

A 65-year-old woman is evaluated for a 1-day history of fever, headache, and altered mental status. Medical history includes type 2 diabetes mellitus and hypertension treated with glipizide and hydrochlorothiazide. She has no allergies.

On physical examination, the patient appears confused. Temperature is 38.9 °C (102.0 °F), blood pressure is 104/66 mm Hg, pulse rate is 100/min, and respiration rate is 20/min. Her neck is supple, and she has no rashes.

Laboratory studies indicate a leukocyte count of 19,000/µL (19 × 10⁹/L) with 30% band forms and a platelet count of 90,000/µL (90 × 10⁹/L). A non-contrast–enhanced CT scan of the head is normal. Cerebrospinal fluid (CSF) analysis shows a leukocyte count of 1300/µL (1300 × 10⁶/L) with 98% neutrophils, glucose concentration of 20 mg/dL (1.1 mmol/L) (plasma glucose, 120 mg/dL [6.7 mmol/L]), and protein level of 200 mg/dL (2000 mg/L). CSF Gram stain results are negative.

After providing adjunctive dexamethasone, which of the following empiric antimicrobial regimens should be initiated in this patient?

(A) Ceftriaxone

(B) Penicillin G

(C) Vancomycin, ampicillin, and ceftriaxone

(D) Vancomycin plus ceftriaxone

(E) Vancomycin plus trimethoprim-sulfamethoxazole

Item 104

A 40-year-old man is hospitalized with a 1-day history of left upper extremity weakness. The patient was treated for gonorrhea when he was 17 years old.

On physical examination, he is awake and alert. Vital signs, including temperature, are normal. Motor strength is 2/5 in the left upper extremity, and deep tendon reflexes are brisker in the left upper extremity than in the right. Motor strength and reflexes are normal on the right. The remainder of the neurologic examination is normal.

CT scan of the head is normal. Lumbar puncture is performed, and cerebrospinal fluid findings indicate a leukocyte count of 48/µL (48 × 10⁶/L) with 100% mononuclear cells, a protein level of 82 mg/dL (820 mg/L), and a glucose concentration of 62 mg/dL (3.4 mmol/L) (plasma glucose, normal); there are no erythrocytes, and the VDRL is pending.

A rapid plasma reagin test for syphilis is reactive at a 1:256 dilution, and a fluorescent treponemal antibody absorbtion (FTA-ABS) assay is also reactive. A rapid HIV test is negative.

Which of the following is the most appropriate treatment?

(A) Amoxicillin and probenecid, orally for 21 days

(B) Aqueous penicillin, intravenously for 10 to 14 days

(C) Azithromycin, orally in a single dose

(D) Benzathine penicillin G, intramuscularly in a single dose

Item 105

A 40-year-old woman is evaluated in the emergency department for a 2-week history of headache, low-grade fever, and malaise. She is a commercial sex worker and was recently tested for HIV in the hospital's outpatient clinic.

On physical examination, she is in mild distress from a headache. Temperature is 37.2 °C (99.0 °F). Some small shotty cervical lymph nodes are palpable bilaterally. Her neck is supple, and neurologic examination reveals no focal deficit.

Laboratory studies:

Leukocyte count	2000/μL (2.0 × 10⁹/L)
Serologic testing for HIV antibodies	Positive
CD4 cell count	20/μL
HIV RNA viral load	150,000 copies/mL

Lumbar puncture is performed. Cerebrospinal fluid results are as follows:

Appearance	Clear
Leukocyte count	5/μL (5 x 10⁶/L) with 100% lymphocytes
Protein	65 mg/dL (650 mg/L)
Glucose	65 mg/dL (3.6 mmol/L)
Gram stain	Negative
Cryptococcal antigen	Positive

In addition to oral flucytosine, which of the following is the most appropriate initial parenteral treatment?

(A) Amphotericin B
(B) Caspofungin
(C) Fluconazole
(D) Methylprednisolone

Item 106

A 36-year-old woman is evaluated for repeated episodes of sinusitis. Five years ago, she had a prolonged episode of maxillary sinusitis requiring treatment with amoxicillin. Since then, she has had three episodes of sinusitis and two episodes of bacterial pneumonia that have responded well to antibiotic therapy. The patient is otherwise well. Her parents are alive and well, but a maternal aunt died in her 20s of pneumonia.

On physical examination, vital signs are normal. BMI is 26. Pulmonary examination reveals a few crackles at the right posterolateral lung base. Complete blood count, serum electrolytes, renal function tests, and HIV serologies are normal.

Radiographs of the chest reveal diffuse, right lower lobe densities. A CT scan of the head shows mucosal thickening in the maxillary, sphenoid, and ethmoid sinuses, and a CT scan of the chest reveals bronchiectasis and bullous changes in the right lower lobe.

Which of the following is the most appropriate next diagnostic step?

(A) Bone marrow aspirate
(B) Bronchoscopy with bronchoalveolar lavage
(C) HIV RNA viral load testing
(D) Quantitative immunoglobulin assay
(E) T-cell subset panel

Item 107

A 42-year-old man is evaluated for a low-grade fever, sore throat, and malaise of 2 weeks' duration. The patient underwent liver transplantation 9 months ago for liver failure

caused by chronic hepatitis C infection. He had good recovery of hepatic function after the surgery and soon began feeling well and gaining weight until recently. Medications are sirolimus, prednisone, and mycophenolate mofetil.

On physical examination, temperature is 38.3 °C (101.0 °F), blood pressure is 130/82 mm Hg, pulse rate is 98/min, and respiration rate is 14/min. Diffuse lymphadenopathy is present, and splenomegaly is noted on abdominal examination.

His leukocyte, erythrocyte, and platelet counts have decreased, and his liver chemistry values have increased compared with his values following transplantation and prior to his current symptoms. A liver biopsy shows no signs of rejection, but lymphocytes are infiltrating into the periportal areas. Lymph node biopsy shows hyperplasia, and fluorescence-activated cell-sorting analysis indicates monoclonal proliferation of B cells.

Infection with which of the following is most likely to explain this patient's new findings?

(A) Cytomegalovirus
(B) Epstein-Barr virus
(C) Hepatitis C virus
(D) Human herpesvirus-6

Item 108

A 57-year-old man is evaluated for a 2-day history of fever, severe myalgia, and a frontal headache. He denies cough, diarrhea, abdominal pain, or urinary tract symptoms. He returned 1 week ago from a vacation in Puerto Rico. He slept in a well-screened room under mosquito netting.

On physical examination, the patient is moderately ill appearing. Temperature is 39.2 °C (102.6 °F), blood pressure is 108/75 mm Hg, pulse rate is 96/min, and respiration rate is 18/min. There is a maculopapular rash on his trunk. The remainder of the examination is normal.

Laboratory studies:

Hemoglobin	14.8 g/dL (148 g/L)
Leukocyte count	3700/μL (3.7 × 10⁹/L)
Platelet count	99,000/μL (99 × 10⁹/L)
Creatinine	1.1 mg/dL (97.2 μmol/L)
Alanine aminotransferase	84 U/L
Aspartate aminotransferase	92 U/L
INR	1.1
Activated partial thromboplastin time	27 s
Urinalysis	Normal

Which of the following is the most likely diagnosis?

(A) Chikungunya
(B) Dengue
(C) Influenza
(D) Malaria
(E) Typhoid fever

Item 109

A 43-year-old woman is evaluated after she noticed a "poppy seed"–sized tick on her right lower extremity last night, which she removed easily. She believes she got the bite yesterday during her first visit this season to a local park and states that the tick was not there before yesterday. This morning, she awoke to find a dime-sized, nonpainful erythematous patch at the site where the tick had been embedded. She is otherwise well with no fever, myalgia, or headache, and she takes no medications.

On physical examination, vital signs, including temperature, are normal. There is no lymphadenopathy. A 0.5-cm erythematous macule is noted on the right lower extremity, just above the lateral malleolus. The remaining skin examination is normal.

Which of the follow is the most appropriate management?

(A) Doxycycline for 3 weeks
(B) Serologic testing for Lyme disease
(C) Single-dose doxycycline
(D) Reassurance

Item 110

A 29-year-old woman is hospitalized because of a 4-day history of fever, chills, myalgia, and a nonproductive cough. The patient has a 10-year history of heroin use; her last usage was 1 day ago. Medical history is otherwise unremarkable, including no allergies.

Temperature is 39.0 °C (102.0 °F); other vital signs are normal. BMI is 27. Needle track marks are present on both arms. Cardiac examination discloses an early grade 2/6 systolic murmur at the base. The remainder of the examination is normal.

Laboratory studies:

Hemoglobin	10.4 g/dL (104 g/L)
Leukocyte count	14,000/µL (14 × 10⁹/L) with a normal differential
Platelet count	190,000/µL (190 × 10⁹/L)
Creatinine	1.4 mg/dL (123.8 µmol/L)

A chest radiograph shows one round 2-cm lesion in each lung with cavitation of the lesion in the left lung. An electrocardiogram is normal, and a transthoracic echocardiogram shows no valvular lesions, although the study is technically limited.

After blood culture specimens are obtained, vancomycin, 1 g intravenously every 12 hours, is begun. Within 48 hours, all the initial blood cultures are growing *Staphylococcus aureus* that is susceptible to oxacillin, the cephalosporins, tetracycline, and the fluoroquinolones and is resistant to penicillin G, ampicillin, and erythromycin. The strain is susceptible to clindamycin, and the clindamycin disk induction test (D test) is negative.

Which of the following is most appropriate at this time?

(A) Continue vancomycin
(B) Switch to clindamycin
(C) Switch to linezolid
(D) Switch to oxacillin

Item 111

A 50-year-old previously healthy woman is evaluated in January for the acute onset of fever, right-sided headache, and personality changes.

On physical examination, the patient is disoriented. Temperature is 38.3 °C (101.0 °F), and the remaining vital signs are normal. The neck is supple, and there are no focal neurologic findings.

Complete blood count and metabolic profile are normal. Emergent CT scan of the head without contrast reveals swelling of the right temporal lobe. Cerebrospinal fluid analysis indicates a leukocyte count of 50/µL (50 × 10⁶/L) with 100% lymphocytes, a glucose concentration of 60 mg/dL (3.3 mmol/L) (plasma glucose of 90 mg/dL [5.0 mmol/L]), and a protein level of 120 mg/dL (1200 mg/L). Gram stain results are negative.

Which of the following antimicrobial agents should be initiated?

(A) Acyclovir
(B) Ceftriaxone
(C) Doxycycline
(D) Voriconazole

Item 112

A 19-year-old female college freshman is evaluated in the emergency department for a 1-day history of headache, fever, and stiff neck.

On physical examination, temperature is 39.3 °C (102.7 °F), and blood pressure is 80/50 mm Hg. The patient is unable to flex her neck and has photophobia. All cranial nerves are intact, and the remainder of the neurologic examination is normal.

Cerebrospinal fluid analysis shows a leukocyte count of 13,259/µL (13,259 × 10⁶/L) with 85% neutrophils, a glucose concentration of 40 mg/dL (2.2 mmol/L) (plasma glucose 95 mg/dL [5.3 mmol/L]), and a protein level of 230 mg/dL (2300 mg/L). Gram stain shows many neutrophils and gram-negative diplococci.

In addition to placing the patient in a private room and instituting appropriate antimicrobial therapy, use of which of the following is the most appropriate next step in infection-control management?

(A) Face mask
(B) High-filter mask
(C) Nonsterile gloves and gown
(D) Sterile gloves and gown

Item 113

A 65-year-old man presents in September with acute-onset lower extremity weakness accompanied by fever and lethargy. The patient recalls recently having gotten several mosquito bites and also having found a dead crow on his front lawn.

On physical examination, temperature is 38.3 °C (101.0 °F). Bilateral flaccid paralysis of the lower extremities is noted on neurologic examination.

Cerebrospinal fluid (CSF) analysis reveals a leukocyte count of 400/µL (400 × 10⁶/L) with 90% lymphocytes, a glucose concentration of 89 mg/dL (4.9 mmol/L), and a protein level of 100 mg/dL (1000 mg/L). MRI of the brain reveals T2-weighted hyperintense lesions in the basal ganglia, thalamus, and midbrain.

Which of the following diagnostic tests will most quickly establish the cause of this patient's findings?

(A) Brain biopsy
(B) CSF IgM antibody assay
(C) CSF polymerase chain reaction test
(D) Serum IgG antibody assay
(E) Serum IgM antibody assay

Item 114

A 26-year-old man is evaluated in the emergency department for the acute onset of a nonproductive cough and right-sided pleuritic chest pain of 2 days' duration. The patient is an injection drug user, with his last use approximately 4 days ago. Results of his most recent HIV test 2 months ago were negative. The remainder of the medical history is noncontributory, and he takes no medications.

On physical examination, temperature is 39.4 °C (103.0 °F), blood pressure is 120/80 mm Hg, pulse rate is 100/min, and respiration rate is 20/min. Cardiopulmonary examination reveals clear lungs and a grade 3/6 holosystolic murmur heard best at the right sternal border that increases on inspiration.

Laboratory studies indicate a hematocrit of 39%, a leukocyte count of 17,000/µL (17 × 10⁹/L) with 15% band forms, and a platelet count of 160,000/µL (160 × 10⁹/L). Chest radiograph reveals small infiltrates in the left upper lobe, right upper lobe, and right lower lobe. Blood cultures are obtained.

Which of the following empiric antimicrobial regimens should be initiated?

(A) Azithromycin plus ceftriaxone
(B) Levofloxacin plus clindamycin
(C) Piperacillin/tazobactam plus aztreonam
(D) Trimethoprim-sulfamethoxazole plus prednisone
(E) Vancomycin plus cefepime

Item 115

A 25-year-old woman who is 28 weeks pregnant has a positive urine culture detected during a routine prenatal visit. She has not had fever, urinary frequency, or dysuria and is not taking any medications other than prenatal vitamins. She has never had a urinary tract infection before and has no medical problems.

On physical examination, vital signs, including temperature, are normal. There is no costovertebral angle tenderness.

The urine culture shows greater than 10⁵ colony-forming units/mL of *Escherichia coli* that are sensitive to

nitrofurantoin and ciprofloxacin but resistant to cefazolin, trimethoprim-sulfamethoxazole, and ampicillin.

Which of the following is the most appropriate treatment?

(A) Ampicillin
(B) Ciprofloxacin
(C) Nitrofurantoin
(D) Trimethoprim
(E) Observation

Item 116

A 50-year-old man is evaluated in the emergency department for a 2-day history of fever, headache, diffuse body aches, abdominal pain, severe malaise, and mouth sores followed by a painful rash that began on his face and trunk and progressed to his arms and legs. The patient had chickenpox as a child. Medical history is otherwise unremarkable.

On physical examination, he appears acutely ill. Temperature is 39.0 °C (102.2 °F), blood pressure is 110/50 mm Hg, pulse rate is 110/min, and respiration rate is 20/min. Hard papular lesions are present in a confluent distribution on the face, hands, and feet and are more scattered on the anterior trunk and back.

Which of the following is the most appropriate management for close contacts of this patient?

(A) Acyclovir prophylaxis
(B) Cidofovir prophylaxis
(C) Hyperimmune globulin injection
(D) *Vaccinia* vaccination

Item 117

A 56-year-old woman with diabetes mellitus is evaluated in the emergency department for fever, chills, and hyperglycemia. She is up-to-date on all immunizations. Current medications include insulin glargine and insulin aspart and aspirin.

On physical examination, temperature is 39.0 °C (102.3 °F), blood pressure is 90/60 mm Hg, pulse rate is 104/min, and respiration rate is 21/min; BMI is 28. There is fissuring in the web spaces between many of the toes of both feet. A 4- × 3-cm necrotic ulcerative lesion extending from the first and second toe to the plantar aspect of foot, with significant warmth and extensive surrounding erythema, is noted. Dorsalis pedis pulses are decreased bilaterally. Sensation over the distal lower extremities is decreased.

Laboratory studies:

Hemoglobin	13.0 g/dL (130 g/L)
Leukocyte count	25,000/µL (25 × 10⁹/L)
Platelet count	175,000/µL (175 × 10⁹/L)
Erythrocyte sedimentation rate	100 mm/h
Plasma glucose	440 mg/dL (24.4 mmol/L)
Creatinine	1.8 mg/dL (159.1 µmol/L) (1.2 mg/dL [106.0 µmol/L] 3 months ago)

The rest of the comprehensive metabolic panel, including serum aminotransferase concentrations, is normal. An MRI of the foot is ordered.

Which of the following is the best empiric antibiotic treatment option?

(A) Ceftazidime
(B) Ciprofloxacin
(C) Vancomycin plus imipenem
(D) Vancomycin plus metronidazole

Item 118

A 48-year-old woman with breast cancer is hospitalized with fever and chills. She previously had breast-conserving surgery and was receiving adjuvant chemotherapy. Peripheral blood cultures and cultures from the chemotherapy port are obtained. All specimens are positive for coagulase-negative staphylococci. The patient is reluctant to have the port removed because of the convenience it affords her.

Vancomycin, twice daily, is begun and quickly controls the fever and chills. All blood culture specimens drawn after starting antibiotic therapy are negative, and drug levels are at target values.

After 5 days of in-hospital vancomycin, the patient is ready for discharge and will complete the 14-day antibiotic course at home. She weighs 58 kg (128 lb). Her serum creatinine level is 1.0 mg/dL (88.4 µmol/L).

After the patient has been home for 5 days (day 10 of the 14-day regimen), the home infusion aide reports a serum creatinine level of 0.9 mg/dL (79.6 µmol/L).

Which of the following is the most appropriate management of the antibiotic therapy?

(A) Adjust the vancomycin dose to a peak level of greater than 40 µg/mL
(B) Adjust the vancomycin dose to a trough level of greater than 20 µg/mL
(C) Complete vancomycin therapy without drug-level monitoring
(D) Reduce the vancomycin dose by 50%

Answers and Critiques

Item 1   Answer: C

Educational Objective: Treat complications of central venous catheter–related nosocomial methicillin-resistant *Staphylococcus aureus* cellulitis and bacteremia in a patient allergic to vancomycin.

This patient has nosocomially acquired methicillin-resistant *Staphylococcus aureus* (MRSA)–associated cellulitis, bacteremia, and tricuspid valve infective endocarditis secondary to a peripherally inserted central catheter. In addition to catheter removal, this patient requires a 6-week course of intravenous antibiotics. Daptomycin is a lipopeptide agent with very broad bactericidal activity against gram-positive pathogens, including those resistant to other drug classes, such as MRSA and vancomycin-resistant enterococci. It has a novel mechanism of action in that it binds to the bacterial membrane and, in a calcium-dependent manner, causes electrical depolarization of the cell resulting in leakage of potassium and rapid cell death. Resistance is rare, and cross-resistance between daptomycin and other agents that are active against gram-positive organisms is absent. Daptomycin is currently approved for treatment for bacteremia and right-sided endocarditis. Daptomycin may cause muscle toxicity when given twice daily, but changing to once-daily administration appears to reduce this risk.

By definition, methicillin resistance means that this organism is resistant to oxacillin; nafcillin; and other β-lactam agents, including cefazolin.

Clindamycin, a bacteriostatic agent, is not included in the consensus guidelines for treatment of MRSA-associated infective endocarditis. Clindamycin monotherapy has been associated with treatment failure and relapse when used to treat methicillin-susceptible *S. aureus* bacteremia and infective endocarditis.

KEY POINT

- **Daptomycin is appropriate treatment of methicillin-resistant *Staphylococcus aureus*–associated bacteremia and right-sided infective endocarditis; regular assessment for signs of myopathy is indicated with this agent.**

Bibliography

Cosgrove SE, Fowler VG Jr. Management of methicillin-resistant Staphylococcus aureus bacteremia [erratum in Clin Infect Dis. 2008;47(3):437]. Clin Infect Dis. 2008;46(Suppl 5):S386-393. [PMID: 18462094]

Item 2   Answer: A

Educational Objective: Understand the principles of tuberculin skin testing in a patient who received bacille Calmette-Guérin (BCG) vaccination.

This health care worker has latent tuberculosis infection and should receive a chest radiograph. She received bacille Calmette-Guérin (BCG) vaccination in Africa more than 20 years ago. Receipt of this vaccination should not influence interpretation of the tuberculin skin test. BCG vaccination is used in many countries with a high prevalence of tuberculosis to prevent childhood tuberculous meningitis and miliary disease. Tuberculin reactivity caused by BCG vaccination wanes with the passage of time and is unlikely to persist more than 10 years after vaccination in the absence of *Mycobacterium tuberculosis* infection; therefore, tuberculin skin testing reactions in persons vaccinated with BCG should be interpreted using the same criteria as used in those who have not received the vaccine. This patient's tuberculin skin testing results should be interpreted as positive (16 mm) and are indicative of latent or active tuberculosis infection. Consequently, this individual should receive a chest radiograph to exclude the presence of active tuberculous disease. If radiographic results are negative, treatment for latent tuberculosis infection consisting of isoniazid therapy with vitamin B_6 (pyridoxine) supplementation should be offered.

Four-drug therapy (isoniazid, rifampin, pyrazinamide, and ethambutol), which is appropriate in patients with active tuberculosis, is not indicated in this patient. For a person with no symptoms and little chance of having isoniazid-resistant *M. tuberculosis* infection, isoniazid with pyridoxine for 9 months is reasonable for management of latent tuberculosis infection. For people with a high probability of having isoniazid resistance (for example, known contacts of patients with isoniazid-resistant tuberculosis), rifampin would be a reasonable alternative. Although the combination of rifampin and pyrazinamide is effective in eradicating latent tuberculosis, there is a fairly high rate of serious hepatotoxicity associated with this combination. There is no hurry to begin preemptive treatment in this patient, and the exclusion of active tuberculosis is essential before contemplating single-drug treatment.

Treatment of latent tuberculosis infection substantially reduces the risk that tuberculosis infection will progress to active disease; therefore, providing no additional evaluation or therapy would not be appropriate. Patients exposed to tuberculosis in the distant past may have an initial negative skin test; performing a second test 7 to 21 days after the first may be helpful in reducing the false-negative response rate. Such two-step testing often "boosts" a negative test result to positive as the immune system recalls its previous exposure, thus divulging a true-positive result. Two-step testing may be particularly helpful in older persons and in distinguishing new from old exposures in annual employee-testing programs. Because this patient has a positive tuberculin skin test, repeating the tuberculin skin test is unnecessary and will not alter management.

> **KEY POINT**
> - Tuberculin skin testing reactions in persons who received the bacille Calmette-Guérin (BCG) vaccine should be interpreted using the same criteria as for those who have not received the vaccine.

Bibliography

The role of BCG vaccine in the prevention and control of tuberculosis in the United States: a joint statement by the Advisory Council for the Elimination of Tuberculosis and the Advisory Committee on Immunization Practices. MMWR Recomm Rep. 1996;45(RR-4):1-18. [PMID: 8602127]

Item 3   Answer: D

Educational Objective: Diagnose tularemia as a result of a possible bioterrorism attack.

This patient's clinical findings are most compatible with pneumonia due to *Francisella tularensis*, a gram-negative bacillus that causes tularemia and may require special cultivation techniques to grow in the clinical laboratory. There are many forms of tularemia, including ulceroglandular, glandular, typhoidal, oculoglandular, pharyngeal, and pneumonic. Tularemia due to a bioterrorism event would most likely be pneumonic from release of aerosolized *F. tularensis*. Victims would develop a nonspecific febrile illness 3 to 5 days after exposure, but the incubation period can be as long as 21 days. Symptoms develop abruptly and include headache, malaise, chest pain, sore throat, abdominal pain, myalgia, and a dry, nonproductive cough; coryza may be prominent. More than 40% of patients do not develop tachycardia or fever. When it occurs, fever classically persists for several days, resolves, and then recurs. Mortality rates are low following treatment with gentamicin or streptomycin. The effectiveness of prophylactic antibiotics for close contacts is unknown.

Inhalational anthrax is characterized by a flu-like prodrome with malaise, fever, headache, a nonproductive cough, substernal chest pain, myalgia, nausea, and abdominal pain. The second phase develops over the next 24 to 36 hours and is fulminant. Severe dyspnea, respiratory distress, and shock occur, and about 50% of patients with advanced disease have meningitis. Enlarged hilar and mediastinal lymph nodes are highly characteristic of inhalational anthrax and result in a widened mediastinum. Pleural effusions are also prominent. In addition, blood culture specimens would probably quickly grow the causative organism, *Bacillus anthracis*.

The epidemiologic features of this patient's illness suggest a possible mass-casualty bioterrorism event, making mycoplasmal, pneumococcal, or staphylococcal pneumonia less likely.

> **KEY POINT**
> - Pneumonic tularemia is a nonspecific febrile illness characterized by abrupt onset of fever, headache, malaise, chest pain, sore throat, abdominal pain, myalgia, and a dry, nonproductive cough.

Bibliography

Dennis DT, Inglesby TV, Henderson DA, et al; Working Group on Civilian Biodefense. Tularemia as a biological weapon: medical and public health management. JAMA. 2001;285(21):2763-2773. [PMID: 11386933]

Item 4   Answer: C

Educational Objective: Diagnose *Pneumocystis jirovecii* pneumonia in an immunosuppressed patient following transplantation.

This patient's presentation is typical for *Pneumocystis jirovecii* pneumonia in the setting of immunosuppressive therapy. Because of her allergy to sulfonamides, the patient was not given trimethoprim-sulfamethoxazole, and the alternative medications are less effective. The presentation of *P. jirovecii* pneumonia in the setting of immunosuppressive therapy differs from that in patients with AIDS. In AIDS, the onset of signs and symptoms is usually much slower, and the disease may progress over months before a diagnosis is established. Alternatively, in both immunosuppressed transplant patients and patients with cancer, the onset tends to be much more acute, with the time between no symptoms and severe symptoms as short as 2 or 3 days. The cough in these patients is usually not productive, arterial oxygen saturation is usually reduced, routine laboratory tests are often normal, and systemic signs, such as fever, are variable. In patients for whom a sputum specimen cannot be obtained, bronchoscopy with bronchoalveolar lavage is diagnostic in more than 90% of cases.

Aspergillus fumigatus would not be expected to cause diffuse pneumonia or to have an onset as acute as that demonstrated in this patient. The chest radiograph in patients with aspergillosis may be normal but more often shows nodules, patchy infiltrates, or cavitary lesions.

Candida glabrata almost never causes primary pneumonia.

Bacterial pneumonia would be more likely to have an acute onset and be associated with a productive cough and focal, rather than diffuse, infiltrates on a chest radiograph.

KEY POINT

- *Pneumocystis jirovecii* pneumonia occurs commonly in immunosuppressed transplant patients and cancer patients, especially when prophylaxis is not given.

Bibliography

Bollée G, Sarfati C, Thiéry G, et al. Clinical picture of Pneumocystis jiroveci pneumonia in cancer patients. Chest. 2007;132(4):1305-1310. [PMID: 17934116]

Item 5   Answer: C

Educational Objective: Diagnose progressive multifocal leukoencephalopathy in a patient with advanced AIDS.

Progressive multifocal leukoencephalopathy (PML) is a demyelinating disease of the central nervous system (CNS) caused by the polyomavirus JC virus (JCV). It occurs almost exclusively in severely immunocompromised patients, including those with advanced HIV-1 infection. Clinical findings of PML include dementia, hemiparesis or paralysis of one extremity, ataxia, hemianopia, and diplopia. The characteristic MRI appearance of these lesions is hyperintense (white) areas on T2-weighted images and fluid-attenuated inversion recovery sequences (FLAIR) and hypointense (dark) areas on T1-weighted images. There is usually no mass effect. In patients with advanced HIV/AIDS, the probability of PML exceeds 80% in those with white matter lesions with no mass effect. The treatment approach involves commencement of highly active antiretroviral therapy to reverse the immunosuppression that interferes with the normal host response to the JCV.

CNS lymphoma occurs in approximately 2% to 12% of HIV-infected patients, typically when the CD4 cell count is less than $200/\mu L$ and, often, less than $50/\mu L$. CNS lymphoma is typically associated with mass effect on MRI.

Cytomegalovirus encephalitis is a concern in patients with advanced HIV infection and the new onset of dementia or other signs of global decline in cognitive function. The imaging usually reveals periventricular or meningeal abnormalities rather than white matter lesions as seen in this patient. The histopathologic findings on brain biopsy can establish a definitive diagnosis, but newer data suggest a potential strong supportive role for cytomegalovirus detection by cerebrospinal fluid-polymerase chain reaction testing.

In patients with HIV infection and CD4 cell counts of less than $200/\mu L$, localized or focal encephalitis is the most common presentation of toxoplasmosis. Toxoplasmosis is the most common cause of a focal brain lesion in patients with HIV infection, and multiple lesions are the rule. Like CNS lymphoma, *Toxoplasma* lesions are typically associated with a mass effect, which is absent in this patient.

KEY POINT

- Progressive multifocal leukoencephalopathy is a demyelinating disease that usually manifests in patients with advanced HIV/AIDS infection.

Bibliography

National Institutes of Health (NIH), Centers for Disease Control and Prevention (CDC), HIV Medical Association of the Infectious Disease Society of America (HIVMA/IDSA). http://aidsinfo.nih.gov/contentfiles/Adult_OI.pdf. Published June 18, 2008. Accessed July 29, 2009.

Item 6   Answer: B

Educational Objective: Treat a patient with a mild, non–limb-threatening, diabetic foot infection caused by aerobic gram-positive cocci.

This patient without evidence of a systemic illness has a mild diabetic foot infection most likely due to aerobic gram-positive bacteria such as *Staphylococcus aureus*, *Streptococcus agalactiae*, and *Streptococcus pyogenes* and does not require initial coverage for aerobic gram-negative bacilli and anaerobic bacteria. The infection is considered mild because it is limited to the skin and superficial subcutaneous tissues and is characterized by inflammation but with erythema/cellulitis extending less than 2 cm around the ulcer and no other local complications.

Diabetic foot ulcers that are chronic, were previously treated with antibiotics, are associated with extensive surrounding cellulitis (>2 cm), or extend to the fascia or bone in a systemically stable patient are considered moderate in severity; treatment should include antibiotic coverage against aerobic gram-negative bacilli in addition to staphylococci, streptococci, enterococci, and, possibly, anaerobes. These diabetic foot infections may be treated with oral or parenteral therapy depending on whether deep tissues are involved.

Parenteral therapy against staphylococci, streptococci, aerobic gram-negative bacilli, and anaerobes is indicated in severe life-threatening diabetic foot infections in patients with systemic toxicity or metabolic abnormalities but is not indicated in this patient.

KEY POINT

- Mild diabetic foot infections in patients without a history of chronic nonhealing ulcers or prior antibiotic use can be treated initially with a narrower antibiotic regimen directed against aerobic gram-positive cocci, such as staphylococci and streptococci.

Bibliography

Lavery LA, Armstrong DG, Murdoch DP, Peters EJ, Lipsky BA. Validation of the Infectious Diseases Society of America's diabetic foot infection classification system. Clin Infect Dis. 2007;44(4):562-565. [PMID: 17243061]

Item 7   Answer: D

Educational Objective: Treat a patient with pelvic inflammatory disease.

This patient's clinical findings are compatible with pelvic inflammatory disease (PID), and she should receive intramuscularly delivered ceftriaxone and oral doxycycline. PID is a polymicrobial infection of the endometrium, fallopian tubes, and ovaries; diagnosis is based on the presence of abdominal discomfort, uterine or adnexal tenderness, or cervical motion tenderness. Other diagnostic criteria include temperature higher than 38.3 °C (101.0 °F), cervical or vaginal mucopurulent discharge, leukocytes in vaginal secretions, and documentation of gonorrheal or chlamydial infection. PID is most likely to occur within 7 days of the onset of menses. All women with suspected PID should be tested for infection with gonorrhea and chlamydia and undergo pregnancy testing. In severe cases, imaging should be performed to exclude a tubo-ovarian abscess. Ambulatory patients are treated with ceftriaxone and doxycycline with or without metronidazole. Duration of treatment is 14 days. Patients with PID should be hospitalized if there is (1) no clinical improvement after 48 to 72 hours of antibiotics; (2) an inability to tolerate oral antibiotics; (3) severe illness with nausea, vomiting, or high fever; (4) suspected intra-abdominal abscess; (4) pregnancy; or (5) noncompliance with outpatient therapy.

Ampicillin and gentamicin do not reliably treat gonorrhea and chlamydial infection and therefore are not adequate antibiotic therapy for patients with PID. Azithromycin alone is sufficient treatment for chlamydial infection but is no longer recommended as initial treatment for gonorrheal infection owing to the high prevalence of gonorrhea strains with decreased susceptibility. Cefoxitin alone is sufficient treatment for gonorrheal but not chlamydial infection and is not recommended.

Metronidazole is not effective treatment alone for gonorrhea or chlamydial infection but is often added to standard PID treatment regimens if the risk of anaerobic infection may be increased. At-risk patients may have evidence of a tubo-ovarian abscess on CT scan or a history of recent gynecologic instrumentation.

KEY POINT

- Pelvic inflammatory disease is diagnosed by clinical criteria, including abdominal discomfort, uterine or adnexal tenderness, or cervical motion tenderness, in young, sexually active women.

Bibliography

Centers for Disease Control and Prevention (CDC). Update to CDC's sexually transmitted diseases treatment guidelines, 2006: fluoroquinolones no longer recommended for treatment of gonococcal infections. MMWR Morb Mortal Wkly Rep. 2007;56(14): 332-336. [PMID: 17431378]

Item 8   Answer: D

Educational Objective: Select the appropriate culture technique for a patient with diabetes mellitus and osteomyelitis of the foot.

Contact with bone (when using a sterile, blunt, stainless steel probe) in the depth of an infected pedal ulcer in patients with diabetes mellitus is strongly correlated with the presence of underlying osteomyelitis, with a positive predictive value of 90%. Patients with diabetes require bone biopsy to obtain deep pathogens, identification of which is the only way to establish a definitive diagnosis and guide therapy. Although it may seem intuitive that drainage from a superficial site such as an ulcer or a sinus tract would contain the causative pathogens, superficial cultures usually do not include the deep organisms responsible for the infection. Failure to identify the causative deep-bone pathogens may lead to spread of infection to adjacent bones or soft tissues and the need for extensive debridement or amputation. The one exception is *Staphylococcus aureus*, which, even if found in superficial cultures, correlates well with findings on deep cultures.

This patient appears well enough to wait for the bone biopsy to be completed before starting empiric antibiotic therapy (and adjusting the antibiotics based on culture results) or until bone culture results become available. Empiric therapy should include activity against streptococci, methicillin-resistant *S. aureus* (MRSA), aerobic gram-negative bacilli, and anaerobes. Therapy with imipenem alone will not adequately cover MRSA, vancomycin and ceftazidime will not adequately cover anaerobic bacteria, and vancomycin and metronidazole will not adequately cover gram-negative organisms.

KEY POINT

- Cultures obtained from a sinus tract or ulcer base often do not reflect the bacterial etiology of an underlying osteomyelitis; bone biopsy is indicated to identify the causative pathogens and guide antibiotic therapy.

Bibliography

Senneville E, Mellie H, Beltrand E, et al. Culture of percutaneous bone biopsy specimens for diagnosis of diabetic foot osteomyelitis: concordance with ulcer swab cultures. Clin Infect Dis. 2006;42(1): 57-62. [PMID: 16323092]

Item 9   Answer: A

Educational Objective: Diagnose Creutzfeldt-Jakob disease.

This patient's clinical findings are typical for Creutzfeldt-Jakob disease (CJD) and fulfill the World Health Organization criteria for a probable diagnosis. Patients with a probable diagnosis of CJD must meet all of the following four criteria: (1) progressive dementia; (2) at least two of the following four clinical features: myoclonus, visual or cerebellar disturbance, pyramidal/extrapyramidal dysfunction, or akinetic mutism; (3) a typical electroencephalogram with the characteristic pattern of periodic sharp wave complexes, and/or a positive 14-3-3 cerebrospinal fluid (CSF) assay with a clinical duration to death of less than 2 years; and (4) an alternative diagnosis ruled out by routine investigations. Routine laboratory evaluation is typically normal, and CSF findings are nonspecific. CJD is unique in that it can be sporadic, familial, or iatrogenic. Iatrogenic cases have been associated with contaminated neurosurgical instruments, dura mater transplants, cadaveric pituitary hormones, corneal transplants (such as in this patient), and liver transplants. When the clinical scenario is convincing, a brain biopsy is unnecessary.

The typical presenting findings of HIV encephalopathy include memory impairment and psychomotor slowing, depression, and movement disorders. The neurologic manifestations of late Lyme disease include a mild neurologic syndrome that is manifested primarily by subtle cognitive changes (Lyme encephalopathy). The most common clinical manifestations of West Nile virus encephalitis include meningitis, flaccid paralysis, and fever. None of these entities manifests the akinetic mutism and myoclonus that are this patient's most prominent findings.

KEY POINT

- Iatrogenic cases of Creutzfeldt-Jakob disease typically develop many years after exposure and are associated with contaminated neurosurgical instruments, dura mater transplants, cadaveric pituitary hormones, corneal transplants, and liver transplants.

Bibliography
Heckmann JG, Lang CJ, Petruch F, et al. Neundorfer B. Transmission of Creutzfeldt-Jakob disease via a corneal transplant. J Neurol Neurosurg Psychiatry. 1997;63(3):388-390. [PMID: 9328261]

Item 10　　Answer:　A

Educational Objective: Diagnose botulism resulting from a terrorism attack.

Cranial nerve deficits and progressive descending weakness without fever or mental status changes are characteristic of botulism, which is caused by a neurotoxin produced by *Clostridium botulinum*, a gram-positive, spore-forming rod. The toxin produces three types of botulism: foodborne, wound, and gastrointestinal. However, experts suggest that aerosolized toxin would most likely be used by terrorists. The five "Ds" describe the major symptoms of botulism: (1) diplopia; (2) dysphonia; (3) dysarthria; (4) dysphagia; and (5) descending, symmetric flaccid paralysis that develops 12 to 72 hours after exposure. As the paralysis progresses, respiratory failure may occur and require mechanical ventilation.

Guillain-Barré syndrome (GBS) is an immune-mediated demyelinating polyneuropathy resulting in rapidly progressive ascending proximal and distal extremity weakness. Symptoms associated with GBS typically evolve over 2 to 4 weeks. In patients with GBS, lumbar puncture of cerebrospinal fluid (CSF) reveals an elevated protein level with a normal leukocyte count.

Myasthenia gravis is characterized by fatigable weakness with a predilection for ocular, bulbar, neck, proximal, and respiratory muscles. Symptoms of this condition are traditionally worsened by fatigue, exertion, a rise in body temperature, stress, and intercurrent infections. A diagnosis of myasthenia gravis frequently may be established by acetylcholine receptor antibody assays. CSF analysis in patients with myasthenia gravis is normal.

In patients with bulbar poliomyelitis, the neurologic symptoms may include weakness of one muscle group, but asymmetric involvement of the proximal arms worse than that in the legs is often present; sensation is normal and reflexes are absent. Bulbar involvement is common. Neurologic symptoms are usually preceded by fever, and CSF findings reveal a pleocytosis consistent with aseptic meningitis.

KEY POINT

- The five "Ds" describe the major symptoms of botulism: (1) diplopia; (2) dysphonia; (3) dysarthria; (4) dysphagia; and (5) descending, symmetric flaccid paralysis that develops 12 to 72 hours after exposure.

Bibliography
Arnon SS, Schechter R, Inglesby TV, et al; Working Group on Civilian Biodefense. Botulinum toxin as a biological weapon: medical and public health management [erratum in JAMA. 2001;285(16): 2081]. JAMA. 2001;285(8):1059-70. [PMID: 11209178]

Item 11　　Answer:　C

Educational Objective: Diagnose acute HIV infection.

This patient's prolonged febrile syndrome in the setting of HIV risk factors should raise concerns for recent infection with HIV. The most appropriate test for diagnosing acute HIV is the detection of HIV RNA, which is the most sensitive test for detecting HIV infection during the acute symptomatic phase. Tests for HIV-specific antigens, such as p24, can also detect the presence of virus in the acute setting. Antibodies to HIV do not commonly occur until about 6 weeks after infection and may therefore be negative during the acute symptomatic phase. In addition to the acute retroviral syndrome, this patient must be evaluated for secondary syphilis using the rapid plasma reagin test. Secondary syphilis and acute retroviral syndrome should always be considered in sexually active patients with rash, fever, and generalized lymphadenopathy. Other causes of a mononucleosis syndrome should also be considered if these tests are inconclusive.

The CD4 cell count may be profoundly depressed in patients with acute HIV infection, but the CD4 cell count can be both insensitive in the diagnosis of acute infection and depressed by various other, non–HIV-1 infectious agents.

Although acute HIV infection can mimic the signs and symptoms of mononucleosis, testing for Epstein-Barr virus infection is a less immediate concern in this patient who has multiple risk factors for HIV infection.

The histopathology of the rash in acute HIV infection is nonspecific and is not useful in diagnosis; therefore, a skin biopsy is not indicated.

KEY POINT

- Because antibodies to HIV are not detectable until about 6 weeks after infection, the measurement of HIV RNA viral load is the most sensitive test for infection during the acute stage.

Bibliography

Kahn JO, Walker BD. Acute human immunodeficiency virus type 1 infection. N Engl J Med. 1998;339(1):33-39. [PMID: 9647878]

Item 12   Answer: C

Educational Objective: Empirically treat a patient with a presumed bacterial brain abscess secondary to a dental focus of infection.

This patient has a bacterial brain abscess, the pathogenesis of which is most likely from a contiguous focus of infection in the mouth. Severe headache is the most common symptom of a brain abscess and is usually localized to the same side of the head as the abscess. Headache may have an acute or gradual onset and is typically unrelieved with usual analgesia. Meningeal signs are absent in most patients with brain abscess but may be present if the abscess has leaked into a ventricle. Abscesses that are associated with significant increases in intracranial pressure typically cause findings of increased intracranial pressure, including alteration of mental status, which is a poor prognostic sign. The frequency of isolation of certain organisms and the pathogenesis of infection should be considered in the empiric approach to antimicrobial therapy. Given the location of the initial infection and the demonstration of bone invasion in this patient, the most likely cause is an *Actinomyces* species. However, considering the likelihood of mixed infection from the primary source in the mouth, the empiric regimen should also include treatment for streptococci and other anaerobes. Penicillin G would treat *Actinomyces* and streptococci but not the β-lactamase-producing strains of *Bacteroides fragilis*, for which metronidazole is the agent of choice.

There are limited data on central nervous system penetration of clindamycin into brain abscesses. Trimethoprim-sulfamethoxazole, or the combination of vancomycin plus gentamicin, would not be appropriate to treat the spectrum of likely organisms in this patient.

KEY POINT

- Optimal empiric therapy for a bacterial brain abscess from a dental focus of infection is the combination of penicillin G and metronidazole.

Bibliography

Lu CH, Chang EN, Lui CC. Strategies for the management of bacterial brain abscess. J Clin Neurosci. 2006;13(10):979-985. [PMID: 17056261]

Item 13   Answer: B

Educational Objective: Evaluate a patient with vertebral osteomyelitis.

The next management step is MRI of the lumbar spine. Vertebral osteomyelitis is an infection of the spine that must be considered in any patient with new-onset back pain and fever. Patients with acute hematogenous osteomyelitis are more likely to present with acute pain and fever than are patients with chronic contiguous osteomyelitis (for example, foot ulcer–associated osteomyelitis). In adults, hematogenous osteomyelitis most often involves the intervertebral disk space and two adjacent vertebrae. Potential sources of hematogenous infection include the genitourinary tract (particularly following instrumentation), skin (injection drug use), infected intravascular devices, and endocarditis, but often, the source of the infection cannot be identified. In patients with hematogenous osteomyelitis, the leukocyte count is typically normal, but the erythrocyte sedimentation rate is elevated in 80% to 90% of patients, often greater than 100 mm/h.

MRI is the most appropriate imaging study for patients with suspected vertebral osteomyelitis and is a more sensitive study than CT scans or plain radiographs. In addition, MRI can detect an epidural abscess or a paravertebral or psoas abscess that might require surgical drainage. If MRI cannot be performed (for example, in patients with pacemakers or metal prosthetic devices) or if results are inconclusive, a gallium nuclear study is very sensitive and specific in this setting.

Three-phase bone scintigraphy using labeled technetium can occasionally be helpful in diagnosing osteomyelitis but is associated with false-positive results in patients with other causes of back pain including fracture as well as false-negative results if the infection is early. Three-phase bone scintigraphy is an inferior diagnostic test compared to MRI scanning but may be appropriate when the initial MRI imaging result is indeterminate.

KEY POINT

- The diagnosis of vertebral osteomyelitis must be considered in any patient who presents with new-onset back pain and fever.

Bibliography
An HS, Seldromridge JA. Spinal Infections: diagnostic tests and imaging studies; Clin Orthopedic Relat Rec. Clin Orthop Relat Res. 2006;444:27-33. [PMID: 16523124]

Item 14   Answer: B

Educational Objective: Diagnose and treat esophageal candidiasis in a patient with HIV infection.

This patient should be started on fluconazole. He is at risk for development of opportunistic infections because of his low CD4 cell count (<100/µL). Candidiasis is the most common esophageal disorder in patients with HIV infection. Approximately two thirds of patients with *Candida* esophagitis have concomitant thrush, which is characterized by fluffy plaques most often occurring on the tongue, buccal mucosa, and soft palate. White patches confined to the tongue are less suspicious for thrush and can be physiologic or a sign of leukoplakia. Because of the strong association between oral and esophageal candidiasis, patients with symptomatic thrush should receive a brief course of systemic antifungal therapy. Owing to its excellent efficacy, ease of administration, and low cost, oral fluconazole is the preferred therapy.

Amphotericin B and its lipid relatives are also effective in treating thrush and *Candida* esophagitis, but besides being available only intravenously, their side-effect profile is highly unfavorable.

Gastroesophageal reflux disease is relatively uncommon in patients with HIV infection and would be characterized by heartburn rather than dysphagia and odynophagia; therefore, omeprazole is not indicated.

Corticosteroids are contraindicated in patients with infectious esophagitis.

For patients with herpes simplex or cytomegalovirus esophagitis, antivirals such as valganciclovir can provide excellent relief; however, these infections occur less commonly than fungal esophagitis. If his symptoms do not improve after several days of fluconazole therapy, diagnostic upper endoscopy is indicated. Upper endoscopy would also have been indicated initially if his dysphagia had been so severe that he was unable to swallow.

> **KEY POINT**
> • Patients with HIV infection and odynophagia associated with oral thrush should receive an empiric trial of fluconazole.

Bibliography
Pappas PG, Rex JH, Sobel JD, et al; Infectious Diseases Society of America. Guidelines for treatment of candidiasis. Clin Infect Dis. 2004;38(2):161-189. [PMID: 14699449]

Item 15   Answer: C

Educational Objective: Diagnose infection with postsurgical *Mycobacterium abscessus.*

This patient has a typical presentation for a soft tissue infection with a rapidly growing mycobacterium (RGM),

Mycobacterium abscessus. This organism is found throughout the world and is endemic in the United States. Wound infection with RGM is uncommon but can be catastrophic if not recognized and treated appropriately. The most distinguishing characteristics of the infections are nodules, often purple in color, and chronic abscess or sinuses. Skin and subcutaneous infections with RGM should be strongly considered in clinical situations demonstrating chronic purulent drainage, a lack of a convincing pathogen on routine culture, and association with implanted prosthetic devices. A lack of response to treatment and the failure to isolate a convincing pathogen should prompt further diagnostic evaluation consisting of staining and special culturing for mycobacteria followed by sensitivity testing to determine the appropriate antimicrobial therapy.

Candida albicans might be considered as a causative agent in this setting, but this organism did not grow on the original culture and grew in only small amounts on subsequent cultures, suggesting that it was a colonizer selected by the antibiotic treatment. Other possible pathogens for such chronic draining skin infections include environmental fungi and *Nocardia asteroides*; however, these are not likely as nosocomial pathogens. *Staphylococcus aureus* is easily identified on routine culture and is almost always susceptible to vancomycin.

Inoculation infection with *Mycobacterium tuberculosis* might be a consideration in this patient; however, it occurs infrequently, even in endemic parts of the world, and is not particularly associated with rapidly progressive postoperative wound infections.

> **KEY POINT**
> • Skin and subcutaneous infections with rapidly growing mycobacteria should be strongly considered in clinical situations demonstrating chronic purulent drainage, a lack of a convincing pathogen on routine culture, and association with implanted prosthetic devices.

Bibliography
Rahav G, Pitlik S, Amitai Z, et al. An outbreak of Mycobacterium Jacuzzi infection following insertion of breast implants. Clin Infect Dis. 2006;43(7):823-830. [PMID: 16941361]

Item 16   Answer: E

Educational Objective: Manage a patient with severe herpes simplex encephalitis.

Predictors of adverse outcome in patients with herpes simplex encephalitis include age older than 30 years, Glasgow Coma Scale score of less than 6, and duration of symptoms before starting acyclovir therapy of greater than 4 days. The recommended duration of acyclovir therapy in adults with herpes simplex encephalitis is 14 to 21 days. A negative cerebrospinal fluid (CSF) polymerase chain reaction (PCR) result at the end of therapy has been associated with a better outcome, suggesting that another CSF specimen should be subjected to PCR testing for herpes simplex virus at the conclusion of therapy in patients who have not had the appropriate clinical response. If the result is positive, acyclovir therapy should be continued as it should in this patient given his suboptimal response despite appropriate therapy and persistently positive PCR result at 14 days of therapy.

Brain biopsy is not indicated because the diagnosis is not in question despite the lack of symptomatic improvement. A brain biopsy would not impact future management decisions and is associated with the potential for adverse effects.

Resistance to acyclovir in herpes simplex encephalitis would be very rare, and the data on use of alternative antiviral therapies such as foscarnet or ganciclovir are anecdotal at best and indicate an association with greater potential for side effects. There are also limited data on the use of adjunctive dexamethasone in patients with herpes simplex encephalitis.

KEY POINT

- **In patients with confirmed herpes simplex encephalitis with suboptimal response to a course of acyclovir, positive findings on repeat cerebrospinal fluid-polymerase chain reaction testing should prompt continuation of acyclovir therapy.**

Bibliography

Tunkel AR, Glaser CA, Bloch KC, et al; Infectious Diseases Society of America. The management of encephalitis: clinical practice guidelines by the Infectious Diseases Society of America. Clin Infect Dis. 2008;47(3):303-327. [PMID: 18582201]

Item 17   Answer: D

Educational Objective: Diagnose *Vibrio vulnificus*–associated necrotizing fasciitis.

This patient most likely has necrotizing fasciitis secondary to *Vibrio vulnificus*. In addition, this patient has chronic hepatitis C infection with evidence of portal hypertension. *V. vulnificus* infections should be considered in patients with liver disease who present with septic physiology and hemorrhagic bullous lesions after potential exposure to this aquatic, gram-negative rod. Wound infection typically occurs by inoculation through the skin, and sepsis or septicemia occurs after consumption of raw shellfish (particularly oysters). This organism thrives in warm salt water or brackish water such as the Gulf of Mexico, and most infections are noted when sea water temperatures are warmer. Surgical intervention, aggressive supportive therapy, and adjunctive antibiotics are often required.

Tetanus, a disease caused by toxins elaborated by the anaerobic bacterium *Clostridium tetani*, can result from inoculation of the infectious agent through an open wound. However, the short incubation period and lack of other clinical findings, including trismus, opisthotonus,

dysphagia, risus sardonicus, or a rigid abdomen, make this diagnosis very unlikely in this patient.

Pasteurella multocida is a gram-negative rod that can cause cellulitis, but it is usually associated with cat bites and scratches.

Rickettsia rickettsii is the organism responsible for Rocky Mountain spotted fever (RMSF). Symptoms including rash, fever, headache, gastrointestinal symptoms, and myalgia are common. Initially, the rash of RMSF is erythematous and maculopapular before progressing to a petechial appearance. It typically begins on the wrists, ankles, palms, and soles before spreading centripetally. This patient's presentation is not consistent with RMSF.

KEY POINT

- **Necrotizing *Vibrio vulnificus* skin infection should be considered in cirrhotic patients who present with septic physiology and hemorrhagic bullous lesions after exposure of wounds to warm brackish water or seafood drippings or after consumption of raw shellfish contaminated with this organism.**

Bibliography

Dechet AM, Yu PA, Koram N, Painter J. Nonfoodborne Vibrio infections: an important cause of morbidity and mortality in the United States, 1997-2006. Clin Infect Dis. 2008;46(7):970-976. [PMID: 18444811]

Item 18   Answer: D

Educational Objective: Manage a patient with respiratory colonization with *Mycobacterium avium* complex.

This patient required no further treatment. Nontuberculous mycobacteria such as *Mycobacterium avium* complex (MAC) are ubiquitous in the environment and can act as both contaminants and colonizers of sputum cultures. This is distinct from *Mycobacterium tuberculosis*, which, when isolated from a properly handled clinical specimen, is always thought to be a pathogen. When nontuberculous mycobacteria are isolated from the sputum, whether the bacteria are pathogenic must be determined. The presence of a compatible clinical illness, repeated isolation of the organism in high colony counts, and no alternative explanation for the illness are suggestive of pathogenic infection. Compatible infectious syndromes include superinfection resulting in pulmonary cavitation in patients with pre-existing pulmonary disease; persistent cough and pulmonary nodules without cavitation (also called "Lady Windermere syndrome"); disseminated infection with positive blood and stool cultures in patients with AIDS; and lymphadenitis. A hypersensitivity pneumonitis due to MAC following hot-tub exposure has been reported. In this patient, MAC is clearly not a pathogen because there is an alternative diagnosis (probable pneumococcal pneumonia), very few nontuberculous mycobacterial organisms on the culture, and no manifestations of compatible illness associated with MAC infection.

Initiating therapy with clarithromycin, rifampin, and ethambutol for at least 1 year is effective treatment for MAC infection; however this patient does not have a MAC infection and should not receive this prolonged antimicrobial course.

Initiation of isoniazid, rifampin, pyrazinamide, and ethambutol would be appropriate for active *M. tuberculosis* infection, but there is no indication that this infection is present in this patient.

KEY POINT

- *Mycobacterium avium* complex–compatible infectious syndromes include superinfection resulting in pulmonary cavitation in patients with pre-existing pulmonary disease; persistent cough and pulmonary nodules without cavitation; disseminated infection with positive blood and stool cultures in patients with AIDS; and lymphadenitis.

Bibliography

Griffith DE, Aksamit T, Brown-Elliott BA, et al; ATS Mycobacterial Diseases Subcommittee; American Thoracic Society; Infectious Disease Society of America. An official ATS/IDSA statement: diagnosis, treatment, and prevention of nontuberculous mycobacterial diseases. Am J Respir Crit Care Med. 2007;175(4):367-416. [PMID: 17277290]

Item 19   Answer: E

Educational Objective: Treat a patient with suspected *Pseudallescheria* infection.

This patient likely has infection with *Pseudallescheria boydii*, or its asexual form, *Scedosporium apiospermum*. Several fungi have the appearance of slender hyphal forms with acute angle branching in histologic specimens, with the most common of these being *Aspergillus* species. However, *Aspergillus* infection is not likely in this patient because *Aspergillus* polymerase chain reaction (PCR) results were negative. Of the other organisms with an appearance such as that described in this patient's histologic findings, *Pseudallescheria* or *Scedosporium* species is also commonly found in immunocompromised hosts such as this patient. Empiric therapy should be initiated in this patient pending culture results. *Pseudallescheria* and *Scedosporium species* are resistant to all forms of amphotericin B; therefore, one of the triazoles such as voriconazole would be the most appropriate therapy. Voriconazole would also be an optimal therapeutic choice for patients with aspergillosis.

Flucytosine has no role in the treatment of patients with suspected *Pseudallescheria* or *Scedosporium* infection because these organisms are highly resistant to this agent.

KEY POINT

- *Pseudallescheria boydii* and *Scedosporium apiospermum* are resistant to amphotericin B but are sensitive to the triazoles.

Bibliography

Cortez KJ, Roilides E, Quiroz-Telles F, et al. Infections caused by Scedosporium spp. Clin Microbiol Rev. 2008;21(1):157-97. [PMID: 18202441]

Item 20   Answer: A

Educational Objective: Treat inhalational anthrax.

This patient's clinical presentation is compatible with inhalational anthrax. The Centers for Disease Control and Prevention's recommended treatment includes a fluoroquinolone or doxycycline plus one or two additional agents (for example, penicillin, erythromycin, vancomycin, rifampin, or clindamycin) pending results of antimicrobial susceptibility testing.

The inhalational form of anthrax is most likely to be associated with bioterrorism. Inhaled spores migrate to mediastinal lymph nodes, where they germinate, disseminate, and produce toxins that cause edema and cell death with hemorrhage. The prodrome is described as flu-like with malaise, fever, headache, a nonproductive cough, substernal chest pain, myalgia, nausea, and abdominal pain. The second phase develops over the next 24 to 36 hours and is fulminant. Severe dyspnea, respiratory distress, and shock occur, and about 50% of patients with advanced disease have meningitis. Enlarged hilar and mediastinal lymph nodes are highly characteristic of inhalational anthrax and result in a widened mediastinum. Pleural effusions are also prominent. *Bacillus anthracis* is also suggested by the initial report of the buffy coat Gram stain.

The other antibiotics or antibiotic combinations are not recommended for the treatment of inhalational anthrax because they do not contain either a fluoroquinolone or doxycycline.

KEY POINT

- The initial therapy for inhalational anthrax should include a fluoroquinolone or doxycycline plus one or two additional agents (for example, penicillin, erythromycin, vancomycin, rifampin, or clindamycin).

Bibliography

Inglesby TV, O'Toole T, Henderson DA, et al; Working Group on Civilian Biodefense. Anthrax as a biological weapon, 2002: updated recommendations for management [erratum in JAMA. 2002;288 (15):1849]. JAMA. 2002;287(17):2236-2252. [PMID: 11980524]

Item 21   Answer: D

Educational Objective: Diagnose a staphylococcal posttransplantation wound infection.

This patient's symptoms are most likely attributable to a postoperative wound infection considering the recent surgery, rapid onset of high fever, leukocytosis, wound erythema and tenderness, presence of peri-incisional fluid, and lack of signs and symptoms supporting other likely problems in the immediate postoperative period. In patients receiving solid organ transplants, infections in the immediate postoperative period are similar to those occurring in patients who have undergone other types of surgery. Posttransplantation wound infections from staphylococci (coagulase-negative and *Staphylococcus aureus*), hemolytic streptococci, or enteric bacteria occur commonly.

Candidal wound infection would be less likely than staphylococcal wound infection in this patient because of the acuity of onset, leukocytosis, and high fever. Candidal wound infections are very uncommon and would be expected to be more chronic in nature.

Cytomegalovirus (CMV) infection is unlikely because it would rarely become clinically apparent this soon after surgery and with such a short duration of immunosuppressive therapy. Because the donor and recipient are both serologically positive for CMV, CMV infection might well occur between the second and sixth month after surgery unless prophylaxis is given.

Pneumocystis jirovecii pneumonia is unlikely to be responsible for this patient's current signs and symptoms because it is not likely to occur this soon after transplantation, and this patient demonstrates no respiratory signs and symptoms and has a normal pulmonary examination and chest radiograph.

> **KEY POINT**
>
> - Infections in the immediate posttransplantation period are usually the same as those occurring after other kinds of surgery and include staphylococci (coagulase-negative and *Staphylococcus aureus*), hemolytic streptococci, or enteric bacterial wound infection.

Bibliography

Fishman JA. Infection in solid-organ transplant recipients. N Engl J Med. 2007;357(25):2601-2614. [PMID: 18094380]

Item 22   Answer: D

Educational Objective: Treat a patient with a bacterial brain abscess secondary to sinusitis.

This patient has developed a bacterial brain abscess from a contiguous focus of infection in the sinuses. After appropriate neuroimaging is performed, lesions should be excised or stereotactically aspirated. Once abscess material is aspirated for microbiologic and histologic studies, empiric antimicrobial therapy should be initiated based on the most likely pathogen(s). In this circumstance, the most likely organisms to be found in the abscess are streptococci, *Bacteroides* species, Enterobacteriaceae (including *Escherichia coli*), *Staphylococcus aureus*, and *Haemophilus* species. The initiation of empiric therapy with vancomycin, metronidazole, and ceftriaxone was appropriate. However, once culture results became available, there was no need to continue vancomycin because no staphylococci were isolated. Even

though the final culture only demonstrated *E. coli*, anaerobic species (including *Bacteroides fragilis*) possibly would not have been isolated. Therefore, metronidazole and ceftriaxone should be continued.

Imipenem should not be used in this patient because it may confer an increased risk for seizures in the setting of a central nervous system mass lesion. Levofloxacin has no significant antianaerobic activity, treatment of which is necessary in this patient.

> **KEY POINT**
>
> - Empiric therapy for a bacterial brain abscess in a patient with underlying sinusitis should include vancomycin, metronidazole, and a third-generation cephalosporin.

Bibliography

Carpenter J, Stapleton S, Holliman R. Retrospective analysis of 49 cases of brain abscess and review of the literature. Eur J Clin Microbiol Infect Dis. 2007;26(1):1-11. [PMID: 17180609]

Item 23   Answer: C

Educational Objective: Manage a pregnant woman with HIV infection.

This patient should receive immediate therapy with zidovudine, lamivudine, and lopinavir-ritonavir. Antiretroviral therapy is recommended in all pregnant women with HIV infection, regardless of virologic, immunologic, or clinical parameters, to prevent mother-to-child transmission. Therefore, initiating antiretroviral treatment at delivery or when the CD4 cell count drops below 500/µL is not appropriate. Recommendations regarding preferred treatment of HIV-infected women are complex. In general, the treatment principles used in management of nonpregnant adults with HIV infection also apply to pregnant women with HIV infection; however, the benefits versus the risks to the woman, fetus, and infant must be weighed and the toxicity data carefully considered before therapy is chosen. In nonpregnant patients with HIV infection, three-drug antiretroviral therapy consisting of two nucleoside analogue reverse transcriptase inhibitors and a protease inhibitor or non-nucleoside reverse transcriptase inhibitor is recommended.

Some agents are harmful to the mother or the fetus and must be avoided during pregnancy. For example, early fetal exposure to efavirenz-containing regimens has been reported to cause neural tube defects. Efavirenz is the only antiretroviral agent listed as a U.S. Food and Drug Administration pregnancy risk category D drug. Therefore, therapy with zidovudine-lamivudine and efavirenz would be inappropriate in this patient.

> **KEY POINT**
>
> - Antiretroviral therapy, excluding efavirenz, is recommended in all pregnant women with HIV infection, regardless of virologic, immunologic, or clinical parameters, to prevent mother-to-child transmission.

Bibliography

Public Health Service Task Force. Recommendations for Use of Anti-retroviral Drugs in Pregnant HIV-Infected Women for Maternal Health and Interventions to Reduce Perinatal HIV Transmission in the United States. http://aidsinfo.nih.gov/contentfiles/PerinatalGL.pdf. Published April 29, 2009. Accessed on July 29, 2009.

Item 24   Answer: B
Educational Objective: Manage a patient with cutaneous Kaposi sarcoma lesions.

This patient with early-stage, but untreated, HIV infection has developed localized cutaneous Kaposi sarcoma, which is caused by human herpesvirus 8. It occurs almost exclusively in men who have sex with men and can develop even before CD4 cell depletion has occurred. Based on his lack of symptoms, normal examination findings, and laboratory test results, he does not have extensive cutaneous or mucosal disease and has a low likelihood of visceral involvement. However, because Kaposi sarcoma is an AIDS-related complication, highly active antiretroviral therapy (HAART) should be started now. Kaposi sarcoma frequently regresses and sometimes resolves completely when HAART is initiated.

Chemotherapy, combined with HAART, should be considered for patients with visceral Kaposi sarcoma and may be a useful adjunctive therapy in patients with widely disseminated cutaneous disease.

Local treatment, such as intralesional injection of vinblastine or topical alitretinoin (9-*cis*-retinoic acid), may be useful in the treatment of symptomatic, bulky, or cosmetically disfiguring Kaposi sarcoma lesions, but this treatment does not prevent the progression of lesions and is not a substitute for HAART in patients with AIDS-defining illnesses. Continuing to monitor his CD4 cell count and viral load only is not the best management option; HAART therapy should be initiated.

> **KEY POINT**
> - Kaposi sarcoma is an AIDS-related complication that requires the initiation of highly active antiretroviral therapy.

Bibliography

The National Institutes of Health (NIH), The Centers for Disease Control and Prevention (CDC), and the HIV Medical Association of the Infectious Disease Society of America (HIVMA/IDSA). Guidelines for Prevention and Treatment of Opportunistic Infections in HIV-infected Adults and Adolescents. http://aidsinfo.nih.gov/contentfiles/Adult_OI.pdf. Published June 18, 2008. Accessed July 29, 2009.

Item 25   Answer: E
Educational Objective: Treat a patient with a cerebrospinal fluid shunt infection.

This patient has a cerebrospinal fluid (CSF) shunt infection. Ventriculo-peritoneal shunt infections can be difficult to diagnose owing to the variability of the clinical presentation.

Symptoms may reflect increased intracranial pressure (headache, nausea, vomiting, lethargy, or altered mental status) as the result of shunt obstruction or even signs of peritonitis. Classic meningeal irritative symptoms may be absent, and fever may or may not be present. This patient has fever and signs of increased intracranial pressure and laboratory findings confirming the diagnosis of shunt infection. The most likely causative microorganisms are coagulase-negative staphylococci (especially *Staphylococcus epidermidis*), *S. aureus*, diphtheroids (including *Propionibacterium acnes*), and gram-negative bacilli (including *Pseudomonas aeruginosa*). Empiric therapy with vancomycin to cover staphylococci and diphtheroids and ceftazidime, cefepime, or meropenem to treat the gram-negative bacilli, is appropriate pending culture results. Trimethoprim-sulfamethoxazole; trimethoprim-sulfamethoxazole plus rifampin; vancomycin; and vancomycin, ampicillin, plus ceftriaxone do not provide a broad enough spectrum of in vitro activity for the possible infectious pathogens in this patient.

> **KEY POINT**
> - Empiric treatment for cerebrospinal fluid shunt infection should include agents with activity against staphylococci, diphtheroids, and aerobic gram-negative bacilli.

Bibliography

Tunkel AR, Hartman BJ, Kaplan SL, et al. Practice guidelines for the management of bacterial meningitis. Clin Infect Dis. 2004;39(9):1267-1284. [PMID: 15494903]

Item 26   Answer: E
Educational Objective: Diagnose West Nile virus encephalitis.

This patient most likely has West Nile virus encephalitis, which has been identified as an important cause of encephalitis in the United States. Nearly all states have reported cases of West Nile virus neuroinvasive disease, but most occur in the Midwest and the Western states in the later summer or early fall. Transmission is usually via a mosquito vector but may also occur through transfusion, transplantation, and breast feeding. There is an increased incidence of encephalitis in patients older than 50 years, and clinical features include tremors, myoclonus, parkinsonism, and poliomyelitis-like flaccid paralysis that can be mistaken for Guillain-Barré syndrome. MRI of the brain may display a characteristic pattern of mixed intensity or hypodense lesions on T1-weighted images in the thalamus, basal ganglia, and midbrain, which are hyperintense on T2-weighted images. Given the clinical presentation and neuroimaging results, the most likely diagnosis is West Nile virus encephalitis.

Listeria monocytogenes causes disease in neonates, immunosuppressed and elderly adults, and pregnant women. Previously healthy adults occasionally become infected, and symptomatic. *L. monocytogenes* may rarely cause a rhombencephalitis with clinical features of ataxia, cranial nerve deficits, and nystagmus.

Toxoplasma gondii causes extrapyramidal symptoms and signs such as delirium, dementia, or brain stem injury signs and symptoms. *T. gondii* encephalitis is restricted to immunocompromised patients, such as individuals with advanced HIV infection. None of these conditions are supported by this patient's symptoms and findings.

Tropheryma whippelii is the etiologic agent of Whipple disease. The four cardinal manifestations of Whipple disease include arthralgia, weight loss, diarrhea, and abdominal pain. The joint symptoms typically present early in the disease course, and weight loss and the less common neurologic manifestations occur in late-stage disease. The most common central nervous system manifestations are dementia, ophthalmoplegia, myoclonus, and cerebellar ataxia; oculomasticatory myorhythmia (pendular vergence oscillations of the eyes and synchronous contractions of the masticatory muscles) is thought to be pathognomonic.

Varicella zoster virus encephalitis usually leads to focal neurologic deficits and seizures, which are absent in this patient. Varicella zoster virus encephalitis may or may not be associated with the typical vesicular rash.

KEY POINT

- **Clinical features of West Nile virus encephalitis may include tremors, myoclonus, parkinsonism, and poliomyelitis-like flaccid paralysis.**

Bibliography

Bode AV, Sejvar JJ, Pape J, Campbell GL, Marfin AA. West Nile virus disease: a descriptive study of 228 patients hospitalized in a 4-county region of Colorado in 2003. Clin Infect Dis. 2006;42(9): 1234-1240. [PMID: 16586381]

Item 27   Answer: D

Educational Objective: Treat a patient with secondary-stage syphilis and a penicillin allergy.

This patient has secondary-stage syphilis. Primary-stage syphilis is characterized by an ulcerative lesion (chancre) that develops approximately 3 weeks after infection occurs, has a clean appearance with heaped-up borders, and is usually painless. It is often unrecognized. The primary chancre resolves spontaneously. Secondary syphilis develops 2 to 8 weeks after the appearance of the primary chancre (but signs of secondary-stage syphilis may coincide with genital ulceration) and is characterized by widespread hematogenous dissemination involving many organs, most often the skin, liver, and lymph nodes. The rash in most patients with secondary-stage syphilis is a maculopapular rash involving the palms of the hands and the soles of the feet. Secondary syphilis also resolves spontaneously. The later stages of syphilis comprise early and late latent infection and tertiary manifestations including cardiovascular and neurologic complications.

The optimal agent for treating all forms of syphilis is penicillin, although the precise regimen and duration vary according to disease stage. Doxycycline has been used successfully to treat primary and secondary syphilis in patients with penicillin allergy. Doxycycline is the recommended antibiotic for nonpregnant patients with these stages of syphilis who report adverse reactions to penicillin.

Any penicillin formulation, with or without the addition of a corticosteroid such as methylprednisolone, is considered unsafe in patients with a significant penicillin allergy, unless desensitization occurs. Based on small clinical trials, The Centers for Disease Control and Prevention guidelines list ceftriaxone as one alternative to benzathine penicillin in patients with a history of minor penicillin allergy. However, this patient's urticaria, wheezing, and dyspnea signify a more serious allergic reaction, and ceftriaxone should definitely be avoided. Erythromycin has a high failure rate in patients with syphilis and therefore is not indicated.

KEY POINT

- **Doxycycline is the preferred alternative treatment for early-stage syphilis in nonpregnant patients with penicillin allergy.**

Bibliography

Centers for Disease Control and Prevention, Workowski KA, Berman SM. Sexually transmitted diseases treatment guidelines, 2006 [erratum in MMWR Recomm Rep. 2006;55(36):997]. MMWR Recomm Rep. 2006;55(RR-11):1-94. [PMID: 16888612]

Item 28   Answer: B

Educational Objective: Treat toxoplasmosis empirically.

In addition to empiric treatment for central nervous system toxoplasmosis, this patient needs urgent determination of his immune status to help focus appropriate preventive treatments for HIV infection–associated processes. Assuming that he has a CD4 cell count of less than $200/\mu L$, localized or focal encephalitis would be the most common presentation of toxoplasmosis. Diagnosis and early treatment are essential, because untreated toxoplasmosis is fatal in immunocompromised patients. In this patient, presumptive therapy for toxoplasmosis encephalitis with sulfadiazine, pyrimethamine, and folinic acid should be initiated.

A definitive diagnosis of toxoplasmosis may depend on obtaining tissue biopsy specimens showing tachyzoites, but brain biopsy is associated with morbidity and is not justified when a strong suspicion of toxoplasmosis is present and treatment has not yet been tried. Were he to have a positive antibody test for *Toxoplasma gondii*, that would further strengthen the presumptive diagnosis of toxoplasmosis. However, some patients who acquire *T. gondii* at a time when they have severely depressed immune function from advanced HIV infection will not produce antibody even in the setting of florid toxoplasmosis. In addition to close clinical follow-up, a repeat neuroradiologic study should be performed 10 to 14 days after antitoxoplasmosis therapy initiation. If there is no reduction in the size or number of lesions, an alternative diagnosis should be considered, and brain biopsy should be performed.

Corticosteroids can provide quick relief from increased intracranial pressure, but they are potentially harmful in patients with active opportunistic infections.

CT scanning might show the same lesions, but, usually, MRI is more sensitive for detecting central nervous system lesions in patients with HIV-1 infection.

The more exotic imaging modalities of thallium 201–labeled single-photon emission computed tomography (SPECT) and positron emission tomography are usually abnormal in patients with cerebral toxoplasmosis, but they cannot confirm the diagnosis with certainty and may not be widely available.

KEY POINT

- A presumptive diagnosis of cerebral toxoplasmosis can be made in HIV-1– infected patients when brain imaging reveals characteristic multiple ring-enhancing lesions, especially when serologic tests for anti-*Toxoplasma* antibodies are positive; empiric treatment is appropriate.

Bibliography

Guidelines for prevention and treatment of opportunistic infections in HIV-infected adults and adolescents. Available at http://aidsinfo.nih.gov/contentfiles/Adult_OI.pdf. Published June 18, 2008. Accessed on July 29, 2009.

Item 29   Answer: A

Educational Objective: Select the appropriate antimicrobial therapy for a patient with *Listeria monocytogenes* meningitis.

This patient has underlying conditions that increase her risk for *Listeria* bacteremia and meningitis. Listeriosis is associated with extremes of age (neonates and patients >50 years), alcoholism, malignancy, immune suppression, diabetes mellitus, hepatic disease, renal disease, iron overload, collagen vascular disorders, pregnancy, HIV infection, and the use of antitumor necrosis factor α agents. No controlled trials have been conducted to establish the antimicrobial therapy of choice for treatment of central nervous system listeriosis. Treatment for definitive *Listeria* meningitis should consist of ampicillin or penicillin G, combined with an aminoglycoside because of in vitro synergy and enhanced killing in vivo, as documented in various animal models of *Listeria* infection. Ceftriaxone, chloramphenicol, and vancomycin plus gentamicin do not have the appropriate clinical efficacy in patients with *Listeria* meningitis.

KEY POINT

- Treatment for proven *Listeria monocytogenes* meningitis is ampicillin or penicillin G, combined with an aminoglycoside.

Bibliography

Clauss HE, Lorber B. Central nervous system infection with *Listeria monocytogenes*. Curr Infect Dis Rep. 2008;10(4):300-308. [PMID: 18765103]

Item 30   Answer: E

Educational Objective: Treat patients with *Aspergillus* pneumonia.

This immunosuppressed patient has pulmonary *Aspergillus* infection and requires the addition of voriconazole to his therapeutic regimen. Pulmonary infection is the most common presentation of *Aspergillus* in a neutropenic patient. Typically, these patients have received broad-spectrum empiric antibiotic therapy for the treatment of fever during an episode of neutropenia, and, possibly, amphotericin B, without clinical response. In addition to fever, patients typically have cough, brown or tan sputum, and chest pain. The presence of hemoptysis, suggesting the diagnosis of pulmonary embolism, may represent intravascular invasion of *Aspergillus* and pulmonary infarction. The chest radiograph may be normal, but more often shows nodules, patchy infiltrates, or even cavitary lesions. The diagnosis is suggested by narrow, septate hyphae with acute angle branching but should be confirmed with culture. *Aspergillus* grows rapidly, and identification can usually be made in 1 to 3 days. In critically ill patients, a more rapid diagnosis can be confirmed with bronchoalveolar lavage. Echinocandins and other triazoles appear to have good activity against *Aspergillus* species, but voriconazole remains the best studied in this setting and is the most appropriate treatment for this patient.

Although amphotericin B deoxycholate (the standard form of amphotericin B) and the liposomal preparation of amphotericin B were the previous gold standards of treatment of aspergillosis, recent studies have revealed an advantage of voriconazole. Fluconazole and ketoconazole have inadequate activity against *Aspergillus* species and should not be used in this setting.

KEY POINT

- Voriconazole has become the drug of choice for pulmonary aspergillosis in immunosuppressed patients.

Bibliography

Walsh TJ, Anaissie EJ, Denning DW, et al; Infectious Diseases Society of America. Treatment of aspergillosis: clinical practice guidelines of the Infectious Diseases Society of America. Clin Infect Dis. 2008;46(3):327-360. [PMID: 18177225]

Item 31   Answer: B

Educational Objective: Treat acute herpes zoster infection.

This patient has acute herpes zoster. When given within 72 hours of the onset of the herpetic rash, antiviral therapy with acyclovir, valacyclovir, or famciclovir decreases acute pain severity and duration, promotes more rapid healing of the lesions, and possibly decreases postherpetic neuralgia incidence and severity. These benefits appear to be greatest in patients older than 50 years of age. This patient's pain began more than 72 hours ago, but the rash has been present for just 24 hours. Therefore, antiviral therapy will likely be beneficial. Because of their improved bioavailability, valacyclovir and famciclovir are preferred to acyclovir, which is poorly absorbed and requires more pills daily.

Although the benefits of antiviral therapy are established, those of corticosteroids plus acyclovir are not as clear (no studies have been done to date regarding the use of corticosteroids plus valacyclovir or famciclovir). Adding corticosteroids may help accelerate healing of lesions, decrease the time to acute pain resolution, decrease insomnia incidence, help patients return to normal daily activities sooner, and decrease analgesic pain medication needs; however, corticosteroids do not appear to decrease postherpetic neuralgia incidence. Finally, if corticosteroids are given, they should be used only as an adjunct to antiviral agents, never as the sole therapy.

There is no role for antiviral topical creams or ointments (including topical acyclovir or penciclovir) in the management of herpes zoster because they are not as effective as systemic antiviral treatment, and their addition to systemic antiviral treatment does not enhance healing compared with systemic treatment alone.

The bioavailability of valacyclovir and famciclovir is excellent, and treatment of cutaneous herpes zoster infection with intravenous acyclovir is not necessary. It is very reasonable to consider beginning therapy with intravenous acyclovir for patients with severe herpes zoster ophthalmicus or for those who develop central nervous systemic complications of herpes zoster, but this patient does not meet any of these criteria.

A varicella zoster virus vaccine has been approved by the U.S. Food and Drug Administration for immunocompetent adults aged 60 years and older to prevent herpes zoster. The Advisory Committee on Immunization Practices (ACIP) has endorsed the use of the vaccine for the approved indication.

KEY POINT

- In patients with herpes zoster, administration of valacyclovir or famciclovir within 72 hours of development of the rash decreases acute pain severity and duration, promotes more rapid healing of the lesions, and possibly decreases postherpetic neuralgia incidence and severity.

Bibliography

Whitley RJ, Weiss H, Gnann JW, et al. Acyclovir with and without prednisone for the treatment of Herpes zoster. A randomized placebo controlled trial. The National Institute of Allergy and Infectious Disease Collaborative antiviral study group. Ann Intern Med. 1996;125(5):376-383. [PMID: 8702088]

Item 32   Answer: D

Educational Objective: Apply the principles of antibiotic stewardship monitoring.

Antibiotic stewardship is the process of adapting antibiotic usage to newly acquired diagnostic information in an effort to reduce overall drug toxicity to the patient and minimize adverse effects to the patient and the hospital flora. The early use of aggressive antibiotic treatment is widely accepted for critically ill patients before confirmation of a specific diagnosis. In this patient, the infection source was difficult to determine, and use of broad-spectrum antibiotics (including those for *Pseudomonas* coverage) was prudent. However, once the diagnosis is known, excessively broad coverage is no longer beneficial because the risk of selecting for resistant colonizing organisms is increased. Willingness to de-escalate therapy can be challenging in a patient who has responded well to broad-spectrum antibiotic coverage. However, failure to curtail excess antibiotic use is an ecologic hazard for that patient and for the medical unit as a whole. Although de-escalation has been tested most often in patients with nosocomial pneumonia (for which an ultimate microbial diagnosis can almost always be established), this principle is now being applied more broadly.

The cost difference between the two regimens is minimal because generic versions of all three drugs are available. Changing to nafcillin will reduce *Pseudomonas* coverage rather than increase coverage for this pathogen. However, this is an acceptable risk because *Pseudomonas* is easy to cultivate in the laboratory and, even when present, may represent colonization in a critically ill hospitalized patient.

The number of daily infusions of the two regimens is comparable (nafcillin every 4 to 6 hours and cefepime and vancomycin every 12 hours). This may be affected by variations in renal function, which will tend to reduce the number of infusions of cefepime and vancomycin but will have no impact on nafcillin.

Changing to nafcillin alone will not reduce the risk of drug toxicity, which is increased only when greatly excessive vancomycin doses are administered.

KEY POINT

- Antibiotic stewardship is the process of adapting antibiotic usage to newly acquired diagnostic information in an effort to reduce overall drug toxicity to the patient and minimize adverse effects to the patient and the hospital flora.

Bibliography

Rello J, Vidaur L, Sandiumenge A, et al. De-escalation therapy in ventilator-associated pneumonia. Crit Care Med. 2004;32(11):2183-2190. [PMID: 15640629]

Item 33   Answer: B

Educational Objective: Treat pyelonephritis.

This patient has pyelonephritis. Pyelonephritis is associated with the abrupt onset of fever, chills, sweats, nausea, vomiting, diarrhea, and flank or abdominal pain; hypotension and septic shock may occur in severe cases. Bacteriuria and pyuria are the gold standard for diagnosing pyelonephritis if these findings are associated with a suggestive history and physical examination findings. Leukocyte casts in the urine are suggestive of pyelonephritis but are uncommonly detected. In clinically ill patients, blood cultures should be obtained. Hypotensive patients with pyelonephritis should receive intravenous fluids.

Treatment of pyelonephritis consists of antibiotics for 7 to 14 days. Patients who are acutely ill, nauseated, or vomiting should receive parenteral therapy initially and can begin receiving oral therapy once oral intake is tolerated. The standard therapy in nonpregnant women is a fluoroquinolone (such as levofloxacin). Alternatives to fluoroquinolone antibiotics include extended-spectrum cephalosporins or penicillins, but oral options may be more limited for patients with a contraindication to fluoroquinolones. Eradication of bacteriuria in patients treated for pyelonephritis can be confirmed through repeat urinalysis and urine culture. Imaging studies should be used only if an alternative diagnosis or a urologic complication is suspected.

Ampicillin and amoxicillin are not used as initial therapy of acute pyelonephritis because of the high rates of resistance to these agents. Nitrofurantoin does not achieve levels sufficiently high for pyelonephritis treatment.

Until recently, trimethoprim or the combination of trimethoprim-sulfamethoxazole was highly effective for treating acute pyelonephritis. The increased frequency of resistant strains of *Escherichia coli* and other gram-negative bacteria to these antimicrobial agents has led to a preference for initial therapy with fluoroquinolones except in pregnant women because fluoroquinolone antibiotics are Food and Drug Administration pregnancy risk category C drugs.

KEY POINT

- **Standard outpatient management for pyelonephritis in women who are not pregnant is an oral fluoroquinolone.**

Bibliography

Drekonja DM, Johnson JR. Urinary tract infections. Prim Care. 2008;35(2):345-367. [PMID: 18486719]

Item 34   Answer: A

Educational Objective: Manage a patient with repeated neisserial infections and a normal total hemolytic complement (CH_{50}) level.

Three episodes of meningococcal meningitis in the same individual are highly unusual and suggestive of a defect in the complement system; measurement of C9 and the alternative and lectin pathway components is indicated. Patients with deficiencies in the terminal complement components (C5-C9) are predisposed to infection with neisserial species, including *Neisseria meningitidis.* Properdin, factor D, and mannose-binding lectin (MBL) deficiencies occur in patients with multiple neisserial infections. Therefore, performing an assay to detect deficiencies in these complement levels and pathway components is appropriate, particularly in patients who do not have evidence of a terminal complement deficiency.

Lymphocyte subsets and quantitative immunoglobulin or immunoglobulin subsets have not been documented to cause selective susceptibility to *Neisseria.* Such tests are therefore not indicated in this patient.

Streptococcus pneumoniae is the most common cause of bacterial meningitis in the United States. Pneumococcal meningitis may develop in conjunction with other suppurative foci of infection such as pneumonia, otitis media, mastoiditis, sinusitis, and endocarditis, or following head trauma with leak of cerebrospinal fluid. An MRI of the brain and spinal cord could identify a meningeal defect responsible for repeated episodes of pneumococcal meningitis but would not be expected to yield an explanation for the multiple episodes of meningococcal meningitis in this patient.

CH_{50} measurement is a good screening test for classical complement components C1 through C8 but will not detect C9 or alternative or lectin pathway component deficiencies. Therefore, a patient with a normal CH_{50} level does not have a deficiency of the classical pathway from C1 through C8, and repeat measurement is unlikely to be helpful.

KEY POINT

- **Classic and alternative and lectin pathways of the complement system may be responsible for unusual susceptibility to neisserial infections.**

Bibliography

Manuel O, Tarr PE, Venetz JP, Trendelenburg M, Meylan PR, Pascual M. Meningococcal disease in a kidney transplant recipient with mannose-binding lectin deficiency. Transpl Infect Dis. 2007;9(3):214-218. [PMID: 17692067]

Item 35   Answer: B

Educational Objective: Treat nongonococcal urethritis.

This patient has nongonococcal urethritis. Nongonococcal urethritis is defined by two criteria: the presence of urethritis (dysuria or a thin mucoid discharge) and leukocytes on Gram stain of the discharge. Urine dipstick testing that is positive for leukocyte esterase also indicates urethritis and may be a readily available test in many settings. The diagnosis is further supported in this patient by the absence of gram-negative diplococci (*Neisseria gonorrhoeae*) on the Gram-stained specimen. The Centers for Disease Control and Prevention's recommended treatment is azithromycin, 1 g orally for 1 dose, or doxycycline, 100 mg orally twice daily for 7 days. Sexual partners should be identified and treated. Acyclovir, penicillin, cefixime, and metronidazole are not effective treatments for nongonococcal urethritis.

Oral acyclovir is appropriate treatment for genital herpes. Genital herpes lesions typically begin as vesicles that ulcerate and are quite painful. The initial infection is often the most severe and can be accompanied by local lymphadenopathy and systemic symptoms. Genital herpes may cause dysuria but not a urethral discharge.

Benzathine penicillin G is effective for treating syphilis. The primary ulcerative lesion (chancre) develops approximately 3 weeks after infection occurs, has a clean appearance with heaped-up borders, and is usually painless. The chancre resolves spontaneously, and the infection progresses to secondary syphilis. Secondary syphilis develops 2 to 8 weeks after the appearance of the primary chancre and is characterized by widespread hematogenous dissemination involving many organs but most often is recognized as a generalized maculopapular rash, generalized lymphadenopathy, and constitutional symptoms. Secondary syphilis also resolves spontaneously. Urethritis is not a feature of early syphilis.

Cefixime is appropriate treatment for gonorrhea. Men with gonococcal urethritis typically have dysuria associated with copious mucopurulent discharge. Gram stain typically demonstrates numerous gram-negative intracellular diplococci (Gram stain sensitivity, 95%).

Metronidazole is effective treatment for bacterial vaginosis and trichomoniasis (infection caused by *Trichomonas vaginalis*). Trichomoniasis is a sexually transmitted disease, whereas bacterial vaginosis is not. Most men with trichomoniasis are asymptomatic.

KEY POINT

- **Azithromycin is the recommended therapy for nongonococcal urethritis.**

Bibliography

Centers for Disease Control and Prevention, Workowski KA, Berman SM. Sexually transmitted diseases treatment guidelines, 2006 [erratum in MMWR Recomm Rep. 2006;55(36):997]. MMWR Recomm Rep. 2006;55(RR-11):1-94. [PMID: 16888612]

Item 36   Answer: C

Educational Objective: Diagnose acute pulmonary histoplasmosis.

This is a typical case of large-inoculum, acute histoplasmosis caused by inhalation of many spores. The organism *Histoplasma capsulatum* can be found in soil contaminated with bird or bat droppings, such as chicken coops, abandoned buildings, roosting sites for birds, caves, and wooded lots. In this case, the infection probably occurred while the patient was cleaning out the chicken coop on his farm. Many patients with histoplasmosis are asymptomatic; fever, chills, headache, myalgia, anorexia, cough, or chest pain can occur in patients with symptomatic histoplasmosis from 2 to 4 weeks after exposure. The presence of several calcifications in the lungs, mediastinum, and spleen in this patient likely resulted from episodes of inhaling small numbers of *H. capsulatum* spores in the past. In North America, multiple splenic calcifications are almost always caused by infection with *H. capsulatum*. The *Histoplasma* urinary antigen detection test is highly sensitive and specific for detecting histoplasmosis in patients such as this as well as in those with disseminated histoplasmosis and pulmonary histoplasmosis when more than a small amount of lung tissue is involved.

Bronchoscopy or lung biopsy may be needed in some cases when less invasive testing fails to establish a diagnosis.

Histoplasma serologic testing is not specific for detection of active infection and often cross-reacts with other fungal infections such as blastomycosis.

Fungal blood cultures are highly unlikely to be positive in a setting such as this because this patient does not have disseminated disease.

Sputum cultures are most sensitive (up to 80%) in the diagnosis of chronic pulmonary histoplasmosis but are relatively insensitive (approximately 50%) in patients with diffuse acute pulmonary disease such as that present in this patient.

Therapy is usually not necessary for patients with acute pulmonary histoplasmosis. Spontaneous recovery typically occurs within several weeks in immunocompetent patients.

KEY POINT

- ***Histoplasma* urinary antigen detection is highly sensitive and specific for identifying many forms of histoplasmosis.**

Bibliography

Durkin MM, Connolly PA, Wheat LJ. Comparison of radioimmunoassay and enzyme-linked immunoassay methods for detection of Histoplasma capsulatum var. capsulatum antigen. J Clin Microbiol. 1997;35(9):2252-2255. [PMID: 9276396]

Item 37   Answer: C

Educational Objective: Manage a patient after exposure to acute varicella virus.

This patient should undergo serologic testing for varicella virus antibodies. More than 90% of adults in the United States have serologic evidence of immunity to varicella, including a large percentage of those without a personal history of chickenpox. Although chickenpox in adults can be a more serious problem than that in healthy children, the two most vulnerable groups of adults are pregnant women and immunocompromised individuals. These populations are at increased risk for development of varicella infection complications, including a severe form of pneumonia and encephalitis, both of which are associated with high morbidity. For those healthy adults who are not pregnant, the problems associated with chickenpox exposure are less pressing. Confirming existing immunity will not only allay anxiety about the current exposure, but will also provide reassurance that subsequent exposures (including those during pregnancy) are not a cause for concern. If the results of the serologic tests show that she is not immune because of lack of prior disease or vaccination, there is time to consider other strategies. These include preemptive varicella vaccination and early intervention with antiviral agents at the first sign of possible chickenpox within the 10 to 21 days following exposure.

No evidence suggests that the use of the zoster vaccine (the same virus as in the varicella vaccine) is superior to the varicella vaccine in this setting. Clinical trials of the zoster vaccine have been performed only in older adults.

The use of routine immune globulin (which is in somewhat short supply) is unlikely to be helpful because the titer of anti–varicella zoster virus antibodies in pooled lots of immune globulin will not give protective titers against varicella. The varicella-zoster immune globulin, VZIG, has been used in settings in which immunocompromised or pregnant adults were exposed to chickenpox. However, the availability of VZIG is very limited because its manufacture by the Massachusetts Public Health Biological Laboratories was discontinued in 2006, and the use of the as-yet unlicensed replacement would not be justified for this patient's exposure.

> **KEY POINT**
> - The first days of evaluation of a healthy adult recently exposed to a person with chickenpox allows time for assessment of existing immunity and preemptive vaccination.

Bibliography

Macartney K, McIntyre P. Vaccines for post-exposure prophylaxis against varicella (chickenpox) in children and adults. Cochrane Database Syst Rev. 2008;(3):CD001833. [PMID: 18646079]

Item 38   Answer: C
Educational Objective: Treat uncomplicated gonorrhea.

This patient has uncomplicated urethral gonorrhea. The recommended therapy is ceftriaxone (125 mg by intramuscular injection) or another third-generation cephalosporin plus concomitant treatment for chlamydial infection with doxycycline orally for 7 days. The prevalence of coinfection with *Chlamydia trachomatis* may be substantial among persons with gonorrhea, thus mandating dual treatment unless concomitant chlamydial infection can be ruled out with highly sensitive tests.

According to the Gonococcal Isolate Surveillance Project, nearly 7% of gonorrhea isolates now have decreased susceptibility to azithromycin; therefore, azithromycin is not recommended by the Centers for Disease Control and Prevention (CDC) as first-line therapy except in patients with severe penicillin allergy who cannot undergo a β-lactam desensitization protocol. Additionally, the dose of azithromycin required to treat uncomplicated gonorrhea is more expensive than other regimens and is associated with a high incidence of gastrointestinal side effects. Ciprofloxacin is no longer recommended by the CDC because of the increased frequency of fluoroquinolone resistance.

Although penicillin was once the treatment of choice for gonorrhea, increased resistance based on β-lactamase as well as altered penicillin-binding proteins has made penicillin a drug of historical, rather than clinical, interest. In addition, benzathine penicillin G is a slow-release product used mostly for syphilis therapy. The correct product for gonorrhea was procaine penicillin (sometimes given in combination with benzathine penicillin G to treat incubating syphilis).

> **KEY POINT**
> - Ceftriaxone or another third-generation cephalosporin is the recommended treatment for uncomplicated gonorrhea in addition to empiric therapy for *Chlamydia trachomatis* infection.

Bibliography

Updated recommended treatment regimens for gonococcal infections and associated conditions - United States, April 2007. www.cdc.gov/std/treatment/2006/updated-regimens.htm. Published April 13, 2007. Accessed on January 31, 2009.

Item 39   Answer: B
Educational Objective: Diagnose hypersensitivity pneumonitis.

This patient most likely has hypersensitivity pneumonitis (extrinsic allergic alveolitis) caused by exposure to *Mycobacterium avium* complex (MAC) from the hot tub, also known as "hot tub lung." There are many causes of hypersensitivity pneumonitis, and the offending agent is generally suggested by the exposure obtained in the history. Hot tub lung presents as an interstitial pneumonia in immunocompetent individuals and can be easily misdiagnosed as an infection with an atypical agent such as *Mycoplasma pneumoniae* or *Chlamydophila pneumoniae*. However, infectious pneumonias very rarely recur after response to treatment, and three episodes of pneumonia over the course of 2 months is unlikely in a healthy person. The chest radiograph in hypersensitivity pneumonitis typically shows a micronodular interstitial pattern in the lower and mid-lung zones, and the serum lactate dehydrogenase level is often elevated during the acute phase of the illness and normalizes with improvement. Most patients with hot tub lung will grow MAC on respiratory specimens; the hot tub water can also be cultured to confirm the diagnosis. Treatment includes prevention of re-exposure to MAC by ensuring adequate chlorination of hot tubs to prevent bacterial growth and corticosteroids in patients whose condition is severe or not rapidly improving.

This patient's clinical scenario does not represent a true infection with MAC and should not be treated with ethambutol and clarithromycin. Most patients improve without treatment, and antibiotics are of no benefit.

> **KEY POINT**
> - Treatment of "hot tub lung" includes prevention of re-exposure and systemic corticosteroids in severe cases.

Bibliography

Cappelluti E, Fraire AE, Schaefer OP. A case of "hot tub lung" due to Mycobacterium avium complex in an immunocompetent host. Arch Intern Med. 2003;163(7):845-848. [PMID: 12695276]

Item 40   Answer: D

Educational Objective: Manage cryptosporidiosis in a woman with mild immunosuppression secondary to HIV infection.

There are few effective treatments for cryptosporidiosis in patients with HIV-1 infection, and the goal is to increase CD4 cell counts to higher than 100/µL. The natural course of cryptosporidiosis is the slow resolution of diarrhea without fever, toxic appearance, or evidence of inflammation. The risks of this disease are related to the fluid and electrolyte losses that can accompany the diarrhea, and this is compounded when patients cannot maintain oral intake or already have a significant wasting illness. This patient has none of these features and should easily be managed with watchful waiting.

The use of stool tests for diarrhea is complicated by the low yield and slow turnaround time for return of results. Processing of stool cultures normally takes at least 2 days after the stool reaches the laboratory. Rapid tests for *Giardia* and *Cryptosporidium* can be done within hours and can be helpful in both epidemic and sporadic cases. Most stool tests for viruses are labor intensive except for rotavirus, which is not commonly a cause of adult diarrhea.

Nitazoxanide is a modestly effective agent approved by the U.S. Food and Drug Administration for the treatment of cryptosporidial disease in children younger than 12 years and for cryptosporidial disease in adults without HIV infection. Drugs that offer no or marginal activity for *Cryptosporidium* but might be useful for other infections should be used only in patients for whom there is documentation of these infectious agents. Examples include the use of trimethoprim-sulfamethoxazole for the treatment of *Isospora belli* and paromomycin for the treatment of intestinal amebiasis. Although anecdotal reports suggest that paromomycin might be useful for cryptosporidiosis in patients with HIV-1 infection, this agent is not a good empiric first-line choice for patients with diarrhea.

KEY POINT

- **There are few effective treatments for cryptosporidiosis in patients with HIV-1 infection, and the goal is to increase CD4 cell counts to higher than 100/µL.**

Bibliography

Abubakar I, Aliyu SH, Arumugam C, Usman NK, Hunter PR. Treatment of cryptosporidiosis in immunocompromised individuals: systematic review and meta-analysis. Br J Clin Pharmacol. 2007;63(4):387-393. [PMID: 17335543]

Item 41   Answer: C

Educational Objective: Treat a patient with dual vector-borne infections.

Babesia species is transmitted by an *Ixodes scapularis* tick bite. *Ixodes* ticks can be doubly and triply infected with *Babesia*, *Borrelia burgdorferi*, and *Anaplasma phagocytophilum*, and, occasionally, humans can develop simultaneous infections with more than one of these organisms. Dual infection should be suspected in patients who are receiving treatment for one documented infection but are not recovering at the expected rate. Human granulocytic anaplasmosis (HGA), the syndrome caused by *A. phagocytophilum* infection, typically manifests with fever, headache, and myalgia. In particular, leukopenia is suggestive of infection with *A. phagocytophilum,* for which doxycycline is the treatment of choice. HGA can be confirmed serologically using the indirect fluorescent antibody test on acute and convalescent titers, or a buffy coat can be examined for intracytoplasmic inclusions (morulae), which are found in 20% to 80% patients with HGA.

This patient's history, physical examination, and laboratory studies are not suggestive of an untreated bacterial infection, and β-lactam antibiotics such as cefepime combined with vancomycin have no efficacy against ehrlichial organisms. Corticosteroids have no established role in treating babesial or ehrlichial infections.

Atovaquone with azithromycin and clindamycin with quinine have similar efficacy in the treatment of babesiosis, although there is more clinical experience with the latter. There is no evidence that switching from one of these regimens to the other is of benefit in the treatment of babesiosis.

KEY POINT

- **Patients who do not respond to recommended treatment for a documented case of Lyme disease, babesiosis, or ehrlichiosis may have dual or triple infection with another of these vector-borne agents.**

Bibliography

Wormser, GP, Dattwyler, RJ, Shapiro, ED, et al. The Clinical Assessment, Treatment, and Prevention of Lyme disease, Human Granulocytic Anaplasmosis, and Babesiosis: Clinical Practice Guidelines by the Infectious Diseases Society of America. Clin Infect Dis. 2006;43(9):1089-1134. [PMID: 17029130]

Item 42   Answer: A

Educational Objective: Diagnose *Aeromonas hydrophila*–associated skin and soft tissue infection.

This patient most likely has a necrotizing skin and soft tissue infection secondary to *Aeromonas hydrophila*. This gram-negative bacterium is found in freshwater environments, although it may also be present in brackish water. Infections are more likely to occur during warmer weather. Soft tissue involvement and bacteremia/sepsis can develop in patients with underlying immunocompromising diseases, including cirrhosis and cancer. This patient's history of heavy alcohol use and abnormal liver chemistry tests suggest the possibility of cirrhosis. The clinical presentations of infection with *Vibrio vulnificus* and *Aeromonas species* can be quite similar and should be considered in cirrhotic patients who present with sepsis and necrotizing fasciitis. Wound infection typically occurs by inoculation through the skin. Patients with invasive necrotizing skin infections due to *Aeromonas* usually require surgical intervention and aggressive supportive therapy. This organism is often susceptible to fluoroquinolones, trimethoprim-sulfamethoxazole, tetracyclines, imipenem, aminoglycosides, and third- or fourth-generation cephalosporins.

Pasteurella multocida– and *Capnocytophaga canimorsus*–induced skin and soft tissue infections are associated with animal bites or scratches and do not typically cause necrotizing fasciitis with hemorrhagic bullae.

Vibrio cholerae infection can cause severe gastrointestinal illness characterized by watery diarrhea and nausea but does not cause necrotizing fasciitis.

KEY POINT

- Skin and soft tissue infections due to *Aeromonas* species should be considered when trauma occurs in a warm, freshwater environment.

Bibliography

Tsai YH, Hsu RW, Huang TJ, et al. Necrotizing soft-tissue infections and sepsis caused by Vibrio vulnificus compared with those caused by Aeromonas species. Journal Bone Joint Surg Am. 2007;89(3): 631-636. [PMID: 17332113]

Item 43   Answer: B

Educational Objective: Manage a patient with severe community-acquired pneumonia.

This patient has severe community-acquired pneumonia and should be admitted to the intensive care unit (ICU). Direct admission to the ICU is required for patients with septic shock requiring vasopressors or with acute respiratory failure requiring intubation and mechanical ventilation (major criteria). Although the patient is severely ill, he does not yet meet these major criteria and, therefore, the need for ICU admission is less straightforward. A combined working group of the Infectious Diseases Society of America and the American Thoracic Society developed consensus guidelines recommending that patients with community-acquired pneumonia with at least three of the following minor criteria be admitted to the ICU: respiration rate greater than 30/min; arterial P_{O_2}/F_{IO_2} ratio of less than or equal to 250; multilobar infiltrates; confusion/disorientation; uremia (blood urea nitrogen level ≥20 mg/dL [7.1 mmol/L]); leukopenia (leukocyte count <4000/µL [4 × 10⁹/L]); thrombocytopenia (platelet count <100,000/µL [100 × 10⁹/L]); hypothermia (core temperature <36.0 ºC [96.8 ºF]); and hypotension requiring aggressive fluid resuscitation. These minor criteria may be used as a guide to determine who would benefit most from ICU admission, but prospective validation of these criteria is needed.

KEY POINT

- Intensive care unit admission should be considered for patients with community-acquired pneumonia who meet at least three of the following criteria: respiration rate greater than 30/min; arterial P_{O_2}/F_{IO_2} ratio of less than or equal to 250; multilobar infiltrates; confusion; a blood urea nitrogen level of 20 mg/dL (7.1 mmol/L) or greater; leukocyte count less than 4000/µL (4 × 10⁹/L); platelet count less than 100,000/µL (100 × 10⁹/L); core temperature less than 36.0 ºC (96.8 ºF); and hypotension requiring aggressive fluid resuscitation.

Bibliography

Marrie TM, Shariatzadeh MR. Community-acquired pneumonia requiring admission to an intensive care unit: a descriptive study. Medicine (Baltimore). 2007;86(2):103-111. [PMID: 17435590]

Item 44   Answer: D

Educational Objective: Understand preventive measures to reduce surgical site infections.

Prospective randomized studies have found that tight glucose control during the perioperative period in diabetic patients undergoing cardiac surgery was associated with reduced infection risk. Aggressive glucose control in the perioperative period can be achieved using a continuous intravenous insulin infusion. In these studies, serum glucose was maintained at a level of less than 200 mg/dL (11.1 mmol/L).

Evidence suggests that preoperative or postoperative anemia is associated with increased mortality and hospital length of stay. Patients who require transfusions before surgery have an increased risk of infectious complications. This patient does not require a preoperative blood transfusion, and if one were required, it might actually increase, not decrease, his risk for infection.

A randomized trial in patients undergoing urgent or cardiac surgery who were hypothermic or normothermic showed no difference in the rate of surgical site infections (SSIs). Most experts now advocate for maintenance of perioperative normothermia to reduce the risk of SSIs, and there is no evidence suggesting that maintaining hypothermia decreases SSI rates.

The use of nasal mupirocin for the prevention of SSIs is controversial and is not supported by prospective randomized studies. However, in a subgroup analysis of patients with proven staphylococcal nasal carriage, treatment with mupirocin ointment significantly reduced SSI rates compared with rates in noncarriers. Protocols describe the use of ointment in the nares for 5 days prior to surgery. It is unlikely that application of mupirocin just before surgery would have much effect on SSIs, even in staphylococcal nasal carriers. No analysis has determined if identification and treatment of nasal carriers is cost-effective.

- **Peripoperative glucose control with insulin infusion reduces the risk of surgical site infections for patients with diabetes who are undergoing cardiac surgery.**

Bibliography

Gagliardi AR, Eskicioglu C, McKenzie M, Fenech D, Nathens A, McLeod R. Identifying opportunities for quality improvement in surgical site infection prevention. Am J Infect Control. 2009;37(5): 398-402. [PMID: 19201509]

Item 45 Answer: C

Educational Objective: Treat *Plasmodium falciparum* malarial infection.

This patient likely has *Plasmodium falciparum* malaria. Quinine combined with pyrimethamine-sulfadoxine, clindamycin, or doxycycline is the most commonly used regimen in patients who can take oral therapy; atovaquone-proguanil can also be used.

At least two thirds of malaria acquired in Africa is caused by *Plasmodia falciparum*, and 95% of infected patients present within 2 months of return from travel. This patient's disease can be safely assumed to be *P. falciparum* malaria because of his recent travel to Africa and the degree of parasitemia. Findings of a high-grade parasitemia (>5%) and only ring forms on the malarial smear are characteristic of *P. falciparum* infection. Because *Plasmodium vivax* and *Plasmodium ovale* infect only reticulocytes, the degree of parasitemia is usually less than 1%. *Plasmodium malariae* infects only older erythrocytes and has a similarly low degree of parasitemia. The high fatality rate associated with *P. falciparum* is related to a unique characteristic of parasitized erythrocytes that includes the formation of "knobby surfaces," allowing them to stick to endothelial surfaces and other non-infected erythrocytes, resulting in decreased microvascular flow and organ dysfunction. Patients with severe malaria should be monitored for hypoglycemia, which may be caused by the malaria itself (parasites metabolize glucose for energy) or quinine treatment. Artemisinin derivatives, such as artemether, with doxycycline or lumefantrine, are an increasingly suggested option for patients with severe disease (cerebral malaria, organ failure, or a parasitemia >10%).

P. falciparum infection should be assumed to be resistant to chloroquine unless the infection was acquired in the Western Hemisphere north of Panama or in the Middle East. Only *P. vivax* and *P. ovale* have a latent liver form (hypnozoite) that requires primaquine for cure.

Pyrimethamine-sulfadoxine had been an effective treatment for malaria; however, increasing drug resistance has made this an undesirable alternative.

- ***Plasmodium falciparum* infection should be assumed to be resistant to chloroquine unless it was acquired in the Western Hemisphere north of Panama or in the Middle East.**

Bibliography

Rosenthal PJ. Artesunate for the treatment of severe falciparum malaria. N Engl J Med. 2008;358(17):1829-1836. [PMID: 18434652]

Item 46 Answer: C

Educational Objective: Evaluate a foot infection in a patient with diabetes mellitus.

MRI is the preferred imaging study for patients such as this one with foot infection. Foot infections are a significant cause of morbidity in patients with diabetes mellitus and, if untreated, can progress to osteomyelitis that may require amputation for cure. Appropriate assessment of diabetic foot infections is therefore essential. Unless bone is visible, physical examination findings are often inconclusive for diagnosing osteomyelitis. Plain radiographs are insensitive and may show soft tissue swelling but no bony abnormalities for 2 or more weeks after infection has developed. In addition, this patient had a negative metal-probe test (a positive test has a predictive value of 90% for diagnosing osteomyelitis). Although her ulcer is limited to the plantar surface, the cellulitis is more diffuse, which implies a more extensive process requiring rapid assessment and treatment.

A CT scan is neither as sensitive nor specific as MRI and is indicated only when MRI cannot be performed (for example, in patients with pacemakers or metal prosthetic devices). Indium-labeled leukocyte scan and triple-phase technetium bone scan are very sensitive but not specific for diagnosing osteomyelitis and are associated with high false-positive rates, especially when an overlying cellulitis or soft tissue infection is present.

- **MRI is the most sensitive and specific study for diagnosing foot infection–associated osteomyelitis.**

Bibliography

Kapoor A, Page S, Lavalley M, Gale DR, Felson DT. Magnetic resonance imaging for diagnosing foot osteomyelitis: a meta-analysis. Arch Intern Med. 2007;167(2):125-132. [PMID: 17242312]

Item 47 Answer: D

Educational Objective: Understand the effects of polyomavirus BK virus activation in patients with transplanted kidneys.

This presentation is typical for polyomavirus BK virus–induced nephropathy in a patient with a transplanted kidney. Polyomavirus BK virus is acquired asymptomatically early in childhood by as many as 90% of all persons. The virus persists throughout life but rarely causes problems in normal hosts. However, it may result in serious disorders in immunosuppressed patients and is an important cause of kidney allograft failure. The virus may be reactivated in 30% or more of kidney transplant recipients as evidenced by shedding of "decoy cells" (tubular or transitional cells with intranuclear viral inclusions) or viremia, which may be characterized by fatigue, myalgia, and malaise. Further confirmation can be obtained by identifying the virus in urine or blood or by kidney biopsy, which is the gold-standard diagnostic test. Quantification of the virus is useful in assessing and managing the effects of treatment, which may include reducing immunosuppressive therapy or using experimental medications, such as leflunomide, cidofovir, or fluoroquinolones.

After the first posttransplantation month, cytomegalovirus (CMV) is one of the infectious agents most likely to affect graft survival and cause life-threatening complications. CMV infection typically involves the gastrointestinal tract and is associated with fever, pain, ulcerations, and hepatitis. CMV alone does not lead to nephropathy, although it may have additive effects in the presence of the BK virus.

The Epstein-Barr virus may cause posttransplantation lymphoproliferative disease, but it is not known to cause nephropathy. Posttransplantation lymphoproliferative disease is characterized by symptoms suggestive of infectious mononucleosis followed by a progressive deteriorating course that may involve the brain, liver, bone marrow, and transplanted organ.

Human herpesvirus-8 infection causes Kaposi sarcoma and is associated with Castleman disease and primary effusion lymphoma but does not appear to cause hepatitis, encephalitis, or nephropathy.

Polyomavirus JC virus may cause progressive multifocal leukoencephalopathy but not renal disease in patients with transplanted kidneys.

KEY POINT

- **Polyomavirus BK virus is a common cause of nephropathy in patients with transplanted kidneys.**

Bibliography
Bonvoisin C, Weekers L, Xhignesse P, Grosch S, Milicevic M, Krzesinski JM. Polyomavirus in renal transplantation: a hot problem. Transplantation. 2008;85(7 Suppl):S42-48. [PMID: 18401263]

Item 48   Answer: B
Educational Objective: Treat a deep soft tissue infection in a patient with gastroparesis and vomiting.

This patient's health is significantly impaired by malnutrition, use of corticosteroids, and advanced diabetes mellitus. Therefore, in addition to draining the thigh abscess, administering antibiotics was appropriate. This patient's early aggressive antibiotic treatment was meant to address the results of the Gram stain of the surgical drainage fluid and the uncertainty regarding the infecting microbe. Although imipenem and vancomycin are appropriate empiric antibiotics in the hospital, ertapenem is a more efficient and convenient drug for home care. In

addition to having a good spectrum of activity for *Klebsiella*, ertapenem can be given once daily at home, which is much easier than the six daily infusions required for imipenem and vancomycin administration.

Colistin has the necessary spectrum of activity for *Klebsiella* but is potentially too nephrotoxic and neurotoxic for use when other agents are available.

Linezolid is approved by the U.S. Food and Drug Administration for treatment of vancomycin-resistant *Enterococcus faecium* infections (including bacteremia), community-acquired and nosocomial pneumonia, and skin and skin structure infections. Oxazolidinones are active against most gram-positive organisms such as streptococci, enterococci, and staphylococci, including strains resistant to other classes of antibiotics. Linezolid also has in vitro activity against some anaerobes, such as *Fusobacterium*, *Prevotella*, *Porphyromonas*, *Bacteroides*, and *Peptostreptococcus* species. However, linezolid does not have a spectrum of activity that covers *Klebsiella* and is therefore inappropriate.

KEY POINT

- **Parenteral ertapenem is an effective and convenient drug for home care in a patient with a soft tissue infection.**

Bibliography
Graham DR, Lucasti C, Malafaia O, et al. Ertapenem once daily versus piperacillin-tazobactam 4 times per day for treatment of complicated skin and skin-structure infections in adults: Results of a prospective, randomized, double-blind multicenter study. Clin Infect Dis. 2002;34(11):1460-1468. [PMID: 12015692]

Item 49   Answer: B
Educational Objective: Treat acyclovir-resistant genital herpes simplex virus infection.

This patient has acyclovir-resistant genital herpes simplex virus infection, which typically occurs in immunocompromised patients; resistance in immunocompetent patients is rare. Foscarnet, which acts by a different mechanism than acyclovir, is the drug of choice for treating acyclovir-resistant genital herpes. Resistance to foscarnet has been reported but is unrelated to acyclovir resistance.

The recognition of drug resistance is important because it can result in serious, even life-threatening, disease in immunocompromised patients. Resistance should be suspected if herpetic lesions do not resolve within 7 to 10 days after the initiation of adequate antiviral therapy. Resistance is most commonly reported for acyclovir, but this may simply be because acyclovir has been available for clinical use longer than the other drugs in this family. If resistance is suspected, a viral culture should be obtained and the specimen submitted for in vitro susceptibility testing; the correlation between in vitro resistance and clinical response is good.

Antiviral agents that work by a mechanism similar to acyclovir, such as famciclovir, penciclovir, and valacyclovir, are unlikely to control this patient's infection.

- **Foscarnet is the drug of choice for treating acyclovir-resistant genital herpes simplex virus infection.**

Bibliography

Balfour HH Jr, Benson C, Braun J, et al. Management of acyclovir-resistant herpes simplex and varicella-zoster virus infections J Acquir Immune Defic Syndr. 1994;7(3):254-260. [PMID: 8106965]

Item 50   Answer: A

Educational Objective: Diagnose cryptococcal meningitis in an immunologically normal patient.

Cryptococcus neoformans is the organism most likely to cause meningitis of subacute or chronic onset. Cerebrospinal fluid (CSF) cryptococcal polysaccharide antigen assay and CSF-VDRL testing for syphilis should be done in all patients with chronic meningitis. The clinical manifestations of cryptococcal meningitis vary greatly but may include headache, fever, neck stiffness, and change in mental status and may develop over several months before the diagnosis is established. CSF results in a patient with chronic meningitis are always abnormal, but these abnormalities are rarely diagnostic. The opening pressure is generally elevated, and cell counts are relatively low, with a predominance of lymphocytes; glucose tends to be low, and protein is elevated. The cryptococcal polysaccharide antigen test can establish the diagnosis of cryptococcal meningitis soon after lumbar puncture is performed. A positive antigen test is 90% sensitive for the diagnosis of cryptococcal meningitis in immunocompetent patients and would permit early therapy. The diagnosis is confirmed with a positive cryptococcal culture from the CSF.

In symptomatic neurosyphilis, the CSF VDRL is highly specific but not very sensitive. A negative fluorescent treponemal antibody absorption test excludes the diagnosis of neurosyphilis. Neurosyphilis has become a rare disease, but it is important to rule out in the right clinical setting because treatment can prevent further deterioration. This patient has an extremely low possibility of neurosyphilis because syphilitic meningitis is almost invariably accompanied by positive serum tests for syphilis, which were all negative in this case.

Neisseria meningitidis and *Streptococcus pneumoniae* cause acute meningitis that would rarely result in symptoms for more than several days (and sometimes just hours) before causing profound illness. This patient's symptoms lasted for several months before he sought medical care, which is more characteristic of chronic meningitis than acute meningitis caused by *N. meningitidis* and *S. pneumoniae*.

Testing for *Histoplasma* in this patient would be unnecessary because *Histoplasma*-associated meningitis is extremely less common than cryptococcal meningitis. But even if histoplasmosis testing were desirable, serum antibody tests would have limited utility, and the organism

would need to be demonstrated on stain, culture, or with direct tests such as urinary antigen or polymerase chain reaction technology.

- **The cerebrospinal cryptococcal polysaccharide antigen test can establish the diagnosis of cryptococcal meningitis soon after the lumbar puncture is performed.**

Bibliography

Pukkila-Worley R, Mylonakis E. Epidemiology and management of cryptococcal meningitis: developments and challenges. Expert Opin Pharmacother. 2008;9(4):551-560. [PMID: 18312157]

Item 51   Answer: A

Educational Objective: Manage a patient with suspected Rocky Mountain spotted fever.

This patient, who has been to an endemic area for Rocky Mountain spotted fever (RMSF), presents with a flu-like illness during the summer. He also has thrombocytopenia and hyponatremia, findings not unusual in patients with RMSF. Because of the nonspecific nature of its symptoms, RMSF should be strongly considered in patients such as this one with a nonspecific febrile illness within 3 weeks of potential tick exposure, and immediate treatment with doxycycline should be given pending results of diagnostic studies. Many people with tick-borne infection do not recall a specific tick bite, and only 15% of people with RMSF have a rash at the time of presentation. Up to 90% of patients do eventually develop the characteristic blanching erythematous macules located around the wrists and ankles that spread centripetally; in some patients, the rash may become maculopapular with central petechiae. The most commonly available diagnostic test for RMSF is a convalescent serology, but this test can be used only to confirm the diagnosis after treatment is given for the presumptive diagnosis. Data are clear that early treatment is associated with a better outcome for this potentially fatal infection.

Although this patient's presentation is compatible with influenza, this disease does not generally occur in temperate regions of the world during the summer; therefore, oseltamivir is not indicated in this patient.

Although vancomycin and ceftriaxone are broad-spectrum antibiotics, they are not effective against *Rickettsia* species. In some settings of very severe illness, drugs such as these might be included as part of empiric therapy until microbiologic data are known; however, doxycycline would also be included in such a regimen.

- **Rocky Mountain spotted fever should be strongly considered in patients with a nonspecific febrile illness within 3 weeks of potential tick exposure; although rash eventually develops in 90% of patients, it occurs in only 15% on presentation.**

Bibliography

Kirkland, KB, Wilkinson, WE, Sexton, DJ. Therapeutic delay and mortality in cases of Rocky Mountain spotted fever. Clin Infect Dis 1995; 20:1118.

Item 52 Answer: D

Educational Objective: Manage recurrent cystitis.

This patient most likely has a recurrent urinary tract infection (UTI). Self-treatment with trimethoprim-sulfamethoxazole on development of symptoms is appropriate. Recurrent UTIs are common in women and are believed to represent new infection rather than a relapse of a previous episode. Although evaluation for subtle predisposing factors such as anatomic urinary tract abnormalities is seldom useful, inquiring about behavioral practices can be helpful. Sexual intercourse is a risk factor for acute or recurrent UTIs as is the use of spermicides or spermicides plus a diaphragm. Most women are able to diagnose a UTI accurately and begin antimicrobial treatment without being seen by a physician. Self-treatment is highly effective in compliant women. One study found that women correctly diagnosed more than 90% of recurrent infections and that self-treatment was effective in more than 95% of patients—numbers that rival those of physician-initiated therapy. Self-management at first onset of symptoms is a feasible, safe, and convenient option for this young, otherwise healthy woman with recurrent cystitis. Trimethoprim-sulfamethoxazole, 160 mg/800 mg twice daily for 3 days, is effective for treating uncomplicated cystitis. In addition, the reported 12% resistance of *Escherichia coli* to this agent is low enough that other antibiotics do not need to be considered.

This patient's recurrent infections do not seem to be related to sexual intercourse; therefore, postcoital prophylactic ciprofloxacin therapy may not be indicated. Additionally, her infections may not occur frequently enough to warrant ciprofloxacin prophylaxis after intercourse. A 10-day course of ciprofloxacin is indicated only if pyelonephritis is documented. Some sources may recommend chronic suppressive therapy for patients with more than two UTIs per year; however, this approach may increase the risk of infection with antibiotic-resistant bacteria.

KEY POINT

- **Short-course antibiotic self-treatment is appropriate for young, otherwise healthy women with recurrent cystitis.**

Bibliography

Drekonja DM, Johnson JR. Urinary tract infections. Prim Care. 2008;35(2):345-367. [PMID: 18486719]

Item 53 Answer: A

Educational Objective: Treat a patient with severe *Clostridium difficile* infection.

This patient most likely has severe *Clostridium difficile* infection (CDI), and treatment with oral vancomycin and intravenous metronidazole should be initiated. The greatest risk of *C. difficile* exposure is in health care settings. This patient demonstrated common features of severe CDI, including abdominal tenderness and distension and the absence of bowel sounds. Systemic findings, such as fever, leukocytosis, mental status changes, and renal insufficiency, are common in those with moderate or severe disease. Her laboratory findings were also consistent with severe CDI (leukocytosis, renal insufficiency, and hypoalbuminemia). Surgical consultation is imperative in patients with severe CDI, and colectomy can be lifesaving.

In patients with severe CDI and possible ileus, intravenous metronidazole should be administered in combination with oral vancomycin. The delayed transit time of orally administered antibiotics necessitates the addition of adjuvant intravenous treatment with metronidazole. Metronidazole, when not contraindicated, is preferred over vancomycin because of vancomycin's higher cost and the concern for the development of vancomycin-resistant enterococci (VRE). Multiple randomized, comparative studies have documented the efficacy of oral vancomycin for CDI, and recent prospective trials have found oral vancomycin to be superior to metronidazole for severe disease. Although metronidazole may be administered intravenously or orally, oral administration is the preferred route in patients without ileus (mild disease). Bactericidal fecal levels of vancomycin are readily achievable in patients with CDI treated orally; however, because of the poor concentration of these levels in stool after intravenous administration, vancomycin should not be given by this route.

KEY POINT

- **In patients with severe *Clostridium difficile* infection and possible ileus, intravenous metronidazole should be administered in combination with oral vancomycin.**

Bibliography

Bartlett JG. Clinical practice. Antibiotic-associated diarrhea. N Engl J Med. 2002;346(5):334-339. [PMID: 11821511]

Item 54 Answer: B

Educational Objective: Diagnose meningococcal meningitis.

This patient's illness is most consistent with meningococcal infection, which is characterized by the sudden onset of fever, myalgia, headache, and rash in a previously healthy patient. Early in its course, meningococcal disease may be indistinguishable from other common viral illnesses; however the rapidity with which the disease worsens (often over hours) and progresses to septic shock differentiates it from these other illnesses. A petechial rash is most common and may coalesce to form purpuric lesions.

The diagnosis is established based on clinical presentation and confirmed with blood and cerebrospinal fluid

(CSF) cultures. It is likely that this student received meningococcal vaccine because it is recommended for all adolescents aged 11 to 18 years and frequently is administered before entrance to college. The current vaccines are immunogenic and effective at preventing disease due to serogroups A, C, Y, and W-135. Unfortunately, none of the current vaccines is effective against serogroup B, which is also a common cause of disease occurring in the United States.

Meningitis caused by *Listeria monocytogenes* is associated with extremes of age (neonates and persons age >50 years), alcoholism, malignancy, immunosuppression, diabetes mellitus, hepatic failure, renal failure, iron overload, collagen vascular disorders, and HIV infection. The clinical presentation of *Listeria* meningoencephalitis ranges from a mild illness with fever and mental status changes to a fulminant course with coma.

The classic presentation of Rocky Mountain spotted fever is a severe headache, fever, myalgia, and arthralgia. Thrombocytopenia and acute kidney injury can occur. A maculopapular rash develops 3 to 5 days later (hardly ever on the first day of illness, as in this patient). It begins on the wrists and ankles and may involve the palms and soles. Rocky Mountain spotted fever is transmitted by the American dog tick in the spring and early summer, which is inconsistent with the timing of this patient's presentation.

Viral (aseptic) meningitis can present similarly to bacterial meningitis with the classic findings of fever, headache and stiff neck, and photophobia and may be associated with a maculopapular eruption. However, acute viral meningitis is rarely associated with the combination of findings indicating early organ dysfunction such as metabolic acidosis and acute kidney injury.

KEY POINT

- **Meningococcal infection should be considered in the differential diagnosis of any previously healthy patient who presents with acute-onset fever, headache, and myalgia.**

Bibliography

van de Beek D, de Gans J, Tunkel AR, Wijdicks EF. Community-acquired bacterial meningitis in adults. N Engl J Med. 2006; 354(1):44-53. [PMID: 16394301]

Item 55   Answer: E

Educational Objective: Manage a patient with Lyme disease after completion of initial recommended therapy.

This patient requires no additional antibiotic or antimicrobial therapy. His initial presentation, including systemic symptoms, recent exposure to ticks in an endemic area, and characteristic erythema migrans rash, are typical for early Lyme disease. Erythema migrans is an erythematous macule or patch that develops within 1 to 2 weeks in 80% of individuals after inoculation by an infected tick, gradually expands over days, and can develop in more than one site.

Early Lyme disease is usually diagnosed clinically because serologic test results are often negative at presentation and can become positive with clinical improvement.

This patient's fever and rash resolved with doxycycline, the preferred treatment for Lyme disease, and the return of his nonspecific symptoms is not indicative of active *Borrelia burgdorferi* infection. Seroreactivity often persists for at least months after successful antibiotic treatment of early infection and for years after treatment of late infection.

Chronic subjective conditions such as malaise, achiness, headaches, and forgetfulness develop in 10% to 30% of patients with Lyme disease after adequate treatment and usually remit spontaneously. The mechanism for development of these symptoms is not well understood. Nonetheless, the Infectious Diseases Society of America, the American Academy of Neurology Quality Standards Subcommittee, and the Ad Hoc International Lyme Disease Group have concluded that additional and prolonged antibiotic treatment beyond the initial treatment course in patients with Lyme disease is not effective and is associated with significant adverse effects.

KEY POINT

- **Seroreactivity often persists for at least months after successful antibiotic treatment of early Lyme disease and for years after treatment of late infection, and treatment beyond the initial course is not indicated and is associated with significant adverse effects.**

Bibliography

Klempner MS, Hu LT, Evans J, et al. Two controlled trials of antibiotic treatment in patients with persistent symptoms and a history of Lyme disease. N Engl J Med. 2001;345(2):85-92. [PMID: 11450676]

Item 56   Answer: C

Educational Objective: Evaluate a patient with a voriconazole–calcineurin inhibitor drug interaction.

The most likely cause of this patient's deteriorating condition as characterized by decreased kidney function, tremor, hypertension, anorexia, nausea, and vomiting is increased blood levels of cyclosporine. This is an expected consequence of adding an azole agent to the patient's therapeutic regimen. Drugs such as diltiazem, ofloxacin, and others also would be expected to cause increased cyclosporine levels because of their effects on the cytochrome P-450 enzymes. These drug interactions would be anticipated to raise the cyclosporine levels into the toxic range and result in the findings described in this patient. In this setting, the dose of cyclosporine should be reduced and cyclosporine blood levels followed closely. Some transplantation programs make use of the effects of azoles by prescribing ketoconazole, an inexpensive azole, to allow reductions in the dose of the more expensive cyclosporine.

Although organ transplant patients on immunosuppression are always at greater risk for bacterial infections, bacterial blood cultures are not indicated in this patient because he is afebrile, and bacteremia would not explain the hypertension and tremor.

Performing blood cultures for fungi would not provide any further useful information and is not indicated. The diagnosis of a fungal infection has already been established, the organisms are unlikely to be in the bloodstream, and the patient is already being treated with an effective regimen. In addition, *Aspergillus* fungemia does not cause hypertension and tremor.

The patient's symptoms are not those of voriconazole toxicity, and the voriconazole levels would not be expected to be high in this setting. Voriconazole may cause visual disturbances, mental status changes, and various gastrointestinal symptoms, but the symptom complex in this patient is typical of cyclosporine overdosage.

> **KEY POINT**
>
> • In patients receiving immunosuppressive therapy consisting of cyclosporine, the addition of drugs including diltiazem, ofloxacin, and voriconazole increases cyclosporine levels because of their effects on the cytochrome P-450 enzymes.

Bibliography

Page RL 2nd, Miller GG, Lindenfeld J. Drug therapy in the heart transplant recipient: part IV: drug-drug interactions. Circulation. 2005;111(2):230-239. [PMID: 15657387]

Item 57   Answer: C

Educational Objective: Evaluate a patient with herpes simplex encephalitis.

This patient presents with the syndrome of encephalitis, the cause of which is most likely herpes simplex virus type 1. The development of nucleic acid amplification tests, such as polymerase chain reaction (PCR), has markedly increased the ability to diagnose central nervous system viral infections, especially those caused by the herpesviruses. The usefulness of PCR assays on cerebrospinal fluid (CSF) for the diagnosis of herpes simplex encephalitis has been reliably demonstrated, with sensitivities and specificities of 96% to 98% and 95% to 99%, respectively, making it the best rapidly available diagnostic test in this setting.

Before PCR assays, brain biopsy was the only definitive way to establish the diagnosis of herpes simplex encephalitis, but it is associated with intracranial hemorrhage and brain edema at the biopsy site. Currently, brain biopsy has a limited role in the etiologic diagnosis of encephalitis and should be considered only in patients who continue to deteriorate neurologically despite treatment with acyclovir, which suggests an alternative diagnosis.

CSF antibody studies will show a fourfold or greater rise in antibody titer after 10 days to 2 weeks, retrospectively

confirming an acute infection, but they are not helpful in the early diagnosis of herpes simplex encephalitis.

Electroencephalography is nonspecific, although in more than 80% of cases of herpes simplex encephalitis, there is a temporal focus demonstrating periodic lateralizing epileptiform discharges.

Although MRI of the brain is useful for detecting the early changes of encephalitis, it also does not necessarily assist in determining a specific cause or guide therapy.

> **KEY POINT**
>
> • Cerebrospinal fluid polymerase chain reaction is the most sensitive and specific test for the diagnosis of herpes simplex encephalitis.

Bibliography

DeBiasi RL, Tyler KL. Molecular methods for diagnosis of viral encephalitis. Clin Microbiol Rev. 2004;17(4):903-925. [PMID: 15489354]

Item 58   Answer: A

Educational Objective: Prevent infection in a patient with a human bite to the hand.

This patient has experienced a human bite wound and should receive treatment with amoxicillin-clavulanate because it has a spectrum that closely matches the major bacteria causing infection in this setting. Irrigation and debridement as needed are part of the management strategy for wounds, including human and animal bite–related wounds. But even vigorous local cleansing may not eradicate bacteria that have been inoculated deeper into the tissues. This high incidence of infection with human bite wounds and subsequent complications to the hand warrant antibiotic prophylaxis and not observation.

The microbiology associated with human bite wounds is often polymicrobial. Signs and symptoms of infection are indolent on presentation, typically developing 1 week after injury. Antibiotic prophylaxis should be provided for all patients as soon as possible after a human bite regardless of wound appearance because of the risk of irreversible damage to deep structures, such as joints, bones, nerves, and tendons. The evidence for the benefit of prophylaxis is particularly significant for patients with human bite wounds that penetrate beyond the epidermal layer or those involving the hands, feet, and skin overlying joints or cartilage. Antibiotic prophylaxis should be polymicrobial in its coverage and usually consists of the oral β-lactam/β-lactamase inhibitor combination amoxicillin-clavulanate for 3 to 5 days.

Eikenella corrodens, a fairly common pathogen in human bite wounds, is resistant to clindamycin, aminoglycosides, macrolides, and first-generation cephalosporins. Thus, these antibiotics are not good choices for antimicrobial prophylaxis in this patient.

Human bite wounds are tetanus prone; however, this patient has received tetanus immunization within the past year and does not require tetanus immunization now.

> **KEY POINT**
>
> - Management of early human bite wounds, particularly those that penetrate beyond the epidermal layer or involve the hands, feet, and skin overlying joints or cartilage, includes irrigation, debridement when needed for removal of nonviable tissue, and prophylaxis with a broad-spectrum antimicrobial agent such as amoxicillin-clavulanate.

Bibliography

Medeiros I, Saconato H. Antibiotic prophylaxis for mammalian bites. Cochrane Database Syst Rev. 2001;(2):CD001738. [PMID: 11406003]

Item 59   Answer: D

Educational Objective: Treat a patient with *Pneumocystis jirovecii* pneumonia.

This patient should receive trimethoprim-sulfamethoxazole and prednisone. His signs and symptoms, including fever, nonproductive cough, and progressive dyspnea, are highly suggestive of *Pneumocystis jirovecii* pneumonia. Because other infections may have similar clinical manifestations, bronchoscopy to confirm the specific diagnosis of *Pneumocystis* pneumonia in addition to initiation of empiric treatment for the presumptive diagnosis is indicated, especially in patients with moderate-to-severe disease. Because organisms persist in clinical specimens for days or weeks after therapy initiation, empiric therapy can be started before diagnostic specimens are obtained. The mainstay of treatment is intravenous or oral trimethoprim-sulfamethoxazole.

Alveolar-arterial (A-a) oxygen gradient determination is crucial because the degree of impairment is the most important prognostic indicator in this setting. Corticosteroid administration within the first 72 hours of commencing treatment for *P. jirovecii* pneumonia can decrease morbidity and mortality. Patients such as this one with an A-a oxygen gradient of greater than 35 mm Hg or those with an arterial Po_2 of less than 70 mm Hg on ambient air should receive corticosteroid therapy when antimicrobial therapy is initiated.

Ceftriaxone and azithromycin would be appropriate for patients with community-acquired pneumonia, but this patient lacks the acute onset and focal radiographic findings associated with bacterial pneumonia, and the sputum Gram stain was not purulent and failed to identify a predominant organism, thus further lowering the probability of community-acquired pneumonia.

Trimethoprim-sulfamethoxazole therapy without a corticosteroid would not be appropriate in this patient given his A-a oxygen gradient of greater than 35 mm Hg.

Approximately 13% to 18% of patients with documented *Pneumocystis* pneumonia have a concurrent cause of pulmonary dysfunction, including tuberculosis, Kaposi sarcoma, and bacterial pneumonia. This patient's subacute course and chest radiograph showing diffuse bilateral pulmonary infiltrates argue against tuberculosis; therefore, immediate treatment with isoniazid, rifampin, pyrazinamide, and ethambutol is not indicated.

> **KEY POINT**
>
> - Patients with *Pneumocystis jirovecii* pneumonia with an arterial Po_2 of less than 70 mm Hg or an alveolar-arterial oxygen gradient of greater than 35 mm Hg should receive adjunctive corticosteroids within the first 72 hours of antimicrobial treatment.

Bibliography

Guidelines for prevention and treatment of opportunistic infections in HIV-infected adults and adolescents. http://aidsinfo.nih.gov/contentfiles/Adult_OI.pdf. Published June 18, 2008. Accessed on July 29 2009.

Item 60   Answer: E

Educational Objective: Manage a patient with suspected variant Creutzfeldt-Jakob disease.

Variant Creutzfeldt-Jakob disease (vCJD) was first reported in England in 1995 and is caused by bovine-to-human transmission of bovine spongiform encephalopathy. There are many features that distinguish vCJD from CJD, including presentation at a younger age; disease onset marked by psychiatric symptoms, which can lead to a mistaken diagnosis of depression; a slower disease progression; and the presence of PrPSc (an abnormal form of prion protein) in tonsillar biopsies. A brain biopsy is required to confirm a diagnosis of CJD and will also establish the diagnosis of vCJD, but it is more invasive than a tonsillar biopsy, which will provide the presumptive diagnosis in this patient.

Corneal biopsy is one way to establish the diagnosis of rabies. Rabies encephalitis is much more rapidly progressive than is vCJD and is characterized by hydrophobia, aerophobia, pharyngeal spasms, and hyperactivity followed by coma, respiratory and vascular collapse, and death within 2 weeks after coma onset. This patient's chronic symptoms are not compatible with rabies.

Intravenous acyclovir is appropriate in patients with herpes simplex encephalitis. Clinical features of herpes simplex encephalitis include fever, hemicranial headache, language and behavioral abnormalities, memory impairment, cranial nerve deficits, and seizures as well as MRI findings characterized by edema and hemorrhage in the temporal lobes and hypodense areas and nonhomogeneous contrast enhancement. However, this patient's clinical tempo and findings are not consistent with herpes encephalitis, and acyclovir has no therapeutic role for vCJD. In fact, there is no effective treatment for vCJD, including corticosteroids.

- Variant Creutzfeldt-Jakob disease (vCJD) is characterized by early-onset psychiatric symptoms suggestive of depression, an earlier age of onset than CJD, an absence of periodic sharp waves on electroencephalogram, and presumptive diagnosis by tonsillar biopsy.

Bibliography

Hilton DA, Sutak J, Smith ME, et al. Specificity of lymphoreticular accumulation of prion protein for variant Creutzfeldt-Jakob disease. J Clin Pathol. 2004;57(3):300-302. [PMID: 14990604]

Item 61   Answer: C

Educational Objective: Treat a patient with suspected *Clostridium difficile* infection.

This patient most likely has *Clostridium difficile* infection (CDI). Empiric therapy with metronidazole is appropriate.

Laboratory confirmation of CDI can be challenging. A high clinical index of suspicion should override an initial negative test result, and empiric therapy and isolation should be initiated in clinically suggestive settings. The processing of a single stool specimen for toxin detection at the onset of symptoms is generally sufficient to establish the diagnosis, especially when the test method has good sensitivity and specificity. This patient's initial tests for CDI were most likely falsely negative, possibly for several reasons. First, the sensitivity of the enzyme-linked immunosorbent assay (ELISA) is relatively low (65% to 80%). Second, *C. difficile* toxins can be degraded at room temperature by proteases. Any delay during specimen transport could result in toxin inactivation. Lastly, approximately 10% of CDI occurs in the ascending colon. Patients with right-sided CDI may not have detectable *C. difficile* toxin. The probability of *C. difficile* infection is high in this patient, and empiric therapy with metronidazole is indicated. It would be prudent to instruct the patient to stop the potentially offending antibiotic if he is still taking it.

Ciprofloxacin could be used to treat gastroenteritis caused by enteric pathogens, such as *Shigella* and *Campylobacter*; however, because this patient's culture was negative, this therapy is not indicated and might prove harmful if the strain of *C. difficile* is fluoroquinolone resistant.

Loperamide could be used for acute or chronic diarrhea, but it is contraindicated in patients with CDI.

Providing no treatment would be inappropriate in this patient with probable CDI; empiric therapy is warranted.

- Because of the high rate of false-negative results in the evaluation of patients with suspected *Clostridium difficile* infection, a high clinical index of suspicion should override a negative test result, and empiric therapy and isolation should be initiated in clinically suggestive settings.

Bibliography

Manabe YC, Vinetz JM, Moore RD, Merz C, Charache P, Bartlett JG. Clostridium difficile colitis: an efficient clinical approach to diagnosis. Ann Intern Med. 1995;123(11):835-840. [PMID: 7486465]

Item 62   Answer: B

Educational Objective: Treat disseminated gonococcal infection.

This patient most likely has disseminated gonococcal infection (DGI). Initial treatment of DGI should include parenteral therapy with ceftriaxone or a comparable third-generation cephalosporin.

DGI may cause septic or sterile immune-mediated arthritis and tenosynovitis and frequently involves the knees, hips, and wrists but not the spine. Dermatitis associated with sparse peripheral necrotic pustules also is common. A characteristic prodrome of migratory arthralgia and tenosynovitis may precede the settling of the synovitis in one or several joints.

Genitourinary symptoms associated with DGI usually are absent in women, and genital infection in women may have occurred long before systemic dissemination. Patients with rectal and pharyngeal colonization of *Neisseria gonorrhoeae* in the setting of DGI are commonly asymptomatic. In all patients in whom DGI is clinically suspected, routine culture of the rectum and pharynx, as well as the blood and the joints, is indicated.

On diagnosis of DGI, prompt evaluation for additional sexually transmitted diseases, including syphilis and HIV, is indicated. Empiric treatment for *Chlamydia trachomatis* infection also should be considered, because coinfection with *N. gonorrhoeae* and *C. trachomatis* is common. Patients with DGI are frequently asymptomatic, and this condition can cause infertility if untreated. Sexual partners of patients with DGI also should be treated.

Acyclovir is an effective treatment for herpes simplex infection. However, herpes simplex is most likely to cause painful vesicular and erosive disease of the genitalia, not papules and necrotic pustules on the cutaneous surfaces, and herpes simplex is not associated with a migratory arthritis.

Fluoroquinolones such as ciprofloxacin are no longer recommended by the Centers for Disease Control and Prevention for the treatment of gonorrhea because of the high resistance rate. Gentamicin is not indicated because *N. gonorrhoeae* is not consistently susceptible to this agent.

- Disseminated gonococcal infection may cause arthritis and tenosynovitis and is often associated with sparse peripheral necrotic pustules.

Bibliography

Centers for Disease Control and Prevention, Workowski KA, Berman SM. Sexually transmitted diseases treatment guidelines, 2006. MMWR Recomm Rep. 2006;55(RR-11). [PMID: 16888612]

Item 63   Answer: A

Educational Objective: Diagnose *Plasmodium falciparum* infection in a returning traveler from southern Africa.

This patient is most likely infected with *Plasmodium falciparum*. There are four species of human malaria: *P. falciparum, P. malariae, P. ovale,* and *P. vivax*. A fifth species, *P. knowlesi,* which infects monkeys residing in the forests of Malaysia, is now recognized to infect humans. Approximately 1500 cases of malaria are diagnosed in the United States each year, and most are in travelers who do not take or are not adherent to chemoprophylaxis. A few of these returning travelers will die.

There are several clues to the correct diagnosis of *P. falciparum* infection. Because *P. falciparum* is capable of parasitizing erythrocytes of all ages, the percent of parasitized cells can be quite high, typically over 5%, but in some individuals, as high as 50% or more. *P. vivax* and *P. ovale* parasitize reticulocytes, and *P. malariae,* only old erythrocytes; consequently, the degree of parasitemia is usually 1% or less. Because malaria parasites anaerobically metabolize glucose for energy, hypoglycemia and lactic acidosis may develop, and the degree of perturbation is directly related to the degree of parasitemia. *P. falciparum* produces erythrocyte membrane changes that promote the formation of "sticky" membrane knobs that allows adherence to endothelial surfaces and other erythrocytes, resulting in decreased microvascular blood flow and organ dysfunction. When this occurs in the brain (cerebral malaria), patients may develop confusion, agitation, seizures, and coma; death is the outcome if this condition not treated. *P. ovale, P. vivax,* and *P. malariae* do not cause cytoadherence, and infected patients appear less ill than those infected with *P. falciparum*. Like *P. falciparum, P. knowlesi* can infect erythrocytes of all ages, producing high rates of parasitemia and severe illness. However, *P. knowlesi* is restricted to the forests of Malaysia.

KEY POINT

- *Plasmodium falciparum* and *Plasmodium knowlesi* are the only causes of malaria associated with high rates of parasitemia (>5%) and severe disease; *P. knowlesi* is restricted to the forests of Malaysia.

Bibliography

Griffith KS, Lewis LS, Mali S, Parise ME. Treatment of malaria in the United States: a systematic review. JAMA. 2007;297(20):2264-2277. [PMID: 17519416]

Item 64   Answer: D

Educational Objective: Treat influenza virus infection.

This patient most likely has influenza virus infection. In the Northern Hemisphere, most cases of influenza occur from November to as late as May. The key features of this infection are profound myalgia, high fever, and nonproductive cough. Two classes of antivirals have efficacy against some strains of influenza: the adamantanes (amantadine and rimantadine) and the neuraminidase inhibitors (zanamivir and oseltamivir). Influenza type B is intrinsically resistant to the adamantanes. Influenza type A adamantane resistance has been steadily increasing since 1994. Because antiviral testing results indicate high levels of resistance to amantadine and rimantadine, neither was recommended for the treatment or chemoprophylaxis of influenza A in the United States during the 2007-2008 influenza season. During the 2008-2009 influenza season, an increasing percentage of influenza A (human H1N1) was resistant to oseltamivir, but all were susceptible to zanamivir, amantadine, and rimantadine. This resulted in a health advisory issued by the Centers for Disease Control and Prevention in December 2008 recommending zanamivir (an inhaled agent) as the preferred antiviral agent if rapid diagnostic testing for influenza was not done or if it was negative for influenza but the clinical suspicion for influenza was strong. For patients who cannot take zanamivir (presence of reactive airways disease or age younger than 7 years), oseltamivir (an oral agent) plus rimantadine are recommended as preferred therapy. When administered within 2 days of illness onset to otherwise healthy children or adults, effective antiviral therapy reduced the duration, and, possibly, the severity, of uncomplicated influenza A and B illness by approximately 1 day compared with placebo.

KEY POINT

- Single-agent therapy (amantadine, rimantadine or oseltamivir) was not recommended for the treatment or chemoprophylaxis of influenza A in the United States during the 2008-2009 influenza season owing to high resistance levels, but zanamivir continued to have activity against both influenza A and B during the 2008-2009 influenza season and could be used as a single agent.

Bibliography

CDC Health Advisory. CDC Issues Interim Recommendations for the Use of Influenza Antiviral Medications in the Setting of Oseltamivir Resistance among Circulating Influenza A (H1N1) Viruses, 2008-09 Influenza Season. http://www2a.cdc.gov/HAN/ArchiveSys/ViewMsgV.asp?AlertNum=00279. Published December 19, 2008. Accessed on February 16, 2009.

Item 65   Answer: D

Educational Objective: Select the appropriate empiric antimicrobial therapy in a patient with a secondary bacterial pneumonia following influenza.

This patient has community-acquired pneumonia that developed after influenza virus infection and requires treatment with vancomycin plus levofloxacin. Bacterial infections complicating influenza should be considered in patients whose condition deteriorates rapidly or seems to initially improve and then deteriorate. Given his age and underlying conditions, the most likely infecting organisms would be *Streptococcus pneumoniae*, *Haemophilus influenzae*, *Moraxella catarrhalis*, and *Legionella* species. However, his prior episode of influenza also increases his risk for developing a secondary pneumonia caused by *Staphylococcus aureus* or group A β-hemolytic streptococci. Although his infection was community acquired, given the increase in *S. aureus* pneumonia caused by community-associated methicillin-resistant *S. aureus* (CA-MRSA), vancomycin or linezolid should be added to the empiric regimen pending culture results and in vitro susceptibility testing. Vancomycin plus levofloxacin is the only regimen that treats the entire spectrum of organisms that need to be considered.

Azithromycin plus ceftriaxone, clindamycin plus levofloxacin, and piperacillin-tazobactam do not include appropriate coverage for CA-MRSA. Although clindamycin may treat some strains of CA-MRSA, resistance to this agent has emerged during therapy.

KEY POINT

- Empiric therapy for *Staphylococcus aureus* pneumonia should be vancomycin or linezolid to treat for the possibility of infection caused by a methicillin-resistant strain.

Bibliography

Mandell LA, Wunderink RG, Anzueto A, et al. Infectious Diseases Society of America/American Thoracic Society consensus guidelines on the management of community-acquired pneumonia in adults. Clin Infect Dis. 2007;44(Suppl 2):S27-S72. [PMID: 17278083]

Item 66 Answer: C

Educational Objective: Treat a patient with a cat bite and a severe penicillin allergy.

This patient presents with a necrotic, infected wound of the right leg secondary to a cat bite and requires treatment with ciprofloxacin and clindamycin. Irrigation and debridement as appropriate are also indicated in the management of this type of wound. Wounds such as that experienced by this patient are often polymicrobial, including multiple aerobic and anaerobic bacteria. The facultative anaerobic gram-negative rod, *Pasteurella multocida*, is the most commonly found microbe in the oral flora of the cat. This patient's clinical presentation is consistent with a serious skin and soft tissue infection warranting intravenous antibiotics. Although agents such as ampicillin-sulbactam or cefoxitin or carbapenems such as imipenem or ertapenem would be reasonable choices in a patient without a history of anaphylaxis to penicillin, only clindamycin plus a fluoroquinolone such as ciprofloxacin is recommended for this patient. Doxycycline or trimethoprim-sulfamethoxazole could also be considered in addition to an anti-anaerobic agent such as clindamycin when an oral regimen is being

considered. In addition, vancomycin might initially be administered owing to the emergence of methicillin-resistant *Staphylococcus aureus* in many communities.

This patient's history of anaphylaxis following penicillin administration makes a β-lactam/β-lactamase inhibitor combination such as ampicillin-sulbactam, the second-generation cephalosporin cefoxitin (a β-lactam agent), or imipenem (a β-lactam agent) inappropriate choices. Erythromycin is not a good choice because of its limited spectrum of coverage, including poor in vitro activity against *P. multocida*.

KEY POINT

- In the absence of penicillin allergy, β-lactam agents are recommended for infected patients with cat bite wounds, whereas a fluoroquinolone plus clindamycin is recommended for those with severe penicillin allergy.

Bibliography

Stevens DL, Bisno AL, Chambers HF, Everett ED, et al; Infectious Diseases Society of America. Practice guidelines for the diagnosis and management of skin and soft tissue infections [erratum in Clin Infect Dis. 2006;42(8):1219]. Clin Infect Dis. 2005;41(10):1373-1406. [PMID: 16231249]

Item 67 Answer: B

Educational Objective: Treat bacterial vaginosis.

This patient has bacterial vaginosis (formerly known as nonspecific vaginitis). The preferred therapy for bacterial vaginosis is metronidazole, 500 mg orally, twice daily for 1 week. Clinical criteria for bacterial vaginosis include a homogeneous, white, noninflammatory discharge that smoothly coats the vaginal walls; the presence of clue cells; a vaginal pH greater than 4.5; and the presence of a fishy odor to the vaginal discharge before or after the addition of 10% potassium hydroxide. Symptomatic patients who have at least three of these criteria should receive treatment with metronidazole or clindamycin, either orally or vaginally. Topical metronidazole gel for 5 days is as effective as 7 days of oral therapy.

Single-dose azithromycin is an effective, although expensive, therapy for *Chlamydia* cervicitis. Cervicitis is associated with a mucopurulent discharge from the cervical os. This patient's cervix was normal on examination, making cervicitis unlikely and treatment with azithromycin unnecessary.

A single dose of metronidazole is insufficient for treating bacterial vaginosis, is associated with higher recurrence rates, and is no longer recommended.

Topically applied miconazole is an effective therapy for vaginal candidiasis. Typical symptoms include pruritus, external and internal erythema, and a nonodorous, white, curd-like discharge. Lack of pruritus makes vaginal candidiasis less likely, and the presence of inflammation and lack of an odor would make this diagnosis more likely. The absence of yeast or pseudohyphae on the wet mount reduces the likelihood of candidal infection. This patient does not have candidal vaginitis and does not require treatment with miconazole.

KEY POINT
- First-line therapy for bacterial vaginosis is metronidazole orally for 7 days or metronidazole vaginal gel for 5 days.

Bibliography

Centers for Disease Control and Prevention, Workowski KA, Berman SM. Sexually transmitted diseases treatment guidelines, 2006 [erratum in MMWR Recomm Rep. 2006;55(36):997]. MMWR Recomm Rep. 2006;55(RR-11):1-94. [PMID: 16888612]

Item 68   Answer: D

Educational Objective: Treat a patient in the developing world who has bacterial meningitis.

This patient has acute bacterial meningitis as demonstrated by his clinical presentation and cerebrospinal fluid results. In all patients of his age group, the most likely infecting pathogen is *Streptococcus pneumoniae*. However, because he has acquired the infection in Vietnam, *Streptococcus suis* must also be considered as a possible infecting pathogen. Considering he may have a highly penicillin-resistant pneumococcal strain of meningitis, antimicrobial therapy with vancomycin, ceftriaxone, and dexamethasone is the most appropriate regimen. In a recent randomized, prospective, placebo-controlled trial of adjunctive dexamethasone in adult patients in Vietnam where most cases of meningitis were caused by *S. suis*, adjunctive dexamethasone led to a significant reduction in the risk of death at 1 month and risk of disability at 6 months in patients with *proven* bacterial meningitis. However, use of adjunctive dexamethasone in patients with *probable* bacterial meningitis was significantly associated with an increased risk of death at 1 month, likely explained by cases of tuberculous meningitis in the treatment group. Similar benefits of adjunctive dexamethasone were not demonstrated in another prospective, randomized, placebo-controlled trial in Malawi, although 90% of these patients were HIV-positive, and a delay in presentation may have contributed to the poor outcome. In developed countries, the benefit of dexamethasone administration was limited to those individuals with pneumococcal meningitis with a Glasgow Coma Scale score of 8 to 11 in one study; patients with other causes of meningitis and with good neurologic function at diagnosis did not benefit from dexamethasone. Despite this, the Infectious Diseases Society of America recommends early dexamethasone administration (before the first dose of antibiotic) to all patients with confirmed or suspected pneumococcal meningitis.

Ampicillin, ceftriaxone, plus dexamethasone would not be effective against highly penicillin-resistant pneumococcal strains that cause meningitis, which may be present in this patient.

Therapeutic regimens consisting of vancomycin plus ceftriaxone, as well as vancomycin, ceftriaxone, plus rifampin, do not include dexamethasone and therefore would not be the most effective treatment for this patient.

KEY POINT
- Adjunctive dexamethasone is appropriate in patients in the developing world with pneumococcal or *Streptococcus suis* meningitis; adjunctive dexamethasone may be of no benefit to patients with bacterial meningitis and advanced HIV infection, nonstreptococcal meningitis, and those in whom diagnosis and management are delayed.

Bibliography

Mai NTH, Chau TTH, Thwaites G, et al. Dexamethasone in Vietnamese adolescents and adults with bacterial meningitis. N Engl J Med. 2007;357(24):2431-2440. [PMID: 18077808]

Item 69   Answer: B

Educational Objective: Institute effective infection-control measures in the setting of tuberculosis.

This foreign-born patient most likely has reactivation of pulmonary tuberculosis. Tuberculosis is a communicable disease and is inhaled into the respiratory system via airborne droplets. A diagnosis of pulmonary tuberculosis should be considered in any patient with cough for greater than 3 weeks, loss of appetite, unexplained weight loss, night sweats, hoarseness, fever, fatigue, or chest pain. The index of suspicion should be substantially high for patients who spent time in developing countries, geographic areas of the United States such as Miami or New York City, or in a correctional facility.

Initially, the most important management is protection from potential tuberculosis exposure with airborne precautions, including placement of the patient into a negative-pressure room and use of respiratory protection by health care workers. Acceptable protection includes a "respirator," which refers to an N95 or higher filtering facepiece respirator or a powered air-purifying respirator. Within health care settings, tuberculosis airborne precautions should be immediately initiated in patients with symptoms or signs consistent with tuberculosis or in those with documented infectious tuberculosis who have not completed antituberculosis treatment. Such patients should continue to be managed with airborne precautions until they are determined to be noninfectious (clinical response to a standard multidrug antituberculosis treatment regimen or until an alternative diagnosis is made). If the alternative diagnosis cannot be clearly established, even with three negative sputum smear results, empiric treatment of tuberculosis should be strongly considered.

Although chest radiograph and sputum acid-fast bacilli stain and culture would be performed in a setting such as this, they would not be done before implementation of effective airborne precautions to reduce the risk for transmission of infection to health care workers and other patients. Performing tuberculin skin testing can help to establish a diagnosis of tuberculosis; however, such testing would not differentiate active from latent tuberculosis and should not be performed before airborne precautions are instituted.

Bibliography

Jensen PA, Lambert LA, Iademarco MF, Ridzon R; CDC. Guidelines for preventing the transmission of Mycobacterium tuberculosis in health-care settings, 2005. MMWR Recomm Rep. 2005;54(RR-17):1-141. [PMID: 16382216]

Item 70   Answer: B

Educational Objective: Diagnose acute coccidioidomycosis ("valley fever").

This is a typical case of acute coccidioidomycosis, also known as "valley fever." *Coccidioides immitis* is a dimorphic fungus that lives in soil in parts of Arizona, California, New Mexico, and west Texas, as well as parts of northern Mexico (the Sonoran Desert). Because most cases are characterized by subclinical or mild disease, patients often do not seek medical care; however, some patients, such as this one, have more severe disease. Acute or subacute pneumonia, with or without pleural effusions or empyema, is the most common form of acute coccidioidomycosis that physicians encounter. Late sequelae that present as pulmonary nodules or cavitary disease occur in as many as 10% of patients with these infections. Infections in extrapulmonary sites such as the skin or central nervous system occur in less than 1% of patients with coccidioidomycosis. Organisms may be recovered from sputum or bronchoalveolar lavage specimens, pleural fluid, and, occasionally, blood. Demonstration of spherules with endospores is diagnostic.

The clinical presentation of blastomycosis is not consistent with that of this patient, and the disease would usually follow a more chronic course resembling that of histoplasmosis.

Cryptococcus neoformans would not be expected to cause bilateral pneumonia with pleural effusions in an immunocompetent host. It would more likely cause single, slowly growing or stationary lesions, often causing few or no symptoms.

Fusarium oxysporum does not cause disease in immunocompetent hosts.

Inhalation of a large number of *Histoplasma capsulatum* spores could conceivably have caused this patient's constellation of symptoms and findings, but this organism is not endemic to Arizona (although it is found in Pennsylvania).

Bibliography

Spinello IM, Munoz A, Johnson RH. Pulmonary coccidioidomycosis. Semin Respir Crit Care Med. 2008;29(2):166-173. [PMID: 18365998]

Item 71   Answer: D

Educational Objective: Treat recurrent *Clostridium difficile* infection.

This patient with recurrent *Clostridium difficile* infection (CDI) should receive oral vancomycin followed by tapering doses of vancomycin. About 20% to 25% of patients with CDI will relapse after initial treatment, with as many as 5% having more than six recurrences. Metronidazole has been recommended as initial therapy for CDI since the late 1990s and continues to be the first choice for all but seriously ill patients and those with fulminant infections or multiple (two or more) recurrences of CDI. The first recurrence can be treated in the same way as a first episode according to disease severity. Antibiotic resistance does not appear to be an issue. Recurrence is likely due to the germination of persistent *C. difficile* spores in the colon after treatment or reinfection. Repeated, prolonged courses of metronidazole are not recommended beyond treatment of the first recurrence or for durations exceeding 14 days because of the potential for hepatotoxicity and peripheral neuropathy. Therefore, because this patient is now experiencing her third episode of CDI, any therapeutic regimen including metronidazole would be inappropriate. In patients with multiple recurrences, tapered or pulse dosing of oral vancomycin has been the most widely used regimen. Although studies have been small, CDI treatment consisting of a 10- to 14-day course of oral vancomycin followed by tapering or pulsing doses of vancomycin over a 4- to 6-week period resulted in significant reductions in multiply recurrent disease.

Vancomycin must be given orally because it is not secreted into the bowel after intravenous administration.

Bibliography

McFarland LV, Elmer GW, Surawicz CM. Breaking the cycle: treatment strategies for 163 cases of recurrent Clostridium difficile disease. Am J Gastroenterol. 2002;97(7):1769-1775. [PMID: 12135033]

Item 72   Answer: C

Educational Objective: Manage a patient with an epidural abscess and paralytic symptoms.

This patient has a spinal epidural abscess and vertebral osteomyelitis. Given his history of injection drug use, he likely has infective endocarditis with continuous bacteremia, leading to seeding of his lumbar spine and development of the epidural fluid collection. The likely infecting organisms are *Staphylococcus aureus* and gram-negative bacilli, and appropriate empiric antimicrobial therapy has been initiated.

Patients with spinal epidural abscess and neurologic dysfunction require urgent laminectomy with decompression and drainage, although surgery is not likely to be a viable therapeutic option in patients who have experienced complete paralysis of longer than 24 to 36 hours' duration; some experts, however, would perform surgical therapy in patients in whom complete paralysis has lasted fewer than 72 hours. Given that this patient's symptoms of paralysis lasted only 12 hours prior to presentation, emergent laminectomy is indicated to attempt to reverse the neurologic deficits.

CT-guided aspiration would likely identify the causative microorganism (approximately 90% of cultures are positive) but would be inadequate to treat the neurologic dysfunction. Electromyography would offer no other information and would not further guide the management of this patient.

Lumbar puncture for cerebrospinal fluid examination is not necessary and will not contribute to the management of this patient. Typical findings include an elevated protein level and pleocytosis, and Gram stain and cultures are negative in more than 75% to 80% of patients.

KEY POINT

- Emergent laminectomy should be performed in patients with spinal epidural abscess and neurologic dysfunction of less than 24 to 36 hours' duration.

Bibliography

Darouiche RO. Spinal epidural abscess. N Engl J Med. 2006;355(19): 2012-2020. [PMID: 17093252]

Item 73   Answer: D

Educational Objective: Manage a patient with herpes simplex encephalitis and an initially negative cerebrospinal fluid herpes simplex virus polymerase chain reaction result.

This patient most likely has herpes simplex encephalitis. Patients with herpes simplex encephalitis may have an initially negative cerebrospinal fluid polymerase chain reaction (PCR) result that becomes positive when the test is repeated 1 to 3 days after initiation of treatment. The presence of less than 10 leukocytes/μL (10×10^6/L) in the cerebrospinal fluid has been associated with a higher likelihood of a negative cerebrospinal fluid PCR result. Therefore, in undiagnosed cases in which patients have clinical features of herpes simplex encephalitis or temporal lobe lesions on neuroimaging, repeating the PCR 3 to 7 days later on a second cerebrospinal fluid specimen to evaluate for herpes simplex encephalitis should be considered. If cerebrospinal fluid results are negative at that time, then discontinuation of acyclovir therapy would be warranted. Until that time, it would be premature to discontinue acyclovir therapy.

Ganciclovir is an antiviral drug used to treat other serious herpesvirus infections, including those caused by cytomegalovirus and human herpesvirus 6. These viruses may cause encephalitis but most often occur in immunocompromised patients. Because this patient is not immunocompromised and herpes simplex encephalitis is the most likely diagnosis, adding ganciclovir is not indicated. Ganciclovir would be a second-line option for the treatment of herpes simplex encephalitis.

Brain biopsy of the temporal lobe might be considered if the patient's condition failed to improve with adequate acyclovir therapy and an alternative diagnosis was being considered. Brain biopsy is an invasive procedure and confers the risk for intracerebral hemorrhage and edema. It is premature to consider performing brain biopsy before repeating the PCR assay for herpes simplex virus infection and assessing the patient's response to acyclovir.

KEY POINT

- In patients with an initially negative cerebrospinal fluid polymerase chain reaction (PCR) result and compatible clinical or radiologic findings for herpes simplex encephalitis, performing a repeat PCR on a second cerebrospinal fluid specimen 3 to 7 days after treatment initiation should be considered.

Bibliography

Tunkel AR, Glaser CA, Bloch KC, et al; Infectious Diseases Society of America. The management of encephalitis: clinical practice guidelines by the Infectious Diseases Society of America. Clin Infect Dis. 2008;47(3):303-327. [PMID: 18582201]

Item 74   Answer: C

Educational Objective: Manage a patient with suspected vertebral osteomyelitis.

In a patient with suspected vertebral osteomyelitis, a microbiologic diagnosis must be established to guide antibiotic therapy. Because the infection is often hematogenous, blood cultures should be obtained initially in all patients. Cultures are positive in up to 75% of patients, and identification of *Staphylococcus aureus*, which is the most frequent cause of vertebral osteomyelitis, may obviate the need for a bone biopsy. However, if the imaging studies suggest vertebral osteomyelitis but the blood cultures are negative, CT-guided percutaneous needle biopsy should be performed.

Because this procedure is only about 50% sensitive, antibiotics should be withheld until a microbiologic diagnosis is made. If results of the first needle biopsy culture are nondiagnostic, the study should be repeated. If the second results are also nondiagnostic, either an empiric course of antibiotics should be started or an open biopsy should be performed. Obtaining another set of blood cultures will not clarify the diagnosis.

This patient is stable enough to wait for the results of the CT-guided needle biopsy to direct appropriate antibiotic therapy.

Empiric ceftriaxone will provide adequate coverage for most gram-negative and streptococcal organisms responsible for vertebral osteomyelitis but will provide no coverage for methicillin-resistant *S. aureus* (MRSA). If after needle biopsy attempts, the patient truly has culture-negative osteomyelitis and an open biopsy is not feasible, an empiric course of antibiotics, possibly including vancomycin and a third-generation cephalosporin such as ceftriaxone or ceftazidime or vancomycin and a fluoroquinolone, can be given. Starting empiric nafcillin would be a good choice if the infective organism were a susceptible staphylococcus; however, nafcillin will not adequately cover infections caused by MRSA or gram-negative organisms.

KEY POINT

- In patients with imaging studies suggestive of vertebral osteomyelitis but negative blood culture results, CT-guided percutaneous needle biopsy is indicated to establish a microbiologic diagnosis.

Bibliography
An HS, Seldromridge JA. Spinal Infections: diagnostic tests and imaging studies. Clin Orthopedic Relat Rec. 2006;444:27-33. [PMID: 16523124]

Item 75   Answer: E
Educational Objective: Diagnose pneumonic plague as the likely cause of a mass-casualty bioterrorism event.

The most likely diagnosis is pneumonic plague caused by the gram-negative bacillus *Yersinia pestis*. This organism may induce overwhelming sepsis in an otherwise healthy person, whether exposure is due to a bioterrorism attack or to aerosols from an infected animal (the naturally occurring form). Plague occurs in three forms: (1) bubonic plague, which is transmitted from rodents to humans by fleas and is associated with a bubo (lymphadenitis); (2) septicemic plague, which progresses from the bubonic form; and (3) pneumonic plague, which results from inhalation of *Y. pestis*. Patients with pneumonic plague present with high fever,

headache, myalgia, dyspnea, hemoptysis, and sepsis 2 to 4 days after exposure to aerosols of *Y. pestis*. Sputum is "watery" and may be blood tinged, and findings of a patchy bronchopneumonia are found on chest radiograph. The mortality rate approaches 100% if patients are not treated within 24 hours of developing symptoms. The diagnosis can be established by isolating the causative microorganism from blood, respiratory secretions, skin, or cerebrospinal fluid. Wayson stain demonstrates the typical bipolar staining, which resembles a "closed safety pin." Gram stain shows small gram-negative coccobacilli.

Tularemia is a zoonotic infection that occurs worldwide and is acquired in humans by contact with infected animals or ingestion or inhalation of the causative microorganism; it usually infects the lymph nodes, lungs, spleen, liver, and kidneys. Bacteremia is common. Pneumonic tularemia may have a clinical presentation similar to pneumonic plague, but the bacteria would not be described as shaped like "safety pins."

Salmonella species can cause acute illness, but most cases occur in the presence of diarrhea, and they do not cause pneumonia. Overwhelming sepsis due to *Staphylococcus aureus* or *Streptococcus pneumoniae* would be associated with gram-positive organisms on Gram stain, making this diagnosis unlikely.

KEY POINT

- *Yersinia pestis*, a potential agent of bioterrorism, is a gram-negative bacillus that causes pneumonia and overwhelming sepsis (pneumonic plague).

Bibliography
Inglesby TV, Dennis DT, Henderson DA, et al. Plague as a biological weapon: medical and public health management. Working Group on Civilian Biodefense. JAMA. 2000;283(17):2281-2290. [PMID: 10807389]

Item 76   Answer: A
Educational Objective: Diagnose posttransplant-related cytomegalovirus infection.

This patient's clinical scenario is most consistent with an exacerbation of gastrointestinal cytomegalovirus (CMV) infection resulting in perforation. Gastrointestinal manifestations in CMV infection vary widely, and presentation depends on the anatomic location of the infection but most commonly includes fever, pain, ulceration, hemorrhage, and perforation. CMV infection occurs most commonly in the second through sixth month after transplantation, and CMV-associated gastrointestinal disease occurs often in this setting. The period of 5 months after transplantation to development of symptoms suggestive of bowel perforation is consistent with CMV infection.

Escherichia coli O127 infection would cause diarrhea, and in some individuals, possibly, thrombotic thrombocytopenic purpura-hemolytic uremic syndrome, but it would not cause bowel perforation.

Giardia lamblia does not cause bowel perforation.

Herpes simplex virus infection would not cause perforating gastrointestinal lesions.

Strongyloides hyperinfection syndrome is a consideration in any immunosuppressed patient who presents with sepsis or pulmonary or gastrointestinal symptoms. The larvae may migrate through the intestinal wall and travel to the lungs, brain, or other sites. Enteric bacteria may migrate along with the larvae and also cause serious infection; therefore, *Strongyloides* infection should be considered in any patient with signs of bacterial sepsis or pulmonary, gastrointestinal, or central nervous system disease, including meningitis. However, this patient's intestinal perforation is not consistent with *Strongyloides stercoralis* infection or its hyperinfection syndrome. Although *Strongyloides* does perforate through the intestinal wall as it migrates to lung and other tissues, it rarely causes the signs and symptoms of macroscopic perforation as demonstrated in this patient.

KEY POINT

- **Cytomegalovirus (CMV) infection occurs most commonly in the second through sixth month after transplantation, and CMV-associated gastrointestinal disease is common in this setting.**

Bibliography

Fishman JA. Infection in solid-organ transplant recipients. N Engl J Med. 2007;357(25):2601-2614. [PMID: 18094380]

Item 77   Answer: B

Educational Objective: Diagnose genital herpes simplex virus infection.

This patient has the classic findings of primary genital herpes simplex virus (HSV) infection. HSV-1 or HSV-2 may cause the infection, but HSV-2 is the more common pathogen. Genital herpes lesions typically begin as vesicles that ulcerate and are quite painful. The initial infection is often the most severe and can be accompanied by local lymphadenopathy and systemic symptoms. Recurrences vary in frequency and are typically less severe than the initial episode. Many recurrences are subclinical but are nonetheless contagious. The diagnosis of genital herpes is often suspected on clinical grounds but may be confirmed by viral culture or serologic testing if the diagnosis is in doubt. Viral culture for HSV-1 and HSV-2 is a rapid test, with results often available by the next day. The specificity of viral culture approaches 100%, but the sensitivity varies with the quality of specimen handling and the age of the lesion (older, crusted lesions have lower yield). Direct tests such as the Tzanck smear are easy to perform, but they should be used only if more specific immunologic tests are not available. The use of all these tests depends on the availability of testing technology. Type-specific HSV-2 antibody will be negative in true primary infection, and although a positive HSV-2 antibody test indicates previous infection (symptomatic or asymptomatic), it does not necessarily explain the cause of concomitant genital lesions.

Chancroid is a relatively uncommon sexually transmitted disease caused by *Haemophilus ducreyi*. Infection is characterized by the presences of ragged, purulent, painful ulcers associated with tender lymph nodes that may suppurate. The superficial vesicles and erosions of herpes simplex virus infection are not easily mistaken for the deep, ragged ulcers of chancroid.

The primary ulcerative lesion (chancre) in patients with syphilis develops approximately 3 weeks after infection occurs, has a clean appearance with heaped-up borders, and is usually painless and often unrecognized, particularly in women. Multiple small painful vesicles and erosions argue strongly against this diagnosis.

Symptoms of vulvovaginal candidiasis include pruritus, external and internal erythema, and nonodorous, white, curd-like discharge. Lack of pruritus makes vulvovaginal candidiasis less likely, and the presence of inflammation and lack of an odor would make such a diagnosis more likely. Candidal infection does not cause painful genital ulcers.

KEY POINT

- **Primary genital herpes simplex virus infection is characterized by fever, headache, and painful, ulcerated, vesicular lesions.**

Bibliography

Cernik C, Gallina K, Brodell RT. The treatment of herpes simplex infections: an evidence-based review. Arch Intern Med. 2008; 168(11):1137-1144. [PMID: 18541820]

Item 78   Answer: D

Educational Objective: Understand measures to prevent the spread of *Clostridium difficile* infection.

Environmental contamination with vegetative *Clostridium difficile* and *C. difficile* spores frequently occurs. *C. difficile* is transmitted to other patients through the hands and clothes of health care workers and from common equipment that is used on patients without cleaning. A combination of interventions "bundled" together have been shown to be effective at reducing many hospital-acquired infections. The use of a *C. difficile* bundle consisting of barrier precautions, enhanced cleaning with bleach, and traditional soap-and-water hand hygiene is useful in preventing the spread of *C. difficile*. Soap and water are not sporicidal, but the mechanics of hand washing effectively removes spores. Barrier precautions such as wearing nonsterile gloves and a gown and using dedicated equipment have been recommended for *C. difficile* control by the Centers for Disease Control and Prevention and have been shown to be effective.

Airborne precautions are recommended for patients with known or suspected illnesses transmitted by airborne droplet nuclei such as tuberculosis, measles, varicella, or disseminated varicella zoster virus infection. Patients must be isolated in a private room with negative air pressure, the door must remain closed, and all entering persons must wear masks with a filtering capacity of 95%. Transported patients must wear masks. Alcohol-based hand hygiene products do not kill spores and are ineffective at removing them from hands.

Droplet precautions are recommended for patients with known or suspected illnesses transmitted by large-particle droplets such as *Neisseria meningitidis* infections and influenza. Patients are isolated in private rooms, and hospital personnel wear face masks when within 3 feet of the patient.

Because *C. difficile* is not spread through aerosols or large droplets, wearing a mask (droplet precautions) or instituting negative room pressure (airborne precautions) would not be useful.

KEY POINT

- A *Clostridium difficile* "bundle" consisting of barrier precautions, enhanced cleaning with bleach, and traditional soap-and-water hand hygiene is useful in preventing the spread of *C. difficile*.

Bibliography
Dubberke ER, Gerding DN, Classen D, Arias KM, Podgorny K, Anderson DJ, et al. Strategies to prevent clostridium difficile infections in acute care hospitals. Infect Control Hosp Epidemiol. 2008 Oct;29 Suppl 1:S81-92. PMID: 18840091

Item 79   Answer: B
Educational Objective: Diagnose HIV-associated nephropathy.

HIV-associated nephropathy (HIVAN) is a renal syndrome that develops in HIV-positive persons and is prevalent among black patients; it is usually a manifestation of advanced HIV disease and high viral loads. The most common cause of HIV nephropathy is collapsing focal glomerulosclerosis, found in approximately 60% of patients who undergo biopsy. The typical clinical presentation of HIVAN is heavy proteinuria, typically in the nephrotic range; renal dysfunction; and rapid progression to renal failure. The renal ultrasound typically shows increased echogenicity, which is a nonspecific finding of many diffuse renal diseases, and no evidence of obstruction. Most HIV-positive patients with renal disease and heavy proteinuria undergo biopsy because many have a glomerular disease other than collapsing focal glomerulosclerosis, particularly patients who are not black. There is no treatment for collapsing focal glomerulosclerosis, but highly active antiretroviral therapy (HAART) and an angiotensin-converting enzyme inhibitor are initiated in most patients to help control proteinuria. The presentation and progression of collapsing focal glomerulosclerosis may be different in patients who are receiving HAART.

Acute interstitial nephritis is a heterogeneous group of disorders that most commonly develop after exposure to drugs but also may result from various infectious and inflammatory conditions. The urine sediment may reveal pyuria, leukocyte casts, microscopic hematuria, and tubular-range proteinuria, but not nephrotic-range proteinuria. Patients with IgA nephropathy and postinfectious glomerulonephritis typically present with the nephritic syndrome (rather than the nephrotic syndrome), which is characterized by hematuria, erythrocyte casts, mild proteinuria, and hypertension.

KEY POINT

- The most common cause of HIV-associated nephropathy is collapsing focal glomerulosclerosis, which is characterized by heavy proteinuria, renal dysfunction, and rapid progression to renal failure.

Bibliography
Wingston JA, Bruggeman LA, Ross MD, et al. Nephropathy and establishment of a renal reservoir of HIV type 1 during primary infection. N Engl J Med. 2001;344(26):1979-1984. [PMID 11430327]

Item 80   Answer: C
Educational Objective: Treat epididymitis.

This patient has epididymitis based on the acute onset of pain and urethral discharge. Ultrasound findings suggesting epididymal inflammation without reduced or altered blood flow to the testes characteristic of torsion are confirmatory. Treatment with ceftriaxone and doxycycline is required.

In sexually active men younger than aged 35 years, the cause of epididymitis is most commonly a sexually acquired infection that has ascended through the urethra, namely *Chlamydia trachomatis* or *Neisseria gonorrhoeae*. The Centers for Disease Control and Prevention recommends ceftriaxone and doxycycline treatment, and this therapy is generally considered sufficient treatment for most men younger than the age of 35 years. For men older than 35 years or men who practice receptive anal intercourse, infection with coliform bacteria must also be considered, and the addition of a fluoroquinolone such as ofloxacin is often recommended. However, the use of ofloxacin alone will not be effective in treating gonorrheal infection because many organisms are now resistant to fluoroquinolone antibiotics.

Ampicillin and gentamicin are much less effective than are ceftriaxone and doxycycline and are not recommended. Azithromycin is not considered a first-line treatment for sexually transmitted epididymitis because of the decreased susceptibility of gonorrheal infection to this agent. Combining azithromycin with ceftriaxone is as effective as ceftriaxone and doxycycline but is more expensive and more likely to cause gastrointestinal upset.

KEY POINT

- In men younger than 35 years, epididymitis is most commonly caused by infection with *Chlamydia trachomatis* or *Neisseria gonorrhoeae*.

Bibliography
Centers for Disease Control and Prevention, Workowski KA, Berman SM. Sexually transmitted diseases treatment guidelines, 2006 [erratum in MMWR Recomm Rep. 2006;55(36):997]. MMWR Recomm Rep. 2006;55(RR-11). [PMID: 16888612]

Item 81   Answer: A

Educational Objective: Manage a patient with cranial subdural empyema.

This patient has a cranial subdural empyema resulting from paranasal sinusitis. Subdural empyema is a medical and surgical emergency requiring adequate decompression of the brain and complete evacuation of the empyema. The neuroimaging procedure of choice is MRI, which will show the fluid collection and can also differentiate empyema from most sterile effusions and subdural hematomas. Whether the empyema should be evacuated by craniotomy or burr-hole drainage is not clear, although retrospective studies have shown that mortality is higher in patients treated with burr-hole drainage only. In one study of 699 patients, the mortality rate was 23.3% in patients treated with burr-hole drainage compared with 8.4% in those treated with craniotomy. However, patients who received burr-hole drainage may have been more ill than those who underwent craniotomy alone and might not have been candidates for craniotomy. Burr-hole drainage is generally recommended only for patients with septic shock or localized parafalcine collections and in children with subdural empyema secondary to bacterial meningitis because the pus is thin, and there is usually no brain swelling in these patients.

CT-guided needle aspiration might be considered because it can help identify the infecting organism, but this patient clearly has evidence of increased intracranial pressure due to a mass effect of the empyema; therefore, CT-guided needle aspiration is inadequate treatment. Aspiration alone cannot adequately remove the empyema or prevent its recurrence.

Lumbar puncture is contraindicated because it confers a significant risk for brain herniation.

Mannitol might provide some treatment for increased intracranial pressure but would not be effective without surgical drainage.

KEY POINT

- **In patients with subdural empyema, craniotomy is the optimal procedure for drainage of the empyema.**

Bibliography

Osborn MK, Steinberg JP. Subdural empyema and other suppurative complications of paranasal sinusitis. Lancet Infect Dis. 2007;7(1): 62-67. [PMID: 17182345]

Item 82   Answer: B

Educational Objective: Diagnose immune reconstitution inflammatory syndrome.

Immune reconstitution inflammatory syndrome (IRIS) is a paradoxical deterioration in clinical status in patients with HIV infection occurring after highly active antiretroviral therapy (HAART) initiation, with most cases developing within a few weeks to a few months of commencement of HAART. IRIS can present in two different situations: as an exacerbation of a partially or successfully treated opportunistic infection or as a previously undiagnosed or subclinical infection.

The signs and symptoms of tuberculous IRIS may include high fevers, new or worsening lymphadenopathy, worsening of pulmonary symptoms, and a new or increasing pleural effusion. This patient had fever and cervical lymphadenopathy without worsening pulmonary disease. Principles of management include identification of the syndrome plus consideration of temporary HAART cessation in patients in whom potentially life-threatening forms of IRIS develop, such as in those with severe neurologic disease. Most patients with IRIS are managed with antimicrobial therapy to reduce the antigen load of the triggering pathogen, short-term therapy with NSAIDs or corticosteroids to decrease inflammation, and HAART continuation.

Lymphoma is always a likely diagnosis in a young person with cervical lymphadenopathy. However, lymphoma does not typically present with the sudden appearance of tender, fluctuant lymphadenopathy. Furthermore, the temporal association of fever and lymphadenopathy with HAART initiation in a patient with known tuberculosis is most consistent with IRIS.

Kaposi sarcoma can affect any organ in the body, including the lymph nodes. However, Kaposi sarcoma typically affects the lower extremities, face, oral mucosa, genitalia, gastrointestinal tract, and lungs. The absence of any involvement in these areas makes the diagnosis of Kaposi sarcoma unlikely.

The optimal time for initiation of antiretroviral therapy during tuberculosis treatment is currently unknown. Current guidelines suggest waiting 4 to 8 weeks before initiating HAART. Patients already receiving HAART when antituberculosis treatment is started require a careful assessment to evaluate for potential drug-drug interactions.

KEY POINT

- **Immune reconstitution inflammatory syndrome presents as a paradoxical deterioration in the clinical status of a patient with HIV infection after initiation of highly active antiretroviral therapy.**

Bibliography

Battegay M, Drechsler H. Clinical spectrum of the immune restoration inflammatory syndrome. Curr Opin HIV AIDS. 2006;1(1):56-61. [PMID: 19372785]

Item 83   Answer: C

Educational Objective: Treat documented *Streptococcus pyogenes* necrotizing fasciitis and toxic shock syndrome.

This patient most likely has group A β-hemolytic streptococcal (*Streptococcus pyogenes*) necrotizing fasciitis and toxic shock syndrome, likely as a complication of her recent varicella virus infection; she now requires treatment with penicillin and clindamycin. The "woody" induration noted with palpation of the subcutaneous tissues is characteristic. This patient meets the diagnostic criteria for streptococcal toxic shock syndrome based on isolation of the organism from a sterile site in the setting of hypotension, acute kidney injury, elevated serum aminotransferase concentrations, thrombocytopenia, and soft tissue necrosis. Surgical debridement is the most important therapeutic intervention for patients with necrotizing fasciitis. Vancomycin plus piperacillin-tazobactam, vancomycin plus cefepime and metronidazole, or vancomycin plus a carbapenem agent such as imipenem or meropenem are acceptable empiric initial choices because of their coverage of staphylococci, streptococci, anaerobes, and gram-negative bacilli. Once *S. pyogenes* is confirmed as the causative agent, parenteral clindamycin and penicillin are recommended. Although this organism is penicillin susceptible, clindamycin is added because of its ability to suppress toxin production by *S. pyogenes* and its continued activity when *S. pyogenes* bacteria are in the stationary phase of growth, a condition often encountered in necrotizing infections in which large numbers of bacteria are present and no longer reproducing.

Intravenous immune globulin therapy has been used to treat necrotizing fasciitis caused by group A β-hemolytic *S. pyogenes* because of its ability to neutralize streptococcal extracellular toxins; however, this therapy is considered adjunctive and should not be used in lieu of targeted antibiotic therapy.

Metronidazole and ciprofloxacin would be reasonable empiric coverage for infections caused by intestinal or genital flora but lack reliable activity against methicillin-resistant staphylococci.

Vancomycin plus cefepime and metronidazole is an appropriate empiric antibiotic regimen; however, once the microbial cause has been identified, the antibiotic choice should be narrowed. Therefore, this regimen would be inappropriate.

KEY POINT

- Group A β-hemolytic *Streptococcus pyogenes* necrotizing fasciitis with or without associated toxic shock syndrome should be treated with aggressive supportive measures, surgical intervention, and an antibiotic regimen consisting of penicillin and clindamycin; adjunctive intravenous immune globulin may also be helpful.

Bibliography

Anaya DA, Pellinger EP. Necrotizing soft tissue infection: diagnosis and management. Clin Infect Dis. 2007;44(5):705-710. [PMID: 17278065]

Item 84   Answer: C

Educational Objective: Provide disease-prevention advice to a traveler to Africa.

Bed netting is a very effective and relatively inexpensive method of preventing mosquito-transmitted diseases such as malaria. Multiple studies have consistently shown the benefit of sleeping under bed netting for the prevention of malaria

transmission, particularly when the netting is treated with permethrin, an extraordinarily effective insecticide. Because the *Anopheles* mosquito predominantly bites between dusk and dawn, all travelers to malaria-endemic areas should sleep in rooms with good screening and/or bed netting.

Carbonated water such as soda is generally safe to drink (as are beer and wine) although it should not be poured into a glass containing locally made ice. Drinks made from boiled water, such as hot tea, also are safe.

In laboratory conditions, DEET-containing insect repellents prevented mosquito bites for more than 300 minutes compared with citronella, which protected for less than 30 minutes.

Air handling on commercial aircraft includes mixing outside sterile air with cabin air, high-efficiency particulate-absorbing filtering, and ceiling-to-floor laminar flow. The use of these measures results in an extremely low risk for acquiring tuberculosis on an aircraft; therefore, wearing an in-flight mask for tuberculosis prevention is not necessary.

KEY POINT

- Bed netting is a very effective and relatively inexpensive method of preventing mosquito-transmitted diseases such as malaria.

Bibliography

Mangili A, Gendreau M. Transmission of infectious disease during commercial air travel. Lancet. 2005;365(9463):989-996. [PMID: 15767002]

Item 85   Answer: D

Educational Objective: Treat trichomonal vaginitis.

This patient most likely has trichomonal vaginitis and should be treated with metronidazole. This condition is characterized by vaginal irritation, pruritus, pain, or unusual discharge. All patients infected with *Trichomonas vaginalis* and their sexual partners should receive treatment with a single 2-g dose of metronidazole, which is usually effective; in patients who do not respond to this regimen, a 7-day treatment course is appropriate.

A microscopic examination of vaginal discharge with a drop of 0.9% saline solution (wet mount) can help to identify motile organisms with flagella (trichomonads) and epithelial cells covered with bacteria obscuring the cell borders (clue cells). Additional examination of the secretions with a drop of 10% potassium hydroxide is useful in identifying the fishy odor of bacterial vaginosis (whiff test) or the filaments of *Candida* species. The microscopic findings shown are consistent with trichomonal vaginitis. *T. vaginalis* infection is sexually transmitted. The chronicity and natural history of trichomonal vaginitis are not well understood. Most men with this infection are asymptomatic and most women with this infection are symptomatic; a diffuse, malodorous, yellow-green vaginal discharge is common.

Doxycycline and fluconazole are not indicated for treating trichomonal vaginitis. Topical application of metronidazole has not been shown to be effective.

- **Trichomonal vaginitis is identified by finding motile protozoa on a wet mount preparation.**

Bibliography

Centers for Disease Control and Prevention, Workowski KA, Berman SM. Sexually transmitted diseases treatment guidelines, 2006 [erratum in MMWR Recomm Rep. 2006;55(36):997]. MMWR Recomm Rep. 2006;55(RR-11):1-94. [PMID: 16888612]

Item 86   Answer: A

Educational Objective: Treat a patient with lung abscess following aspiration pneumonia.

This patient's history of alcohol abuse and alcohol-withdrawal seizures puts her at risk for aspiration pneumonia. She now presents with a lung abscess, characterized radiologically by a cavity with an air-fluid level, which probably occurred as a complication of aspiration pneumonia. Lung abscesses are polymicrobial infections caused by anaerobic bacteria that are normally present in the mouth; microaerophilic streptococci, viridans streptococci, and gram-negative enteric pathogens have also been implicated. In studies using sample techniques that avoid oral contamination, anaerobes are found in about 90% of patients with lung abscess and are the only organisms isolated in about half. Possible anaerobes in patients with lung abscess as a complication of aspiration pneumonia include *Peptostreptococcus* species, *Fusobacterium nucleatum*, *Prevotella melaninogenica*, and *Bacteroides* species (including *B. fragilis*). Of the choices listed, only ampicillin-sulbactam would have a broad enough spectrum to cover the likely pathogens.

Of the other antimicrobial choices, levofloxacin and aztreonam would not be effective in treating oral anaerobes, and ceftriaxone would be effective in treating some oral anaerobic species but not β-lactamase–producing strains.

Although metronidazole is highly active in vitro against most anaerobes, it is not active against microaerophilic streptococci and some anaerobic cocci.

- **Patients with lung abscess as a complication of aspiration pneumonia require treatment with an antimicrobial agent effective against β-lactamase–producing strains of oral anaerobes.**

Bibliography

Mandell LA, Wunderink RG, Anzueto A, et al. Infectious Diseases Society of America/American Thoracic Society consensus guidelines on the management of community-acquired pneumonia in adults. Clin Infect Dis. 2007;44(Suppl 2):S27-S72. [PMID: 17278083]

Item 87   Answer: D

Educational Objective: Manage a patient with suspected multidrug-resistant tuberculosis.

A diagnosis of pulmonary tuberculosis should be considered in any patient with cough for greater than 3 weeks, loss of appetite, unexplained weight loss, night sweats, bloody sputum or hemoptysis, hoarseness, fever, fatigue, or chest pain. The index of suspicion should be substantially higher for patients who spent time in developing countries or residing in geographic areas of the United States such as Miami or New York City that have been hot spots for multidrug-resistant tuberculosis or have spent time in a correctional facility in the United States or abroad.

Four-drug therapy is used in patients with suspected, previously untreated tuberculosis in whom resistance patterns are unknown to allow coverage for possible multidrug resistance, followed by de-escalation of antimicrobial therapy once drug susceptibility is known. Isoniazid, rifampin, pyrazinamide, and ethambutol are usually appropriate first-line drugs. All four drugs are used during the first 2 months of treatment, and, depending on susceptibility testing results, treatment continues with isoniazid and rifampin for the remaining 7 months, for a total of 9 months of treatment. Rifabutin should be substituted for rifampin in this patient's regimen if he is diagnosed with HIV infection and begins highly active antiretroviral therapy with protease inhibitors. Rifampin will decrease the levels of the protease inhibitors, but the degree of this decrease is unpredictable. Rifampin can cause similar problems in patients taking medication to prevent the rejection of transplanted organs, and frequent monitoring of drug levels is required in these patients.

Drug-resistant tuberculosis is resistant to at least one first-line antituberculosis drug. Multidrug-resistant tuberculosis is resistant to more than one antituberculosis drug and at least isoniazid and rifampin. Suspected or proven drug-resistant tuberculosis should be managed by an expert.

Treatment with fluoroquinolones, pyrazinamide, ethambutol, ethionamide, and cycloserine would be appropriate only after multidrug-resistant tuberculosis is confirmed. Fluoroquinolones, ethionamide, and cycloserine are considered second-line therapies and should be used only if resistance has been documented. Ethionamide and cycloserine are less effective and more toxic than the first-line drugs.

Isoniazid alone is not acceptable because isoniazid monotherapy is typically used to treat latent tuberculosis when multidrug-resistant tuberculosis is not suspected.

Dual therapy with isoniazid and rifampin is typically used to complete a full course of therapy in patients with susceptible tuberculosis but not to initiate therapy in patients with active tuberculosis.

- **The initial therapeutic regimen for all adults with previously untreated tuberculosis consists of a 2-month initial phase of isoniazid, rifampin, pyrazinamide, and ethambutol pending drug susceptibility test results.**

Bibliography

American Thoracic Society, Centers for Disease Control and Prevention (CDC). Update: adverse event data and revised American Thoracic Society/CDC recommendations against the use of rifampin and pyrazinamide for treatment of latent tuberculosis infection—United States, 2003. MMWR. 2003;52(31):735-739. [PMID: 12904741]

Item 88   Answer: B
Educational Objective: Diagnose disseminated cryptococcal disease based on dermatologic findings.

Cutaneous cryptococcosis, caused by the encapsulated yeast, *Cryptococcus neoformans,* is generally associated with concomitant systemic infection. A high index of suspicion is therefore mandatory in affected patients because cryptococcal skin involvement is nonspecific and produces a variety of lesions, including papules, nodules, plaques, vesicles, bullae, pustules, abscesses, cellulitis, ulcers, and purpura. The most typical lesions are asymptomatic and resemble molluscum contagiosum (also found commonly with HIV infection) and appear as small umbilicated papules with surrounding erythema most commonly on the face and scalp. Cryptococcal infection may occasionally be differentiated from molluscum contagiosum by the presence of a hemorrhagic center and an acute onset in the former. Diagnosis is confirmed by skin biopsy and fungal cultures.

Cytomegalovirus infection and *Mycobacterium avium* complex infection typically present as disseminated disease without skin lesions and are therefore not the most likely diagnoses in this patient.

Herpes simplex virus infection is usually characterized by the appearance of painful vesicles that lead to ulcerations on the oral mucosa or genital area, and the lesions typically are not asymptomatic, widespread, or concentrated on the face and scalp as they are in this patient.

KEY POINT

- Cutaneous involvement of cryptococcosis in patients with HIV infection/AIDS is a sign of disseminated cryptococcal infection and requires a high index of suspicion in affected patients.

Bibliography
Murakawa GJ, Kerschmann R, Berger T. Cutaneous Cryptococcus infections and AIDS: report of 12 cases and review of the literature. Arch Dermatol. 1996;132(5):545-548. [PMID: 8624151]

Item 89   Answer: B
Educational Objective: Treat a critically ill patient with community-acquired pneumonia and severe penicillin allergy.

This patient has community-acquired pneumonia characterized by cough, sputum production, fever, rhonchi, and pulmonary infiltrates on the chest radiograph. He is critically ill, requiring admission to the intensive care unit (ICU). All patients from the community who are admitted to the ICU should receive antimicrobial therapy for *Streptococcus pneumoniae* and *Legionella* species, as well as

Haemophilus influenzae and Enterobacteriaceae organisms, using a potent antipneumococcal β-lactam agent (cefotaxime, ceftriaxone, or ampicillin-sulbactam) and a macrolide or a fluoroquinolone. Therapy with a respiratory fluoroquinolone alone has not been established for treatment of severe community-acquired pneumonia, and combination therapy is recommended for at least 48 hours or until results of diagnostic tests are known. For penicillin-allergic patients, a respiratory fluoroquinolone and aztreonam are recommended.

Cefotaxime, ceftriaxone, or ampicillin-sulbactam cannot be used because of the patient's severe penicillin allergy. Vancomycin plus gentamicin would not be effective in treating *Legionella* pneumonia, and trimethoprim-sulfamethoxazole would not provide a broad enough spectrum of treatment for the likely infecting organisms.

KEY POINT

- A potent antipneumococcal β-lactam agent and a macrolide or a fluoroquinolone are recommended for patients with severe community-acquired pneumonia who require intensive care unit admission; for penicillin-allergic patients, a respiratory fluoroquinolone and aztreonam are recommended.

Bibliography
Mandell LA, Wunderink RG, Anzueto A, et al. Infectious Diseases Society of America/American Thoracic Society consensus guidelines on the management of community-acquired pneumonia in adults. Clin Infect Dis. 2007;44(Suppl 2):S27-72. [PMID: 17278083]

Item 90   Answer: A
Educational Objective: Diagnose *Capnocytophaga canimorsus*–associated overwhelming sepsis.

This splenectomized patient most likely has overwhelming sepsis due to *Capnocytophaga canimorsus,* a member of the normal oral flora of dogs. Life-threatening infection with this gram-negative bacillus has been associated with dog bites in immunosuppressed patients, including those who have undergone splenectomy and those who abuse alcohol or have cirrhosis. The predisposition to infection with this organism in patients with asplenia is due to impaired ability to clear intravascular bacteria and impaired antibody production. The mortality rate is high in patients with *C. canimorsus* sepsis, requiring prompt management with antibiotics such as a β-lactam/β-lactamase inhibitor combination, supportive care, and possible surgical debridement.

Escherichia coli is not classically associated with dog bites.

Salmonella species have been associated with infections after contact with pet reptiles such as turtles and snakes. Gastroenteritis is a common feature of infection in these individuals and is not consistent with the symptoms found in this patient.

Staphylococcus aureus and *Streptococcus pyogenes* can cause necrotizing skin infections with associated shock; however, both are gram-positive cocci in contrast to the gram-negative bacilli that were isolated from the blood cultures of this patient.

KEY POINT

- *Capnocytophaga canimorsus* should be suspected as a cause of sepsis in an asplenic patient or in a patient who abuses alcohol or has cirrhosis and has recently experienced a dog bite.

Bibliography

Janda JM, Graves MH, Lindquist D, Probert WS. Diagnosing Capnocytophaga canimorsus infections. Emerg Infect Dis. 2006;12(2):340-342. [PMID: 16494769]

Item 91   Answer: C

Educational Objective: Understand that *Streptococcus pneumoniae* is the most common cause of bacterial meningitis in patients with a basilar skull fracture and cerebrospinal fluid leak.

This patient has a basilar skull fracture with cerebrospinal fluid (CSF) leak, which is manifested clinically as rhinorrhea. The rhinorrhea is the result of a dural defect that has been created because of the trauma. *Streptococcus pneumoniae* is the most common etiologic agent of bacterial meningitis in patients who have experienced a basilar skull fracture with CSF leak; other possible infecting organisms include *Haemophilus influenzae* and group A β-hemolytic streptococci. Pending culture results, empiric antimicrobial therapy targeted towards *S. pneumoniae* should be initiated with vancomycin plus a third-generation cephalosporin to treat for the possibility of highly penicillin G–resistant pneumococci. Adjunctive dexamethasone should also be initiated prior to or concomitant with the first antimicrobial dose, because the use of dexamethasone has been associated with reduction of both mortality and adverse outcomes in adult patients with pneumococcal meningitis.

The efficacy of meropenem as monotherapy in the treatment of meningitis caused by highly penicillin G–resistant pneumococci has not been established. Vancomycin alone would not adequately treat *Haemophilus influenzae*.

KEY POINT

- *Streptococcus pneumoniae* is the most common etiologic agent of meningitis in patients with a basilar skull fracture and cerebrospinal fluid leak.

Bibliography

van de Beek D, de Gans J, Tunkel AR, Wijkicks EFM. Community-acquired bacterial meningitis in adults. N Engl J Med. 2006;354 (1):44-53. [PMID: 16394301]

Item 92   Answer: A

Educational Objective: Treat herpes simplex encephalitis.

Herpes simplex encephalitis is the most common cause of sporadic encephalitis, and typical manifestations include rapid onset of fever, headache, seizures, focal neurologic signs, and impaired consciousness. This patient most likely has herpes simplex virus encephalitis based on the fever, seizure, CT scan, and lumbar puncture findings. The diagnosis is established by polymerase chain reaction showing herpes simplex virus DNA in the cerebrospinal fluid. Herpes simplex encephalitis is a disease with devastating consequences, and early empiric treatment is recommended. Intravenous acyclovir is the recommended initial therapy for this infection.

Although cidofovir is an effective antiviral agent, its long half-life and significant toxicity profile make it unsuitable as initial therapy.

Levofloxacin, penicillin G, and the combination of ceftriaxone, vancomycin, and ampicillin are antibacterial agents. The CSF results are not compatible with bacterial meningitis.

KEY POINT

- Herpes simplex encephalitis should be considered in an otherwise healthy patient who presents with fever, headache, and seizures.

Bibliography

McGrath N, Anderson NE, Croxson MC, Powell KF. Herpes simplex encephalitis treated with acyclovir: diagnosis and long term outcome. J Neurol Neurosurg Psychiatry. 1997;63(3):321-326. [PMID: 9328248]

Item 93   Answer: D

Educational Objective: Treat a patient with asymptomatic bacteriuria.

This patient requires no treatment with antibiotics even if a urinalysis indicates pyuria. Asymptomatic bacteriuria does not cause symptoms of a urinary tract infection but is detected when the results of a urine culture grow greater than 10^5 colony-forming units/mL. This condition is not uncommon, especially among adult women and the elderly, and rarely requires treatment. Screening for asymptomatic bacteriuria is generally recommended before transurethral resection of the prostate, urinary tract instrumentation involving biopsy, or other tissue trauma resulting in mucosal bleeding. Screening is not recommended for simple catheter placement or cystoscopy without biopsy or in most asymptomatic ambulatory patients. Pregnant women are screened for asymptomatic bacteriuria, which is associated with low birth weight and prematurity.

Asymptomatic bacteriuria is only treated in the following circumstances: in pregnant women, in patients who recently had an indwelling catheter removed, before an invasive urologic procedure, in neutropenic patients, or in patients with a urinary tract obstruction. Chronic prophylactic antibiotic therapy is beneficial in pregnant women with recurrent asymptomatic bacteriuria; if untreated, 20% to 40% of patients will progress to symptomatic urinary tract infection, including pyelonephritis.

KEY POINT

- Although asymptomatic bacteriuria in adult patients usually does not require treatment, pregnant women should be treated to decrease the risk of pyelonephritis.

Bibliography

Lin K, Fajardo K; U.S. Preventive Services Task Force. Screening for Asymptomatic Bacteriuria in Adults: Evidence for the U.S. Preventive Services Task Force Reaffirmation Recommendation Statement. Ann Intern Med. 2008;149(1):W20-W24. [PMID: 18591632]

Item 94   Answer: B

Educational Objective: Evaluate a patient with pulmonary aspergillosis using polymerase chain reaction testing.

CT-guided needle biopsy with polymerase chain reaction (PCR) is the best next diagnostic test for this patient who may have chronic invasive aspergillosis, an indolent form of pulmonary aspergillosis. These patients typically have pulmonary disease and present with cough, hemoptysis, and low-grade fever, and the chest radiograph shows a slowly progressive infiltrate, nodule, or mass. Chronic invasive aspergillosis may be associated with an aspergilloma.

PCR has been shown to be highly sensitive and specific and may yield results quickly to demonstrate the presence of *Aspergillus* in tissues. The sensitivity and speed at which results become available exceed that of culture.

Cultures from deep-body specimens are reliable but are difficult to obtain and take several days to grow. Blood cultures are rarely positive, even if the patient has a serious infection.

Galactomannan antigen detection serum assays are significantly less sensitive and much less specific than PCR on tissue specimens. Repeat bronchoscopy and bronchoalveolar lavage would not be expected to be more successful at obtaining the lesion than the first attempt in this patient, especially with a peripheral lesion.

KEY POINT

- Polymerase chain reaction testing for *Aspergillus* antigens is a sensitive and specific test for use on tissue specimens.

Bibliography

Rickerts V, Mousset S, Lambrecht E, et al. Comparison of histopathological analysis, culture, and polymerase chain reaction assays to detect invasive mold infections from biopsy specimens. Clin Infect Dis. 2007;44(8):1078-1083. [PMID: 17366453]

Item 95   Answer: E

Educational Objective: Evaluate a patient with recurrent meningococcal infections.

This patient presented acutely with meningococcal meningitis as demonstrated by his clinical manifestations of fever, headache, neck stiffness, and confusion and cerebrospinal fluid analysis and culture results. But he also has a history of a prior *Neisseria meningitidis* infection. Patients with deficiencies in certain complement components, including C5, C6, C7, C8, and perhaps C9, the so-called membrane-attack complex, have a markedly increased incidence of recurrent neisserial infection, including that caused by *N. meningitidis*. However, mortality rates in patients with complement-component deficiencies and invasive meningococcal disease are lower than those in patients with an intact complement system (3% versus 19% in the general population). Because meningococcal meningitis occurs in approximately 39% of patients with late complement-component deficiencies, a screening test for complement function (such as the CH_{50}) should be performed in patients with recurrent neisserial disease. However, the CH_{50} will not detect deficiency of the C9 complement component.

Metrizamide cisternography and MRI of the brain might detect structural defects that would lead to recurrent meningitis but not those that would likely be caused by *N. meningitidis*.

Quantitative immunoglobulin deficiencies might be present in patients with recurrent pneumococcal infections or other encapsulated organisms. Nitroblue tetrazolium reduction is a test for diagnosing chronic granulomatous disease, a condition characterized by the inability of phagocytes (neutrophils, monocytes, and macrophages) to destroy microbial organisms once phagocytosed, which leads to infection with catalase-positive organisms. Neither of these tests is appropriate for this patient with recurrent neisserial infections.

KEY POINT

- A screening test for complement function should be performed in patients with recurrent neisserial infections.

Bibliography

Overturf GD. Indications for the immunological evaluation of patients with meningitis. Clin Infect Dis. 2003;36(2):189-194. [PMID: 12522751]

Item 96   Answer: A

Educational Objective: Recognize the most common fungal cause of chemotherapy-related neutropenia.

Patients with fever and marked neutropenia, such as this patient with cancer who is undergoing chemotherapy, are more susceptible to many bacterial, viral, and fungal infections than those without these findings. The cause of his pulmonary lesions is *Aspergillus fumigatus* because bronchoalveolar lavage fluid from the affected area yielded no bacteria, but fungal cultures were growing a mold. Statistically, the most likely organism in this setting is *Aspergillus*. The major manifestation of invasive aspergillosis pulmonary infection is fever in the setting of neutropenia and broad-spectrum antibiotic therapy. Common symptoms include chest pain, cough, and hemoptysis. Findings on chest radiography are variable and include nodules, patchy infiltrates, or cavities. Other fungi, such as *Pseudallescheria*, *Mucor*, or others, may also occur in this setting, but *Aspergillus* species is the most common.

Candida species rarely cause a primary pneumonia, and these species grow with smooth colonies that do not resemble molds on culture.

Histoplasma capsulatum may cause disease in immunosuppressed patients but far less often than *Aspergillus*. In addition, the progression of disease in patients with *H. capsulatum* infection would be slower than that demonstrated in this patient.

Nocardia asteroides may cause cavitary pulmonary disease and multiple lesions, but it does not resemble a mold on culture, and it also occurs less often than *Aspergillus* infection.

> **KEY POINT**
>
> - *Aspergillus* is the most common fungus to cause pulmonary disease in immunosuppressed patients, especially those with neutropenia.

Bibliography

Upton A, Kirby KA, Carpenter P, Boeckh M, Marr KA. Invasive aspergillosis following hematopoietic cell transplantation: outcomes and prognostic factors associated with mortality. Clin Infect Dis. 2007;44(4):531-540. [PMID: 17243056]

Item 97   Answer: C

Educational Objective: Diagnose *Legionella pneumophila* pneumonia.

This patient most likely has *Legionella* pneumonia as supported by multiple similar cases on the cruise ship, her underlying risk factors, clinical presentation, and hyponatremia. Risk factors for Legionnaires disease include smoking, diabetes mellitus, hematologic malignancy, other types of cancer, chronic kidney disease, and HIV infection. Symptoms of *Legionella* pneumonia may include cough with nonproductive, mildly productive, and/or blood-streaked sputum and chest pain. Gastrointestinal symptoms are prominent and often include diarrhea, abdominal pain, nausea, and vomiting. Most patients are lethargic and have headache, and some may be obtunded. High fever is common, with an oral temperature greater than 40.0 °C (104.0 °F) suggestive of Legionnaires disease. Hyponatremia is found more often in patients with Legionnaires disease than it is in patients with pneumonia from other causes.

Urinary antigen tests are commercially available for the detection of *Legionella pneumophila* serogroup 1. Prior studies of patients with culture-proven Legionnaires disease indicate that the urinary antigen test has a sensitivity of 70% to 90% and a specificity of nearly 99% for detection of *L. pneumophila* serogroup 1; the urine is positive on day 1 of illness and continues to be positive for weeks. However, urinary antigen tests do not detect other *Legionella* species. Therefore, a negative test result cannot be used to exclude the diagnosis of *Legionella* pneumonia.

Legionella species would not be isolated from blood cultures or thoracentesis fluid; therefore, neither of these tests is warranted in this patient.

Patients with acute influenza typically present with high fever, myalgia, and malaise accompanied by cough and sore throat. Primary influenza pneumonia is a rare complication of influenza and tends to occur in patients with heart failure, elevated left atrial pressures, and chronic pulmonary disease.

Most patients with pulmonary tuberculosis present with a subacute or chronic presentation of cough, weight loss, low-grade fever, mild systemic symptoms, and, possibly, blood-tinged sputum. However, some patients develop high fever, severe inanition, and large quantities of blood-tinged sputum. The radiographic changes of reactivation tuberculosis include upper pulmonary lobe infiltrates, cavitation, and volume loss, and pleural effusions may be indicative of pleural tuberculosis. This patient's clinical presentation and radiographic findings are not consistent with influenza or tuberculosis; therefore, nasal swab for influenza and acid-fast bacilli testing for tuberculosis would not be appropriate. In patients with primary influenza pneumonia, the chest radiograph usually reveals bilateral interstitial findings consistent with adult respiratory distress syndrome, but no consolidation.

> **KEY POINT**
>
> - Urinary antigen tests for detection of *Legionella pneumophila* serogroup 1 have a sensitivity of 70% to 90% and specificity of nearly 99%, but these tests do not detect other *Legionella* species; therefore, a negative test cannot be used to exclude the diagnosis of *Legionella* pneumonia.

Bibliography

Murdoch DR. Diagnosis of *Legionella* infection. Clin Infect Dis. 2003;36(1):64-69. [PMID: 12491204]

Item 98   Answer: A

Educational Objective: Treat disseminated herpes zoster infection.

This patient most likely has disseminated herpes zoster infection, which is a medical emergency, and requires high-dose, intravenous acyclovir. He has typical lesions in a dermatomal pattern but also has multiple lesions outside the dermatomal area (cutaneous dissemination). When this occurs in an immunocompromised patient, visceral dissemination of the herpes zoster lesions must also be considered. Visceral dissemination can include pneumonitis, hepatitis, and meningoencephalitis. This patient's confusion, hypoxemia, abnormal chest radiograph findings, elevated aminotransferase levels, and abnormal cerebrospinal fluid findings could all be explained by disseminated herpes zoster.

Acyclovir-resistant herpes zoster occasionally occurs in HIV-infected individuals. These patients with herpes zoster infections may not respond to prolonged courses of acyclovir. In this circumstance, foscarnet is usually recommended, but success in controlling the infection is variable. Foscarnet is associated with significant toxicity and is not a first-line drug for the treatment of herpes zoster infection.

Valganciclovir has not been studied as a treatment for herpes zoster infection, although valacyclovir is often used as the preferred oral treatment for immunocompromised patients with herpes zoster infection despite a small risk of thrombotic thrombocytopenic purpura associated with high doses of valacyclovir.

Herpes zoster vaccine has been approved for use by the U.S. Food and Drug Administration, and the Advisory Committee on Immunization Practices (ACIP) recommends herpes zoster vaccination for all immunocompetent people aged 60 years and older. The herpes zoster vaccine is a live vaccine and is not indicated in immunosuppressed patients or as a treatment for herpes zoster infection.

> **KEY POINT**
>
> - Intravenous acyclovir is the treatment of choice for immunocompromised patients with disseminated herpes zoster infection.

Bibliography
Wareham DW, Breuer J. Herpes zoster. BMJ. 2007;334(7605):1211-1215. [PMID: 17556477]

Item 99   Answer: D

Educational Objective: Diagnose *Rickettsia africae* infection (African tick bite fever).

This patient's presentation is typical for African tick bite fever caused by *Rickettsia africae*. Rickettsial illness is generally mild and is characterized by nonspecific symptoms of fever, headache, and myalgia that are similar to those occurring in many diseases endemic to that part of the world, such as malaria and typhoid fever. The leukocyte count in patients with *R. africae* is generally normal, and mild alanine and aspartate aminotransferase elevations are common. The presence of a solitary or multiple crusted, ulcerated papules (tache noir or eschar, referring to the necrotic scab on top of the papule); regional lymphadenopathy; and a generalized, faint vesicular or maculopapular rash is suggestive of *R. africae*. Isolation of the rickettsial organism can be performed at specialized laboratories, or acute and convalescent sera can confirm a clinical

diagnosis. Treatment consists of doxycycline, and recovery is prompt and complete.

Dengue is caused by a mosquito-borne flavivirus. It occurs commonly throughout much of the developing world and results in an acute illness characterized by headache, fever, and severe myalgia. A maculopapular rash may occur in patients with dengue. However, patients with dengue do not have an eschar.

Leishmania major is one organism of the *Leishmania* species that can cause localized cutaneous ulcers. The ulcer is typically painless, and the edges are often raised or "rolled." However, unlike this patient, patients with *L. major* do not have systemic symptoms or other cutaneous manifestations.

Mycobacterium marinum causes cutaneous nodules and, occasionally, ulcers, after an inoculation related to salt or fresh water exposure. There are no systemic symptoms. This patient's signs and symptoms are more consistent with *R. africae* than *M. marinum*.

Vibrio vulnificus is a gram-negative bacillus that can cause severe wound infections. Inoculation with this organism is related to salt water exposure–associated trauma. Iron is a cofactor for this organism's virulence; therefore, *V. vulnificus* is particularly associated with cirrhosis, especially due to hemochromatosis. Infection causes necrotizing fasciitis, often with bullae and myositis, rather than a cutaneous ulcer, as seen in this patient.

> **KEY POINT**
>
> - A crusted ulcerated papule and regional lymphadenopathy after recent return from Africa are suggestive of *Rickettsia africae* infection (African tick bite fever).

Bibliography
Oostvogel PM, van Doornum GJ, Ferreira R, Vink J, Fenollar F, Raoult D. African tickbite fever in travelers, Swaziland. Emerg Infect Dis. 2007;13(2):353-355. [PMID: 17479918]

Item 100   Answer: B

Educational Objective: Diagnose atazanavir-induced hyperbilirubinemia.

This patient has indirect hyperbilirubinemia, demonstrated by an indirect bilirubin level greater than 50% of the total bilirubin level, and normal serum aminotransferase levels. The most common laboratory abnormality associated with atazanavir is indirect hyperbilirubinemia without serum aminotransferase elevations. The elevation is due to competitive inhibition of the UGT1A1 enzyme. This enzyme is necessary for the glucuronidation of bilirubin, which facilitates its elimination in the bile. Indirect hyperbilirubinemia has been reported frequently in clinical trials involving atazanavir but has infrequently led to its discontinuation.

The characteristic features of AIDS cholangiopathy include upper abdominal pain, diarrhea, fever, and liver chemistry studies consistent with an obstructive disorder (primarily direct hyperbilirubinemia). AIDS cholangiopathy is most often due to infection with *Cryptosporidium* or cytomegalovirus and occurs most often in persons at risk for opportunistic infections with CD4 cell counts of less than 100/µL. *Cryptosporidium* may infect the biliary tract, including the ampulla, and cause stricturing that mimics sclerosing cholangitis. Endoscopic retrograde cholangiopancreatography is confirmatory. This patient is asymptomatic, has no biochemical evidence of biliary obstruction, and has a CD4 cell count of greater than 500/µL, making AIDS cholangiopathy an unlikely diagnosis.

A common bile duct stone can lead to hyperbilirubinemia, but typically, the elevation is due to direct, not indirect, bilirubin. Patients with acute common bile duct obstruction due to a gallstone often have pain.

Autoimmune hemolytic anemia is not compatible with this patient's normal hemoglobin level and normal reticulocyte count.

This patient has a positive anti-hepatitis B surface antigen titer but a negative hepatitis B surface antigen titer, documenting past, but not current, infection. In addition, hepatitis would be associated with hyperbilirubinemia and an elevated serum aminotransferase level, the latter of which is absent in this patient.

KEY POINT

- Indirect hyperbilirubinemia is a common and reversible adverse event associated with the protease inhibitors atazanavir and indinavir.

Bibliography
Busti AJ, Hall RG, Margolis DM. Atazanavir for the treatment of Human Immunodeficiency Infection. Pharmacotherapy. 2004;24 (12):1732-1747. [PMID: 15585441]

Item 101   Answer: C

Educational Objective: Manage a needlestick injury from a source who is HIV- and hepatitis C virus–positive.

After needlestick injury, injured persons should immediately wash the area with soap and water and report to the employee health department or specified area for needlestick evaluation. Baseline serologies and postexposure HIV prophylaxis should be done immediately, with follow-up serologies done as indicated.

Recommendations for postexposure HIV prophylaxis are based on severity of exposure and the source HIV class. Severity is divided into two categories: less severe is defined as exposure to a solid needle with superficial injury; and more severe is defined as exposure to a large-bore hollow needle, deep puncture, visible blood on device, or needle used in a patient's artery or vein. An HIV class 1 exposure is defined as exposure to an asymptomatic source or to a source in whom the viral load is low (for example, <1500 HIV RNA copies/mL). An HIV class 2 exposure is defined as exposure to a source with symptomatic HIV infection,

AIDS, acute seroconversion, or a known high viral load. For low-risk exposure, prophylaxis with two nucleosides is recommended. This physician's exposure was more severe, and the source's class is 2; therefore, the recipient of the needlestick should be offered postexposure prophylaxis with three or more antiretroviral agents. Assistance with choosing a regimen can be obtained by calling the National Clinicians' Post-Exposure Prophylaxis Hotline at 888-448-4911.

Currently, there is no vaccine or immune globulin therapy to protect against hepatitis C virus transmission. Postexposure treatment with interferon alfa-2b, with or without ribavirin, has not been shown to have efficacy in this setting. This patient has been immunized against hepatitis B, and her hepatitis B surface antibody titer is being checked. If her antibody titer is adequate, no treatment is necessary; if inadequate, a single dose of hepatitis B immune globulin and vaccine booster would be administered.

KEY POINT

- After needlestick injury, injured persons should immediately wash the area with soap and water and report to the employee health department or specified area for needlestick evaluation; if HIV prophylaxis is indicated, it should begin immediately.

Bibliography
Updated U.S. Public Health Service Guidelines for the Management of Occupational Exposures to HIV and Recommendations for Post exposure Prophylaxis. MMWR Recomm Rep. 2005;54(RR-9):1-17. [PMID: 16195697]

Item 102   Answer: A

Educational Objective: Select the appropriate empiric antimicrobial therapy in a patient with pneumonia and no comorbidities.

The most common pathogens identified from recent studies of patients with mild community-acquired pneumonia (CAP) were *Streptococcus pneumoniae*, *Mycoplasma pneumoniae*, and *Chlamydophila pneumoniae*. Macrolides have long been commonly prescribed for treatment of outpatients with CAP, and numerous randomized clinical trials have demonstrated the efficacy of clarithromycin or azithromycin as monotherapy. Erythromycin is a less expensive macrolide but not generally recommended owing to the need for more frequent dosing, more gastrointestinal upset, and lack of coverage for *Haemophilus influenzae*.

Influenza virus symptoms typically consist of fever (usually high), headache, extreme fatigue, nonproductive cough, sore throat, nasal congestion, rhinorrhea, myalgia, and, occasionally, gastrointestinal symptoms, with most cases of influenza occurring from November through April in the Northern Hemisphere. Because the patient's symptoms and findings are more consistent with CAP than influenza virus infection, antiviral therapy with oseltamivir is not indicated.

The use of fluoroquinolones to treat ambulatory patients with CAP without comorbidities is discouraged because of the concern that widespread use would lead to the development of resistance.

Penicillin would not be effective in treating *M. pneumoniae* and *C. pneumoniae* and is therefore not appropriate in this patient.

KEY POINT

- Macrolides (clarithromycin or azithromycin) are efficacious as monotherapy for treatment of mild community-acquired pneumonia; use of fluoroquinolones to treat ambulatory patients with community-acquired pneumonia without comorbidities is discouraged to avoid resistance.

Bibliography

Mandell LA, Wunderink RG, Anzueto A, et al. Infectious Diseases Society of America/American Thoracic Society consensus guidelines on the management of community-acquired pneumonia in adults. Clin Infect Dis. 2007;44(Suppl 2):S27-72. [PMID: 17278083]

Item 103   Answer: C

Educational Objective: Select the appropriate empiric antimicrobial therapy for an elderly patient with bacterial meningitis.

This patient likely has bacterial meningitis and requires therapy with vancomycin, ampicillin, and ceftriaxone. Bacterial meningitis in adults is characterized by fever, headache, nuchal rigidity, and signs of cerebral dysfunction. In elderly patients such as this one, insidious onset with lethargy or obtundation and variable signs of meningeal irritation may be present, particularly in the setting of diabetes mellitus. This patient's symptoms and cerebrospinal fluid results are consistent with acute bacterial meningitis. The most likely etiologic agents are *Streptococcus pneumoniae*, *Listeria monocytogenes*, *Neisseria meningitidis*, and aerobic gram-negative bacilli. Pending culture results and results of in vitro susceptibility testing, empiric treatment with antimicrobial therapy consisting of vancomycin, ampicillin, and ceftriaxone for infection caused by penicillin-resistant pneumococci and *L. monocytogenes* is necessary.

Intravenous ceftriaxone or intravenous penicillin G alone might not provide adequate cerebrospinal fluid concentrations for treatment of penicillin-resistant pneumococci. Most infectious disease experts would recommend vancomycin plus ceftriaxone for the treatment of penicillin-resistant pneumococci; however, this combination would not adequately treat meningitis caused by *L. monocytogenes*, which requires the addition of ampicillin. Trimethoprim-sulfamethoxazole does treat *Listeria* meningitis, and the combination of vancomycin plus trimethoprim-sulfamethoxazole would be potentially inadequate treatment for pneumococcal meningitis.

KEY POINT

- Empiric therapy of acute bacterial meningitis in an older adult should target *Streptococcus pneumoniae*, *Listeria monocytogenes*, *Neisseria meningitidis*, and aerobic gram-negative bacilli; the empiric antibiotic regimen should include a third-generation cephalosporin, vancomycin, and ampicillin.

Bibliography

Tunkel AR, Hartman BJ, Kaplan SL, et al. Practice guidelines for the management of bacterial meningitis. Clin Infect Dis. 2004;39(9):1267-1284. [PMID: 15494903]

Item 104   Answer: B

Educational Objective: Treat neurosyphilis.

This patient's presentation (symptoms compatible with a stroke, a reactive serologic test for syphilis, and elevated cerebrospinal fluid [CSF] mononuclear cells and protein level) is compatible with meningovascular syphilis, which is a classic form of neurosyphilis. The most appropriate therapy recommended by the Centers for Disease Control and Prevention (CDC) is intravenous aqueous penicillin G, 3 to 4 million units every 4 hours, or 18 to 24 million units per day by continuous infusion for 10 to 14 days. Syphilis diagnosis is usually based on clinical presentation and specific and nonspecific test results. Specific treponemal serologic studies include the fluorescent treponemal antibody absorption (FTA-ABS) assay and the microhemagglutination assay—*Treponema pallidum* (MHA-TP), and nonspecific studies include the rapid plasma reagin (RPR) test and Venereal Disease Research Laboratory (VDRL) test. The CSF-VDRL is only 30% to 50% sensitive in diagnosing neurosyphilis; therefore, treatment for neurosyphilis is indicated, regardless of the CSF-VDRL results. Neurologic examination and lumbar puncture should be performed 3 to 6 months after treatment and every 6 months thereafter until the CSF leukocyte count is normal and the CSF-VDRL (if initially reactive) becomes nonreactive.

Amoxicillin and probenecid require frequent dosing and offer no advantage over aqueous penicillin G. Neither is recommended by the CDC as a treatment for neurosyphilis. Single-dose azithromycin and benzathine penicillin G are not adequate treatments for neurosyphilis.

KEY POINT

- Recommended treatment for neurosyphilis is intravenous aqueous penicillin G for 10 to 14 days.

Bibliography

Centers for Disease Control and Prevention, Workowski KA, Berman SM, Sexually transmitted diseases treatment guidelines, 2006 [erratum in MMWR Recomm Rep. 2006;55(36):997]. MMWR Recomm Rep. 2006;55(RR-11). [PMID: 16888612]

Item 105   Answer: A

Educational Objective: Manage a patient with cryptococcal meningitis and HIV infection/AIDS.

This patient most likely has cryptococcal meningoencephalitis, an AIDS-defining illness, and requires amphotericin B with flucytosine. The most common presentation of cryptococcosis is subacute meningitis with fever, headache, and malaise. Most cases in HIV-infected patients occur when the CD4 cell count is less than 50/µL. The classic meningeal signs and symptoms occur in fewer than 25% to 35% of patients. Some patients have other signs of disseminated disease, including cough, rash, or lymphadenopathy. Most have a normal physical examination on presentation, with fewer than 25% having altered mentation. The recommended standard initial treatment for patients with cryptococcal meningitis is amphotericin B with flucytosine. Adding flucytosine to amphotericin B is associated with a more rapid sterilization of the cerebrospinal fluid (CSF) than treatment with amphotericin B alone. If after 2 weeks the patient demonstrates a clinical response and sterile CSF, amphotericin B and flucytosine can be discontinued, and high-dose fluconazole can be substituted. If after 8 weeks of high-dose fluconazole therapy, the patient continues to respond to therapy, maintenance therapy with lower-dose fluconazole can be continued for a minimum of 1 year. This patient should be started on highly active antiretroviral therapy, and if her CD4 cell count recovers, discontinuation of fluconazole can be considered.

Caspofungin is an echinocandin, which is part of a class of drugs that have no activity against *Cryptococcus* species.

Fluconazole combined with flucytosine is an alternative to amphotericin B plus flucytosine but is inferior to amphotericin B and flucytosine and is recommended only for highly compliant, asymptomatic patients unable to tolerate standard treatment.

Corticosteroids may play a role in a subset of patients with extremely high CSF pressure, intractable headache, and cranial nerve dysfunction, but the main component of treatment in this setting is lowering CSF pressure by serial lumbar punctures. Corticosteroids and flucytosine alone would be insufficient treatment because rapid resistance to flucytosine monotherapy has been described.

KEY POINT

- **The recommended initial standard treatment for cryptococcal meningitis associated with HIV infection is a combination of amphotericin B and flucytosine.**

Bibliography

Prevention and Treatment of Opportunistic Infections in Adults and Adolescents Guidelines. http://aidsinfo.nih.gov/contentfiles/Adult_OI.pdf.v Published June 18, 2008. Accessed on July 29, 2009.

Item 106   Answer: D

Educational Objective: Diagnose and treat patients with common variable immunodeficiency.

This patient's presentation is typical for common variable immunodeficiency (CVI). Performing a quantitative immunoglobulin assay would be the most appropriate next step in the evaluation of this patient. CVI is the most common form of severe antibody deficiency and is characterized by impaired B-cell differentiation and defective synthesis of immunoglobulin. Multiple bacterial or viral sinopulmonary infections are most often seen in these patients. The diagnosis of CVI is made by demonstrating low total serum concentrations of IgG, IgA, and/or IgM. Affected patients will also have absent or minimal response to immunization. Other diseases associated with low immunoglobulin levels must be excluded.

Bronchiectasis is a common sequela of bacterial pneumonia in patients with CVI. There is often a history of more than one family member with CVI as is likely in the case of this patient and her maternal aunt.

A bone marrow biopsy would not be expected to divulge the cause of this patient's underlying problems because there are no indications of hematologic defects or likelihood of culturing organisms from the bone marrow.

Bronchoscopy would not be likely to yield the underlying cause of this patient's chronic problem, especially in a patient in whom sinus infections are the most prominent finding.

This patient has negative HIV serologies and does not require HIV RNA viral load testing.

A patient with T-cell defects would be more likely to have opportunistic infections (cytomegalovirus, herpesviruses, mycobacteria, *Candida*, *Cryptococcus*, and *Pneumocystis*) than the multiple bacterial or viral sinopulmonary infections that this patient has experienced. Consequently, performing a T-cell subset panel is not indicated.

KEY POINT

- **The most common presentation of patients with common variable immunodeficiency is multiple sinopulmonary infections.**

Bibliography

Oksenhendler E, Gérard L, Fieschi C, et al; DEFI Study Group. Infections in 252 patients with common variable immunodeficiency. Clin Infect Dis. 2008;46(10):1547-1554. [PMID: 18419489]

Item 107   Answer: B

Educational Objective: Evaluate a patient with posttransplantation lymphoproliferative disease caused by Epstein-Barr virus infection.

This patient has posttransplantation lymphoproliferative disease caused by reactivation of the Epstein-Barr virus. This disease may be characterized by progressive infectious mononucleosis, cytopenia, and B-cell monoclonal proliferation. The onset of symptoms suggestive of infectious mononucleosis followed by a progressive deteriorating course often occurs in patients with this disease. This disorder can be associated with relentless worsening of the initial symptoms, often resulting in development of pancytopenia; arrest of individual hematopoietic cell lines; infection of the transplanted organ, liver, or brain; B-cell lymphoma; or death. The syndrome may resolve with reduction of immunosuppressive therapy.

Cytomegalovirus (CMV) infection is not associated with development of monoclonal proliferation of B cells and most commonly involves the gastrointestinal tract from the esophagus to the colon, with fever, pain, ulceration, hemorrhage, and, possibly, perforation.

Almost all adults are seropositive for human herpesvirus-6 (HHV-6), and, as with all of the other known human herpesviruses, the virus remains latent throughout life. As with many of the herpesviruses, HHV-6 reactivation may occur later in life, especially in an older, immunodeficient patient. Transplant recipients frequently develop HHV-6 reactivation and may show evidence of hepatitis, encephalitis, and pulmonary disease. This patient's clinical symptoms and findings are not compatible with HHV-6 infection.

Hepatitis C virus can be expected to return in the transplanted liver, but it is often quite manageable clinically. The overall prognosis for patients with hepatitis C virus who require transplant is similar to that of other liver transplant recipients. When hepatitis C does cause posttransplantation problems, it is almost always direct liver toxicity rather than the syndrome described in this patient.

KEY POINT

- Posttransplantation lymphoproliferative disease caused by the Epstein-Barr virus commonly occurs after solid organ and hematopoietic stem cell transplantation and may be characterized by progressive infectious mononucleosis, cytopenia, and B-cell monoclonal proliferation.

Bibliography
Koch DG, Christiansen L, Lazarchick J, Stuart R, Willner IR, Reuben A. Posttransplantation lymphoproliferative disorder—the great mimic in liver transplantation: appraisal of the clinicopathologic spectrum and the role of Epstein-Barr virus. Liver Transpl. 2007;13(6):904-912. [PMID: 17539010]

Item 108   Answer: B

Educational Objective: Diagnose dengue.

This patient's clinical scenario is typical for dengue. Dengue is the most common mosquito-borne infection. Dengue is becoming increasingly common in the Caribbean, Central and South America, and most other tropical regions, and an occasional case has occurred in the southern United States in recent years. The vector for dengue is the *Aedes aegypti* mosquito, a day-biting species. Patients with dengue may be asymptomatic or may have a severe influenza-like illness with prominent fever, headache, and characteristic severe myalgia. A maculopapular truncal rash develops in as many as 50% of patients. Mild leukopenia and thrombocytopenia and small elevations in serum alanine and aspartate aminotransferase levels are common. If there is evidence of elevated hematocrit and bleeding, the condition is called *dengue hemorrhagic fever,* and if there is hypotension, *dengue shock syndrome.* The diagnosis is made on clinical and epidemiologic grounds and may be confirmed by the presence of a fourfold or greater increase in serum dengue virus antibody levels. There is no specific therapy or vaccine for dengue, and treatment is therefore symptomatic and supportive.

Chikungunya is another *Aedes* mosquito-borne disease that is similar in clinical presentation to dengue. Chikungunya is endemic to Asia and Africa but not the Western Hemisphere.

Influenza presents as a nonfocal febrile illness, often with headaches and myalgia; however, a rash, thrombocytopenia, and elevated aminotransferase levels are not part of the syndrome.

Malaria should always be considered in any febrile, returning traveler; however, malaria does not occur in Puerto Rico and is not characterized by a rash.

Typhoid fever occurs throughout the world. This condition also typically presents as a nonfocal febrile illness with leukopenia and mildly elevated alanine and aspartate aminotransferase levels. However, the rash of typhoid fever is characterized by faint, scanty, erythematous macules on the trunk (rose spots), usually does not appear until the second week of the illness, and is associated with abdominal pain. The diagnosis of typhoid fever is established by positive blood, stool, and/or urine cultures.

KEY POINT

- Patients with dengue may be asymptomatic or may have a severe influenza-like illness with prominent fever, headache, and characteristic severe myalgia; a maculopapular truncal rash (50% of patients); and mild leukopenia and thrombocytopenia and small elevations in serum alanine and aspartate aminotransferase levels.

Bibliography
Wilder-Smith A, Schwartz E. Dengue in travelers. N Engl J Med. 2005;353(9):924-932. [PMID: 16135837]

Item 109   Answer: D

Educational Objective: Manage a patient with a tick bite.

This patient's lesion was caused by direct irritation from a tick bite, and she should be assured that it is not erythema migrans, the skin finding of early Lyme disease. The local irritation from a tick bite occurs within a day of the bite, is asymptomatic or mildly pruritic, is not associated with systemic symptoms, is small (generally, less than 1 cm), and clears spontaneously over several days. Conversely, erythema migrans develops within days to weeks (average, 1 week) after a tick bite, grows over days to at least 5 cm, can be tender, is often associated with pruritus and systemic symptoms such as arthralgia and fever, and can take several weeks to resolve if untreated. Because this rash is not erythema migrans, the patient should not be treated with a prolonged course of doxycycline.

Single-dose doxycycline has been shown to decrease the risk of Lyme disease transmission after a tick bite; however, transmission of *Borrelia burgdorferi,* the bacterium that causes Lyme disease, does not begin immediately after attachment. The Infectious Diseases Society of America guidelines suggest that only patients who have had a tick bite with attachment for longer than 36 hours should be considered for antimicrobial prophylaxis, which is not the case in this patient; therefore, single-dose doxycycline prophylaxis is not indicated.

Even if the tick were attached for longer than 36 hours, it can take several weeks for positive serologic results to develop in patients with Lyme disease; therefore, serologic testing would not be useful in this patient.

KEY POINT

- **The local irritation from a tick bite occurs within 24 hours of the bite, is not accompanied by symptoms, measures generally less than 1 cm, and resolves spontaneously over several days; transmission of *Borrelia burgdorferi* does not occur until the tick has been attached for at least 36 hours.**

Bibliography
Wormser, GP, Dattwyler, RJ, Shapiro, ED, et al. The clinical assessment, treatment, and prevention of Lyme disease, human granulocytic anaplasmosis, and babesiosis: clinical practice guidelines by the Infectious Diseases Society of America [erratum in Clin Infect Dis. 2007;45(7):941]. Clin Infect Dis. 2006;43(9):1089-1134. [PMID: 17029130]

Item 110   Answer: D

Educational Objective: Treat methicillin-susceptible *Staphylococcus aureus* right-sided endocarditis.

This patient has complicated bacteremia most likely resulting from right-sided endocarditis. Treatment requires using the most effective drug with the fewest side effects, and vancomycin should therefore be changed to oxacillin. Penicillins have never been shown to be less effective than other antibiotics for treating susceptible strains of *Staphylococcus aureus,* their safety profile is well documented, and they are reasonably inexpensive. In the rare setting in which an isolate of *S. aureus* is susceptible to penicillin G, this would be the drug of choice.

Both vancomycin and daptomycin have been used to treat *S. aureus* bacteremia and endocarditis. Although both

are effective for treating methicillin-resistant *S. aureus* (MRSA) strains, they show no clinical superiority for treating methicillin-susceptible *S. aureus* (MSSA). Patients with MSSA infections appear to have a slower response to vancomycin than to the semi-synthetic penicillins such as oxacillin or to the cephalosporins, and this accounts for the preference of β-lactam versus vancomycin therapy in patients with MSSA.

Clindamycin may be effective in vitro, and this patient's negative clindamycin disk induction test (D test) establishes that resistance is unlikely to develop during treatment. However, the failure rate is higher for clindamycin than for other drugs used to treat endocarditis, presumably owing to inconsistent killing by clindamycin, which usually shows only bacteriostatic, rather than bactericidal, activity for many strains of susceptible *S. aureus.*

Linezolid has been used with some success and some failure in patients with staphylococcal bacteremia. Because of concerns about its efficacy, it is usually reserved for patients who do not respond to first-line therapy.

KEY POINT

- **Synthetic penicillins, such as oxacillin and nafcillin, are appropriate for treating patients with methicillin-susceptible *Staphylococcus aureus* bacteremia and endocarditis.**

Bibliography
Fowler VG Jr., Boucher HW, Corey GR, et al; The S. aureus Endocarditis and Bacteremia Study Group. Daptomycin versus standard therapy for bacteremia and endocarditis caused by Staphylococcus aureus. N Engl J Med. 2006;355(7):653-665. [PMID: 16914701]

Item 111   Answer: A

Educational Objective: Treat a patient with herpes simplex encephalitis.

This patient's temporal lobe swelling combined with her clinical presentation and cerebrospinal fluid (CSF) analysis is most suggestive of herpes simplex encephalitis. Acyclovir (at a dose of 10 mg/kg every 8 hours in adults with normal renal function) is the treatment of choice for suspected or proven herpes simplex encephalitis, although morbidity and mortality (mortality rate of 28% 18 months after treatment) remain high even with appropriate treatment.

In patients with encephalitis of unknown cause and clinical clues suggestive of ehrlichial (leukopenia, thrombocytopenia, and elevated serum aminotransferases) or rickettsial (rash beginning on the wrists and ankles) infection during the appropriate season, doxycycline should be added to the treatment regimen; however, this patient presents in January and would not have had tick exposure.

Treatment for bacterial meningitis should also be added to the treatment regimen when the clinical setting is appropriate. Bacterial meningitis in adults is characterized by fever, headache, nuchal rigidity, and signs of cerebral dysfunction. In elderly patients, insidious onset with lethargy or obtundation and variable signs of meningeal disease may be present, particularly in patients with diabetes mellitus; however, this patient's lack of nuchal rigidity, CSF findings, and abnormal CT scan are most consistent with encephalitis rather than meningitis. Therefore, ceftriaxone is not indicated.

Empiric voriconazole therapy for a possible fungal infection would not be given without a strong suspicion of a fungal cause or a clear diagnosis. The two major fungal infections considered in the differential diagnosis are cryptococcosis and coccidioidomycosis. Fungal meningitis tends to be an indolent infection with symptoms developing over days to weeks, often in immunocompromised patients. This patient's abrupt onset of fever and personality changes and focal findings on CT scan are not consistent with fungal meningitis.

KEY POINT
- Acyclovir is the treatment of choice for all patients with suspected encephalitis, pending results of diagnostic studies.

Bibliography
Tunkel AR, Glaser CA, Bloch KC, et al; Infectious Diseases Society of America. The management of encephalitis: clinical practice guidelines by the Infectious Diseases Society of America. Clin Infect Dis. 2008;47(3):303-327. [PMID: 18582201]

Item 112   Answer: A
Educational Objective: Institute infection-control measures in a patient with *Neisseria meningitidis* meningitis.

This patient has *Neisseria meningitidis* meningitis. Droplet precautions should be initiated when this diagnosis is suspected and require that health care workers within 6 to 10 feet of the index patient wear a face mask. Appropriate infection control measures for all patients include hand hygiene and standard precautions.

The human nasopharynx is the only known reservoir for meningococcal meningitis. Meningococci are spread from person to person by respiratory droplets of infected nasopharyngeal secretions. Persons with significant exposure to the index patient (same household, day-care center, or anyone with direct contact with a patient's oral secretions) should receive chemoprophylaxis with appropriate antibiotics. Significant health care exposure includes personnel with potential for intimate contact (within 3 feet) of the patient's respiratory secretions.

Rifampin and fluoroquinolones are the antimicrobials commonly used to eradicate meningococci from the nasopharynx. Three cases of ciprofloxacin resistance were identified in North Dakota and Minnesota in 2007-2008, triggering a regional health advisory recommending that ciprofloxacin chemoprophylaxis not be used. However, areas with only a single sporadic case of ciprofloxacin-resistant *N. meningitidis* should continue to follow current recommendations.

For infection spread by direct contact with the patient (for example, vancomycin-resistant enterococci), additional infection control measures include patient placement into a private room or with those who have a similar infection and the use of nonsterile gloves and gowns for direct contact with the patient or any infective material. Airborne infection precautions are appropriate for illnesses transmitted by airborne droplet nuclei (for example, tuberculosis, measles, and varicella). Additional infection control measures include placement into a private room, typically in a pressure-negative room, and special masks with a filtering capacity of 95% of particulates (N-95 respirator or a Powered Air Purifying Respirator [PAPR]).

KEY POINT
- Droplet precautions, which require that health care workers wear a face mask for close contact with infectious patients and don the mask on room entry, are indicated when meningococcal meningitis is suspected.

Bibliography
Siegel JD, Rhinehart E, Jackson M, Chiarello L; The Healthcare Infection Control Practices Advisory Committee. Guideline for Isolation Precautions: Preventing Transmission of Infectious Agents in Healthcare Settings. www.cdc.gov/ncidod/dhqp/pdf/guidelines/Isolation2007.pdf. Published 2007. Accessed on August 14, 2009.

Item 113   Answer: B
Educational Objective: Evaluate a patient with West Nile virus encephalitis.

This patient most likely has West Nile virus encephalitis, which can present with a poliomyelitis-like flaccid paralysis that may be irreversible. The other epidemiologic clues include the report of mosquito bites in the late summer and early fall and a dead bird in the yard. Wild birds can maintain high viral titers and serve as amplifying hosts. Although most birds remain asymptomatic, crows, ravens, and jays experience a high mortality rate from the infection. In patients with encephalitis caused by flaviviruses (such as West Nile virus), the detection of cerebrospinal fluid (CSF) IgM antibodies is considered diagnostic of neuroinvasive disease. IgM antibodies are identified in approximately 90% of patients with neuroinvasive disease caused by West Nile virus. Conversely, results of CSF polymerase chain reaction testing are positive in less than 60% of serologically confirmed cases. Although acute and convalescent titers of serum IgM and IgG capture enzyme-linked immunosorbent assays may be used to diagnose arboviral encephalitis, there may be cross-reactivity, especially among the flaviviruses, and they do not provide immediate diagnostic information. Serum IgM antibody may persist for 6 months or longer after West Nile virus infection and, even in the setting of positive results, it may be impossible to distinguish current infection from an unrelated past infection.

Brain biopsy is an invasive procedure associated with definable risks and would only be indicated if the diagnosis could not be established by other means.

KEY POINT

- **Cerebrospinal fluid IgM antibody assay is the best test for diagnosing West Nile virus encephalitis.**

Bibliography

Solomon T. Flavivirus encephalitis. N Engl J Med. 2004;351(4):370-378. [PMID: 15269317]

Item 114   Answer: E

Educational Objective: Treat an injection drug user with tricuspid valve endocarditis and multilobar pneumonia.

This injection drug user most likely has tricuspid valve endocarditis as suggested by the right lower sternal border systolic murmur that increases with inspiration. He has developed septic pulmonary emboli to both lung fields leading to multilobar pneumonia. Septic pulmonary emboli are common in tricuspid endocarditis, occurring in up to 75% of patients. In this instance, the most likely infecting organism is *Staphylococcus aureus*, and treatment of a possible methicillin-resistant strain must be initiated pending culture and in vitro susceptibility results. Vancomycin plus cefepime would provide appropriate coverage for endocarditis caused by *S. aureus*, gram-negative bacilli, and other likely infectious causes of pneumonia, especially *Streptococcus pneumoniae*.

Azithromycin plus ceftriaxone, levofloxacin plus clindamycin, and piperacillin/tazobactam plus aztreonam do not provide appropriate coverage for methicillin-resistant *S. aureus* and are therefore not appropriate for this patient. Although trimethoprim-sulfamethoxazole plus prednisone would treat *Pneumocystis jirovecii* pneumonia, such a diagnosis is unlikely in this patient given his clinical presentation. In HIV-infected patients, *Pneumocystis* pneumonia typically has a subacute onset of cough, fever, and dyspnea. The most common radiographic abnormalities are diffuse, bilateral, interstitial, or alveolar infiltrates. This patient's acute onset of symptoms, multilobar pneumonia, and presence of a heart murmur are not compatible with *Pneumocystis* pneumonia.

KEY POINT

- **Treatment for septic pulmonary emboli from an infected tricuspid valve in an injection drug user should include empiric therapy for methicillin-resistant *Staphylococcus aureus*.**

Bibliography

Chambers HF, Korzeniowski OM, Sande MA. Staphylococcus aureus endocarditis: clinical manifestations in addicts and nonaddicts. Medicine (Baltimore). 1983;62(3):170-177. [PMID: 6843356]

Item 115   Answer: C

Educational Objective: Treat asymptomatic bacteriuria in a pregnant patient.

Pregnant women are screened for asymptomatic bacteriuria, which is associated with low birth weight, prematurity, and an increased risk for pyelonephritis. This pregnant woman has asymptomatic bacteriuria that now requires treatment. The most appropriate antibiotic for this patient is nitrofurantoin, which is a Food and Drug Administration pregnancy risk category B drug. Ampicillin and amoxicillin are both pregnancy risk category B drugs, but based on susceptibility test results are not likely to be effective in this patient. Ciprofloxacin and trimethoprim are both pregnancy risk category C drugs and are therefore not indicated.

Urine cultures should be obtained after treatment in pregnant women with asymptomatic bacteriuria to confirm eradication of bacteria. Confirming the sterility of the urine can be done by repeating urine cultures at intervals until delivery.

KEY POINT

- **Asymptomatic bacteriuria during pregnancy is associated with low birth weight, prematurity, and an increased risk for pyelonephritis.**

Bibliography

Drekonja DM, Johnson JR. Urinary tract infections. Prim Care. 2008;35(2):345-367. [PMID: 18486719]

Item 116   Answer: D

Educational Objective: Manage close contacts of a patient with smallpox (variola).

This patient's findings are compatible with smallpox (variola) infection, which is a public health emergency and indicative of a bioterrorism attack. Smallpox is highly contagious and has a mortality rate of 30%. The incubation period ranges from 7 to 17 days, with a mean of 12 days. Patients initially present with high fever, malaise, vomiting, headache, backache, and severe abdominal pain. In the ordinary form of smallpox, characteristic lesions appear simultaneously, primarily on the extremities and face, but also on the oropharynx. The lesions are at the same stage in any one part of the body and evolve from macules to papules to pustules before finally forming scabs after about 8 days. Polymerase chain reaction testing in a public reference laboratory confirms the diagnosis. Patients with suspected or confirmed smallpox infection should be placed in respiratory and contact isolation. There is no proven treatment for smallpox other than supportive care.

Immediate vaccination of close contacts (ring vaccination) is the appropriate response to a community outbreak of smallpox.

Acyclovir has no effect against variola, and cidofovir has not been tested as a prophylactic agent for this infection.

Passive immunization with hyperimmune globulin is an effective prophylaxis for smallpox, but supplies are too limited to be of practical use in epidemic-control efforts.

The Centers for Disease Control and Prevention has drafted a response plan for patients with possible smallpox (www.bt.cdc.gov/agent/smallpox/response-plan/index.asp).

KEY POINT

- **The lesions of smallpox usually appear first on the face and chest and then spread to the extremities; lesions are at the same stage in any one part of the body and evolve from macules to papules to pustules before finally forming scabs after about 8 days.**

Bibliography

Henderson DA, Inglesby TV, Bartlett JG, et al. Smallpox as a biological weapon: medical and public health management. Working Group on Civilian Biodefense. JAMA. 1999;281(22):2127-2137. [PMID: 10367824]

Item 117   Answer: C

Educational Objective: Treat a patient with a severe, life-threatening diabetic foot infection.

This patient has a severe limb- and life-threatening diabetic foot infection as evidenced by her systemic symptoms, hypotension, tachycardia, and multiple metabolic derangements; she requires treatment with vancomycin plus imipenem. The lower-extremity findings of decreased foot pulses indicate peripheral arterial disease, and the decreased sensation reflects a sensory neuropathy. In addition, the fissures between the toes are a likely portal of entry for infection. The size of the wound and the increased erythrocyte sedimentation rate suggest potential bone infection.

These severe infections are polymicrobial and can include anaerobes, aerobic gram-positive cocci, and aerobic gram-negative bacilli. In addition to supportive care, assessment for peripheral arterial disease, and surgical consultation for debridement, this patient requires broad-spectrum antibiotics directed against these pathogens, including methicillin-resistant *Staphylococcus aureus.* The best therapeutic choice includes vancomycin, which provides coverage against gram-positive organisms, and imipenem, which has excellent activity against gram-negative aerobic organisms and anaerobic bacteria.

Ceftazidime, a third-generation cephalosporin, and ciprofloxacin, a fluoroquinolone, are active against aerobic gram-negative bacilli including *Enterobacteriaceae* and *Pseudomonas aeruginosa.* However, they are not reliably active against gram-positive aerobic bacteria and anaerobes. The addition of vancomycin and metronidazole to either of these agents would provide adequate coverage.

Metronidazole provides coverage against anaerobic bacteria, and vancomycin provides coverage against aerobic gram-positive cocci. However, neither provides adequate coverage against aerobic gram-negative bacilli. The addition of ceftazidime, cefepime, or ciprofloxacin would provide this activity.

KEY POINT

- **Severe life-threatening diabetic foot infections are usually polymicrobial and require empiric broad-spectrum antibiotic coverage against aerobic gram-positive cocci, aerobic gram-negative bacilli, and anaerobic bacteria.**

Bibliography

Lipsky BA, Berendt AR, Deery HG, et al; Infectious Diseases Society of America. Diagnosis and treatment of diabetic foot infections. Clin Infect Dis. 2004;39(7):885-910. [PMID: 15472838]

Item 118   Answer: C

Educational Objective: Determine whether therapeutic drug monitoring can be safely discontinued in a patient receiving vancomycin at home.

The rapid and accurate measurement of vancomycin serum levels is now widely available, but the rationale for monitoring can still be confusing. This patient requires only four more doses of vancomycin. Her outcome has been satisfactory, kidney function is unaltered, and the infection is not considered severe. Therefore, additional monitoring is not needed. Dosing based on algorithms (including the patient's weight, age, and kidney function) is usually associated with predictably good drug levels. Patients who have already achieved target drug levels do not require additional measurements.

Controversy continues about when to measure vancomycin serum levels for patients with serious *Staphylococcus aureus* infections or with infection caused by any organism that has a relatively high vancomycin minimal inhibitory concentration (MIC). Measurements are indicated for patients with fluctuating renal function. When monitoring is needed, peak levels are rarely obtained because they correlate poorly with predicting outcome or determining toxicity. Since vancomycin is considered a time-dependent antibiotic, maintaining trough levels above the MIC, with a target level of 10 µg/mL to 20 µg/mL, is more relevant than achieving high peak levels. Similarly, reducing the dose to avoid toxicity is unlikely to be helpful and may result in therapeutic failure.

KEY POINT

- **Patients taking vancomycin do not need constant monitoring of drug levels if renal function is stable and initial levels were satisfactory.**

Bibliography

Cunha BA. Vancomycin revisited: a reappraisal of clinical use. Crit Care Clin. 2008;24(2):393-420. [PMID: 18361953]

Index

Note: Page numbers followed by f and t denote figures and tables, respectively. Test questions are indicated by a Q.